Crossing the River

Crossing

the River

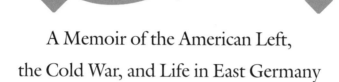

A Memoir of the American Left,

the Cold War, and Life in East Germany

VICTOR GROSSMAN

(Stephen Wechsler)

Edited with an Afterword by Mark Solomon

University of Massachusetts Press

Amherst and Boston

LC 2002151875
ISBN 1-55849-371-9 (library cloth ed.); 385-9 (paper)
Designed by Richard Hendel
Set in Carter Cone Galliard by Graphic Composition, Inc.
Printed and bound by Thomson Shore, Inc.

Library of Congress Cataloging-in-Publication Data

Grossman, Victor, 1928–
Crossing the river : a memoir of the American left, the Cold War, and life in East
Germany / Victor Grossman (Stephen Wechsler) ; edited with an afterword by
Mark Solomon.
p. cm.
Includes bibliographical references.
ISBN 1-55849-371-9 (alk. paper) — ISBN 1-55849-385-9 (pbk. : alk. paper)
1. Grossman, Victor, 1928– 2. Defectors — United States — Biography.
3. Defectors — Germany (East) — Biography. 4. Cold War. 5. Germany (East) —
Description and travel. I. Solomon, Mark. II. Title.
CT275.G7796 A3 2003
943'.1087'092 — dc21
2002151875

British Library Cataloguing in Publication data are available.

The author wishes to thank
Mark Solomon, professor of history emeritus, Simmons College,
and Paul M. Wright, editor, University of Massachusetts Press,
for their efforts on behalf of this book.

*I dedicate this book gratefully to the
courageous men and women in the past, noted and
nameless, who gave me inspiration — among them my
favorite authors: the Jewish German Heinrich Heine,
who wrote: "Every age believes its battles to be more
important than those preceding it. This is the proper
faith of every age. . . . And we too wish to live and die
in this religion of freedom"; and the Missouri
American Mark Twain, among whose myriad of wise
and witty sayings are: "A lie can travel half way
around the world while the truth is putting on its shoes"
and "I would rather have my ignorance than another
man's knowledge, because I have got so much
more of it."*

*As for the present, I thank the person who
helped me keep my feet on the ground and whose endless
love permitted me to keep slogging along —
my wife Renate.*

CONTENTS

Illustrations follow page 154.

I
Crossing the Border

In rivers, the water that you touch is the last of

what has passed and the first of that which comes;

so with time present.

Leonardo da Vinci (from his Notebooks)

FLIGHT (I)

My life before my wild flight had not really been so bad. If it had not been for that one registered letter I might even have led a normal American life. And then again, perhaps not.

When the letter arrived I was working in a U.S. Army camp in Fürth, in Bavaria, helping to supply the drivers of jeeps and army trucks with spare parts. A technical idiot, I was one of the few Americans who could not even drive a car and hardly knew a carburetor from an exhaust pipe. Despite this, I was in good spirits upon returning from a furlough in Scandinavia, for I had stopped in Copenhagen long enough to fall in love with a Danish girl with a red coat.

Should I try to stay in Denmark after my two years in the army were completed? Would I be permitted to remain? If so, how would I make a living? If I did return to the United States, how could I earn my keep and get along in my troubled homeland? It was 1952; I was twenty-four and needed some direction in my life.

I had just begun to reconsider these questions when the solution arrived, hard and rough, if not fully unexpected. The friendly mail corporal told me that there was no mail except a registered letter, which I would have to pick up myself. I looked at my watch. The regimental post office had closed at 5:30. Who would send me a registered letter? Was it perhaps the terrible message I had been fearing the past three months? I just had to wait, so I finally settled into a worried sleep.

In the morning I immediately recalled the letter but had to get through half my daily conflict with technology as best I could. After an anxious lunch I walked to the post office and was airily handed a big manila envelope. It came from the army's highest legal authority, the Judge Advocate General over three thousand miles away in Washington. I tremblingly hastened to some spot where I could be alone; my fears were confirmed. The explicit accusations ended with an unmistakable order: on the coming

Monday I was to present myself to the U.S. military court in Nuremberg. It was now Tuesday. I was in bad trouble.

But I had not been arrested. None of my officers had said a word about the matter. Evidently I was not to be brought to Nuremberg in custody or in handcuffs. It appeared that the initial action against me would be administrative. However, I feared that all kinds of terrible crimes could be loaded on in the terrifying period I was living in; I was certain I would end in military prison in West Germany or in Leavenworth. And there would always be a notice on my discharge papers effectively barring me from nearly all attempts to earn a living.

The only solution, born of panic, had been going through my head for three months: I must take off. It didn't matter how or where, but I had to leave. I wanted no taste of military imprisonment; nor did I want to spend my life as a second- or third-class citizen living in constant fear. So I had to leave. Of course the idea was insane, but I saw no choice and when I received the registered letter I made the decision. I would be betraying no one, I would be deserting no wife or children. As for "the cause" in America: if I were in jail I would be damaging it more than helping it. No, everything compelled me to leave, above all, the choking, paralyzing fear of the McCarthy era, the time of the Rosenbergs' trial and their eventual execution.

It was obvious that only one escape route was possible: eastward. But a dozen new questions pulsed through my thoughts. How could I get to the East? I was sure that once before the military court I would be imprisoned or strictly confined. Would I be able to leave our camp at all before Monday? Had the guards at the gates been warned to stop me? If so, could I leave the camp in some riskier way? How soon would I be missed? Could I get across the border — any eastern border — before then? I believed that as soon as I was missed an alarm would be issued and every MP would be looking for me. I had to be quick.

One solution was to slip away on Sunday, when we could leave camp after breakfast and stay out until midnight. I would not be missed for fifteen or sixteen hours. There was a risk in waiting till the last day before reporting to the military court, but Sunday was the best choice.

My first task was to write two letters. If my flight were successful, I would vanish — God only knew for how long. Because I had feared that difficulties might arise ever since my army service began, I had suggested a code to my father before leaving for Europe. If a letter from me began with the words "Dear Ma and Pa" instead of the customary "Mom and Dad" they were to examine the contents carefully, reading every third word; if no message emerged, they should try every fourth word, every fifth word, and so forth, until they found the proper combination and the hidden message.

I sat down in the empty clubroom and nervously began to write my coded letter. I wanted only to say that I was compelled to leave for the East, and they should not worry about me. This message had to be buried in a normal-sounding letter beyond a snooper's grasp. I tried repeatedly but every third word soon proved to be impossible. Every fourth and fifth word were no easier. I had never dreamed that it would be so damned difficult to sandwich some words into a text with another meaning.

It took what seemed hours to build a much shortened text into a letter that sounded anything but normal to me. However, I could do no better. Then I wrote a second letter to Ruth in Copenhagen — not in code but not too open either. I tried to explain that I thought a great deal of her but was forced to flee — so farewell. I decided to send the letters not by military mail but at a German post office in Nuremberg. After the second letter I went to bed — exhausted, worried, fearful. I had done enough for the first day.

While wishing I could fall asleep, I wondered whether I should tell a friend of my decision to leave. When I had raised that possibility with Earl two months earlier, he had looked at me uncomprehendingly and asked, "Are you crazy?" But he was not endangered. I decided against telling anything to anyone. This eliminated the chance that someone would say too much before I reached safety; I was also making no one else responsible for my action. Silence was the best policy, and as inconspicuous an exterior as I could muster. I finally fell asleep.

It was Wednesday; again I had to go to work, try to help without making too many stupid mistakes, and not display the worries wracking my brain. I scrutinized my fellow soldiers for any changes in their relationship to me. Did they know anything? No, they acted just as they always had.

My thoughts turned constantly to where I should attempt to cross the border. It was not far from nearby Hof, but I would still have to approach it on foot. What could I say if U.S. guards picked me up in the vicinity? And when they called my unit and discovered the truth, I would be in even worse hot water. I thought of the only people who might be able to advise me: the Communists. After all, they were my comrades.

But how would they recognize a comrade? U.S. Communists had had no membership cards for years, and even if they had existed, I had been suspended from party membership when I was drafted. After work on Wednesday I went into Nuremberg. No one stopped me at the gate, my pass was checked as cursorily as ever, and I breathed the first sigh of relief in two days. In those years GIs had to wear their uniforms when in Germany or Austria; civilian clothes were permitted only outside the two occupied countries. But going into Communist Party offices in a U.S. Army uniform — the West German party was not yet forbidden at that time, though under sharp attack — was like Daniel entering the lions' den, except that the carnivores waited outside the den.

After mailing my two letters, I dialed the local Communist Party headquarters — still listed in the telephone book. I stuttered into the receiver in worse than my usual heavily accented German, and nervously asked whether I could explain an urgent problem. Could I meet someone, perhaps at the main railway station, and explain why I could not now speak more openly? The answer was inevitable: "No, that is impossible." Anyone with a question to discuss could come to the party office at any time. I knew how unconvincing I sounded, and that the comrades feared provocations of any kind. I understood, yes, but I cursed to myself anyway. I was certain that the telephone connection was tapped. There was little else to say, so I hung up — but decided to risk going to their office the next evening and enter if the surroundings did not look too dangerous.

All Thursday I was consumed by worries about what I could say if I did go in. That evening I came to a quiet sidestreet outside the downtown area, with several apartment buildings and large villas. The party offices were in one such villa, separated from the street by a fence and a large iron gate. Just beyond a side fence was a larger building whose windows stared provocatively into the party building. I had often been warned in the United States that the FBI stationed agents in buildings facing party offices so all visitors could be checked or filmed. Now I felt like a goldfish, observed from all sides.

I was ushered into a sparsely furnished room. To my surprise and fright the big window was wide open, permitting a perfect view from the building next door. After stammering a few words about this which were not understood, I sat opposite the party secretary, positioning myself to show as little of my face as possible to onlookers, and tried to explain my situation.

Not daring to take the Judge Advocate General's letter with me, I had only one flimsy bit of evidence as to who I was. Before I left the United States, my old friend Mike Gold, the well-known *Daily Worker* columnist and author of the sad but vibrant *Jews without Money,* had said that if I ever got to Paris I should visit the acclaimed French writer Louis Aragon. He scribbled a short note, introducing me as a young friend and comrade. I now hoped that any active Communist would recognize the name of Mike Gold, and certainly Aragon, and would then trust me. Though written in a barely legible hand, the hasty signature would certainly have sufficed for Aragon, who knew Gold well. But offered by a strange American soldier struggling with the Bavarian dialect to a party secretary in Bavaria who did not speak English — what could these lines really convey?

I tried to explain what had happened to me — no easy matter. He understood at least the general drift. Then I told him that I needed to know the best and safest way to cross the border to East Germany. "What should I do?" he asked. "I cannot help you. All I have myself is a bicycle."

I wasn't asking for anyone to take me across (how happy I would have been for such an offer; perhaps I really was hoping for that). No, I said, all I wanted was advice on where best to cross over. But he would not or could not help me; no advice, no travel routes, nothing. In one final attempt I reminded him that many victims of fascism — frequently Communists — had been forced to flee across borders during the 1930s and 1940s and had been aided by comrades in neighboring countries, even without documentary proof. Though, for all I knew, he may once have been in such a situation, that did not help me either. The pained conversation, hobbled by language problems, was doomed to failure. His party was then under fierce attack and was finally outlawed four years later. This man had to assume that any occupation army soldier might be a provocateur, and that even if he were not, the chances of getting even slightly involved in such a matter were simply too risky. I was terribly shaken nonetheless. I was now completely on my own.

My evening had only just begun. As I left the villa and walked toward the street in nervous despair, I passed a man of about thirty coming the other way. He wore Lederhosen and was pushing a bicycle. This man stared at me much too long and searchingly, I thought, though a partially shocked American soldier stumbling out of the Communist Party offices was undoubtedly something to stare at long and searchingly.

But now this man with the Lederhosen, probably a comrade or neighbor, was to follow me for what seemed hours. In my almost hallucinatory state, I saw men with Lederhosen and bicycles everywhere, all looking like the one I had passed, all observing me "inconspicuously," all keeping me within "shadowing" distance.

I had set out to accomplish several things this evening; most important now was the destruction of my accumulated mail. In order not to endanger my correspondents when my locker was searched after flight, I had decided to destroy all letters. But even this had become a huge problem. There were no heating ovens in the camp, and I certainly couldn't light a bonfire for that purpose. I decided to tear them up and throw the shreds into sewers. Now I feared getting caught by the man with the bicycle. I hastened nervously from one corner to another of this ancient, once beautiful city now filled with dark ruins, shredding letters and throwing them down sewers when I thought myself unobserved.

Every few streets I saw the man with the Lederhosen again. Then another pursuer, a man with a light coat and glasses, was undoubtedly following me. One man took up the hunt from another; a third man took up the chase. I wondered whether my imagination was playing tricks on me, turning passersby into pursuers. I was in a cold sweat, my knees trembled, I am sure I had a fever.

I finally got rid of the last of the letters. Now I must hurry back to camp; if I were late in returning, the resultant attention and possible punishment might well ruin all my plans.

The army bus terminal was next to the servicemen's club. I waited for the bus at the club bar and, to my consternation, saw the last people I wanted to meet: my company captain, first sergeant, and another noncommissioned officer at a nearby table. But politeness and caution forced me to go over and greet them. And they had to invite me to take an empty chair at their table. How could I chat with them in my condition? Yet that was just what I had to do.

The captain was not a bad fellow, and we had gotten along as well as possible for a private-first-class and a commissioned officer. His conduct toward me had grown cooler recently though, I believed, and now, at the table, the atmosphere seemed icy. He *must* have been informed that a member of his company had been under scrutiny and would soon have to report for investigation or trial. But you never know anything for sure in the army. Did the first sergeant know the story too? These thoughts raced through my head while we tried to exchange small talk and I prayed silently that the bus would not be late. When it arrived, I managed to get separated from the three men, but back at camp I climbed into bed in a worse state of mind than at any other time in my entire life.

The next day, Friday, brought another crisis. There had been almost no kitchen duty for months—but there was my name now, listed for KP on Sunday. I had told no one, not even the CP secretary, of plans to leave on Sunday. Yet it seemed impossible for this to be coincidental. If I tried to leave on Sunday, they might know who was on KP and stop me at the camp gate. Even if I got through the gate, my absence from the kitchen would cause a search. The big hunt would be on before I had time to get away at all.

What about leaving on Saturday? It would mean less time, since we were only free after lunch. But I would still have thirteen hours to get away before my absence was noticed. And there were certain advantages. Sunday, after all, was the very last day before I had to report and meant cutting things a little close. I must try Saturday.

Now I had to decide my route. I had heard that it was simple to go from West to East by the Berlin subway in those days. But how was I to get to West Berlin? The train trip was long, and there were certainly plenty of controls. One could get a ride there in a military plane, but I didn't know where or how, and even asking for information seemed risky. Too risky.

I recalled that the train to Kassel passed a small stream marking the frontier, so narrow that crossing it looked simple. But how many guards might be patrolling this area? It was quite a distance and somehow did not seem safe or sure enough. I thought of my winter trip to Vienna to visit an old friend and comrade. I had taken the train from Munich. Austria was still divided into four occupation zones in 1952, and I had had my military papers checked by Soviet soldiers. It had been somewhat exciting to see them in their fur caps and red stars for the first time. Perhaps I could travel the same route and ask to go with them when they came through. But I could not recall if there had first been an American control. I also could not be sure of the Soviet response. There were too many questions. I thought of traveling on to Vienna, which was then divided into five sectors, one for each occupying power and one joint four-power sector. But again, the matter seemed too complicated, too distant, too fraught with the danger of checks and controls.

My final choice was probably the stupidest and most dangerous of all.

But it seemed to offer the fewest problems involving checks and controls. The border between the American and Soviet Zones near Linz in Austria was formed by the Danube River. I decided to cross over there, with a boat or raft if I could find one, otherwise by swimming. I could not believe that my fellow soldiers controlled the entire length of the river. And I could endure a swim over long distances. I had made my final decision.

On Friday, with no difficulties at the gate, I went to the main station in Nuremberg. I checked departures to Salzburg, just over the Austrian border, and from there departures to Linz, which I should reach about 11 P.M.

While working at Headquarters Company many months earlier, always in fear that something like this might occur, I had "borrowed" some empty three-day pass forms. I filled out forms for Austria, signing imaginary names. I now had papers which could take me far enough to get to safety if I were not missed and searched for.

What to take? I had a small satchel in which I could put civilian clothes. If I could not reach the other side before 1 A.M. Sunday I would be less conspicuous in "civvies." If I were caught at night in uniform, the MPs would undoubtedly telephone my regiment, recognizable by the shoulder patches on my jacket and shirt. Civilian clothes would clearly be of great advantage.

Yet fear prevented taking them. If the satchel were checked at the gate, how would I explain those clothes, permitted only outside Germany or Austria? I thought of throwing them over the fence and picking them up later or hiding them there until I left. But I was too fearful of being observed. My fears were exaggerated, but I was so distraught that I finally decided to do without the pants, shirt, and jacket.

I decided to take some cartons of cigarettes in my unsuspicious satchel, some to be smoked, others as a means of payment or for making friends. I had destroyed all my letters, but I had taken photos all over Europe and the pictures meant a lot to me. Five rolls of film from Scandinavia had not even been developed, many of them of Ruth in her red coat. I put them in a small, tight metal box with many coins from my European travels.

I still had two unread progressive books I had bought in Copenhagen: Howard Fast's *The American* and Christopher Caudwell's *Illusion and Reality*. I feared taking such "Communistic" literature with me, and also feared leaving them in my locker. I did something I had never done before. With great sadness, I tore them up and buried them in a garbage can.

Friday night, on going to bed, I considered a last question: should I leave a farewell note for my fellow soldiers that could be found later, perhaps under a mattress? I would have liked to tell how I had been forced to leave to counter any lies spread about my departure. I liked many of them, got along with all of them, and had learned a great deal from some of them even without being able to communicate as openly as I might have wished. Yes, I would have liked to write that I was neither a spy nor unpatriotic, but was simply ruled by circumstances beyond my control. But again fear held me back, and perhaps common sense as well. What if they should find the note before I reached the East? I must forget the idea.

There was nothing left to do, nothing left to decide. I could only nervously run through everything in my mind and get as much sleep as possible. Saturday morning I added a few toilet articles to the satchel, made my bed, went to breakfast, and did my four hours of work. Later, I hid the registered letter under my undershirt and put a few personal papers, photo prints, and some cash into a plastic bag which I buttoned into a shirt pocket. In my wallet were only my identification, one of the passes I had filled out, and enough money to pay for tickets and something to eat. I headed for the camp gate. Had no one been warned against me? Was the army so sure of its prey? And if I did get out and finally reach the Danube, would I be able to cross the broad, swift river ahead of me? Or was my plan insane?

[1]

CHILDHOOD

How in the world did I, once the curly-headed little son of an art dealer, ever get into such terrible difficulties? Much of the blame lies perhaps in the decade of the thirties. My first recollection is of a Christmas tree with tiny animals, breathtaking for a three-year-old, but my second one is a long line of sad men awaiting a warm meal. The first newsreel I recall showed disheveled workers during the General Motors sit-down strike. In 1936, Germany had joined Italy to intervene on Franco's side in Spain. I asked my father why the bad guys were "rebels," which sounded revolutionary, while the good guys were "Loyalists." He explained that it was the fascists who had rebelled against a democratic government. I recall later seeing dramatic posters from the Spanish Civil War. Although in Spanish, their hard-hitting message, "No Pasaran," was very clear and helped inscribe the word "Spain" and all its associations indelibly in my soul.

My father sold lithographs, etchings, old maps, and caricatures. But few could afford such things in the 1930s, so he took office jobs to make ends meet. Though not well off, our family did not suffer dire poverty. But we were always moving: Queens, Greenwich Village, the Upper West Side, and Yorkville — to a better flat when we could afford it; mostly to a worse one.

I began my education in 1934 at ancient Public School 9 in Upper Manhattan. In 1935 my father got a concession to sell pictures in the prestigious Putnam Bookshop. We rented a small house in then-suburban Queens, and my parents decided I should learn our traditions, sending me to Jewish weekend school. But the Hebrew chants and prayers were mystifying; so was the story of Ezekiel, which we were to illustrate as homework. Not understanding how bones could join in a graveyard, I drew soup bones, ideal for my dog. When my artistry was rejected, I refused to go back, missing a chance to learn the lore of four thousand years.

My mother's parents came from Estonia; her father had had a tanning business until the czar wanted him in his army—for life. He escaped to America, had a large family, and invested in three houses. But, refusing to bribe building inspectors, he came close to bankruptcy. While doing repair work, he fell from a ladder, leaving his widow and oldest sons to care for the family.

My father's father was involved in an anticzarist conspiracy in Odessa, perhaps with the Jewish Bund. The conspirators were arrested, but he escaped and made it all the way to Connecticut. A scholarly man, he began to teach me Hebrew for my bar mitzvah, but after the first three letters he died, thus ending Passover seders, religious teaching, and any prospect of a bar mitzvah, and with it a sense of belonging to a "chosen people."

Some friends said that Jewish culture or religion was a shield against anti-Semitism. I found other defenses and luckily suffered few attacks. But living among Jews, with the holidays, food, and parents who could speak Yiddish, I did absorb some of the culture. Jewish history had yielded contradictory leanings toward art or business—or rebellion. I inclined toward rebellion; yet I was also drawn to the spirit-nurturing literature, music, and art.

Free Acres must take a good share of the blame for what became of me.

In summer we drove thirty miles to New Jersey's Watchung Mountains where eighty-five families had bungalows on land donated by its owner in 1910 to the Free Acres Association—if the organization were run in a way that conformed to Henry George's ideas. George, a nineteenth-century printer, theoretician, and activist, despised the "unearned increment," artificially inflated land prices, and rent which robbed ordinary folk. Free Acres did conform to George's ideas, and rent was extremely low.

Perhaps a third of the Free Acreites were WASPs, some of the right, some of the left, some just unusual, like elderly Miss Kissam, a vigorous disciple of the then unknown Baha'i sect, or Brownie, always with bicycle, knapsack, and occasional signs of long fasts. One WASP was Thorne Smith, a noted writer of ribald novels (including *Topper*) who drank himself to death during Prohibition.

Of the many Germans, few, if any, were Nazis; Hitlerite efforts to recruit people of German descent had almost no success in Free Acres. Most were "normal citizens," apolitical, fairly conformist, who "just wanted to be good Americans." A few Germans were Communists. Chris Blohm was big, stout, and hearty, and loved kids. His artificial leg made him especially intriguing. He was a Communist Party organizer, known for his help to grateful refugees from fascism living in German sections of New York, dangerous areas sprinkled with Nazi thugs.

Many Free Acreites, like us, were Jewish. They too were a varied mix of Bohemians, solid "bourgeois" citizens who ranged from conservative to left-leaning, and many unabashed leftists: a Trotskyist or two, but mostly Communists.

For us youngsters what mattered most were not nationality or politics, but whether a family was friendly to children or had a nasty dog. But one left-wing Jewish family left a lasting impression. Flo Gitnick, of aristocratic old German Jewish descent, was energetic and sharp-tongued. Step Gitnick, of Russian Jewish background, was gentle and warmhearted. Every summer they prepared a marionette show to take to schools during winter: *Pinocchio, Tom Sawyer, The Prince and the Pauper.* Bill Crawford, a Free Acres oldtimer, carved heads; Flo made clothes and wrote the texts; Step worked on the props. How I loved to watch them. And they talked politics with me as if I were an adult. When I was eight, I asked who they thought was the best candidate. They replied by asking what I thought. Maybe Roosevelt, I answered. They responded: why not Earl Browder?

"Well, I'm really for the Communists, too," I'd reflect. "But maybe we should back FDR so Landon doesn't win."

"You mean back a man who helped big business weather the Depression and who pushed through the AAA, so hogs are slaughtered, wheat burned, and milk poured into the river to raise prices high while people go hungry?"

"But wouldn't Landon be worse?"

"If people always choose the lesser of two evils, evil will always be with us," said Step.

Our white wooden bungalow had two porches scantily protected from New Jersey's giant mosquitoes. There was no electricity or plumbing; I recall the privy with its spiders and penetrating odor. Our rough stone fireplace was a source of much smoke, some warmth, and many daydreams while I listened to the crackling sap and shifting logs.

My mother had unusual ability at word games, which we played under a kerosene lamp in the evenings. She was remarkable in other ways. With two unmarriageable older sisters, she refused to vegetate under the old Jewish tradition that daughters marry in order of age. She fled to dances via the fire escape, worked as a "farmerette" during World War I, and took

art school courses where she met my father, whom she married when he returned from the war. Never content as a housewife, she nevertheless cooked
deliciously, loved coffee and delicacies, and fought an endless battle with
her weight. She also introduced me to the world of books from *Babar* to
Ditte Menschenkind and took me and my brother to plays — dragging us
from our cheap balcony seats into the orchestra. At restaurants she haugh-
tily returned unacceptable dishes while defending her propensity to stir tu-
mult by declaring: "If you don't, you get the worst seats and the worst
food. Everyone steps on you!" Refusing to become a housewife, she worked
as a social worker for an orphan asylum.

My father loved "whodunits," chess, and complex guessing games. If
anyone at supper said, "Guess who I met today," he would ask for three
guesses and, more often than not, uncannily succeed. I seem to have inherited only my mother's appetite, my father's mustache, and an addiction
to crossword puzzles.

My brother, six-and-a-half years my senior, was widely known as the boy
who ate caterpillars. One day he confided to me that he really chewed grass
while deftly tossing a caterpillar over his shoulder. His audience never analyzed the green wad that he spat out. I basked in the reflected glory of such
feats, and on a nobler plane learned from him a love of classical music.

My cousin Helen, whose mother had died, stayed with us whenever
possible. New to country life, she spoke of a "kitty" who rejected her pet-
ting. That was the skunk whose lair was under our house, close by mice,
turtles, snakes, frogs, and the wonderful katydids whose debate lulled us to
sleep. On lucky days a scarlet tanager flew by — bringing a moment of bliss
whose memory remained a symbol of stunning American beauty.

We rolled down the slanting "Common" lawn, arms flailing and laughing in the sweet grass. We had a swimming pool and a beach with a mud
end populated by tadpoles and by leeches, which fetched a penny each
from the local doctor. Afternoons were spent at the pool till we were summoned by our mothers' amazing falsetto calls, or our fathers, just home
from work.

One summer the Gitnicks convinced nonconformist Free Acreites to
start a nudist camp. It was an idea so abhorrent (though mildly amusing)
to so many Americans that it was given the code name "Uncle Sol's."
About forty people, young and old, met one Sunday in a clearing in the
distant woods. For me at six the array of huge buttocks and breasts was

overwhelming but not shocking. But the resident bees objected! They stung where they could—and they had a wide choice. I will never forget watching the adults file past our local doctor to receive blotches of tincture on all parts of their anatomies. The next Sunday the rain poured down and we retreated to an abandoned cabin with no clothes and no joy. We never again visited "Uncle Sol's."

Free Acres offered home-grown entertainment and culture: amateur nights, dances like the Virginia Reel and "Shoo Fly," a water carnival, and parties replete with then popular games. We staged amateur plays in our Open Air Theater with its backless benches and a backdrop of trees, putting on works that ranged from an anti-Nazi drama by Clifford Odets to *A Midsummer Night's Dream,* and Gilbert and Sullivan's *Trial by Jury,* which we performed with bandages covering faces and with the judge unable to sit as a result of a poison ivy attack at rehearsal.

The annual "Shishkebab" was best of all. Everyone sat around a big bonfire, roasting food, chatting, and singing the old songs together late into the night. Such evenings were milestones of childhood which engendered a sense of shared community.

There were "town meetings" on the last Sunday of each month amidst squalling babies and canine quarrels. Squabbles also marked the meetings; scrawny Miss Kissam often scolded my Uncle Sam, who lived next door to us, waving her umbrella menacingly over his head. He stuttered severely when excited, and umbrellas waving over his head certainly excited him. We youngsters didn't understand all the weighty issues at stake, but we got a good show and some understanding of Robert's Rules of Order.

One summer, four of us at age eleven decided to publish a newspaper. It was valuable training, especially in running a mimeograph, a diabolical invention that frequently failed to fill a page with legible text but always managed to cover us with heavy black ink. My job was to do interviews, and the most important was with Mike Gold. Mike was a sallow man, his face lined by struggles with diabetes, poverty, and many an adversary. He was reluctant to say much about his past, mentioning only that "we went to Mexico during the World War." I learned later that his magazine, *The Masses,* had been banned and arrests of socialists had forced him to flee the country. He said little of his part in the battle to save the Italian anarchists Sacco and Vanzetti and nothing of the heartbreak of millions when an electric switch killed the shoemaker and the fishmonger in Massachusetts—and their fine poetry and love of people. Nor did he speak of his role in meetings of writers around the world. But I was impressed by this quiet, modest, harassed man with his gentle ways and by his wise and charming French wife.

Free Acres residents met regularly for the "Forum," where they debated politics heatedly, argued Henry George's Single Tax, and even discussed sex (though no efforts at windows or chimney made this audible to us kids). Gold once spoke on the "Good Gray Poet" Walt Whitman, then still controversial because he broke taboos on sexual themes and wrote verses without rhyme and jingly meter. His poetry was called abstruse, almost incomprehensible, and for some antileftists, suspect, if not quite communist.

After reciting some verses, Mike turned to me, seated up front with my coeditors, and asked if I understood the poem. My thoughts had wandered, but I couldn't let Mike down and said loudly, "Oh, yes!" How could my friends admit less? They too asserted their comprehension. The laughter began with my statement. It became a torrent when a coeditor, the son of the main anti-Whitmanite, undercut his own father by fiercely affirming his understanding of Whitman.

World storms worsened in the late 1930s, but the Depression eased in the United States. The government offered cheap credit and Free Acres' single tax taboos on improving homes were relaxed. Oil heating, electricity, and flush toilets replaced fireplaces, kerosene, and privies. More and more bought cars, making long walks to the store, and even some short walks to neighbors unnecessary. A gap grew between the more and the less prosperous, and led to a gradual "bourgeoisification." A summer day camp was also set up; it was not bad, but our barefoot Huckleberry Finn days were lost forever.

––––––––––

The Putnam Bookshop closed down; we moved from suburbia to a Riverside Drive apartment in Manhattan. That meant another new school and new friends. Allen Abrahams taught me stamp collecting, opening the door to learning about every country from Antigua to Zambeziland. We hated swastika stamps and the Italian issues, but loved the handsome Soviet sports stamps and Hungarian stamps from the short-lived revolution of 1919, featuring pictures of Friedrich Engels and the executed peasant leader Gyorgy Dózsa.

Music became a part of my life. On Saturdays I went to a music school in Greenwich Village to learn the cello and play in the school orchestra. Not being gifted, I found cello practice so torturous that at times I bit the cello neck in despair. My suffering teacher may have secretly done the same. But despite false notes, the music school and orchestra and all the scales and arpeggios pouring from every room were worth the tears.

I spent the summer of 1937 at progressive Camp Manumit, where plucking chickens, eviscerating sheep, and weeding were a departure from Free Acres as well as being a new world for urban kids. After chores, we learned sculpture and linoleum carving, and Ben Himmel, a poor and leftist Jewish refugee from Poland, read us bedtime stories by unknown but unforgettable writers like the Polish author Sienkewicz. On Saturdays he took us on delightful picnics, playing violin along the way like a Chagall figure. When I turned away from the other boys' games with tin soldiers, Ben was impressed. That influenced me, as did my pacifist brother and the 1930s antiwar stance of the left.

Spain again. A friend and I went to the camp's director to suggest a melodrama about the Spanish Civil War. With his help we created a new play without putting a line on paper. It was a naive kids' product, but it explained the Franco revolt, why Mussolini and Hitler aided Franco, and why people came from all over to help the Republic. In 1937 we were optimistic, the play had a happy ending, and our little Mussolini caused great hilarity when dashing across the stage between costume changes with his bottom exposed. I played Hitler, a peasant, and an international volunteer. The little drama is marked indelibly in my memory.

In September, unable to pay our rent, we broke our lease and moved to a cheap apartment further uptown. Until the statute of limitations took effect, my father feared a summons; I was warned not to tell strangers that he was at home. We did not go hungry, but my parents' nerves were becoming alarmingly frayed.

Because of the lease hassle, we rented a neighbor's home at Free Acres in September 1938 and I began seventh grade in a small country school. When I walked into the classroom I got a shock. I had skipped four semesters over the years, and now I saw hulking lads and buxom girls of fourteen. I had rarely met farm or Italian children, and never such big ones. When I responded to an incredulous teacher's question that I was "ten," the class burst into laughter. There was widespread anti-Semitism among Catholics then, and I was warned that tough Johnny Carbo would make "mincemeat" out of me, the new kid from Free Acres, the "radical Jewish hotbed." I pleaded to go back to New York.

But to rural kids I represented the exotic "big city," and I had a supply of smart-alecky jokes which finally helped gain stature with the boys. So I got along — except in athletics where I remained hopelessly inept.

One day in September 1938 the geography class was given "busy work." The teacher let Czech-born Natalie and me listen to a menacingly ranting Hitler demand the Sudetenland. While the sellout of Czechoslovakia was being hailed as a triumph for "peace in our time," tearful Natalie and I took a very different view. Mussolini's propaganda influenced some classmates; most were not interested. But within five years most of these boys were marching off to war.

My parents got fed up with country life and found ways to finance a return to New York. I wept as bitterly at leaving as I had at staying, having shed my urban and ethnic snobbishness. I had learned to get along with and like those Italian farm kids. Even Johnny Carbo had become my friend and protector.

We moved to a run-down flat on the fifth floor of a building on East 88th Street. My brother had gone to the famous private Walden School. Now my mother took me to the Dalton School, aiming to get me a free education at this expensive institution. When she wanted something she usually got it; I soon was in another new school, replete with luxurious facilities from a swimming pool to well-equipped labs to a big library for the children of many wealthy and famous parents.

The school was named after the British Lord Dalton, whose system involved giving the students monthly folders detailing tasks to be completed and a graph to be filled in by teachers after each task, be it reading, homework, lessons. The system aimed to instill self-discipline, independence, and other virtues. I always lagged behind. Was it my late start or perhaps chronic laziness? Whatever the reason, my graph level was constantly low.

But Dalton had good teachers: hard-working, knowledgeable, skilled communicators. Some were even famous like the muralist Rufino Tamayo. Physical education remained my fearful burden. I could neither dribble nor shoot baskets and waited miserably to be chosen last. Baseball was worse — and as for football, I was willing to summon the courage to attempt tackling, but could hardly be mistaken for the "All-American boy" and fretted about the scorn of students for whom defeat meant "lack of manliness."

Much of my education came from hearty, red-headed Dave Binger, who inspired me to read Sherlock Holmes, memorize the Irish poems of Padraic Colum, and absorb zoology — learning every animal from aardvark to Grevy's zebra. While we hovered behind clanging backboards, Dave would ponder with me: "What was here before the beginning of the world?" or "Where does the universe end?" Such mysterious concepts were far more attractive than basketball. Some subjects were earthier. He was fourteen and I was an immature twelve, but we joked knowingly about the girls' emerging breasts. We were men of the world.

My main problem was not yet sex, but money. Classmates invited me to parties at their elegant homes — one with a corps of servants. Dave, like me, lived in a brownstone; but his family occupied the entire five-story building. Once, after a party, I was driven home in a limousine and panicked that the other kids would see where I lived. Despite my pleas to be let out at the corner, I was driven to the door. Luckily my father opened the front door in a bathrobe and it seemed as if we owned the whole building.

Our lack of money did not cow me into silence. But 1940 was miserable for leftists: the vanishing of famous Soviet figures, the Nazi-Soviet nonaggression pact, the division of Poland, and the Soviet war with Finland all engendered rising anti-Soviet sentiment. Except for the "treason trials" in the mid-thirties, liberals had generally acknowledged steadfast Communist resistance to fascism within Germany and Italy, in Spain, and at the League of Nations. Now Communists were being jailed, intellectuals were quitting the party, and Communist-influenced groups were collapsing. Though I was just twelve, as the "only red" at Dalton I was held responsible for Soviet actions and strained for any argument I could find while feverishly honing my debating skills.

I had an indirect triumph when the twenty-one-year-old nephew of our history teacher visited to sing folksongs and songs about the Congress of Industrial Organizations (CIO), which had recently won better conditions and self-confidence for millions. I was one of Dalton's few CIO partisans, but who could resist this fellow's stamping feet, bobbing Adam's apple, rhythmic banjo, and his skill at getting everyone to sing? It was one of Pete Seeger's first concerts.

Only once did my views cause me fear. In May 1940, Hitler's armies smashed through five small Western European countries, blitzkrieged France, and threatened England. The Soviets still had their nonaggression pact with Hitler, and Communists, sadly, were still calling it an imperialist war. I was told that teary-eyed English Miss Downes and Mme. Ernst from France had spoken angrily about me. The report, fortunately, was not true; they didn't blame me. So school life went on and I received my eighth-grade diploma.

After my father opened a gallery in Brentano's Bookshop, we moved to Free Acres to look after the modernizing of our bungalow. We had a new roof, a cellar, hot water, and electricity, but my beloved wild fields became a sedate lawn. And instead of New York's High School of Music and Art, where my cello had gained me acceptance, I wound up riding the school bus to Union County's Dayton High School.

The Nazi war machine ground on through Southern Europe and then, in June 1941, invaded the USSR. Most U.S. commentators accepted Hitler's boast that his army would be in Moscow in six or ten weeks. Not I. I felt certain, just as mistakenly, that fascism would be quickly smashed. It was easy to speculate from afar. While European and Asian homes collapsed in flames, we watched our home being rebuilt and almost forgot the up-heavals overseas.

Financial problems arose again, however, forcing us to rent out our re-built home, and I was never again able to live in Free Acres. In the fall of 1941 we moved back to New York, across the street from the Museum of Natural History, where I spent hours admiring and drawing its beautiful dioramas of African mammals. Our apartment also boasted an abundance of wildlife — from roaches to bedbugs. In 1943 we moved to an even worse flat on 75th Street, where my parents slept on a convertible couch in a cramped living room and did their best to make this tiny, roach-infested flat livable by decorating its walls with our still lifes and etchings.

I attended the then all-boys Bronx High School of Science, whose mostly working-class and lower-middle-class students were bright and ea-ger. A large number were Jewish, some Catholic, a few Protestant, and one or two were African American. All got along well, simply celebrating all re-ligious holidays. I became friendly with a happy kid named Don deKoven whom I avoided taking to my flat. One day he took me to his; it was even shabbier than ours, and that cemented our friendship. We loved to race loudly through subway cars or act out elaborate film clichés. Don's humor was in the inventive Bronx Science mold. At parties he would ostenta-tiously lift a gold pocket watch to his ear, shake it slowly, then violently, then smash it — scattering its parts. He would then coolly brush the parts back into the watch and get it ready for another show. He could also cover all but an ear on the portraits of famous composers and unerringly identify them. And he was fond of lying offhandedly that he was currently "skimming through Kant's *Kritik der reinen Vernunft*."

Teachers at Science were the usual varied lot. But one was particularly memorable: Mr. Falkenstein, whose compelling descriptions of Napoleon III's campaigns were masterpieces of irony. He introduced us to Marxist concepts like "superstructure" and economic "base," and probably did not survive the later purges of left-wing teachers.

I plunged into Bronx Science's rich club life, exploring genetics in the Biology Club, chasing on-the-loose snakes in the Nature Club, plodding with the Birding Club through swamps and sewage outlets to identify "new birds." But the Current Events Club had the greatest impact with its disputes between Social Democrats, Trotskyists, and Communists. The Communists impressed me most; I accepted their invitation to attend meetings of the American Student Union, once a vital part of the huge 1930s youth movement, but now fading after the Soviet-German pact.

On December 7, the world conflagration hit home when the Japanese struck Pearl Harbor. We listened intently as Congress declared war on the Axis. Overnight the United States became allied with the USSR; cries of "Communazi" evaporated and anti-Sovietism had suddenly become "unpatriotic." While the underlying tension between socialism and capitalism remained, the isolation that Communists experienced in 1939 began to diminish.

The Japanese conquered one Pacific Island after another from hardfighting U.S. and allied forces. German armies swept to Moscow's outskirts. A giant counteroffensive broke their grip, but a new Nazi drive reached Stalingrad on the Volga and another neared Suez. Every defeat was shocking, but I never doubted a final victory.

On the home front, my father became an air-raid warden. The worst we had to contend with were blackouts, black markets, scarcities, rising prices, and rationing. There were no battles and falling bombs, and the only concentrations camps were for 100,000 Japanese Americans — while posters caricatured big-toothed "yellow Japs" and even the Communist Party supported the incarceration of citizens of Asian descent. I always despised the flag-waving nationalism which scarred the nation's ideals and was unhappy with some left-wing friends who had opposed the "imperialist war" until the USSR was attacked, and now embraced nationalism and even anti-Japanese racism. Such shifts were too rapid for a thirteen-year-old. But I knew enough of Hitler's genocidal acts to hate fascism more than anything in the world.

Jack Royce was magnetic — the best speaker in the Current Events Club as well as expert in lobbing hilarious puns. One day he asked me if I was interested in joining his Young Communist League club which met weekly on the Upper West Side. At fourteen, I was the youngest of about a dozen members, but soon joined the heated discussions. We were expected to read and sell a pamphlet by Communist leader Earl Browder, asserting that Soviet-American unity and the no-strike truce between capital and labor would continue after the war. I do not recall my views, but I hope I was skeptical.

Devastating bombing of Germany had begun, striking many civilian targets. One member, about to be drafted, evoked Nazi barbarities in Spain and insisted that every German not held in a concentration camp should be bombed. I recall trying to counter with my belief that for those committed to humankind, especially Communists, it might be necessary to fight and even bomb other nations to defend one's existence — but we must never ape the Nazis, whose primary aim was to destroy people. We argued often, but these young people were devoted to winning the war, to stamping out racism, and to making a better world for the good of all its people, especially working people. For better or worse, I had hitched my star firmly to this hundred-year-old movement, with a developed theory and active advocates around the world.

On Sundays, I also began visiting a different kind of club. The Ethical Culture Society, a secular, humanitarian organization, had invited high school students to explore topical issues. Most YCL friends were from lower-middle-class families. Those at the Sunday discussions, also largely Jewish, were from wealthier homes. I fit in with both groups which at the time similarly supported Roosevelt and opposed fascism, racism, and big business.

In 1943 I went to an Ethical Culture summer camp, where we did our bit for the war effort by picking fruits and vegetables. Most campers attended Fieldston, a high school also run by Ethical Culture. Though expensive, it offered scholarships for those from nonwealthy families. My determined mother got one, but I had to repeat the eleventh grade to make a minimum two-year residency. I left that inventive, crazy bunch at "Science" to enter a different and more prosperous world.

Some Fieldstonites were very intelligent and interesting, others were more enthralled with the latest fashions, or films, or who was dating whom. Small, relaxed classes made it easy to make friends, and I soon felt at ease. Some elderly teachers, kept in service by the wartime labor shortage, struggled with poor hearing (students fought to sit on our Latin teacher's deaf side), but they and others also encouraged us to think. I wrote papers on the truncated Mexican Revolution and its memorable figures: hesitant President Madero, stormy Pancho Villa, the fiery mural painters, Zapata on his wheeling steed leading Indian peasants. I delved into Chinese history, and wrote about Sun Yat-sen's 1911 uprising, Chiang Kai-shek's betrayal of the revolution, and the legendary Communist Long March to Northern China. In our final year I took the best course I have had in my life. Elbert Lenrow gave us a grand review of literature from the *Iliad* and *Odyssey* and both Testaments, to the Greek playwrights, Dante, Chaucer, Cervantes, Shakespeare, Milton, Goethe, Whitman, Ibsen, Shaw, Malraux, and others. That engendered a life-long love of literature, for which I am eternally grateful. Mr. Werthman led us through soaring renditions of Schubert and Mendelssohn with the right blend of discipline, humor, and musical brilliance. Even in "Phys Ed," account was taken of those bereft of athletic gifts by placing us in a "Special Squad" that was kidded but never despised.

Fieldston suddenly confronted me with another problem—girls, who had not existed at all-boys' Science. I began to learn the elaborate codes of dating. I gradually discovered that my idea of a great date, involving lively discussions of literature, art, and above all politics, ending with a long romantic kiss which sent me home blissfully to read love poems by Keats or Shelley, somehow was not shared by my seventeen-year-old dates. I could not understand why other far more limited lads had more luck—and the result was many a lonely Saturday evening at home or desultory wanderings with Don or some other all too masculine friend.

During my last school year, girls increasingly occupied my thoughts, and even played a part in my political career. In October 1943 the Young Communist League turned itself into the "broad" progressive American Youth for Democracy, a precursor of Communist leader Earl Browder's later dissolution of the Communist Party into the "Communist Political Association." I was unhappy with the scrapping of the YCL, and paid little attention to the AYD. But when I got an invitation to an AYD gathering in the same hall, with the same name, and the same leader as that of the dissolved YCL club, I was amused and curious — and went.

There I met Dalton students Nina and Eloise. Nina had fought for the right of a black student to use the Dalton pool. She was the petite and intelligent daughter of Martin Gumpert, a German refugee doctor and poet. Eloise had stunning big brown eyes and long, dark hair. Both were pretty, vivacious, and politically engaged, a perfect combination. I could never decide which to pursue — and won neither of them. But my hopes kept me in the group. It turned out that the AYD was just right for me, with its stimulating speakers and exciting discussions among an eclectic brew of leftists. We danced, joked, flirted, collected aluminum for the war effort, sought votes for FDR and scrappy, radical congressman Vito Marcantonio, organized a boycott of a Jim Crow skating rink, and sought (without much success) to recruit black members. We learned more than most young people of the heroism, sacrifice, and suffering of the Soviets, the Yugoslav, Greek, and Italian partisans, and antifascist fighters all over the world.

My brother, who always loved the sea, was now a merchant marine officer. His convoys often came under Nazi attack, and happy were the moments when Walt's little "V-mail" letters arrived to assure us that he was alive and sailing. My father got a job censoring sensitive information out of letters going abroad. I was far more carefree, and discovered the AYD's Folksay Club in Greenwich Village, which ran Saturday night square dances at the left-wing Furriers' Union Hall. During breaks we had impromptu "hootenannies," singing songs that ranged from Woody Guthrie to Hanns Eisler. We sang the antifascist "Peat Bog Soldiers" in English and German, seeking to replicate Paul Robeson's moving rendition of the final line: "One day we will cry rejoicing, homeland dear you're mine at last." We sang "Avanti Popolo" from Italy, "Chee Lai" from China, the Spanish Civil War songs, partisan songs, and the legendary Almanac Singers' rousing pro-labor and anti-Nazi songs, especially their "Round and Round Hitler's Grave." My romantic streak made me love the old ballads. After the dances I joined Tom Paley and Ernie Lieberman, who were to become popular in folk circles, to sing laments like "Barb'ry Allen" and "On Top of Old Smoky." My voice was loud, if not mellow, and my heart was full of love for the music. Those songs, and that environment, drew me into "the movement" far more than scores of ideological arguments.

At Bronx Science, my goal had been zoology. But one evening, at the "Town Hall of the Air" I became emotionally involved with a topic under debate and reflected: do I want to be a zoologist? No, my vital interests were political. Not career politics but "change-the-world" politics, to achieve a world without hunger, war, or mass suffering. Perhaps I could join the labor movement, whose songs I sang, whose struggles I supported, and whose traditions I loved.

I discussed all this with Dick, the able, confident president of the Fieldston student government. He said that I was tying myself down to one political doctrine, perhaps devoting my life to it. What if it's wrong? What if I realized, say at sixty-five, that I'd thrown my life away on an unworthy cause?

After reflecting on that question, which had not occurred to me, I replied that he might be right. Maybe at sixty-five I'd realize that I had been deluded and misled. But the alternative would be to devote my life only to personal advancement. Then it surely would have been wasted. This way, I had a chance that it would be well spent. I don't recall whether Dick found a counterargument; I never did.

My college entrance exam results landed me at my first choice, Harvard. But my father's censor's job had ended; I sorely needed a scholarship, which was granted on the basis of test results, financial need, and an interview at the august and intimidating Harvard Club of New York. Stodgy men exuding an aura of rock-ribbed Republicanism (despite a black-wreathed picture on the wall of FDR, who had died weeks earlier) asked me about my hobbies, my favorite subjects—and my views of the New Deal. I didn't want to lie, but I didn't want to lose the scholarship either. So I said I liked many things Roosevelt had done, but not everything. In response to their question about what I didn't like, I mentioned the Agricultural Adjustment Act. Conservatives despised the AAA, but the left also criticized it for destroying foodstuffs to boost prices. The gentlemen accepted my equivocal answer.

I got the $250-per-semester scholarship, which helped, but was not enough. Additional support came from an unexpected source—a radio quiz for high school seniors. My mother characteristically pressured me into the event that covered a range of subjects from science to history. I made it to the finals, where, though using the wrong method, I stumbled into the right answer to a pivotal math question. Lo and behold—I had won the first prize, one thousand dollars, and happily opened my first checking account.

In June 1945 a world was being transformed. The most destructive carnage in history was winding down and I had been born a year too late to be directly engaged. My nearly heedless teen years seem almost fatuous compared to others. The war and the death camps which cost over fifty million lives did not spare my cousin Jerry, who was captured during the Battle of the Bulge. The Nazis had ordered Jews to step forward if they did not want all captives to be killed. My aunt was not consoled that our nation was largely spared such sacrifices. Her only son — a fine medical student — was gone.

The war in Asia ground on. Expecting to be drafted, we Harvard enrollees attended a special summer semester to at least get started. At seventeen, I embarked on my college career.

FLIGHT (2)

I had no problems leaving the camp, though I ran into three soldiers from the parts depot, and clumsily shammed light chatter. My train chugged past pretty Bavarian towns, but scenery did not interest me. I was constantly expecting someone to tap me on the shoulder. Worried that my five cigarette cartons would look suspicious to customs, I kept a few packs but threw one carton after another out the window.

At Munich I changed trains for Salzburg, recalling a very perfunctory check at the Austrian border on my earlier visit. Would my flight mean tighter controls? Of course not. No one even looked at my papers. One big hurdle had been taken but I was no less distraught. In Salzburg, I changed most of my money for Austrian schillings and bought a ticket to Linz.

On the Linz train I pored nervously over a map and pondered where to get off. Across from Linz was a small area marked as part of the U.S. Military Zone. What if I swam right into that enclave? Another concern: in downtown Linz, the last station in the U.S. Zone, I might face a military control. But if I got off sooner, could I get to the Danube before a 1 A.M. cutoff when soldiers on city streets would surely be questioned?

The problem dissolved when the train passed through the suburbs without stopping and pulled directly into the Linz station. I descended into the dark city without seeing any military controls and began groping toward the Danube, not daring to ask directions. I walked in circles, for all I knew. The big river should not be difficult to find and I simply must find it — soon.

Suddenly, I was on a prosperous, pleasant street. One look at the license plates confirmed my fears; I was in the middle of a U.S. Army housing area, the worst place imaginable. It was past midnight and deserted; but a guard might stop me. I quickly walked through the darkness into a broad field bordered by trees, the kind suggesting wasteland and water. This must be near the Danube. As I moved forward the ground became muddy. Picking my way toward what was surely the river, I suddenly heard from different directions mysterious whistles which did not sound like night birds. There seemed little doubt—these "birds" wore uniforms. Were they communicating about a suspicious intruder? I believed that and decided to quietly retreat from what was likely the river boundary marking the "Iron Curtain," the dangerous, ideologically charged dividing line between East and West. After a panicked walk through a dark grassy field, I heard those whistle tones again from several directions. To this day I wonder: were they echoes of a sleep-deprived imagination, or were they chillingly real?

Uncertain about which way to turn, I squatted at the edge of the field. I had already shed the traveling bag, but the coin-filled metal box was making a loud rattle. If only I had thrown the damned foreign coins away. In the pitch black night, I could not separate them from the photos and film rolls and, in a move that still saddens me today, I exposed the film, buried the box in a shallow hole, and then dozed off, completely exhausted.

I must have napped for over two hours. When I awoke, the eastern sky was paling. People would soon be stirring; they would see my disheveled, muddy clothes, and perhaps turn me in. I moved on toward the sunrise and what seemed the city outskirts. A wall poster announced that the Austrian-Soviet Friendship Society was meeting that very day. Should I try to find an Austrian Communist or a Soviet from across the river? But how could I find the gathering, and how could I avoid a repetition of my sad experience with the Nuremberg party headquarters? I kept walking and at last saw a power plant near a small inlet or canal bordered by gravel embankments. At the end of the inlet was an empty barge; and there, surely was the river. I had reached the Danube—with nothing to stop me from swimming across the river, which did not look too wide or swift.

Just then I spotted a man arriving at the plant building. He seemed to look at me distrustfully. Would he call the police or the U.S. Army? I must get into the water quickly and be ready for underwater swimming. I slid down the embankment thinking that swimming would not be easy; swift undercurrents might spell life and death. I tore off my conspicuous regimental patch; I could not swim with my shoes, so I threw them into the water and watched them sink. With a heavy heart, I threw my new, expensive camera into the canal. I was now left only with socks, pants, a torn shirt, a wallet in my back pocket, the army's letter in my undershirt, and a small waterproof bag with valued items and money in my buttoned shirt pocket.

Leaving nearly all worldly possessions behind, I slid deeper into the cool water and began swimming. Wondering how far I would get, whether I would ever stand on dry land again, and what awaited me, I struck out through the inlet toward the Danube.

[2]
HARVARD YEARS

When I arrived at Harvard, I was awed by the ivy-walled Yard and solid Georgian brick "houses" with their trees and lawns. The university embodied scholarship, learning, and authority in its great names: the Adamses, Roosevelts, Emerson, Thoreau, Lowell, and later John Reed, Dos Passos, Thomas Wolfe, W. E. B. Du Bois. Its clubs were snobbish preserves of blue-blooded WASPs. But just as the New England aristocrats had retreated before waves of immigrants, Harvard had felt the impact of changes wrought by the New Deal, the war, and the GI Bill—opening its doors to Irish and Italian Catholics, Greeks, Jews, and three blacks.

I was closest at first to my Fieldston mates, with whom I laughed, played word games, and argued over classical music (there were Bach and Tchaikovsky factions). We took high culture seriously and combined forces to compete in Harvard Radio's classical music quiz, where first prize was the name and number of a student at Radcliffe, our "sister school." Our clique nearly always won.

In September, I moved into the handsome Dunster House. For the next three years I lived and studied there, rooming with Bronx Science pal Danny Federman and with Jack Duker, the funny, lecherous war veteran son of a cantor. Those two became solid friends who respected my views even when disagreeing with them. I liked "Dukes's" unceasing frivolity and Danny's Freudian ardor. What they surely saw as my Communist obduracy may have moved us apart over the years, but our love of a good laugh and our resistance to crankiness preserved our harmony.

We lived in a traditional Harvard setting—two bedrooms, living room, and bathroom cleaned daily by derisively labeled "biddies." Tuition was $200 a semester, board was $65 and meals about $80. My $250 scholarship did not suffice, but with Spartan living, my quiz money got me through the first year. But we were not perturbed by our scanty finances. Social differences faded when we all streamed to the football stadium, bottles in hand, to laugh at pitched battles for the goalpost after games and the battered students, soaked by water from the fire trucks, who collected goalpost trophies but no lasting injuries.

When the Labour Party of our British professor of government surprisingly won the July 1945 election, even stalwart Churchill partisans applauded. I wondered: would Britain now join the Soviets and oppose Harry Truman's incipient belligerency? The new Labour Party leaders soon dispelled my naiveté. Then, only eleven days later, came the Hiroshima tragedy. Two days after that unprecedented carnage, the Soviets moved against Japan, as promised. The following day, the air force dropped a second atom bomb, this time on Nagasaki. Japan's surrender five days later evoked joy and pandemonium — ironic after two cities had become wastelands of ashes, with 200,000 corpses and even more survivors who envied the dead. The war's end spared us from the draft. But the two atom bombs, I believe, were the first tragic blows in the new cold war.

I soon met AYD member Rowe Gingrich. He was jesting and easygoing, but took his Marxism seriously. Harvard had a Liberal Union, but we hoped to form an AYD chapter to the left of the Union. Rowe met with Marge Metten, the area AYD secretary who had been a legendary leftist at Radcliffe with the fiery persona of Barbra Streisand in *The Way We Were*. He brought back a folder with AYD brochures, injunctions against despised Social Democrats and "Trotskyites," and the name of studious, earnest Betty at Radcliffe to help us get started. When we met Betty, Rowe's folder was gone. We retraced our path to and from the telephone booth where we had called her, but never found the folder.

In the fall, instead of building AYD, Rowe and I decided to join the Harvard Liberal Union. But instead of getting a hearty welcome, we were cross-examined about whether we planned to "bore from within" the HLU. With that, our membership was left in hostile abeyance. So we staked out another project: a coordinating organization for all progressive groups on five or six New England campuses. Little came of it, but I did meet beautiful, magnetic Ann from Smith College who won over nearly everyone she met. Rather than confrontation and attempts to prove others wrong, she sought common ground, such as the widely shared wish to save the planet from atomic destruction. Ann did not alienate or scorn opponents, but won them through respect and willingness to take one or two modest steps together. Little came of our efforts, however, especially after Ann graduated. But something else momentous occurred. One day Rowe asked: "You're a red, aren't you?"

"What do you mean? Sure I am," I answered.

"Then sign this!" And he handed me an application to join the Communist Party.

I swallowed. The cold war glacier was moving inexorably onward; Communists, almost tolerated during the war as friends of "our Soviet ally," were suspect again. The party became the "Communist Political Association" in 1944 and gave up most branches in factories and the Deep South. An open letter from the French Communist Jacques Duclos criticizing this move in June 1945 (many believed he spoke for Stalin) made it possible to reestablish the party, oust Earl Browder, and return to a more militant stand. This hardly enhanced its media popularity. What would I be getting into by joining? Such a fateful step required reflection!

"Are you a red or aren't you? If so, just sign here!"

I signed, paid a 50-cent initiation fee, and, with no other formalities, became a member.

Many influences in my seventeen years led to this step. There was my Depression-era question about why those haunted men stood in line, those "no pasaran!" posters and our play about the heroic international resistance to Spanish fascism, the fight to save the Scottsboro boys and cleanse the nation of racial injustice, Communist resistance to the Nazis, particularly the massive Soviet sacrifices exemplified by Stalingrad and Leningrad. The especially enriching cultural life to which I had been exposed also deepened my belief in a new society which advanced culture and humanity. I was pushed to the decision, yet it was logical enough. It changed my life, but I never felt regret.

Even my Harvard comrades laughed because I got "as involved in an election in Peru" as in events next door. I exalted in victories or mourned defeats in "the good fight," whether in Nepal, Nigeria, or Nicaragua, and felt closer to those fighting them than to many insensitive people nearer home. My first party activity was collecting signatures on the run-down side of Cambridge to qualify two black clergymen for the City Council ballot. I still recall how one elderly woman refused to sign, saying that the last time she signed something her furniture was taken away.

About ten people were at my first party meeting in a married student's apartment. At one point, a student came in, stood around for fifteen minutes, and left. Everyone thought someone else had invited him to the private gathering. Finally, one member said wryly, "That's the biggest provocateur on campus." Future meetings were more secret, not because we preferred it that way, but because we feared very correctly that disclosure of our membership might wreck job chances and bring even worse consequences.

I plunged into peace activity, joining a "Win the Peace" delegation to Washington which still attracted some prominent people, from Paul Robeson to Senator Claude Pepper and R. J. Thomas, the centrist president of the United Auto Workers. That spring the Harvard Liberal Union swerved to the left, partly because of returning war veterans. Rowe and I finally became members. In March, Winston Churchill gave his "Iron Curtain" speech at Fulton, Missouri, urging an Anglo-American crusade against communism. When Harvard decided to award Churchill an honorary doctorate, the HLU organized a protest, and also called for international control of atomic weapons and a break with Franco. The protest won surprising support but also frenetic opposition from rightists, who embraced Churchill as a great war hero and anticommunist. The Conservative Club called a counterprotest; Boston papers smelled a "hot spring" and fanned "townie" resentment against "gownie" Harvard. Everyone expected two clashing marches. Finally, nearly one hundred antiwar demonstrators with high spirits, clever signs, and a wooden atom bomb marched triumphantly through Harvard Yard.

Suddenly another group appeared—not the conservatives, but ten pranksters led by bandaged piper, drummer, and guitar strummer in "Spirit of '76" motif, spoofing us protesters with signs that read "Tippecanoe and Tyler Too" or "Pike's Peak or Bust." The ringleader was the friendly though wacky Shep Ginandes. His notoriety began with a frog dissection, when the female instructor called out: "Come look. Mr. Ginandes has the largest pair of gonads I've ever seen!" The class roared, she blushed, and a legend was born. Now he sought to create a new legend by stealing our march. (Our fury grew when headlines falsely blared: "100 Conservatives Counter Leftist March.") The right-wing marchers never appeared, but there were some skirmishes. A big redhead wrested a placard from a Radcliffe student. I stared. It was my old pal Dave Binger, with whom I had joked, learned zoology, and memorized poetry. I could only call "Dave?" An icy era was unfolding.

My next political adventure was more strenuous. The AYD was campaigning against the big meat companies which were trying to kill price regulation. Back in the 1600s, the Common had been deeded to Boston so that residents might always graze cattle there. We would break a media boycott by bringing a cow to the Common and leaflet the anticipated gawkers. A friendly farmer brought one, not a stolid milk cow, but a frisky heifer. Someone urged that the "Harvard man" take the rope, and the strong-minded young bovine dragged me off on a wild race through the Common. We wound up struggling to get an exhausted heifer onto a rampless truck, while one local paper printed a photo with an unflattering caption.

In 1946 I had my first free summer. My pursuit of union work was foiled when the left-wing United Electrical Workers could not hire me. I had $100 of my prize money left and few hopes of a job. So I decided to leave New York's swelter and head west to see my country.

I hitchhiked to grimy Buffalo, admired the thundering Niagara Falls, and crossed two hundred miles of Canada, my first time on foreign soil. In Detroit I watched the shift change at Ford's massive River Rouge plant and in Chicago found relief from oppressive slums and stockyard stench when my friend Rowe mercifully took me to a beach along Lake Michigan. In Madison, Wisconsin, I visited Jack Royce, who had recruited me into the YCL — and I joined a veterans' rent control demonstration. Across the Mississippi, there were miles of dry plains. I knew not a soul between Madison and San Francisco.

In the Black Hills, an elderly Seventh-day Adventist gave me a few days' lodging for helping with some construction work. He warned that the atom bomb would first hit New York, and tried to convert me. At a rodeo in Sheridan, Wyoming, I sat in the cheap bleachers among owners of nearby ragged tepees and stood for the national anthem while they sat and chatted. Feeling uncomfortable, I sat, stood, then went into a crouch, neither sitting nor standing. A young Native American had me buy him a beer. My next ride told me that I had broken the law.

Yellowstone was paradise. But even paradise can cost too much. Wandering bears kept me from sleeping out, and I had to cadge a mattress or a floor from merciful employees or tourists. After a third night in an empty shack, I hurried on. Finally I crossed the Golden Gate Bridge, and in beautiful San Francisco I found social contacts again — an AYD group and my cousin Helen, whom I had not seen in years. She was visibly nervous, and I later learned that she had just had a baby out of wedlock, which in those years was a "sin." Helen had to give her baby to an elderly family to raise, visiting only weekends and claiming to be a "divorcee."

On the homeward journey, I got stuck in El Monte, near Los Angeles, where the only place to sleep was an unoccupied jail cell. At Boulder Dam, I waited two desperate hours in 114 degree heat, not daring to walk 150 feet to look at the giant dam and lose my spot in a line of hitchhikers. In Albuquerque, I again sought a jail for shelter and wound up on a dirty floor with glaring lights and roaches while drunks and prostitutes were hauled in all night. In Ohio, I luckily caught a ride all the way to New York City. In those six weeks I got rides from farmers, teachers, shop stewards, lonely traveling salesmen, and lots of truck drivers who risked fines or loss of insurance to pick me up. I got only one ride from an African American, in a dilapidated pickup truck in California. Barriers crumbled slowly. But I listened intently as he told me something of his life, and perhaps he sensed that I was less prejudiced than most whites whom he met. Then, before long, it came time to say: "I turn off here, son."

I saw many ugly sights: ragged Indian hovels, urban slums, pollution, self-abnegating tawdriness — like the sleazy burlesque shows which loneliness drove me to in Buffalo and Detroit. I met nasty drivers, including some who hated blacks. Should I argue with them and possibly lose the rest of a ride, or keep my mouth shut? I did both on occasion, but hoped they all noticed my disapproval. An anti-Semite insisted that Jews were running the country. I asked him for examples. He came up with the industrial magnate Henry Kaiser (who was not Jewish) and comedian Eddy Cantor. A year after the war he was repeating the lies which led to gas chambers for millions. Others hadn't had enough of killing, wanting to drop the A-bomb on the Russians "before they drop it on us."

But most people were thoughtful and decent, if perhaps too ready to believe the press or radio. They worried about high prices, scarce jobs, or prospects for new bloodshed. I came to appreciate the vastness and beauty of the country and the diversity, complexity, and often contradictory character of its people. That trip provided memories and sustenance for all my years in exile.

I hurried home to attend an AYD school north of New York. Nat

Brooks, expelled from the University of Michigan for political activity, guided us through student movement history from the tepid 1920s to the upheavals of the 1930s. Long before "political correctness," we sought to purge our speech of unconsciously racist terms like "black as sin," "white lies," "yellow," and "Gyp." Sometimes this was overdone, but it was motivated by our demand for equality and a belief that progress was impossible without purging racist thought and action from our lives. We debated whether there were too many Jews in AYD and concluded that there were not, but too few others. Male chauvinism was probed, especially the downgrading and stereotyping of women as incapable of leading. We ended with "criticism and self-criticism," debating individual strengths and weaknesses. This could become petty and heartless, even repressive. But it could also be cathartic and liberating, ending in unity, mutual respect, and camaraderie. That is how it felt then.

Back in the Harvard Liberal Union, unity was fraying. Conflicts between "fellow travelers" and "Social Democrats" reemerged: Do we support Greek partisans or British-backed royal forces, new Soviet-sponsored Balkan regimes, or ousted monarchs and regents who claimed fidelity to democracy and free enterprise? As disputes sharpened, both sides sought to mobilize sympathizers to attend meetings. The left had a thin majority, buttressed by some who still embraced wartime friendship with the Russians. But many were becoming anti-Soviet, spurred by Stalin's maneuvers and by a deluge of media anticommunism. There were esoteric charges: "Why are the Russians still on Danish Bornholm?" one fellow asked repeatedly. We could countercharge, but could not provide adequate answers for every allegation.

Tensions worsened in 1947. With the Greek partisans not broken, the "Truman Doctrine" was announced: $400 million to destroy the partisans and to fortify Turkey as a bulwark against the Soviets. The press mocked frequent "Nyets" by the outnumbered Russians in the UN while spy scares in Canada and the United States multiplied. Truman's Executive Order 9835 set up the Federal Employee Loyalty Review program, threatening government workers with dismissal for the "wrong" beliefs and the Attorney General Tom Clark issued his list of "subversive" organizations. The McCarthy era began well before that gentleman arrived on the scene.

Many of our supporters began to slide away while our opponents invited anyone they pleased to pay a one-dollar initiation and "vote against the reds." The day of reckoning came at a jammed election meeting. We fore-saw the defeat—but not what preceded it. One of their leaders took the floor, said: "Before we vote I have something of interest," and read excerpts from the papers Rowe and I had left in the telephone booth two years be-fore with those simplistic, sectarian descriptions of professors and students, some now present. There was an uproar. Rowe and I now understood the cold reception we had received when applying for HLU membership.

We lost the vote. When in the majority we had not always distributed positions fairly. With some magnanimity, the winners allowed our friendly Geoff White to remain as head of a minor committee.

Besides politics, I also studied some, majoring in economics, a subject which for me was laden with ideological snares. Economics 101 was fes-tooned with "marginal" graphs and curves, appropriate for future busi-nessmen, but not for me. I was not confident enough to draw my own con-clusions in a course on John Maynard Keynes and had similar problems with New Deal adviser Alvin Hansen's belief that the new International Monetary Fund and the World Bank would solve global ills. Flamboyant John Dunlop taught union history, but discussion usually boiled down to debates between those who wanted management to be nicer to "respon-sible" unions and those who wanted unions and workers to shut up and take whatever was offered. I wanted neither.

Courses in European history and government were informative, but of-ten mistakenly reduced Marxism (whenever it was mentioned) to simple economic determinism. But F. O. Matthiessen, the brilliant literary scholar, ignited my romantic spirit with wonderful images and hidden ideas in Shakespeare. My learning remained spotty, perhaps because I had little confidence in my courses and lacked tangible goals, unlike my roommates Danny and Dukes, who had no doubts about their goals respectively in psychiatry and law.

Our defeat in the HLU led us at last to found a Harvard AYD chap-ter, which required two faculty sponsors and ten members. Professors Kirkley F. Mather, a renowned geologist whose lineage went back to Cot-ton Mather, and Matthiessen, both tenured and supportive, were willing. We received recognition. Harvard was proud of its tolerant traditions.

Tolerance did not extend, however, to a planned AYD magazine, to be edited and published at Harvard, with contributors from other colleges. It was not a Harvard publication, the dean decided, and despite past precedents, forbade it. We turned a hard blow to a well-designed magazine to our advantage: outside the walls we shouted, "Buy the only magazine banned in Harvard Yard." We soon sold out. But the second issue was our last one.

Chairing the AYD chapter, I met guest speakers like Feng Yu-hsiang, the legendary "Christian general" who fought Japan and later broke with Chiang Kai-shek. He denounced Chiang with such juicy invective that the interpreter had to clean it up while Chinese students roared with laughter. Our club also brought to Harvard the jazz musician Sidney Bechet; folksingers Betty Sanders and Oscar Brand; the great singer Woody Guthrie with the words "This machine kills fascists" on his guitar; the magnificent Leadbelly with his rhymed couplets in Louisiana dialect, dance steps, and his anthem "Goodnight, Irene," destined to top the charts months after he died in poverty; Pete Seeger, with his exuberance, sincerity, and depth in all he said or sang.

Our party group revived the prewar John Reed Society, named for the journalist, author, Communist Party founder, and Harvard graduate. It aimed to promote serious Marxist inquiry, but attracted occasional nutty leftist poseurs, like the pipe-puffing Radcliffe student who demanded to know of a speaker on Soviet economics: "What do they do with imbecile children in Russia?" Another speaker, Manny Bloom, New England Communist Party head, allayed our worries by effectively answering questions from sophisticated Harvard students with humor and logic — qualities that were not always typical. Two of the more memorable lecturers were Carl Marzani, who went from intelligence service behind enemy lines in Italy to being one of the first jailed during the cold war, and the German Communist Gerhart Eisler. Eisler had fled Europe one step ahead of the Nazis. When he tried to return after the war, he was labeled in the media as a "Comintern spy." Expecting a big crowd and trouble, we asked friendly Boston seamen to occupy the front row. When Eisler began, two students in Cossack costumes hitherto concealed under their coats ran toward him. They were hustled out, but the local press got its photo of this prearranged "angry student protest." Eisler later slipped out of the country and made it to East Germany.

There was more than politics at Harvard, even for me. The Drama Club's offerings ran from a magnificent rendering of Shaw's *Saint Joan* to an impassioned staging of Odets's *Waiting for Lefty* replete with extras in the audience shouting "Strike, Strike!" I was accepted into the Glee Club and sang magnificent works like Fauré's Requiem and Bach's B minor Mass. But politics came first; I stupidly dropped out, missing a chance to sing Beethoven's Ninth with the Boston Symphony under Serge Koussevitzky.

Before this blunder, I met a dark-haired alto, Marion, and fell in love. Her background was new to me — small-town New Hampshire where her father owned a Greek restaurant. But we connected and talked warmly about college, homes, family, and ultimately politics, especially battle-torn Greece. We went to an AYD dance — a fund-raiser for Spanish exiles and prisoners. That was something new to her: she was surrounded by leftists, Jews, blacks, workers. Admission was according to waist size; people happily pressed coins on adhesive tapes that soon hung to the floor; we heard a moving speech and sang Spanish Civil War songs. Marion was impressed, and impressed my friends with her dark-haired beauty.

My first true love affair foundered. Sex, or rather the lack of it, was the main reason. When Danny's girlfriend visited during permitted afternoon hours we left him alone. My turn had finally come, and I feverishly reminded my roommates about leaving. But daylight shabbiness and my nervousness crushed romance; Marion warded off my advances. I stupidly admitted this and for months my roommates taunted me with parodies of my pleas: "You leaving? You leaving?" Later, on a balmy evening on the deserted Charles River bank, everything seemed right. But in those anxious days before pills and with my immature anxieties I ruined the occasion. I walked an angry woman home in miserable silence. After that my phone calls were in vain. I began to drink and made a fool of myself on various occasions until I came to realize what a nuisance I was becoming. Since then I have never drunk more than a glass or two.

After about a year of unemployment my father got a job managing an army Post exchange, first at Fort Dix, then in Germany. I now had more money, but no home. During holidays I explored New York's still ample and spirited left-wing cultural and social life listed in the *Daily Worker:* films, concerts, parties, dances. The mambo was the new dance craze. I couldn't manage it, but I watched awestruck as a young Puerto Rican woman mamboed with such exuberance and skill that she exhausted one partner after another.

Spirits were lamer at a union rally to protest the anti-labor Taft-Hartley bill. Neither AFL conservatives nor the now-centrist CIO was solid in its opposition, since the bill hurt the left most of all. It was a feeble affair in a half-empty Madison Square Garden with inappropriate music, rambling speeches, and a resolution passed by half-hearted acclamation. It clearly reflected the state of the labor movement in those years of purges. The Taft-Hartley Law made things far worse.

In the meantime, we heard about a youth festival in the spring of 1947 in Prague. Since my parents would pay for the voyage, I was elected an AYD delegate. I left a few days before Secretary of State George Marshall's Harvard speech announcing his plan to help war-torn Europe — and curb communism. I hoped to see and judge things for myself.

The converted troop carrier pulsated with forums and discussions under glistening June weather. I met Dora, a Czech physician of Polish-Jewish background who had volunteered in Spain and also survived Auschwitz. For the first time I saw the infamous tattooed number which she bore on her arm. She had come to the United States to ask emigrant Czechs and Slovaks for aid in rebuilding their homeland. At Le Havre she met her great love for the first time since 1939 — a Polish doctor and volunteer in Spain, who had fought in the European Resistance.

I met my parents, and we spent a week in Paris. One afternoon, wandering alone to see the sights, I came upon an excited crowd at the National Assembly. When the police arrived the crowd joined arms and sang the "Marseillaise." I joined in exuberantly, but when the cops began driving wedges into the crowd I decided to move out, not really knowing what it was all about. As Mark Twain said, "They simply stared at me when I spoke to them in French; I never did succeed in making those idiots understand their own language." I later learned that after the AFL and the CIA split the French union movement, Communists were forced out of the government as a price for Marshall Plan aid. That had inspired the protest.

Driving through wrecked towns in my father's VW Beetle, we crossed the Rhine to Karlsruhe, where my parents occupied half a villa expropriated from a Nazi big shot. The city was filled with unimaginable ruins and rubble. People were thin and shabby; it was not pretty to see a youth pick up a cigarette butt I had just flipped away, or to see elderly people scrape up horse manure in the street. Wooden crosses marked where bodies still lay under the rubble. Could I have pity for all their suffering or only hatred for those who permitted or participated in Nazi crimes? Like many later visitors to Germany I would think, sitting next to any man in the streetcar: "I wonder what he did?"

My mother told me of seeing piles of patents, appropriated by the U.S. Army, that should have been shared with the other occupation powers. She visited a Communist Party meeting and found a small, elderly group already being steam-rollered out of any influence accruing from their resistance to Hitler. The American and British were linking their zones — leading to formation of the Federal Republic. While the cold war was deepening, I looked forward to Prague.

Though hardly bombed, Prague had been freed by a final uprising and many flowered plaques marked spots where antifascists died. It was a beautiful city, with its Wenceslaus Square, Old Town, ancient synagogue, the striking Jan Hus statue, and majestic Hradcany Palace. Hot sausage salesmen hawked "Horki Porki" and had little scissors to cut meat coupons. Contradictions abounded: "narodny podnik" signs indicated nationalized enterprises, while many detours on the city's trams were allegedly caused by the mayor to obstruct the "Communist" festival. Most exciting, Prague was jammed for four weeks with youth from all over the world.

At the opening ceremony we stood next to copper-complexioned Mongolians in striking hats and silk robes. We met sari-clad women from India and Ceylon, men with fezes, turbans, and burnooses from Indonesia, Pakistan, and Arab countries, sandaled Burmese, young people with Polish eagle emblems or Yugoslav stars, Italian students with long-peaked colored hats, each for a different course of study. Even our blue jeans were novelties then.

The two hundred Americans were housed in the "Roosevelt Dormitory" of Karl University. Most were leftists from unions, ethnic groups, or the AYD. About thirty were on the right; many were somewhere in the middle. Our first conflict raged around the exhibition. The Eastern Europeans and some big youth organizations like the French had professional exhibits. The Soviets featured a large Stalin statue; others had busts or blowups of their leaders. We strove to make something out of a motley collection of pictures and objects. But most of us balked at displaying Truman, who symbolized for us repression of Indonesia, Greece, and Spain, and of course use of the atom bomb. We "compromised" with our adversaries by displaying a big portrait of FDR.

Our delegation was a center of attention. At a torchlight parade, better dressed Czechs shouted special greetings to us to signal their pro-Western proclivities. We didn't know — should we respond warmly? Czech plans to attend the Marshall Plan conference had just been dropped hurriedly. The government was struggling to maintain a shaky coalition of centrists, Social Democrats, Catholics, and Communists, who had the largest vote and therefore named the premier.

Tensions were running high. Our assigned interpreters were anti-Nazi leftists, but self-appointed translators from the opposition intruded. A palaver began when the right-wing interpreters refused to escort us to a "Communist" nightspot. Most of us went in and the place was soon jumping. Our black delegates were especially adored as we all sang "American" songs and snakedanced around the room to "Long Way to Tipperary."

Other problems festered. There were whispers about Soviet disputes with Yugoslavia, many of whose delegates were former partisan fighters now building the Samac-Sarajevo Youth Railway to link Bosnia's disparate ethnic communities. Two groups came from Palestine. Zionists who danced and sang songs in Hebrew sought to convince me to escape universal anti-Semitism by settling in a Jewish state. The other group, a Communist-led Arab-Jewish chorus, advocated a united Arab-Jewish land. At a Palestine evening, as the Zionists finished and the joint chorus started, leaflets opposing unity fluttered downward.

Such omens at the time seemed minor. The dominant spirit was friendly and optimistic. India won independence during the festival, and hope remained that after the war's devastation, the Greeks, Spanish, Indonesians, Vietnamese, and the South Africans (their delegation was proudly mixed) would win their freedom. I saw exuberant Greeks toss two surprised Vietnamese into the air — without a common language the only way for the Greeks to express their emotions about their similarly torn countries.

We were nearly overwhelmed by the richness of the dance and music assembled in Prague, including North Korean, Indonesian, and Bulgarian folkdance groups, and went wild over the acrobatic Soviet Moisseyev ensemble. Russian violinist Leonid Kogan and cellist Mstislav Rostropovich performed memorably at a rather formal U.S.-Soviet "friendship meeting."

But personal contact with Soviets was difficult, as their top-notch musicians and athletes were far busier and mixed less than the Americans. However, I did meet two Soviet interpreters, Galya and Alex. At a shooting gallery Galya calmly demolished all targets, and I wondered if she had put that skill to use in the war. In his tiny room Alex proudly offered a taste-less soft drink, and I reflected on what such tiny luxuries meant in his dev-astated country. I later wrote him; a reply from his institute informed me curtly that he was no longer there.

There were more new friends: an Albanian guerrilla whose group had been slaughtered by the Nazis and who survived under a pile of corpses; a South African Xhosa youth leader, a Romanian singer who spoke nine lan-guages, a Burmese student eager to fight for his country's freedom, and many others. For me, camaraderie was easiest to achieve with Commu-nists, thanks to similar ways of viewing a world as yet not riven by splits and revelations.

At the final parade with a hundred thousand young Czechoslovaks, our right-wingers and their Czech friends planned to hand out leaflets de-nouncing the festival, the government, and the Communists. But the night before, they were locked in their rooms just long enough to prevent com-pletion of the leaflet. Czech authorities claimed it might have led to an in-cident with international repercussions.

After the festival, most Americans volunteered for work on reconstruc-tion projects. Some went to Lidice, whose men were murdered, whose women went to concentration camps, and whose children were adopted as "Aryans." I worked on a miners' homes project, with simple Czech food, eight hours with pick and shovel, and a project head who told of Buchenwald concentration camp across the mountains where the underground com-mittee he belonged to had freed the camp just before the Americans arrived.

After our week's work we scattered in all directions. The "opposition" headed home to tell of their travails to a press eager for just such a story about an event it otherwise ignored. Those of us who were to return on a Yugoslav freighter gathered in Venice before heading for Yugoslavia. But delays drained my meager finances, and I experienced marvelous Venice by bumming meals and going without gondola rides or Lido. At last a small boat crossed the Adriatic to Rijeka. Our U.S. passports prohibited entry into Yugoslavia, so we climbed rope ladders directly onto the big chrome ore freighter, *Radnik,* and peered enviously at the shore where unrestricted Canadian delegates roamed over the region and returned full of stories about the Youth Railway.

We were recompensed by a magnificent trip past Dalmatian cliffs, around the Italian boot, and past smoky Mt. Etna. Dolphins leaped at the bow and flying fish sailed over the deck while we lay in the sun and were doused by the waves.

But the harsh realities of a still-darkened world were never far away. A Canadian who had visited Warsaw after the festival told me of a city in ruins. The ghetto, site of the courageous Jewish uprising of 1943, was a desert, with hardly one brick on top of another. Stopping in colonial Algiers, where the contrast between the French area and the Casbah was immense, we wandered through alleys with open sewage and urinals, and donkeys carrying huge bags of garbage. We descended through a maze and found men drinking coffee and staring coldly at us, schoolchildren chanting Koran verses, and brothels where half-dressed women lolled around, visible through open doors. Our guide bargained to have a young woman do a belly dance. But negotiations faltered; suddenly four Senegalese police in fezes herded us out. I felt like a stupid tourist "doing the sights" of a city which wanted only its freedom.

Near the Spanish coast we held a small ceremony, floating bottles with antifascist messages and little candles to light their way toward land. And then, too rapidly, back to home and college.

I settled tardily into new courses and politics. My ties with the Harvard Liberal Union were over and the AYD had faded, owing to icy currents and its inner doubts. Some on the left kept busy with the John Reed Society; some in defiance of the chill wanted a revived Young Communist League; others disagreed.

My attention became centered on our CP branch, whose discussions were punctuated with references to Marxist works. But I had read little more than the *Communist Manifesto*. "What, you never read *Feuerbach*?" So I read Marx's words — that philosophers had interpreted the world; the point was to change it. "You don't know *Anti-Dühring*? Read Marx before you say anything." I learned to nod knowingly to avoid condescension and then read the classics, which were sometimes difficult but often perceptive, even witty and relevant, though we frequently argued about what precisely was relevant.

Our comrades included brilliant students. One was a recognized authority on James Joyce. Sam, a tiny, hunchbacked African American, was a brilliant scholar with gentle humor, but a body so twisted that we carried him and his two canes upstairs to meetings despite his pained protests. We had experts on mathematics, literature, languages, and architecture. Some had returned from military service. One, a middle-class Irish-American, while fighting on Guadalcanal had kept a "light" book in one pocket for foxhole breaks — Dostoyevsky, Thomas Mann, Tolstoy — while in the other pocket for longer stretches he kept Kant, Hegel, Nietzsche, Schopenhauer. He told me of a dramatist new to me: Bertolt Brecht. Our talks about art made me resolve never to reject new trends as alien or incomprehensible — or to accept them simply because they were modern. I hoped for valid standards somewhere between snobbish fads, mass-produced kitsch, and tasteless heroics mislabeled "socialist realism."

New China was more vital to us than the USSR. We followed the advance of the Peoples' Liberation Army on a member's large map; Harry, our chair, suggested naming our branch after the writer and union leader Liu Ting-yi, whose ironic word for party jargon, "bagu," became part of our vocabulary. Few were dogmatic. Harry would chortle: "Our line has changed again, da-di-da-da." But such flipflops, we felt, showed a lack of respect for us and those we hoped to influence. If changes were needed, offer proof and try to explain them honestly, without acting as if nothing had changed. We joked about our uncomfortable state and rationalized: didn't others alter their views? wasn't the world complex and volatile?

Joking was not always easy. Tito had our esteem; now Stalin called Tito a traitor. A friend who was close to us angrily threw a newspaper at me: Prokofiev, Shostakovich, and Khachaturian had been censured because their music was "not popular enough." He could not believe that any politician understood music better than they did. I don't recall my response. But I hope I agreed with him or at least admitted my own confusion. Such approaches might have mitigated charges of blind fanaticism. But they could also open the door to unprincipled retreat. Perhaps that is why wise Catholics whom I knew defended Immaculate Conception. How to be openminded and flexible while defying growing pressure? There were no simple answers.

We admired the Soviets' struggle against Nazism, led by Stalin, and their support for independence movements. We savored Stalin's succinct irony in interviews with the Western press. But some were unhappy with the cultish adulation of the Soviet leader in books and films. I discovered that Geoff White, our "man in the HLU," was also disturbed about this, and once we talked until the break of dawn. Such subjects were touchy; but generally the atmosphere was intellectually honest, without blind discipline, and with humor and flexibility which made for interesting, even attractive meetings.

Our group's atmosphere and effectiveness brought us growth, while the CP's numbers nationally were declining. For an amazing four months, we recruited a new member every week. Before long we were up to thirty, too many to meet in one place, so we split into three groups. I became organizational secretary of one of them. We all attended a Marxist class in Boston, picketed in a meatpackers strike, canvassed for a local black candidate, got up at 4.30 A.M. to distribute flyers for the beleaguered left-wing United Electrical Workers, and appealed to the delegates at the United Steelworkers convention to reject their leaders' new anti-left rules. A left delegate stating such views was beaten up right on the floor. That convention marked the decline of active CIO organizing and commitment to workers' rights, racial equality, and peace.

In the meantime, my interest in my courses dwindled. Few classes were giving me what I felt I needed, nor was I giving them what they needed. I kept my crucial "B" average by a slim margin.

Two days after a congressional conscription bill came up, Harry asked me what action my group had taken. I stared blankly; we hadn't been called upon to act. "What kind of a Communist are you?" he snorted. Did we always wait for orders? Waiting for higher-ups meant never leading or thinking. Weren't we smart enough to make our own decisions when necessary? Conformity and risk avoidance can do damage even in a radical organization. Sure, he added, we need discipline and central planning to have impact. But not doing anything without prior approval can be deadening and mean defeat.

I had never seen him so worked up. I opened my ears and shut my mouth, for he convinced me. I didn't like Harry, but after this scolding I got along with him better; a good storm often clears the air.

One winter evening, one of Harvard's few black students was denied admittance to a student bar and was told that it was a private club. When he tried to join, there were "no more openings." Our Geoff White, still on the HLU executive committee, proposed fighting the case. The HLU leaders, though skeptical about Geoff, could not easily refuse, and allowed him to organize a nightly picket line which became known far beyond Harvard. Some students joined in, others expressed sympathy and did not enter the club. Only a few crossed the line, including my old friend Dave Binger from Dalton. Our party members picketed the most and the longest. In the end we won.

We searched for ways to break out of our growing isolation to challenge the emerging cold war. The Harvard chapter of the American Veterans Committee, formed as an alternative to the conservative veterans' groups, began drifting rightward, eagerly pushing a resolution against the February 1948 "Communist putsch" in Czechoslovakia. A festival friend in Prague wrote me that pro-Western elements in the government had exploited shortages caused by drought and tried to topple their left-wing coalition partners, but were themselves toppled by one million demonstrating workers. My parents, touring in Prague, confirmed this. Left-wingers in the AVC proposed that I tell about these aspects of the event. But I was not a veteran. A compromise was reached: I was given exactly two minutes to speak. Two minutes — to combat a tidal wave! I did what I could.

We tried to work with campus Zionists. The Soviets had supported Israel in 1948, while Britain, France, and the United States backed Arab countries. Israel fought hard and won, but attacked the poorest Arabs, now often refugees. I opposed prejudice against both Jews and Arabs. One Socialist Zionist group, Hashomer Hatzair, rejected anti-Arabism, viewing the British, who played Arabs and Jews against each other, as the real foe. I agreed with them almost completely, though I was never happy about a strictly Jewish state, even when, after the Holocaust, yearning for it was very understandable. Regardless of the aims of muftis or Zionists, the rights of all people, Arab and Jew, had to be upheld.

In early 1948, at a jammed Madison Square Garden, Henry Wallace's Progressive Party was born. The irrepressible comic Zero Mostel slinked onto the stage in Sherlock Holmes getup, and with the FBI honchos in front of the Garden in mind he sang: "Who's gonna investigate the man who investigates the man who investigates me?" Paul Robeson, as always, moved the audience with song and speech, and Wallace, the main event, pleaded for peace and a return to New Deal and antifascist principles.

Wallace was in the presidential race, but getting on the ballot was an immense problem. Massachusetts had a 56,000-signature requirement. For weeks and weeks, countless hours were spent knocking on doors from Lawrence to Boston in search of registered voters. A "Wallace for President" group formed at Harvard. Its chair, Dick Stone (later a Florida senator and ambassador), ferried singing, chanting students all over town; on Boston Common we sang radical Irish songs until a crowd gathered, then plugged, often heatedly, for Wallace.

The Young Progressives of America (YPA) founding meeting in Philadelphia in the summer of 1948 was held jointly with the parent Progressive Party convention. The atmosphere was hectic but joyous with marathon debates on resolutions and intensive efforts to find common ground between Communists and left-liberals. All sides compromised to produce a platform that satisfied nearly everyone. At a giant rally Wallace stood with his running mate, Senator Glen Taylor, who had won his Idaho seat without money, but with vigor, humor, and songs. He surprised us with a risqué parody of "Isle of Capri." We were overjoyed that Taylor, the only union member in the Senate, had joined the ticket. As for his silly song: why be purists in a broad movement? An old friend summed up the mood: "Isn't it great to be fighting *for* something again!"

With that, five of us sped to North Carolina for a week to gather signatures to get on the ballot. In Winston-Salem we got advice from black union organizers who had bucked racism at the Camel plant, winning higher wages and better working conditions for blacks and whites. Later, the union local was disbanded when national leaders and the company joined to smear it as a "Communist front."

Across that state, some heard us out, some didn't. A broad valley filled with tiny cabins housed white families on one side and blacks on the other. I had not seen such poverty since Algiers. We talked about Wallace's program for schools, roads, hospitals, and a one-dollar minimum wage. A ragged young white mother in front of a rickety hut with a clinging child listened unbelievingly with wide eyes as if we were describing heaven. Blacks were easily convinced, but were rarely registered. After hearing of the Progressives' fight for equality, a middle-aged black man warned us not to say that to the whites who worked in the miserable textile factory — still superior to the jobs that blacks held in gas stations, laundries, and as maids. He did not see this as eternal; he wanted changes and was ready to fight. We didn't collect too many signatures, but came away burning with the desire to get votes and build the new party.

That summer of 1948 I stayed in Boston, working to establish area YPA clubs, while sharing a small flat in the vibrant Italian section with Progressive Party organizer Jack Lee. We forged ties with neighbors, many of whose families came from three leftist villages in Italy; we sought support from Armenians in Lawrence and Greeks in Boston, and challenged that city's racial divide by seeking to build a YPA in black Roxbury on interracial principles. Initially we were met with skepticism by young people who were understandably suspicious. Mistrust extended to Jack, who, despite his brown skin, had trouble breaking an icy chill with our topical songs, which clearly were not resonating. It was not until he sang the earthily sarcastic "Put It on the Ground" that things warmed a bit. We organized a dance, which drew some from the neighborhood and youth from other Boston clubs. A few black youths, seeing Jack dance with white women, also took the plunge, a novel and risky act in 1948. They hardly danced with black women, however; nor did the white fellows. We clearly had a way to go in understanding the nation's complex racist heritage. The dance, we thought nonetheless, was a modest start in building a Roxbury YPA. But as Jack was about to say a few words, five cops rushed in. "Mixed dancing" was suspicious, and so were we. Within seconds, the neighborhood people had vanished. They had enough experience with cops!

Jack spoke with deep conviction, but with humor and no "bagu" jargon. That endeared him especially to youth. I also learned a lot about Jewish culture from this friend from Jamaica. He sang popular Hebrew songs like "Hava Nageela" and "Tsena, Tsena," and used Yiddish words I didn't know. He often played Robeson records, and like Robeson, he loved his background and its African component. And like Robeson's, Jack's African roots never prevented him from absorbing and celebrating all peoples' cultures. Perhaps his Afro-Caribbean pride was like my relationship to my Jewish background; not exclusive or nationalistic, but never really absent.

That summer marked the first peacetime draft registration in the nation's history. At a Boston armory protest, a group of thugs tore a pacifist minister's poster urging refusal to register and knocked him to the ground. The police arrested the minister. YPA had devised a carefully worded leaflet: "You have to register, but protest the draft!" That made no difference to the thugs, who turned from the minister to Jack and me—the only ones to show—throwing our leaflets in Jack's face. When the police ordered us to stop leafleting, we refused, asserted our rights, and were arrested, winding up in a cell next to the minister. We were bailed out in an hour, but the story got front page treatment in Boston and coverage that reached Texas, attributing the registration refusal to us and never mentioning the minister. The charges were soon dismissed; my stint in jail was short, but I am still proud of it.

After the court case, we were allowed to rejoin the protest, a final picket line at the armory. About twenty demonstrators faced a large, hostile crowd, incited by vitriolic news stories, and armed with crates of eggs and tomatoes which soon filled the air — hitting us, the signs, and even unfriendly reporters. Most projectiles and invective were aimed at African Americans and a tall Unitarian minister. One ripe tomato landed with red splatter all over the pants of a cop who had just told a complaining newsman: "What tomatoes?" When the mob started grabbing at our signs, we retreated, defensively gripping the sticks attached to the signs. Someone hit me on the back of my neck; everything briefly went black. I came to, with tooth fragments in my mouth, and asked a cop what he intended to do. His only response was an icy, hate-filled stare.

The Progressive Party collected a hundred thousand signatures in Massachusetts, an incredible feat which had required a few hundred canvassers to speak to nearly a million people. The brunt of the job was borne evening after evening by a few like Jack Lee and F. O. Matthiessen. In September the campaign held a large Boston rally. Wallace made a fine speech, after the usual emotional collection which ended with the cry for dollar bills: "Let's hold them high to make a sea of green." But my most vivid memory is a remark by Robeson. The Progressive Party was politically diverse; its Communist participants especially avoided any topics which might cause division. Robeson amazed us by breaking this taboo, mentioning the dream of "a socialist America." After a startled silence, thunderous applause rang through the hall; evidently many non-Communists shared that dream. Only Robeson dared utter it, in a voice seemingly capable of winning trees or stones to our cause.

Hope died in November. We had expected four to six million votes, putting the party on the political map. Truman surprisingly defeated heavily favored Thomas E. Dewey, and even Strom Thurmond's racist candidacy beat Wallace's 1,160,000 votes by about 100,000. World developments hurt Wallace, who refused to buckle to rising anti-Soviet and anti-Chinese hysteria. But Communist rejection of the Marshall Plan, the Czechoslovakian events, Communist advances in China, the Soviet split with Tito, and especially the Berlin Blockade all cut deeply. Critically important, labor split over Truman and the Marshall Plan, with center-right CIO leaders insisting that both be endorsed. The CIO's left was fighting for its life, unable to play a major campaign role. Truman, with media exposure not available to Wallace, had stolen much of Wallace's domestic platform — talking liberal while holding the center. In the crunch, many Wallace backers, fearing Thomas Dewey in the White House, turned to Truman as the "lesser of two evils." The defeat would wreck the Progressive Party and weaken the left disastrously, facilitating its annihilation in the CIO, abetting rampant McCarthyism, and permitting a belligerent foreign policy.

The situation worsened rapidly. Truman's loyalty review program had already undermined the rights of over two million government workers. The "Hollywood Ten" had been convicted of "contempt of Congress" for defying the House Un-American Activities Committee. A fearful Hollywood turned to making cold war duds like *I Married a Communist,* and the rot crept into literature, the arts, science, and education. Even lordly Harvard eventually retreated. Many liberals who had opposed racism and reaction now turned their guns on "Stalinism" to earn their anti-red bona fides, providing an intellectual rationale for Neanderthal McCarthyites, and fronting CIA creations like the Congress for Cultural Freedom.

In those days, we never mentioned names over phones which we suspected were tapped. But Marge Matten, now party youth secretary, had a sweet four-year-old daughter who often answered the phone, knowingly identifying the nervous caller by full name. We ingeniously devised tasty nicknames with the daughter. Our most nervous member, Elmer Manstett, became "Apricot." When he next called, a joyful little voice piped up loudly: "Mommy, it's Apricot Elmer Manstett."

A new party decision was less comical; we were told to destroy membership cards for our own protection. Another event was symptomatic of the darkening landscape. Pitirim Sorokin, a Russian émigré professor, with independent spirit and belief in peace, agreed to appear at one of the last antiwar rallies on campus. But when he rose to speak, loud catcalls made it impossible for him to continue — something new at Harvard.

The changes now affected me directly. I had to take a military service physical. On the psychological questionnaire I exaggerated about chewing my fingernails, but despite "expert" advice could not bring myself to say I was a bed wetter. Attired only in papers hung around my neck, I was prepared for the shrink's first question: do you go out with girls? Yes, I replied. The next question was unsettling: did I ever go out with girls from Brookline? I answered that I did; a friend and I had just dated two Brookline girls. He knew my date, and said that she was his daughter's friend. Did I know his daughter? She was the other girl on my double date, and I said truthfully that I had rather regretted not being with her. He then suggested that I give her a call: "perhaps she can have a party for you." When I saw that he had scored me as eligible, 1A, I thought bitterly: yes, a "farewell party."

Two courses in my final year challenged my views. One, on the USSR, was preparing future Kremlinologists by raising tough issues calculated to puncture pro-Soviet sympathies. The other, by the renowned Austrian Joseph Schumpeter, was on socialist theory and also aimed to give naive enthusiasts hard nuts to crack. Despite doubts I may have had, my views had been under such severe attack that I was suspicious of any critical test. I might have learned more, but "stonewalled" to resist the anti-left offensive. I neglected my studies more and more and sank below the B average required for a scholarship. Luckily I had reached my final semester, so I borrowed $250 from a Radcliffe comrade, enough to finish, and paid her back a year later.

My last exams were in January 1949. With other problems on my mind and wearying of student life with its strangely separate compartments, I did not study hard. But exams must be passed; I spent an unhappy Christmas with books I should have read earlier. Little time was left for my very last exam, and I had to learn a semester's work by making a night of it. At the exam, my mind spun with semi-digested facts. Suddenly I realized I was dozing off. My nerves tautened, my mind ordered what I had crammed, and I finished the exam, winding up with a B. My Harvard education was over.

Before I left Cambridge, Marge Matten visited. She noted that Harvard degrees had clout if the Unamericans didn't get us. But our theoretically workers' party had too few workers, so she asked that we think about passing up other careers to become workers. It wouldn't be easy, she conceded, but she was passing on that request to all graduating students.

Three of us ten who graduated that year decided to try it. Including me.

Harvard has always sought to engender an elite in the arts, science, politics, and business, while many of its students used their degrees to help their careers. The university's curricular flexibility allowed a wide choice of subjects which students with goals like law, medicine, or languages utilized well, but it could leave students without clear-cut goals up in the air, with little more from the four years than a general cultural veneer.

I did not benefit enough from my Harvard education, mistrustful as I was of theories taught in economics, political science, and history. But I learned much from our little party group, whose members were knowledgeable, enthusiastic, devoted, and quick to take fresh initiatives. They were not dogmatists or fanatics but nonconformists with ideals, who looked upon life with optimism and humor.

Our convictions were not based on personal need, but were intellectual; even those one or two from working-class backgrounds tended, as they became intellectuals, to lose their roots and ability to communicate with working people. Nearly all eventually left the Communist movement, in part because of a lack of moorings in working-class experience, mostly because of the terrible things which were to follow: unendurable pressures, tragic disappointments, narrow-mindedness, insularity, and above all the developments in the USSR and the socialist world. It is perhaps surprising that any stayed on. A few did.

There were bitter tragedies. F. O. Matthiessen had hoped to contribute to building a peaceful and socialist future. After the bitter conflicts in Czechoslovakia, a country he hoped would be a bridge to that future, after Wallace's defeat, and after rabid attacks on him by McCarthyites and fools, he jumped to his death. We were also shaken on hearing that our brilliant scholar Sam had given up an endless struggle against his disabilities and against the torment born of racism.

Our group was later consumed by quarrels with party officials over Freud and psychoanalysis. I suspect the party's position was intransigent toward these bright intellectuals. But some students may have been searching for a good excuse to leave.

A few months later, before the group broke up, I returned for an Easter weekend on Cape Cod at a bungalow owned by the parents of a Radcliffe comrade. We had a great time, made our own clam chowder, ate spaghetti, and played "Twenty Questions" and "Botticelli" in front of the fire. The next day, like children, we played "Capture the Flag," forgetting the world and its worries. Before the weekend ended — for me the end of an era — we plucked up our courage and dove into the icy pond for a last quick swim.

FLIGHT (3)

I alternately swam or waded through the shallow canal, aiming for the empty barge and reaching it after twenty minutes of floundering. Its steep sides annulled any idea of climbing on to it—and I feared going on land again. There was nothing left but to start crossing the river. The sapling-covered opposite shore did not seem far, nor was the current strong. Off I went, with a thousand preying anxieties. How should I approach the So-viet soldiers on the other side? Should I emerge with hands raised to avoid being shot at? I did not have long to worry; the water got shallower and I waded out with hands half-raised. No one shot at me, no one could be seen or heard. I walked hesitantly between the saplings, and after a few yards I stopped in amazement. In front of me flowed the river, the real Danube—broad, swift, and beautiful. How could I have believed that the little chan-nel had been the great river which watered eight countries, the longest, most powerful river west of the Volga? I looked on the mighty Danube, filled with awe.

But now I must conquer this speedy, powerful current. At least the fur-ther eastward the current took me, the less chance of landing in the Amer-ican enclave on the other side. I tried not to think about fatal whirlpools, fits of weakness, cramps, or other dangers.

I again stepped into muddy water, swimming slowly and as steadily as I could. I made progress, moving away from the shoreline with every stroke, getting a better view of the broad river as it flowed from Linz. But there was little leisure to admire scenery. I was moving diagonally, pulled by the strong current. Whenever I relaxed I was pushed rapidly downstream. The crawl sapped my strength, so I alternated between breast- and sidestrokes, which were less tiring for my legs and yet kept me moving.

Would I be able to make it to the other side? I never doubted it. Some-how things had always worked out—until they didn't work out. I won-dered how I would be received. Would I be viewed as a hero, invader, or spy? What if I stumbled on the American enclave? God, that would be a

catastrophe, landing me for years in a military prison. It seemed very un-
likely, but I didn't know the lay of the land. Yet the Danube current was my
ally. And slowly, stroke by stroke, I was crossing the broad river.

The other side, drawing closer, showed hills, trees, one or two little
houses, but not a soul. The water was getting muddier. Would the shore be
a mound of mud, impossible to scale? But I had never seen a river without
a riverbank. I found a foothold and waded out of the Danube, water
streaming from my clothes. I had crossed my widest river, and I was ready
to halt, raise my hands, or, if worst came to worst, jump back into the water, letting the current carry me further eastward.

But no one was there, no one noticed this strange wet figure in torn
clothing ducking among the saplings lining the river. Neither a shot nor a
"Halt," in Russian or English. Silence, except for the rush of the water. I
followed indistinct paths and found hoofprints in the soft ground. Were
they cavalry horses — or simply farm animals, come to the river to drink?

I reached the edge of the riverside grove and, keeping hidden, I saw un-
cultivated fields and an asphalt road parallel to the river. A house was visible, but still not a soul. It was early Sunday morning, yet I felt sure that on
the American side there would be patrolling vehicles and armed guards like
those I believed I had heard whistling around me one terrible night ago.
But here was a peaceful scene. A few civilian cars of fairly ancient vintage
passed by. I decided to wait till no cars were in sight, then cross the road to
hills on the other side where I could look down without being seen. I
walked quickly and nonchalantly across the road and up the low hill. I was
out of immediate danger or the eyes of an observer.

I watched and watched. Cars whose license plates I could not read drove
by about every quarter of an hour. But neither a U.S. jeep to hide from nor
a Soviet vehicle to surrender to. My concentration flagged; I was wet, hungry, and tired. I saw blackberry patches nearby and picked berries, keeping
one eye on the road. The tiny paths were thorny and I wore only socks, but
I had eaten so little in twenty-four hours that I could not resist.

I moved along the hillside parallel to the road. There was not much to
see so I kept on, worried that I was moving westward, not eastward. The
sun, now quite high, was drying me quickly. I stopped to check what I had
carried. The registered letter from the Judge Advocate General in Washington in the thick manila envelope that I had kept under my undershirt
was wet around the edges but in almost perfect condition despite forty

minutes or more in water. This was vital; it was my only proof that I had been forced to leave because of my politics. What good fortune that the envelope was virtually waterproof. Water had accumulated inside my Swiss watch, but it still ticked. My wallet in my back pants pocket contained a false three-day pass and some Austrian and West German cash, all intact if damp, while the plastic bag in my shirt pocket was gone, the button opened by the stream. The last photos of family and friends were gone, plus most of my money and items which had seemed important.

I moved on and reached a fork; one road continued along the river, the other turned inland. Traffic was slightly more frequent now. I decided that the best way to avoid the feared enclave was to move away from the Danube, parallel to the inland road but still out of view.

It was nearly noon when I reached another fork. The hills had flattened out; I was exhausted, hot, hungry, and didn't give a damn anymore. I had walked too far to be in any riverside enclave and brazened into the open to read a roadside sign. Three towns were listed, each in a different direction. Urfahr — the name of the enclave — was in the direction I had come from. The other two meant nothing. I decided that the lack of any reference to borders meant I was safe.

Just past the fork was a large house, with an inviting lawn and comfortable-looking benches. I boldly sat down, resting my aching body. I was a disheveled mess, with uncombed hair, a ripped sleeve, badly torn socks, no shoes.

I did not know whether Austrians in the Soviet Zone were pro- or anti-Soviet. At this point I hardly cared as I reclined blissfully. But I could not help reflecting on what I had done. Had it been insane or wise, courageous or cowardly? I was lucky to get across the river safely, but how lucky had I really been? Would I ever see my country again? There were no answers; my physical and mental exhaustion made me lose interest in anything but resting, and possibly dozing, as unwise as that would be.

[3]
WORKING

When I decided to become a worker, my mother was emphatic: "No!" Her family had struggled to climb out of the Lower East Side; she came from an ethnic tradition which viewed only intellectual or business careers as desirable. But disliking the business option, she dreamed of my becoming a journalist or writer. I had a Harvard degree and now I wanted to be a mere worker! My mother sympathized with my political views. (So did my father, more or less, but he was in uniform in West Germany.) But she looked down on workers. Couldn't I accomplish more in anything other than a blue collar?

I wasn't sure either. While certain that labor was decisive, I wondered how I would fit in. I knew nothing about machines and was helpless with tools, didn't bar-hop, play poker, or talk baseball, and lacked a personality that exudes influence. But I was never a snob and I possessed lots of enthusiasm and devotion to a cause. And then, what else could I do?

So I waited in New York to attend a special party school for "going into industry." At a left-wing dance I met Sandra. Unusual for that time, she had her own apartment, which was explained simply: her father was a banker. But she was a leftist, I was not narrow-minded, and ended up staying the night. She had a diaphragm — and the ice, which had threatened to become a glacier, was finally broken.

I struggled to strike a balance between personal and political matters. But political concerns were relentlessly intrusive and nearly all worrisome. The CIO edged back toward the corrupt old AFL. Western European governments, purged of Communists by Marshall Plan pressure, were joining the North Atlantic Treaty Organization. Leading U.S. Communists were on trial for "conspiring to teach and advocate" the overthrow of the government. As for the tragic repression inside the USSR, I knew little.

In March 1949 I ushered at the Conference of Intellectuals for World Peace in New York, sponsored by, among others, Einstein, Thomas Mann, W. E. B. Du Bois, Lillian Hellman, Clifford Odets, and the leading foreign guest, Dmitri Shostakovich. The government failed to mount a counter-conference and the Hearst press failed to ignite large demonstrations against the gathering. In the hall I passed Shostakovich, looking very worried, certainly at the insults from the crowd and media and possibly for other reasons as well. The State Department made it look like a wholly Communist event by giving visas to delegates from the USSR and Eastern Europe, but almost none from Western Europe and the Americas. Peace conferences elsewhere followed, but intimidating waves of anti-Sovietism could not be halted.

At party headquarters, eight or nine former college students studied and debated Marxist concepts, guided by a Hungarian exile, J. Peters, who was later deported as an agent of the "Cominform" (a postwar version of the Comintern). I recall only rebelling mildly at the current party line on the right of blacks to self-determination in the South, which seemed totally unrealistic. Kindly broad-faced Peters defended the line, though gently, and maybe with his own doubts. He closed the course by saying: "Here we used Marxist-Leninist terminology. But when you talk to people, express those ideas in their language. Otherwise, you won't get far with anyone."

Despite my mother's resistance I left for Syracuse to seek work in the huge General Electric plant where the United Electrical Workers, expelled from the CIO, fought to survive against a new right-wing union with backing from government, church, press, and GE — whose plants had been organized by UE in years past.

I got a cheap room at the YMCA and rode the bus every day to the plant. There were never openings. In my room I pored over the Gideon Bible despite a loud jukebox nearby blaring "Ghost Riders in the Sky," making me despise ghost riders forever.

After a few lonely days, I violated the rules, joining leftist students at Syracuse University campaigning to save the "Trenton Six," six black men charged with murder, despite the fact that none matched police descriptions. (In the end, four were acquitted, one died in prison, and one was re-sentenced.) Meanwhile at GE, still no job. A Syracuse comrade finally gave me a note saying: "Mattie Timpken, 92 Jackson," and I hitchhiked 130 miles to big, shabby Buffalo.

At No. 92, on a rundown ghetto veranda, I saw a stout, black, plainly dressed woman of about fifty. Could she help me find Mattie Timpken? "I think I can," she said with a twinkle, "That's me." I had met the chair of the Buffalo party.

The Timpken house was sparsely furnished, with cheap religious prints on the walls. In the next few hours, four generations wandered in and out, relatives, neighbors, comrades — young and old, black and white. Mattie dug up $10 spending money, asked friends to put me up, and said:

"Now, son, this isn't New York and I guess it's not like your college either. Buffalo's no easy street for leftists, things may seem a little tough, but we need every soul who's ready to come here. I'm glad you decided to and I hope you get some satisfaction working here."

The next day I found a small furnished room with a working-class family. And I found a job.

At Fedders-Quigan, near the Niagara River, I dared not mention Harvard on the application, and took a second shift unskilled job starting at 94 cents an hour (82 cents for women). I could be fired without cause during a three-month probation, so I refrained from political contacts. But I looked forward with pride to becoming a member of the United Steelworkers of America.

I soon got used to punching in before 3.30 P.M. and punching out two seconds after midnight. I avoided the highbrow words loved at Harvard but abandoned a few attempts to speak ungrammatically. Yet it was hard to conceal my background. A workmate once asked me: "Haven't you ever thought of college?"

Our little team — Herbert, a young Polish-American who was in charge, Richard, an older German, and I — pushed handtrucks with heavy rolls of brass or copper to men who whizzed them through crimping machines for use as metal ribbons in car coolers. We also tugged heavier pigs of solder over uneven floors to the acrid room where the ribbons were dipped in an acid bath. We rolled barrels of paint, and harder to do, rolled the empties back at a bold slant. Mine always careened into a wall. As low man on the totem pole, I had to chop up cylinders of tar; Herbert and Richard grinned as countless tar splinters stuck all over me. We worked hard to fill demands for parts, rags, and other items. But if all went well we could ease off after 10 P.M. One of us could even doze in a rag bin while the other two watched for nervous, snooping Charley, the shift manager.

My workmates laughed at my clumsiness, but Richard was happy that someone was below him in the pecking order. With his long experience in the plant it was not easy to submit to a younger boss. Though he was a loyal union man, his vision was narrowed to saving for old age. He was full of stories of the war years, when women workers with husbands in the armed services were easy to seduce in dark corners. To listen to him, he must have seduced nearly all of them — not easy to believe when he struggled with toothless jaws to eat his beloved pickled tomatoes. But he had been younger then.

Herbert aspired to foreman, especially since he was about to get married. That didn't stop him telling his own amorous tales, often about puncturing condoms before using them. Was he lying, very religious, or just sadistic? Though we usually got along, Herbert had a brutal strain and made clear who was boss. Hardly class-conscious, he only wanted to move upwards.

I never experienced anti-Semitism after mentioning that I was Jewish. But my workmates noticed that I never used the word "nigger," and the arguments began. The plant employed only five blacks, three men at rough low-paid jobs and two women as sweepers. Neither workmate understood my halting talk of the need for unity, but kept up hackneyed canards about "expensive Cadillacs" and "body odor."

From Richard I learned about merciless pranks and "cheating the company," a practice considered legitimate since, it was agreed, the company always cheated the workers. One man hid a heavy motor under his coat, hanging between his legs from a rope around his waist. At the gate the rope got so tight he fainted — and was caught. As for me, I had no car or home needing purloined parts. I understood the theft, but I wanted instead to organize workers to demand collectively more of what they produced.

One evening I witnessed a prank that would become legendary. The men in the hot, smelly room with acid vats made a dummy with rubber boots, apron, and slouch hat, dozing defiantly in a chair. When shift boss Charley turned up, he circled the lazy worker — scolding, shouting, and finally grabbing. Everyone watched with intense enjoyment, and Charley's aggressiveness softened noticeably in the next weeks.

Our work took us all around the plant. I often joked with three young Italian Americans at the crimping machines, but noticed that they never stopped working. On piecework every lost minute meant lost wages. I got to know the big men who lowered radiator frames into the burning acid and the women at the nearby conveyor, and roared with them at the stunts and banter that pervaded the factory — like the water-filled condoms hung on the conveyors that burst on the women's side amid laughter and indignant cries: "I'm a respectable single girl!"

Workers constantly cut corners in the battle to win back some of the value they created. Finished work was often withheld until times when higher rates were paid, as on Saturdays. I learned how important pencils were to pieceworkers who manipulated extra pay by juggling entries on their work slips. Despite constant jokes about "pencil artistry," it was a serious matter for workers making so little.

Having no family, I could manage. I bought little food or clothing and had few other expenses. Drinkers' families bore the worst burdens. Every payday some wives waited combatively at the gate to get at checks before the barkeepers did. Some were amused, but the wives were deadly earnest.

I was chummy with many but close with none. The time to make friends was after work, but midnight was late to start bar-hopping, and I had never been at ease in bars. Once I went drinking with several men and got a little tight. Strangely, a cello hung behind the bar. I mentioned indiscreetly that I once played the cello, and it was handed to me. It was hopelessly out of tune and my unpracticed hands were even clumsier due to alcohol. I thought suddenly: my God, once I could make music with a cello.

I took no more bar tours. In my lonely room I read some, slept late, bought a quick bite, and went back to work. On Saturday I wanted to go out. There were two downtown weekly square dances in an informal atmosphere with frequent change of partners. But I could never master the seemingly mandatory muscular strut and suggestively joshing tone. On Sundays I took the Lake Erie boat to beautiful Crystal Beach in Canada, where I discovered English-style fish and chips but not what I was looking for.

We were asked one Friday to work Saturday evening at time-and-a-half pay. But when the request was repeated in ensuing weeks I preferred to forgo the extra money. The square dances weren't much but they were something. Next came an implicit threat: whoever did not work Saturday might not be welcome on Monday. I didn't wish to test this threat, so I spent most Saturdays "with Fedders." Needless to say, I never glimpsed Fedders himself or any other top brass in this factory of thirteen hundred employees.

My probation ended; I now earned over a dollar an hour and could not be fired arbitrarily. The taboo on meeting comrades was also over, though my late shift kept me from evening meetings. But I found a daytime sanctuary, indeed, a new home: the Timpken house. I had previously known only black intellectuals; now I also met black workers.

In Florida, Mattie had never found work other than cleaning white families' homes and caring for their children while her own had to fend for themselves. Her oldest son became a boxer, her second daughter, tough and intelligent Billie, was behind-the-scenes manager of a white bar, no easy job for a black woman in the South. When her brother unwisely beat a white boxer, a customer confided that he was in danger from vengeful whites. He slipped north to Buffalo and soon urged the family to follow. They somehow squeezed into an old car and escaped the South.

A couple in Buffalo hired Billie to help the pregnant wife. They insisted that she eat with them instead of in the kitchen. They also invited her to a political rally. For the first time she saw people of different colors mixing in an easy, friendly spirit. Billie's discomfort and distrust evaporated. She went again, became a leading member of the AYD, and was soon an avid Communist. She once told me why things went so quickly: "Just you give a hungry man a steak. Even if he's never seen one before, you don't have to explain."

She was soon organizing youth in town and working in a wartime airplane factory. One day Billie climbed onto the wing of an unfinished plane and lectured on the rights of women, especially black women. She was a passionate speaker with grand gesture and dramatic voice — and an occasional rough word to make a point. She broke some taboos that day.

Mattie threatened to throw her and her propaganda out, and once did. But Billie would not back down; Mattie got curious, and when she became convinced — it was an avalanche. Mattie had ten children, and all but the youngest followed.

I had met the second youngest daughter three years earlier at my AYD school, beautiful and wonderfully self-possessed Bessie-Mae. When a male once facilely talked of "women's work" implying that Bessie-Mae should wash the dishes, everyone in the room got a caustic lecture about equality, women's rights, and the nonexistence of "women's work," possibly excepting the maternity ward. I had never witnessed such pride in being a woman, especially a black woman, and never forgot the lesson about gender equality, driven home many years before the coming new wave of women's liberation.

I often visited a married son who lived upstairs — straightforward, thoughtful steelworker Sam and his pretty wife who had two adorable daughters, one-and-a-half and three years old. Of course, the impish, hyperactive, joyful little girls knew nothing of racial differences. But they helped me drown the racist traces that lurked in nearly every white American, even the most resolutely antiracist. I perhaps loved their sensitive mother as much as I did the little girls, but dared not admit such feelings even to myself.

Another brother lived downstairs with his wife and two children. Like Sam, he was often laid off. If both men had been white, they would not have borne the most onerous work, or been laid off so often. Ben, the oldest and perhaps wisest brother, worked at many trades but once confided his dream of farming, not privately, but in a socialist collective. He later married a white schoolteacher and moved away. Seventeen-year-old Gladys went to an all-black high school and good-naturedly tolerated my squarish ignorance of jazz greats like Dizzy Gillespie and Billy Eckstine.

One generation removed from rural life, the Timpkens spoke a rich, metaphorical language. When we despaired of our rearguard battles against overwhelming odds, Mattie said: "There are some proud, mighty cliffs in the mountains, but the sun and frost make tiny little cracks in them and can bring those proud old cliffs tumbling to the ground, especially if they're given a little help at the right place and the right time."

Mattie was a fighter. She once saw the furniture of a white family down the street being removed. While she argued with the bailiff, she sent her eleven-year-old son to rally neighbors. When enough had gathered, they returned the furniture. The bailiff looked at the crowd and decided to retreat. Mattie's husband passed by, but slipped away trying not to be seen. The fear of losing his job and undermining his family's survival had overcome the compulsion to join in. But Mattie had saved the day and soon had a block committee working to stop more evictions.

I was learning that ghetto life was threatened from all directions: cops, joblessness, crime, alcohol, drugs. But the buoyant, proudly class-conscious Timpken home, with its stream of family and Buffalo radicals constantly coming and going, was a healthy island, not isolated from the ghetto or the rest of the world, but an intense part of both. My own loneliness was lessened by the Timpkens' fortitude, optimism, and humor.

I was assigned to a party branch which met on Sundays for late-shift workers. The chair, who had led jobless marches during the Depression, loved flowery words and rolling phrases. The others, workers recruited since the war, were not always an integral part of party life, and were now slipping away from this besieged little organization. Meetings were dull compared to Harvard, but as the only white and college-trained member, I could hardly give advice, and did not have any to offer anyway. The branch slowly faded away; I hoped my presence did not hasten the process.

So there was no branch for me. But since I was the lone Communist in a mid-sized factory when bigger plants demanded attention, no one seemed concerned. To do something, I began selling the *Sunday Worker,* but was afraid to approach whites, fearing that I might be recognized by someone from my factory and tagged as a "red." I worried about doors slamming in my face, being denounced to the police or FBI, or being assaulted. Spy stories clogged the headlines, and the new Soviet A-bomb stirred paranoid associations between Communists and "Russian atom spies." But blacks had been lied to so much by those in power that few believed cold war rhetoric about defending freedom and democracy. Without being sympathetic to the Soviet Union, they were rarely red-baiters. Of the nearly fifty families I visited every Sunday in a ghetto housing project — a depressing jungle of concrete blocks without grass or trees — only one, that of a civil service employee, ever slammed the door or cursed me out. But few bought the dry *Worker.* The friendliest family chatted, then tried to sell me the *Watchtower.* Unsold *Worker*s piled up in the Timpken house, and I decided it was better to give them away than have them go to waste. One customer told of her travails and extracted money from me. At the end, I had fewer funds than I had when I started. Little came of my rounds, but I had gained insights into the trouble-plagued lives of many Americans.

Several other young comrades came up from New York City or stayed in the area after finishing college. A few went to work at Bethlehem Steel in nearby Lackawanna, where they fought for better conditions, especially for blacks — and were summarily fired if exposed. This influx of "colonizers," called "outside agitators" by hostile local media, drew a sharp response from Mattie: "We're all from the same country. They never lash missionaries. Christian saints went around with epistles and rosaries since St. Paul. Nobody called them outside agitators, and we're working to better people's lives right here and now, on earth."

Jerry, whose background was similar to mine, arrived from New York and we immediately became friends and confidants. I asked why, unlike college, branch meetings were so deadly. Why were Gil, a local party official, and Dominick, a respected labor organizer in the '30s and now head of party union activities, such know-it-alls, always hunting for slips and errors? Jerry didn't like them either, but an old war horse like Dominick could not be cast off.

OK, I replied. But anyone expressing a doubt or asking a question is put down as if he's about to desert or turn renegade. People are almost afraid to criticize anything. Jerry agreed, but said the party was under severe attack, and many were quitting or becoming informers out of fear, ambition, or capitulation to relentless propaganda. Such circumstances fanned suspicion of those who doubted and questioned. It's easier to be tolerant when you're winning; now we're as spiny as cornered porcupines, but had to maintain discipline and hold as many people as possible.

I replied that at Harvard we had discipline, but had open discussion, laughed at our blunders, and won new members. Jerry countered that I had admitted that many Harvard comrades were elitists who did what they liked and fell away in the end. I agreed in part. But survival didn't mean becoming robots or lemmings who scurry over precipices after incompetent leaders like Gil and Dominick. They were driving people away. I knew Communists who would leaflet in blizzards, but who could not think for themselves. I knew others who got knocked off their feet by any change of line, whether it was a blunder or a justified shift in a complicated world. There should be comrades who aren't knocked out either by blizzards or by shifts and who can think for themselves.

"Take a deep breath," Jerry advised. "We can't bake good Communists to meet your specifications. This tough world is made up of human beings, not gods. So we have to struggle along as best we can with the people and leaders we've got and ourselves try to set a good example." There was not much left to say.

On Labor Day weekend of 1949, I went down to New York City to visit with a good friend, Dore Ashton. On Sunday we unexpectedly found ourselves heading north to Peekskill. A week earlier, a Paul Robeson concert had been prevented by a frenzied mob that burned books, destroyed music and chairs, and fought for hours to break through a thin line of men protecting women and children. That spring, Robeson had addressed the World Peace Congress in Paris, where he joined others in pleading for peace. Allegedly he said that black Americans would never join the racists to fight the Soviets, and a torrent of denunciation was unleashed against him. Racism became the visible hand that made Robeson, a national hero years earlier, into Public Enemy No. 1.

The concert had been defiantly rescheduled. As our chartered buses headed north, we saw countless signs and bumper stickers saying "Wake Up, America, Peekskill Did!" and passed a pickup truck laden with stones. "I hope they're not for us," I joked. Finally we drove through a raucous gauntlet shouting "Commies," "Kikes," "Niggers," held back by grinning cops, and then had a wonderful surprise.

Perhaps twenty thousand people filled a grassy basin. Around the entire circumference was a resolute line of unionists and veterans protecting the throng. Robeson stood on a little platform, guarded also by black and white union men and veterans who shielded him. We heard that a sniper had been spotted in the hills. Howard Fast spoke, Hope Foye and Pete Seeger sang, but when Robeson's huge, warm voice poured out "Old Man River" with his line "I'll keep on fighting until I'm dying," there was a roar of joy, approval, and commitment such as I never heard before or since.

Returning to our buses, we found that the drivers had disappeared. Each bus had to find a rider who could handle the vehicle. We selected a black passenger as our "bus leader," and as we drove away we saw state cops descend upon members of the defense line, searching for "concealed weapons" and beating a black veteran viciously with nightsticks. The state police directed all vehicles away from the main road with instructions to drive slowly on a wooded secondary road. We soon learned why. Every fifty yards along the road, each bus or car was pelted with rocks taken from big piles at the rock throwers' feet. Our bus leader asked us to keep calm, told the children to lie down in the aisle and the men to hold their jackets to the windows to stop flying glass. Two-thirds of the windows were smashed, including the windshield. But our amateur driver kept the bus moving through the howling mob.

After the rock-throwing gauntlet, our troubles were not over. The state cops stopped each bus "to check drivers' licenses." Our leader wanted to negotiate; other passengers insisted that the police would rather beat a black man than negotiate. He had to be almost forcibly restrained while one of the whites made a futile attempt to bargain. Evicted from the bus, we were forced to walk through the dark streets of a small town to the station past "patriots" who could only glare because here they were not in big numbers and had no stones.

The media reported hotly that Robeson and his "Communist backers" were to blame for the violence while the police had protected them from the just wrath of angry veterans.

Was Peekskill a victory or a defeat? After the first carnage, the left responded with a magnificently planned second concert for thousands. That surely was a victory for free assembly and defiance of increasingly powerful forces whose outlook was symbolized by the burning of a KKK cross near Peekskill. But the concert was one of the last major left-wing actions for many years as the McCarthy-Nixon eclipse darkened the nation's landscape. Robeson was soon stripped of his passport and barred from film, stage, concert halls, and recordings. Black leaders were pressured to back away or attack him. But he refused to buckle, or to change his views on peace, racial justice, and colonial freedom. Despite its outcome, Peekskill remained a symbol for those who loved him. Dore, hardly far to the left, never forgot Peekskill; I think its memory always affected her outlook. And mine as well.

I returned to pushing copper and brass, solder and paint, and because of my cowardice, or my wisdom, I never mentioned Peekskill to my workmates.

Fedders received a large order for water coolers and began working us as much as eighty-four hours a week. Most pieceworkers rejoiced at nearly triple pay each week, but were soon exhausted, collapsing at every break. Hourly workers warned against that schedule, only to be told that we were jealous of the pieceworkers' high pay. Actually, no one had any choice; the union was too close to management to complain.

After eight weeks the schedule reverted to normal. We awaited Christmas and Fedders's big holiday basket with lots of goodies and a turkey. But I got a surprising "cold turkey": a note with my paycheck regretted that I was no longer needed. It wasn't personal; 250 others, the last hired, got similar slips. Seniority was good in many ways, but it took the jobs of most young workers and three of the five blacks. I was sure that those double workweeks hastened the layoffs.

A few months earlier another New Yorker, big, lusty, red-headed Bill Nuchow, had come upstate to work and got a job at Fedders. I was no longer alone; there had been hope for starting a party branch if only with two members. Now we were both laid off. There were no jobs at the unemployment office, where we were rudely informed that we did not qualify for jobless insurance because we had not worked six months in the previous year. We canvassed countless personnel offices, often lying about our qualifications. Constant refusals began to have an enervating effect. I had no dependents, lived inexpensively, and could always fall back on my degree to seek work. Yet, as my meager savings dwindled, I felt smaller and smaller, like a hat-in-hand beggar. Job-seekers are advised to act as if they owned the world. That's not easy when you're bowing and cringing to every secretary who hands out another useless questionnaire or says curtly, "We're not hiring just now." A terrible feeling. To me, a crime.

To save money, Bill and I moved into a single room below ground level, with one big double bed. Every day we scrambled for the first evening paper and dashed off to any listed job openings. With growing desperation we decided to answer an ad for "Roger's Employment Agency," in a ramshackle building next to Roger's handsome new house and car. We had hardly entered when a piece of paper was thrust into our hands committing us to pay Roger our first week's wages, including overtime and any bonuses. We grumbled—but signed. Bill was sent to a GM assembly plant and I got a job with the American Radiator Company, switching from coolers in the summer to heaters in the winter. Having been turned away from that plant a week earlier, I asked if I would have gotten the job if I had not come through Roger. "Today, yes," was the reply. I lost a week's pay because Roger, probably due to occasional cash lubrication, knew who was hiring each day, and I didn't. Now I knew why he had a new house and car.

I alternated between three shifts—and was blissfully free two evenings out of three. The plant was more modern and more orderly than Fedders, but with only two women and no blacks. I became a crane operator assistant, unloading sheet steel from trucks, or taking steel out to the work hall and delivering it to the shearing benches with a handcrane. I was hopelessly clumsy at this dangerous work; a loose sheet of steel could cut a man in half. Gradually I learned the techniques from my boss, who was patient unless I did something very stupid. He was Polish-American, like the crane operator, who was ill-humored, cynical, and reactionary, but an artist with that crane. From way up high he could nudge things into place and then soar across the huge hall. The crane was like a swift spider gliding across a complicated web; when its metal filigree silhouetted against a moonlit sky, I decided that industrial beauty did exist.

Our breaks were not so lyrical. The only eating place offered goulash or stuffed cabbage and two jukebox songs, "Domino" or "Jealous Heart." Always stuffed cabbage or goulash — my stomach became more jealous than my heart.

One night a beam fell on my toe. With no first-aid at 3 A.M., I waited in agony until the doctor arrived at 8, when he lanced the toenail and sent me home. At my first union meeting I proposed that there be at least a nurse on all three shifts. The leadership was not interested, and neither were the few old stalwarts who automatically backed their leaders. It was time for action: I wrote up a petition for medical aid on all shifts. But there was apathy, little militancy, and considerable fear. When my foot healed I was sent to the painting department. I couldn't learn to spray the parts quickly and my coworker lost out in pay. I decided this was not a good time to wave a petition around.

Fedders was now hiring back laid-off employees. I had to choose between returning or staying where I was, losing six months' seniority either way, and not knowing which job would last. Also, my bed-sharing experiment with Bill had failed. He was being speeded up mercilessly on the GM assembly line. Whenever I got home he was fast asleep, his large bulk diagonally across the bed. When I pushed him he would react as if I were his hated foreman or even worse, his fiancée. I moved back to my old room, and back to Fedders since I would be on straight day shift.

My new mobility coincided with the founding of the Labor Youth League, an echo of the old Young Communist League. Morty Sheer and his wife came up from New York to help get things going. They were good-humored, easygoing, and not dogmatic. We never found a way to reach local white youth, so our club was composed of white "colonizers" and black friends of Gladys, the youngest Timpken daughter. With half of us being white college graduates and the other half noncollege blacks, it was vital for the whites to avoid racist-tinged domination or condescension. Somehow it all worked, largely because of the decency that pervaded both groups. Gladys, though less political than her siblings, was accustomed to relaxed, equal relations between blacks and whites. A young, self confident African American was elected president. There were parties, picnics, and occasional modest demonstrations. The whites learned about Afro-American music, the blacks learned left-wing songs, and we all loved a jazzed-up version of the gospel "Hebrew Children."

Our club soon became embroiled with the virulent racism so widespread at the time. One evening on the Crystal Beach boat, which featured weekend dancing, a young black dared ask a white woman to dance. The following weekend blacks were denied tickets, with the transparent excuse that "only couples" could be admitted. A week later two single white LYLers bought tickets; two black members tried to do the same, and were denied under the "only couples" excuse. Our two whites returned to nail the lie; an argument erupted, and suddenly two policemen charged, one hitting Ben Timpken over the head with his nightstick. With blood streaming down, Ben continued to protest. The second cop aimed a pistol at him. Billie Timpken, in her ninth month of pregnancy, threw her arms around her brother's neck and began to cry loudly. Her "hysteria" may have saved him. The cop put his pistol away but arrested Ben and one white LYLer. They made bail, and charges against our white member were dropped, but it took months and a trial lawyer to get Ben acquitted.

When two comrades made an unprecedented visit to my room, I knew it was about money. We paid party dues, LYL dues, and gave two weeks' pay to the *Daily Worker.* I had saved only about forty dollars for a vacation and now I was being tapped for most of that. But it was hard to say no. A black youth of seventeen had been arrested for burglary and attempted rape, based on unconvincing accusations by an elderly white woman. The LYL sought to bail him out and fund his defense. We were convinced of his innocence, but he would never get a fair trial without publicity and solid legal support. My savings were well spent and never returned, of course. Life in those days was not easy.

The left's one major action after Peekskill was the Stockholm Peace Appeal, which labeled as criminal the first use of atomic weapons by any country. Millions signed all over the world. In the United States, the famous black intellectual W. E. B. Du Bois led the appeal, for which he was arrested for "failing to register as a foreign agent." We LYLers sought signatures, and I returned to my old housing project, where the response was hardly enthusiastic. Atomic war was very distant to people who were oppressed by closer circumstances. But they didn't respond like some whites with "drop the bomb on them before they get too strong." Our timidity in facing whites was fortified by a *Los Angeles Times* editorial: "If approached by a peace petitioner . . . don't punch him in the nose. Reds are used to that. Get his name . . . and phone the FBI." But Bill's fiancée, our only white noncommunist, got the most signatures — in white communities. She had found a way that eluded the rest of us.

My new job at Fedders, enlarging and flanging copper tubes with a drill, required adeptness — never my strong point. Piecework rates would be set when we became proficient at our tasks, and it was in our interest not to work too quickly in order to establish a lower speed as the norm. That suited me fine. The foreman kept asking why I did not produce more than nine or ten pieces a day. I talked to the fellow doing the same job on late shift, and he agreed: "Not too many. I only do thirty-five a day!" I was soon put on other jobs but never could achieve the norm, which others exceeded — even keeping a few pieces in reserve in order to grab a smoke.

There was a lot of kidding among the young, mainly Polish and Italian workers, and some of it had ethnic or religious undertones. The Poles were more religious than the Italians and scolded at the Italians' Friday meat sandwiches, while the Italians joked about dubious celibacy in the priesthood.

But they began to joke, too, about "brown-noses" and "batmen." "Brown-noses" were those older men who worked very hard, even after quitting time, and were considered money-hungry company loyalists. "Batmen" too worked hard, but they didn't believe in killing themselves for the company or working one minute past quitting time. I might have chosen other labels, but I realized that the thinking behind the teasing was like my own. I worked desperately hard to overcome my clumsiness, but fellow workers must have felt that anyone producing as little as I did could not be a company loyalist. And I was always careful — and glad — not to work after the buzzer.

Those "brown-noses" muttered sullenly about wiseguy "batmen." With little class consciousness, many of the old guys were faithful to a company which hardly repaid their loyalty when they were no longer so productive. But they took a craftsman's pride in doing a good job. Sadly, such feelings and conduct helped the company, often at the expense of these same older workers and all the others. I reflected that socialism was the only way out of such dilemmas. Good work would not be self-destructive; skill and pride would better everyone, not just bosses and stockholders. But I could not yet realize how hard it was, even under socialism, to achieve such circumstances and attitudes.

With a day job I could attend union meetings. Only about twenty of the thirteen hundred employees came regularly to such dull, routine gatherings; usually only elected officials, their cronies, and a few devoted old unionists from the 1930s struggles showed up. Ruling the roost were a president with one of the best-paying piece-rate jobs in the factory, a slick tool and dye maker secretary-treasurer with even higher pay, and an elegantly dressed district business agent who saw to it that the locals did not step out of line.

They seemed surprised to see a new and young face. I spoke up at my third meeting, suggesting a campaign for air-conditioning in the hot, fume-filled acid-dip room. There was little response, but I was flabbergasted at the next meeting when I was nominated for compensation agent. Over a year of working with little impact, and now I was offered an official job.

The Taft-Hartley Law required union officials to file noncommunist affidavits; falsifying them carried heavy fines and even jail. But party experts believed that compensation agent was not an elective post and not subject to Taft-Hartley; so I took on the job. I went to a few downtown meetings, helped an old Polish worker file a compensation claim, told others about their rights, and got up early to distribute information booklets at the plant gates. This surprised some workers, since no one had ever before bothered to give them this useful information.

I dreamed of starting a factory paper to attack plant conditions: unsafe machines, poisonous fumes, few lockers, no showers, no lunchroom. The plant was filthy, partly because things that did not bring profits were neglected. The paper would attack unequal pay for women and discrimination against the few blacks who were hired and all who were not. But such a paper was impossible without a party branch and help from others. I did look up a former AYDer, a clear, progressive thinker who knew the plant inside and out. But his new wife had pressured him out of activity, and he turned down all meetings. Thus I could only dream about the paper to battle against the owners for decent conditions and a better life.

On June 25, 1950, the Korean War began and with it came headlines about brutal Russian-backed aggression. The origins of the war were ambiguous; on the day after the fighting erupted a map showed South Korean forces bulging up into the North with no bulge southward. I never saw that map again and soon North Korean troops were clearly moving south, while at home hysteria grew. The Stockholm Appeal ground to an end; American Legion veterans in Buffalo threatened to burn down two newspaper stands which carried the *Daily Worker;* the UE lost an election in a big factory near Buffalo; Julius and Ethel Rosenberg were arrested and the tragic ordeal began that ended in their execution; the top Communist leaders had been sentenced to five years under the Smith Act; every Communist was required to register as a foreign agent under the McCarran Act with up to $10,000 fines and five years in prison for every single day not registered. But registering as "foreign agents" was unthinkable. What could we Communists do but laugh weakly, especially when we later learned that concentration camps — proposed by Senator Hubert Humphrey — were being built for "emergency" roundups? The rabid atmosphere infected the workplace, where a workmate commented knowingly that workers in the USSR slaved twelve hours a day. I kept my mouth shut; a lynch spirit was in the air.

While I was on vacation, candidates for our union elections had been selected, all of them on friendly terms with the company. Unopposed, they were rubber-stamped into office. But I had been dropped as compensation agent without explanation; I was afraid to complain or ask for a reason.

One week before our contract was due to expire, hundreds of determined members jammed a big hall. The business agent, attempting to frighten us, warned darkly that company spies were sure to report what we said but then spoke lengthily and with pathos about the need to help our nation during its struggle against communism. People began to grow restless and suspicious. Someone yelled: "What's in the contract?—Read us the contract!" Finally our oily secretary-treasurer read the result of long bargaining sessions. The draft contained a three-cent increase and little more. This set off loud demands for the floor. When the president sought to call on one of his stooges, an angry-looking man near him began speaking at the same time.

"No, not you," he was told. "I mean that brother there with the brown jacket."

"Whaddaya mean?" the angry man said. "Do you need a brown jacket to talk in this local?"

The crowd shouted: "Let him speak!—Give all sides a chance!—We don't want that lousy contract!" And he spoke.

The argument became white hot. I hadn't planned to speak, but the moment had come, and somehow amidst the noise, I got the floor. I had so much to say and so little time. A strike committee should have been set up even if no strike were planned; links should have been forged with other locals in Buffalo and Fedders plants in other states. A fighting spirit would pressure the company. But with stooges shouting against a strike, I blurted out that none of us wanted a strike but with prices going up so fast a three-cent raise was really like a cut in pay. I then moved that the negotiating committee go back and take nothing less than a 15-cent raise in pay.

The leaders were livid. The president declared, "No second—no motion." But many voices shouted "Second." The brass, sensing strong support for 15 cents, didn't dare go too far out on an unpopular limb. A vote was taken and our dour leader had to admit that the motion had carried, sending the negotiators back to the table—at least pro forma. The crowd left the hall with feelings of anger, struggle, and strength absent for years.

Then the counterattack began. Rumors circulated that Fedders was prepared for a long strike or planned to shift its Buffalo production to anti-union Alabama. Men with families began calculating how many years they would have to work to make up for strike losses after four, six, or eight weeks. Old quarrels resurfaced between hourly and pieceworkers, the former accusing the latter of a lack of militancy, while the latter called the former mindless firebrands. Petty squabbles between shifts about the quality of each others' work, or the day workers' habit of picking the best parts to work on, grew sharper. Older workers claimed the younger men didn't have families to support. Even mild ethnic frictions increased. Some of this was due to increased tension, but I believed the company had fanned divisions, helped along by the local's leaders.

Two days before the contract expired, another meeting was held. Fewer workers attended; many had been discouraged from coming or were fearful or disgusted. The whole atmosphere had changed. The president's cliché-ridden report pointed to almost no new benefits but a new wage offer: six cents now and three cents after a year on a two-year contract. The improvement, due only to our obduracy, was far short of the 15 cents demanded, but this time the leadership had a majority. Fear of a long, hungry strike had withered a fighting spirit. The president was careful in picking speakers, but some opponents, including myself, got the floor and were shouted down while the business agent hinted darkly that opposition bordered on sabotage of the war effort. One young worker resolutely read a statement charging Fedders with maintaining conditions unfit for pigs: filthy toilets, no showers, no decent place to eat. Everyone knew the truth of his charges. But when he spoke against the contract he also was shouted down.

The vote, a foregone conclusion, was a big victory for the company and the corrupt leaders. But forty or fifty workers voted against it; young and old, pieceworkers and hourly workers of many ethnic backgrounds. If only they could stay together and build their ranks for future battles.

The Korean War was hardly conducive to the exercise of constitutional rights without fear of surveillance or reprisal. I got a rude reminder of this where I lived—in a little room in the house of a working-class family. The husband always seemed cool, but the wife was friendly enough when we met on occasion and at times invited me to watch her living room TV. Alone in the house one afternoon I answered the phone, and found myself talking with someone who identified himself as "FBI." When he realized to whom he was speaking, he quickly hung up. I was left with a lot of thinking to do. I had always kept *Daily Worker*s and other party literature in my dresser drawer, covered with clothing, but what landlady is not inquisitive?

Then came an even greater shock. I received my draft notice. A swarm of new questions arose. Would I be sent to Korea? What did the army know of my past, and what would it do about it? Should I refuse to sign the form demanding to know whether I had belonged to any of the scores of groups of all types on the "Attorney General's List of Subversive Organizations"? What if I admitted having been in some of them? What would happen if I did sign?

I decided to report not in Buffalo, where left-wingers were few and well known, but in New York City, where I might escape notice. I quit my job and packed my bags.

The party suspended draftees from membership while they were in military service, providing weak protection if asked about affiliation. But I knew that the army would hardly draw such fine distinctions. I cleared up formalities with the district and with Mattie, the first person I met in Buffalo and a close comrade for seventeen months. In her typical metaphorical manner, Mattie expressed sorrow that we didn't get more done, but urged against being discouraged. We were like travelers on a tedious journey who had reached a first mountaintop where we could see travails and dangers, but also the blurry outlines of a bright future. Many rockslides remained, but we knew our goals — and that was a great solace.

I said good-by to her and others I had known, liked, and sometimes loved, and went on to face new rockslides. I paid a last visit to Niagara Falls and was again amazed at how Lake Erie's dirty water flowed in the Niagara River past drab Buffalo and was transformed by these magnificent water-falls into a mighty power, rushing ever faster, hurtling thunderously down-ward, with high-flying spume and rainbows hovering over the scene.

On my way to New York, I wondered if the seventeen months, for which I was so poorly equipped, had been worth it. Only toward the end did I meet people who might be won to social action. But by then, pro-gressives were being routed. On the other hand, I had had an immense learning experience: finding and making great friends in the black com-munity and learning more about my country's working people. Many of my fellow workers seemed politically backward and afflicted by rampant racism, due partly to right-wing clerical influences but mostly because, like Americans of every class, they were subjected to powerful pressures from all the media. Many wanted to make money, dreamed of climbing the ca-reer ladder, perhaps some day "opening a business of my own." Few suc-ceeded, but the dream shaped their outlook.

I had lost idealized illusions about "noble proletarians." Working people, unlike my student comrades, never spoke of class struggles; but they took part in them every day in the shape of facing a foreman or a work norm, flawed materials, or danger to life and limb. They were in constant gut-wrenching battle for every penny when trying to squeeze a few cents more out of a pay slip, or when the time-keeper came around with his stopwatch. Ever present was the fear of layoffs, firings, or having to strike, with the re-sulting cutbacks in purchasing power for themselves and their families.

Other groups had financial worries. Many professional people were ba-sically workers, like my father, who balanced on the edge of bankruptcy for years. But workers in factories, mines, or building sites were often forced by their work into togetherness. Efforts were constantly made to split them on the basis of color, age, sex, skill, or nationality. But as well as such cen-trifugal forces there were opposite forces which at times brought them into the kind of unity I saw at that first contract meeting. To increase the unifying tendencies it was vital to have leadership with fighting spirit and experience. I had been far too inexperienced and isolated to be useful, while the party at that time was simply fighting to survive.

In the first week of January 1951 I went to the Reception Center in downtown Manhattan, pushed through crowds of young men, parents, wives, and girlfriends and walked through that fateful door. After having my name checked and doublechecked, I lined up with a mixed group of young New Yorkers and climbed onto a bus driving north into the winter night.

FLIGHT (4)

"Come along with me!" said the uniformed Austrian, escorting me to the police station. I pretended not to speak German and said only: "Soviet Kommandantur."

I hadn't spoken any German either with the woman who emerged from the house where I had stopped to rest. I wanted to be absolutely certain that I had not landed in that American enclave across from Linz, so I only asked: "Wo ist Soviet Kommandantur?" She pointed to where I had come from — and clearly wondered if I was trying to avoid the Kommandantur, was blundering, or was crazy. She figured I was a Czech soldier deserting to the West and tried a few words in Czech. I didn't enlighten her, but tramped back along the hot, dusty road, no longer trying to conceal myself. Farmers stared at my torn clothing and shoeless feet. I didn't care and was glad to be apprehended at last in the first village I entered.

I kept up the "Nicht verstehen" act to curious Austrian police — and they finally called the Kommandantur. A friendly man in Lederhosen soon appeared and led me to a jeep. Why was a Soviet employee dressed like that? Was he an interpreter? In my exhausted state I could not think clearly; when he asked me in German who I was and where I came from, I dropped my pretended ignorance and told him. At Soviet headquarters an officer said that was a mistake, giving me insight into relations between Soviet forces and Austrian police, who, as I discovered years later, reported all I said to the U.S. Army.

The officer showed most interest when I mentioned having been stationed at Bad Tölz. I was puzzled, but later learned that our unit had been replaced in the comfortable but isolated military complex, once an SS center, by a Ranger unit made up of pro-Nazi East European "escapees" including remnants of the fascist Vlassov division. But I knew nothing of this and he did not keep me long. I was left in an office with a cot and was finally able to eat and sleep, though a troubling note was the armed soldier at the door. The next day two officers drove me though beautiful mountain scenery marred by the presence of Mauthausen, a concentration camp where thousands of Communists, Jews, and resistance fighters had suffered and died.

We arrived at Soviet Headquarters in Baden near Vienna, driving through red and green entrance arches to a three-story building. One officer said: "I hope you won't mind staying here a little while." "Of course not!" I answered grandly. But I got a shock. I was taken to a grim cellar cell; the door was locked behind me, the window was barred. I saw an armed guard in the corridor for me alone. It was not what I had expected.

[4]
SOLDIER

"You won't be staying here long," said the sergeant to us tired New Yorkers. "Do what I say and don't make trouble and we'll get along." I was back in Massachusetts, at Fort Devens, not far from cities I had visited two-and-a-half years earlier during the Wallace campaign.

The next few days were all about army life: how to wear the uniform, how to salute an officer, stand at attention, march in every direction. But the looming "sixty-four dollar question" overwhelmed my consciousness: "Are you now or have you ever been a member of the Communist Party?" I had a vague notion of refusing to sign when we were marched off to a building where I suddenly found the fateful form in my hand with scores of organizations listed. Aside from the Ku Klux Klan and Imperial Japanese groups, all were leftist, including the Young Communist League, which I had joined at fourteen; American Youth for Democracy, in which I had been a campus chairman; Labor Youth League, which I had joined from the start; Southern Negro Youth Congress, which I supported in 1947 with a one-dollar initiation fee; Joint Anti-Fascist Refugee Appeal, which helped exiled and imprisoned Spanish antifascists. And the Communist Party, which I had joined in 1945.

"Hurry up, men," the sergeant said. He had surely never seen anyone refuse to sign. My fellow inductees had probably never encountered anyone belonging to such loathsome outfits. What should I do? My main impulse was not to attract attention. I signed hastily. Now I must be unobtrusive for two years, hoping that no one would check up on me. Was I visibly shaken? I didn't know. I knew only that I was terribly frightened.

That was an immediate problem. Our group reflected New York's many races and ethnicities. Most inductees searched out "their own," while color lines were always sharper than the religious and nationality divide. As a

Communist I felt a duty to bridge gaps, oppose racism, or at least involve black recruits in barracks doings. In those days even that was "conspicuous behavior." The army "solved" the problem by shipping blacks to separate camps, mostly in the South. Segregation still reigned. We "Caucasians," which included Latinos, white and black, traveled six hundred miles to central Virginia to receive basic training and prepare for war.

The two-story wooden barracks were not fancy; over twenty metal beds were jammed together on each floor and a communal wash room was graced by unpartitioned throne-like toilets. Our unit had been in the Connecticut National Guard, which many had joined to evade the draft only to land in the army after all.

In our group were Italian, Polish, and Irish draftees, some cynical, some devout, some very homesick. The Jews were also a varied lot—one angled clumsily to exploit an injured wrist, another bumbling fellow repeatedly asked questions in an effort to get nothing wrong, not grasping that the army always changes its rules. He teamed with another awkward fellow who faced military life with irony and self-deprecating humor.

Si Haskel, though not religious, attended Jewish services, something I should have done but could not bring myself to. He was bright and witty and became my best friend. Fifty years later he told me that he, too, had been a member of American Youth for Democracy—and kept silent about it.

Army life was unpleasant but bearable. I got used to frenzied Friday night barracks-cleaning "GI parties," Saturday morning "policing" of the area for butts and trash as sergeants shouted: "I don't want to see nothing but assholes and elbows!" and daily marches to the training area to learn about rank, rules, hygiene, camouflage, creeping and crawling, digging foxholes, throwing hand grenades, and above all, care of our rifles. I never got into growling loudly and plunging a bayonet into a straw dummy, a hateful exercise for most draftees, though adored by the glory-dreaming "Regular Army" volunteers.

Political questions were handled by a noncommissioned officer during "Information and Education" sessions. I answered factual questions but otherwise kept quiet. My lips were sealed during one turbulent session, chaired by a raw corporal, on "Why must we fight in Korea?" Our company jester intervened in the fumbling discussion: "You want to know why we're fighting in Korea? Well, I'll tell you." He pointed dramatically: "See these rifles? And you see these helmets? And the uniforms? And the tanks and everything else issued in the army. Some men make billions — and they want to keep making billions. That's why we're in Korea!" His words, said humorously, met with a roar of approving laughter at the expense of the profusely sweating corporal — but also deep down most felt truth in them. The corporal tried some funny remarks and platitudes, but ended the session early. A few weeks later, after basic training, our jester was sent to Korea.

We completed basic training in fourteen weeks and were no longer restricted to camp. But Richmond's segregated buses were repellent and kept me from exploring its social life. Once, on a visit to Washington, I suddenly spied a *Daily Worker* in an empty lot. I found a lonely park bench and read every word of it, clichés, party jargon and all, and most avidly the items about the movement to end the war. Who left it there? I doubt there were fifty subscribers in Washington. On the way back to camp I thought of what lay ahead — and my dread of having to fight Koreans.

If Saturday inspection went without delays I could make a train reaching New York by early evening. Anna, whom I had met before being drafted, was my main reason to make the run. She was tall, pretty, with warm, dark-brown skin, straightened, elaborately coiffeured hair in the fashion of black women in those days, and dark eyes reflecting lively intelligence. We talked about everything from politics to literature, which I missed in army camp.

Going out, we were greeted with stares, dirty looks, and bad service. Progressive gatherings were inadvisable although I changed to civilian clothes in New York. One Sunday evening, after it had become difficult to part, she accompanied me a little too far toward Grand Central Station and a soldier from my company saw us. I'm sure he was shocked, though he never said a word about it, at least not to me. After all, interracial liaisons were as taboo as having a *Daily Worker.*

Anna's girlfriend, the daughter of a Spanish Civil War veteran, was engaged to Earl Albright, a member of my regiment. We found to our joy that we were both of the left and plunged hungrily into political issues and army problems, relieved that our burdensome isolation was lifted a bit.

Our overseas transfer drew near. No one wanted to go to Korea, and many scurried to find previously unaccepted physical defects. My flat feet did not suffice. In an ironic twist, those fellows whose disabilities were finally acknowledged were transferred to laundry, bakery, and service units — only to be sent to Korea, and later into battle. The rest of us received great news: we were going to Germany.

A friend in Headquarters Company suggested I transfer there, where work keeping records was easier, the atmosphere more relaxed, the bureaucracy more limited. Getting the transfer was easy, but the process violated my resolution to "remain inconspicuous." Nonetheless, since no one had shown suspicion thus far and my friend had already spoken to the warrant officer, I decided to take the step.

A clerk's life wasn't bad at all. No more waking up at 4 and waiting around for hours, no more long marches, no more freezing all night in pup tents or snapping to attention at barked orders. Our master sergeant was dense but not domineering, and the warrant officer was interested only in keeping records up to date. Every promotion, transfer, every shot for every disease had to be recorded and kept in long coffin-like crates. The only bad aspect was to see in my own envelope the form with the signed "loyalty oath" and be unable to alter or remove it for fear this might be noticed.

Some of us tried German lessons with a refugee soldier. No pedagogue, he wrote word lists on the blackboard with the German equivalents and told us how to pronounce them. His bored pupils wanted important words. "How do you say 'ass'?" one man yelled, with less anatomical than lascivious interest. But our teacher had left Germany at twelve and was primly bourgeois. He could only come up with "popo," obviously a nursery term. I laughed to think of a GI using this word with some tough German prostitute. That was our first and last lesson.

On a last visit to New York, I said good-by to Anna and my family, and I agreed on a code with my father. Late in October we shipped out on a troop transport from Newport News.

The crossing was marked by miserable weather, cramped quarters, sloshing toilets, and a seasick soldier who groaned loudly until we docked eleven days later. The main deck was jammed with GIs fleeing the pestilential atmosphere below. There were so many men that we were cut to two daily meals with over an hour's wait for each. The food was eaten standing at narrow tables, trays and cups sliding with the moving ship.

At Bremerhaven we boarded a southbound train to Bad Tölz in Bavaria. We were amazed to learn that a castle-like white "kaserne" would be our new quarters, a striking change from our seedy Virginia barracks. We slept three or four men to a room; each room had a toilet with walls and doors. That alone made it feel almost luxurious.

Army life in Germany was better: perfunctory inspections, no saluting officers outside camp, and German employees doing most of the kitchen work. Our unit had a warm office; only rarely did an "Alarm" make us pack the records onto a truck and evacuate camp. "Information and Education" sessions explained how the Russians might invade any day through the "Fulda-Bebra gap." The men took mock bets on who would run the fastest.

We were permitted to leave the kaserne frequently. I took German lessons from a lady who had owned a big estate in what was now Poland and expected great sympathy for her losses; I refrained from arguments. Before long I was her only student.

Unprosperous, normal Bad Tölz, with magnificent views of the Alps and the Isar River, overflowed with cuckoo clocks, which GIs sent home by the dozen. At local pubs I found only elderly Bavarians sipping from glasses with metal beer-warmers and playing Skat, or occasionally the zither. There were also GI haunts where soldiers got what they wanted for a price. But neither the locales nor the ladies were appealing; their English was fluent but frightening.

Once I had guard duty near the laundry and, defying orders, chatted with the young man in charge. He spoke English well and wanted friendship. I eagerly accepted his invitation to visit Christmas Eve, looking forward to learning local customs and surely having a better meal than in the mess hall.

I met his pleasant wife and little daughter, admired the carved nativity scene, and sat down to dinner. This was the first disappointment: many Germans eat potato salad and sausage on Christmas Eve, saving the goose for the next day. After a friendly chat over wine, my host led me to a big closet, and digging mysteriously, produced three big albums, opening them triumphantly: "What do you think of these?"

The photos, once obtained for cigarette coupons, showed Hitler in his limousine, Hitler at home, Hitler at a party rally, Hitler and Göring, Goebbels and Hitler, ad nauseam. My host, clearly proud of them, expected praise or maybe a cash offer. I mumbled a few words, wished the little girl a Merry Christmas and left for the kaserne, my Christmas Eve shattered.

Getting away from sleepy Bad Tölz became a near-obsession. I grabbed every tour available, running to Bavarian palaces and monasteries and from Bolzano in Italy to Innsbruck in Austria. Vienna was memorable because Rowe Gingrich, who had recruited me into the party, had married an Austrian and settled there. In Vienna I found a tiny room and asked the landlady how to get to my friend. "But that's in the Russian Sector!" she said.

I looked shocked but found no barriers, controls, or guards barring entry to that mysterious region. We had a happy reunion and reminisced about how we left the material in the telephone booth and other adventures. His wife, who had fled to Switzerland during the Nazi years, and whose brother was a Communist newspaper editor, was friendly and bright. They invited another young woman to join us for an evening in a wine restaurant, where we ate, drank, and danced. They had to leave at midnight, and I walked the icy, empty streets alone, looking dutifully at St. Stephen's Cathedral and other sights, the most welcome of which was the first café to open for a hot cup of coffee.

In the army occupational tests I had been quick to pick up Morse Code, making me eligible for a radio course in Munich. My friend Si and others urged me to take it. I couldn't explain my fear of being investigated, but the prospect of leaving Bad Tölz was irresistible. Maybe I could later get a job as a railroad telegrapher, joining a conservative but important union, this time as a skilled worker.

Nine of us had a big room in a unit which provided meals and passes but left us alone. After eight hours of Morse Code and the workings of various radio sets, we were free to visit the city, and weekends were entirely free. Despite its ruins, Munich still had beautiful churches, palaces, and a rich cultural life. At the famous, noisy, beer-guzzling Hofbräuhaus, I asked a pretty girl of about eighteen to dance a waltz and later was invited to her home. When I innocently used the familiar *du*, her parents reacted icily: *du* was reserved for intimate relationships in those days. When their big German shepherd walked in, I said respectfully "Kommen Sie her" (Come here), using the formal form of "you." They roared: *du* for the daughter, *Sie* to the dog. I couldn't get anything right. But *du* or *Sie,* our friendship didn't last.

Our coffee and cigarette ration was double what I needed and I made a few marks by selling some to black marketeers. They were an unpleasant bunch, skilled at ripping off GIs — paying with invalid currency, handing over scrap paper wrapped in a five mark note, or pulling other crooked tricks. A kid from Kentucky who rarely broke away from his comic books once ventured out to sell some cartons. When handed a wad of invalid bills he retreated to the kaserne, never to go out again. I quit this sordid game after a while, partly because of falling prices, partly because the dealers had often fought for the Nazis or had been concentration camp guards in the Balkans, Eastern Europe, or North Africa.

With inexpensive GI tickets, I saw a lot of Germany. While I was waiting for a train at Ulm, Einstein's birthplace, a slightly drunken man sat down next to me and said how great it was that our two "Kulturvölker" were getting together again. "But," he intoned, "it wasn't right for your air force to wreck our cities and kill so many women and children." I nodded vaguely and asked what he had done during the war. He replied that he had a good job on the Belgian coast, "sending V-1 rockets over to England." He didn't come close to grasping the horror and contradiction of what he had said and done.

In Hamburg, I saw the contrast between the huge statue of Bismarck, the "Iron Chancellor" and the simple street named for Ernst Thälmann, the murdered Communist leader. Thälmann's name is long gone; Bismarck is still standing. In Stuttgart, I risked attending a celebration of International Women's Day, hungry for even limited contact with progressive Germans. Some muttered at my uniform, but when I talked with them I was drawn into their friendly circle in an emptying street. A girl fetched some *Worker*s from the party newspaper office, which I greedily devoured all night.

Our radio course ended and we returned to beautiful, boring Bad Tölz to begin work as radio men. I was determined to "keep my nose clean" for my last nine army months.

In the meantime, I had accumulated leave time, which I used for a ten-day foray through Italy. In Rome, I watched a young man blanketing the walls with witty election posters for the Communist-Socialist coalition, still close allies. The following day, in Trastevere, Rome's main working-class district, I again ran into the poster man, who insisted on taking me to Young Communist League headquarters to show me off. They were busy — less impressed or more cautious, so he proudly took me to a Soviet film downtown, offering whispered, muddled translations of the Italian subtitles.

Naples encompassed an elegant downtown and squalid slums where heavily laden donkeys trudged around, many people were barefoot, a boy "offered" me his sister, and toddlers with distended stomachs wallowed in gutters of filthy alleyways. Yet I met exuberant men tanning sheepskins who dropped their work when I photographed them and launched a happy conversation in rapid Neapolitan. At the great hall where fish were auctioned, I witnessed a mock battle with flying ice chips, epithets, and roaring laughter. Naples was surely full of contrasts.

My last stop, on May Day (no coincidence), was Bologna, the heart of "Red Emilia." The handsome old city was jammed with crowds waiting for the parade. A man next to me who spoke English was the local correspondent of the Communist Party paper *Unitá*. We discussed one jarring note: anticommunist posters showing a USSR covered by circles marking alleged labor camps. This was forgotten when the first marchers came down the narrow streets, cheered by the onlookers. Students whom I had encountered the evening before waved and called me to join them. I told the newsman that I was a soldier. "Fifty thousand people are marching," he said. "No one will notice you."

I was soon marching, joyously singing Spanish Civil War songs all the way to the People's Park where the mayor waved to each new group: delivery boys on bikes with big baskets over their shoulders, lively pensioners, and women from the Po Valley rice fields, singing the moving songs I recalled from *Bitter Rice*. The signs, floats, and big papier maché monsters attacked capitalism, imperialism, Uncle Sam, or similar foes, but always with humor, never stiffly or didactically.

There was plenty of wine and sausage on sale, and my new friends took me to a table presided over by three old women with bright red bandannas and about five teeth among them. Everything was joyful. When the singing began, I requested the only relevant Italian song I knew, "Avanti Populo." There were embarrassed glances: this was a Communist song while May Day was jointly sponsored. But for a foreigner the three old women made an exception, possibly favored by the wine, and we sang along together.

On the train to Germany I mused that Italians were, by and large, "the salt of the earth." Bologna was a highlight of the trip and of my life. An acid voice interrupted my musings. In my compartment was the German wife of an American sergeant saying how good it was to be going home. Assuming my agreement, she added: "You know, Italians are all so dirty."

When I returned to work, I was in for a surprise. The officer in charge told me to work on the telephone switchboard. This was a troubling development. The next day, little Tom Dalucca, a tough, brash, Brooklyn kid who ran a black market in cigarettes, caught me alone and told me that during my furlough someone in civilian clothes had been asking questions about me. "I told him I didn't know you very well," he said. "When he asked me who did I mentioned Bill Meiser." I thanked him, pretending puzzlement but reflecting gratefully that without knowing why I was being checked, he tried to protect me, to turn the snooper to someone he considered a better friend of mine and, most important, to warn me.

Meiser was a Jewish fellow drafted with me, and that may have induced Tom to believe he would say nothing against me. I indirectly gave Meiser opportunities to hint at what went on. He did not respond. Was he warned not to say anything? I wasn't as friendly with pious and stodgy Meiser as Tom may have thought. I was less friendly in the days that followed.

One evening, I told fellow leftist Earl what had happened. They were after me: "If things really get too hot, there may be nothing left for me to do but flee." He looked at me in shocked amazement. "That means you could never come back! You're completely crazy!" I didn't belabor the issue, mumbled about the difficulty of such decisions, and never mentioned the matter again. Ironically, Earl was transferred to my company, into the job as radio man I was forced to vacate.

Before long, evidently the switchboard was also considered risky, and I was sent to the motor pool to supply vehicle drivers with spare parts; I was in no state of mind to learn and my ignorance was a hopeless liability. To my astonishment, with less than seven months to go, I was sent off for a month's training in supply work, a field in which I was utterly incompetent. Or did they simply want me out of the way? I was glad to leave my suddenly worrisome unit and see new places — though not from behind bars.

Eschwege in Hesse was a picturesque little town. Our commander barked and bullied, but not during long classes where we were taught the dull bureaucracy of a storage and supply system. The town was ringed on three sides by East German territory. On two occasions I saw carloads of people arriving in a flurry of excitement. "They're refugees from the other side," a man explained.

I met a young high school student from the East who was eager to speak with an American in uniform. He claimed that his teacher caught him drawing a pig-like caricature of President Wilhelm Pieck. When they threatened to punish him he decided to "opt for liberty." I knew little about East Germany but did know that Pieck succeeded Thälmann after his jailing and was respected as a militant but gentle antifascist. The youth was puzzled that a GI who even spoke some German didn't congratulate him for his courage. I just walked away.

One Sunday when on a train to Kassel I saw that there seemed only a few yards and a narrow stream between the tracks and the broad stretch of plowed land that marked the West-East border. It should be simple to get out at the next station and wade across. But no, like a man in a burning building, I would jump only if there was no other way out.

When I returned to camp, there was little time to worry for we were leaving Bad Tölz to make way, as I later learned, for the East European Rangers. We drove in long truck columns through Bavaria to Fürth near Nuremberg, where I was to spend the rest of my army career. I did my job as best I could; the men bore my ignorance with tolerance.

I still had ten days of leave and wanted to get far away from my problems. In late July 1952, I headed for Scandinavia. When I crossed the German border, the bright "Dannebröd" flag of Denmark greeted me joyously. Putting on civilian clothes, I entered Copenhagen and roamed from huge shipyards to the Little Mermaid on her rock to seamen's bars. On one old street I found a familiar-looking shop window. Despite the language there was no mistaking books by Marx, Engels, Lenin, Plekhanov, Stalin. Naturally I went in and bought two books in English. The book dealer suggested I talk with Karin, a Communist youth leader who spoke fluent English. We hit it off immediately, and I met her the next day for lunch. I told her that many Germans had learned little from their Nazi nightmare. She said that she met German youth at the 1951 World Youth Festival in East Berlin who hated fascism and were trying to build a socialist country. I was skeptical. She also showed me a speech by the Soviet writer Ilya Ehrenburg, a moving indictment of the cold war, and suggested that I distribute it among GIs, recalling how she, disguised as a prostitute, had left anti-Nazi leaflets in bars frequented by German soldiers. I gulped. "I can get you lots of copies in English. Think it over," she said cheerfully. I had already thought it over. I was in enough trouble now.

Her next suggestion was less problematic: that I visit wonderful Tivoli in the city center which had everything from roller coasters to a symphony hall, great eating places, and a free *commedia dell'arte* pantomime with Pierrette, Pierrot, Columbine, and Pantolone. And there I searched for my own Columbine. I spoke to pretty passersby; some looked alarmed and none responded. I tried French; the second young lady I spoke to, in a bright red coat, answered in an ironic but not hostile tone — in fluent English.

Ruth was charming, witty, and attractive. She told me all about Copenhagen and Denmark, about the tattooed king and the cigar-smoking women. We moved closer and closer together on this delightful summer night, but she wouldn't come to my room in an elderly lady's house, and being a domestic worker from the countryside, she could not take me to her room in her employers' house. The ground was damp that evening, and her pretty new red coat could not be sacrificed either. In a typically masculine way, I wondered about her "morals"; it had certainly been easy to make her acquaintance in Tivoli. What was she doing there at that hour? But I was wise enough and enamored enough to repress such nonsense. She was there for the same reason as I — loneliness.

I wasn't wise enough to remain in Copenhagen and went on to Sweden and Norway. Both countries had impressive bridges, wide vistas, and interesting buildings. But I did not find Copenhagen's quaint charm. Or Ruth. So it was back to Denmark.

Ruth was as nice and as full of fun as ever. Back at Tivoli, we were the only riders on a little roller coaster. The man in charge asked slyly if he should stop the car longer in the dark "Tunnel of Love." And he did.

After a sad, uncertain good-by I got aboard the cramped train back to Germany. Was I really in love or was it another short-lived infatuation? What was Ruth's past like, and did it matter? What about Anna? Could I remain in Denmark? If so, how would I support myself? I knew only that I could never abandon political activity, without which I felt empty and useless. And would the army permit me to decide all these issues in the five months I still owed it? I fell into a tormented sleep, passed Hamburg and Frankfurt, and finally reached Nuremberg and then Fürth. I had hardly been back thirty minutes when our mail corporal told me about the registered letter.

ARRIVAL

Instead of a bed, a wooden platform filled half my cell; the other half had a small table, a chair and, hanging from the ceiling, a light bulb. Standing on the platform I could see a patch of sky through the bars. The guard was my contact with the outside world. When I had to use the toilet I called out the word he taught me: "Ubornaya." His response was "Nachalnik pridyot," "The boss is coming," and I was escorted to the toilet. This was no pure joy; a pile of used newspaper scraps, evidently too much for the plumbing to manage, lay in the corner.

My contact with the guards gradually developed. I thought of every Russian word I knew, including a few words learned in Prague in 1947, some related to the similar Czech. Not enough for probing discussion, but better than nothing. I found the language barrier most porous in the spheres of politics and culture. After I assured the guards that I was an "Amerikansky Kommunist," they were willing to do some rudimentary talking about films and literature. I could say film names like "*Chapayev*" or "*Lenin in October*" so that the guards understood them. This also worked a bit with some authors and books. The simplest-looking Soviet soldier, seemingly primitive in some ways, knew of more books than any American GI I ever met—not only works by Soviet authors like Sholokov, Gorky, Ehrenburg, and Fadeyev (and many I had not heard of) but also Russian classics by Tolstoy, Lermontov, Gogol, and Pushkin, and even Dostoyevsky, who was not in favor during the Stalin years. And the guards knew foreign writers too, especially Hugo, Dumas, and Dickens, Twain, London, and Dreiser.

Our discussions, not exactly peaks of literary exploration, involved repeatedly naming an author or title, like "*Anna Karenina,*" until the other was hopelessly puzzled or suddenly comprehended and said, if it applied: "Da, chital" (Yes, I read it), nodding that it was "ochen khorosho" (very good). It was all strenuous and rather lacked depth, but it taught me a bit about the Soviets and built my vocabulary.

My only other occupation was eating. I have never been choosy, and enjoyed the frequent barley soup and especially the occasional fresh tomato or cucumber. But I literally couldn't stomach herring, which was often the main dish. I did without or got along with boiled potatoes.

After two days, an officer came to question me. Through an interpreter I told him why and how I had come. Some details seemed to puzzle him, and he asked several times what I had done between my swim and the time I had been picked up — suspecting perhaps that I had been in contact with someone in that time. The American enclave on their side of the Danube, it turned out, no longer existed. The Russians didn't seem to know about it. I did not have my map showing the enclave. That would have explained my extreme and ultimately unnecessary caution after the crossing.

Could anyone vouch for me? they asked. I could think only of a camerawoman I had met on a ship in 1947 on my way to the Youth Festival, a daughter of Sun Yat-sen's foreign minister Chen, now living in Moscow, and Rowe Gingrich, whose brother-in-law was a leading Austrian Communist. There were two or three such sessions. Their doubts about my veracity surprised me, and I was not sure that the people I mentioned would be of any use. In my tiny cell I had time to think about the strange direction my life had taken. I recalled the posters I had seen in Bologna, charging that the Soviet Union had labor camps for political prisoners. We had always scorned such charges. What if they were true? No, they couldn't be true. But with nothing to do but count hours and days, I could not convince myself completely and wondered whether I had made the blunder of my life.

At last I was given something to help pass the time and forget my worries. They found three books in English, essays by an unknown American "back to the farm" philosopher, Dreiser's classic *Sister Carrie,* and finally a heavily detailed history of Scotland from 1603 to 1707 by Sir Walter Scott. I read them all twice.

I had been in the cell nearly two weeks when three loud, jovial officers came in, told me in German to cheer up, said my friend in Vienna had just become a father, and asked me to put my foot down on a piece of paper so they could draw a line around it. I assumed they had spoken to Rowe and was glad that someone from my country knew of my whereabouts (he wrote years later that no one had spoken to him). The next day the officers returned with a pair of new black shoes which fitted amazingly well, with underwear, a suit, shirt, raincoat, and a tie — "bright red for your views," they said laughing. I would leave the next day, they promised, and were so friendly and encouraging that my worries faded.

I had waited two days when I was escorted to a strange vehicle. A small closed structure was mounted on the back of a car. Two men sat in the front of this primitive minivan and six in back, three men facing three men. All were armed soldiers or officers to protect or guard me. I was more than curious to know where we were going, but none spoke English or German and I could see little of what was outside the curtained windows.

We drove right through the four-power sector in the center of Vienna. This was nerve-wracking, but we soon left the city and headed in an unknown direction. With the help of my tiny but slightly improved vocabulary, we got acquainted. Our common ground was not books but songs; we were soon singing the Red Army songs I knew from the war years: "Meadowlands," "Kalinka," "Katyusha." The Soviets relished that; so did I.

We came to a railroad crossing late at night. The barrier was down, but no train came. Our officer finally woke the sleeping Austrian guard, who cranked up the gate. I grasped little of what was said, but surely heard mocking references to "western capitalism." I had asked to go to the Soviet Union or Czechoslovakia and tried to recreate a map of Eastern Europe in my mind's eye. Eastward might mean heading to Hungary, the Balkans, or the USSR. Northward could mean Czechoslovakia, Poland, the USSR, or East Germany. I feared the latter; I had read in *Stars and Stripes* about a camp for ex-GIs in an East German town. That was the last thing I wanted. We soon reached a border, and once we crossed over, the atmosphere in our vehicle relaxed. I was able to spot a road sign: it said Ceské Budejovice, a Czech city (Budweis), which eliminated some possibilities. In the morning we stopped near a brook where we stretched, washed, and dove into two suitcases filled with bread, meatballs, tomatoes, and cucumbers. But first vodka and beer at 5 A.M. on an empty stomach. I only pretended to drink.

Where were we headed? I would soon know the answer. We reached the outskirts of Prague, which I had visited five years earlier, but drove on without stopping. That left only Poland or East Germany. We soon reached the Elbe River; we were going to East Germany. As we approached the border I saw the signs confirming that my destination was indeed the "German Democratic Republic." When we reached it, my traveling companions directed me to get out and a young man came over and said in excellent English: "I understand you want more books to read." He gave me two and asked me to follow him. I waved good-by to the group from Austria and climbed into a car already occupied by an elderly, white-haired man and the driver. Off we went along the Elbe and into my first city in the GDR.

We drove only through the outskirts. A country-wide gathering of Young Pioneers was taking place; blue banners and slogans everywhere welcomed the young delegates and called for peace. I had never seen so many peace banners and slogans — for children. The language may have been a bit wooden, but I was moved to tears. If the car had driven closer to the center of that city, I would have seen another argument for peace, overwhelming in its infinite tragedy. I would see it before long — the immense, burnt-out rubble field which had once been the beautiful center of Dresden.

We drove north on the autobahn, toward Berlin, but turned off at Potsdam and stopped at a two-story house on a tree-lined street. I got a shock when I was told to change into pajamas, bathrobe, and slippers, giving up my new clothing, even my watch. I'd get it all back, I was assured, and would remain here "only briefly." My room was almost luxurious, with a carpet, lamps, a big desk, a couch, two beds, and a table and chair for meals. Two big windows had opaque milk glass. I was in great comfort, but complete isolation.

To go to the bathroom, wash, or shave, I again depended on a guard whom I buzzed to escort me to the bathroom door and back to my room. Meals were brought by the cook, and I received a daily pack of cigarettes or long tubular *papirossi*. Every day I had an hour for fresh air in the garden with flower beds, trees, and a fish pool. It was welcome, but strolling around or sitting on a bench for an hour became boring. A wooden fence discouraged further exploration. So did an armed soldier guarding the walk leading to the street. Some violated orders and chatted, One guard suggested jokingly that I try angling for goldfish.

The breath of one guard smelled of vodka, and his eyes and motions were not fully controlled. And this was a Soviet soldier! I was dependent on him; what if a fire broke out, with me on the second floor? Should I complain about this guy? I decided I was no tattletale. His job must be boring; maybe vodka helped him endure it.

I became aware that I was not alone in this mysterious house. Others passed on their way to the bathroom; one man spoke in broken Russian to the guard downstairs. From the garden I saw a man in a blue shirt sitting behind a downstairs milk glass window. One day I found a short hair in the sink, that of an African. Another day I heard someone whistling "Yankee Doodle." Whoever it was seemed to be asking, "Is there another American here?"

Should I whistle back? Here was a fellow American, confined like me. But I was not imprisoned against my will, I had come voluntarily and for some reason was being detained. We were isolated from one another for some reason, too. What kind of people could be sharing this house with me, what kind of American could that be? The chance that someone else had had the same problem and found the same solution seemed unbelievable. Was he some kind of involuntary prisoner? I'd never heard of one. Or was it a trick to test me and my response? I doubted that but decided the best thing was to keep my mouth shut.

As the weeks passed I found solace in books—devouring Soviet-published classics in English: *Jane Eyre, Vanity Fair,* and *Pickwick Papers.* I read Lermontov's *A Hero of Our Time,* Turgenev's *A Nest of the Nobility,* and other books I had heard about from my guards in Austria, current novels like Azhayev's *Far from Moscow,* which would later stir great controversy. After reading everything they had from the USSR, I was given books published by Tauchnitz, the old German publisher of English paperbacks, some very good, some trashy, and one clearly racist, which I self-righteously mentioned at my next interview. I was asked to write a short review, but felt a bit silly, since both book and author were surely long forgotten.

As September passed into October, the weekly interviews kept me going, giving me the chance to say more than "Ubornaya" or goodnight and good morning. The first encounters were with the young man at the border, and then I had meetings with an older man who spoke English with an American accent and must have spent years in America, I thought. He asked me about my background and kept assuring me that I would soon get out of this strange house and into everyday life. It was difficult to find me a room and a job, he plausibly explained. But I grew increasingly impatient, especially when he didn't make promised meetings. At one point, he suggested that I write about my life, and asked why I thought the army had decided to examine my past. He once asked a strange question and gave me a week to think it over: Would I consider going to Western Europe? Was he checking whether I would jump at a chance to get back? Could he be probing my willingness to work as an underground agent?

That seemed preposterous since I was being sought by the army. I'd be quickly discovered, I told him, and then they would really lock me up and throw the key away. I added that there was nothing I feared more than going back to the West. He never raised the matter again.

To further my "political education" he gave me the *Brief History of the Communist Party of the Soviet Union,* which I had read at Harvard. When we met a few weeks later we discussed it; one of his questions was about the author. It was written by a group of historians, I said, while the fourth chapter on dialectical materialism was said to have been written by Stalin. He smiled knowingly. Stalin really wrote the entire book, he assured me.

I had always viewed the Soviet Union as the center of progress and hope and rejoiced at its successes, especially its fight against fascism and its advances in raising living standards. But I had gnawing doubts about the adulation of Stalin. We had reasoned that this was needed in a backward country pulling itself up by its bootstraps and forced to defend itself against massive attacks. But weren't we rationalizing? Given the circumstances, I decided this was not the best time or place to discuss such doubts with Charles, as my interviewer called himself.

Not that he was a forbidding person. He loved to joke, to learn off-color American slang, to tell funny riddles and do tricks with matchsticks. I got along with him and was disappointed when he left long gaps between visits which I filled by consuming more books. With no private radios, Soviet garrisons in those years turned loudspeakers high enough for soldiers in a mile-wide radius to hear. This could be unpleasant, but I got to like some of the music, especially one fiery, rhythmic song sung, I imagined in my growing loneliness, by a woman from the Caucasus. More music was provided by Russian soldiers singing marching songs instead of cadences, with a lead singer calling out a line which the troops answered. One such answer sounded exactly like *leberwurst.*

October dragged on, the leaves changed color, but the food remained the same — tomatoes, cucumbers, macaroni, goulash, meatballs. The repetition was getting on my nerves. I kept reading everything in English, even USSR magazines euphoric about Stalin's seventieth birthday and the lavish cascade of gifts showered upon him. Running out of English material, I started reading in German, but having no dictionary I worked through the reading carefully, writing down each new word, guessing its meaning, and when finding it again, comparing it with my first guess.

Finally, my first outing—down the block to the barber. Surprised that he was Russian, I realized that the whole street, perhaps the whole neighborhood, was a Soviet area. Next was a trip to a department store, also a Soviet facility with German sales personnel. My two English-speaking companions footed the bill for suit, shoes, underwear, the works—adding cryptic advice not to mention these purchases when GDR authorities would later give me new clothing. The younger man asked my advice on a gift for his wife. I nodded tactfully when he chose a big porcelain stag.

For the next outing Charles asked me to choose: Cecilienhof or Sanssouci. The latter had played some role in older history and might be interesting. Cecilienhof was the site of the Potsdam Conference in July 1945, with Churchill (later Attlee), Truman, and Stalin. Important as the conference had been, I was drawn to Sanssouci but left the decision to my guides, who opted for Cecilienhof. In the end the driver found neither, but I saw the appalling ruins of Potsdam, with the remains of a triumphal arch standing sadly amidst rubble and emptiness. Despite missing our goal, my companions were in good spirits. Passing a Soviet statue of a man and woman holding a hammer and sickle aloft, they joked in Russian understandable to all about the lady, who had been granted a more ample bosom than the famous original. I always imagined that Soviets, especially official ones, were very "moral," or prudish. My mental image of them was changing: less moral but more human.

After nearly two months, Charles told me I could soon leave. We spoke of my request to change my name to protect my relatives in those difficult times. He agreed readily, and told me to think of one I liked. When I failed twice to come up with a pseudonym he suggested one; I liked neither Victor nor Grossman but could find no reason to reject them.

A tailor measured me for a new set of clothes. My last day in Potsdam was a Wednesday, the morning after election day in the United States, and I asked if I could listen to the returns on the radio. "Of course," they answered and brought me a set, saying I could have had it earlier if I had only asked. I kicked myself, but that chapter was over. I listened to the big victory reports of Dwight Eisenhower and Richard Nixon over Stevenson and wondered what it be like, after twenty years, to have a Republican in the White House. Not so good, but the last Democrat had been no prize either.

With the remains of my uniform and a suitcase of new clothes, I met three young men who were leaving with me; a merry Welsh trio who had spent several weeks together in a room of the house, playing cards and pulling pranks which made me wonder about their convictions. I caught myself in time when they asked my name. We headed south, and in the early evening arrived in a town called Bautzen. We were furnished clean beds in a dormitory-style hostel at the rail station, given 20 marks each and asked to stay put until morning, when we would be picked up.

The Welshmen wanted to go out "on the town" and drink something stronger than the beer given us in Potsdam. I was dubious; we had been asked to stay where we were. But, not wanting to be a wet blanket and being the only one who spoke German, I went along. It didn't take them long to find the Fuchsbau (Fox Lair), one of the lowest dives in town, and we started spending the 20 marks.

It wasn't only drinks they craved after weeks of enforced chastity. There was one other customer and I was pressed into service as an interpreter. The young woman, about twenty, was rather stout and ugly, but of some interest to me nonetheless; she wore a uniform with a patch saying "Dienst für Deutschland" (Service for Germany) and was returning from a swamp-clearing youth project in the north. I recalled the youth brigades in Czechoslovakia and Yugoslavia during the World Youth Festival, expecting to find the same élan, but found only an interest in these foreign young men. But if I was disappointed, one Welshman, Stump, was not. I suddenly realized he was gone and so was she.

His two friends, slightly inebriated, were certain he would show up, and we returned to our beds. This seemed one hell of a way to start off life under socialism. In the morning a man from the County Council came to pick us up; with him was a contrite, sad-looking Stump. He had taken his new lady-friend to her village, lost his way back, was picked up in a drunken condition and locked up to sleep it off. This brought us all a stern lecture from the councilman, who explained the situation and then gave us each another 20 marks. There was no internment camp here of the kind I had feared; we were free to move around, though only within Bautzen county. He would try to get us jobs as soon as possible; until then we would get pocket money. For a time we would stay in a hotel, with two rooms for the four of us. Room and board were free; we must pay for drinks and cigarettes. Thus, I began life here with a slight foretaste of the promised Utopia of Communism, where money was given "to each according to his needs."

Life had certainly not reached that stage here yet, but I saw no signs of hunger or extreme need in this town of forty thousand. Things were clearly tight; there was rationing of many foods and some textiles, and not too much in the shops. But life seemed normal enough. Walking through the narrow streets I thought of home. I would miss family, friends, and comrades, and would remain worried about Anna. I would miss the dogwood, tulip trees, and Black-eyed Susans, even the narrow path, menaced by poison ivy, that led to our little house at Free Acres, the only real home I ever had, with the song of the katydids and the flash of the scarlet tanager speeding toward the apple tree. Would I ever see them again?

Life in East Germany

We stand for the maintenance of private property. . . .

We shall protect free enterprise as the most expedient,

or rather the sole possible economic order.

Adolf Hitler

We should have had socialism already,

but for the socialists.

George Bernard Shaw

[5]

STARTING IN A NEW LAND

Why the hell was everyone staring at me? The morning had been rough; I had been softened by little heavy work in the U.S. Army, and none with the Soviets. On my second day in this "publicly owned" factory, in the icy December of 1952, I loaded heavy planks onto a handtruck, pushed them into a work hall, unloaded them, and went out into the bitter cold for more. Now I dug hungrily into my meal.

I had not been too useful. I didn't know oak from ash or beech, could not balance planks on my right shoulder while my "brigadier" (team leader) carried the other end on his left one, and barely understood his Hungarian-style German. But I had done my best and now I had lined up for a plate of potatoes and soft white cheese or "Quark." I was not choosy, just hungry. So why were they staring and whispering remarks about the "American"?

My brigadier finally pushed his way through. "How can you eat potatoes without removing the skin?" he asked reproachfully. "No one ever heard of such a thing." So that was it! At home we ate parboiled potatoes in the skin. But now I smiled uncertainly and began peeling. The crowd dispersed.

My adventure was worth a chuckle despite my weary trudge back to Bautzen after work. But questions gnawed at me: God, what am I doing in this place? How did I, an American, a New York Jew at that, wind up lugging heavy planks in a run-down town in remotest East Germany, less than eight years after the war? I had never been anti-German, and this was all my own doing. But how long would I haul planks, with blistered hands and aching shoulders, in a baggy worksuit and baggier underwear supplied by the "German Democratic Republic"? What had I done?

I surveyed dreary sheds in bare, wintry gardens, like Hooverville shacks in Newark's evil-smelling outskirts that I had seen in childhood. The drab buildings did little to cheer me. But as I approached Bautzen's "Old Town" my eyes were drawn to its towers and their gentle mountain background. Despite soot or naked brickwork, I admired the baroque city hall, the cathedral, the dignified old market square, the quaint alleys, the landmarks, centuries older than any at home. Some ancient houses were truly beautiful, but many tiny streets were dirty and neglected. Yet their age and narrowness gave them a mysterious quality. What was around that little curve? And, I reflected, what would the next hour, day, or year bring? Such human questions were urgently relevant to me now.

I emerged from the alleyways and crossed a run-down square, once Piglet Market, now "Platz der Roten Armee"—Square of the Red Army. A drunken figure lurched out of a dissolute saloon. My goal, the Hotel zur Krone, now renamed less royally Hotel Stadt Bautzen, was on a street marked by three street signs: one in faded German, one in Cyrillic letters for Soviet soldiers, and a somewhat newer version in Sorbish. Bautzen and much of Lusatia were officially bilingual; the Slavic Sorb minority which ruled here a millennium ago gained equal status in 1945—verified on all signs.

The once luxurious if faded hotel was home for two months, its rooms and meals free for Western ex-soldiers. For me and the three Welshmen it was a great improvement over being locked up. There was little risk of misusing our right to free meals; the few entrées offered were not expensive. I usually went to bed early, exhausted from work, the early starting hour, and the long walk. The three Welshmen, still without jobs, were on the town again. All the better. I didn't dislike them, but we came from different worlds. Unless they faced me and spoke slowly, I barely understood them. Some words were new: a "bint" was a woman, "to flog" was to sell something "unofficially." We had each received a full complement of clothes, including a warm jacket, even a briefcase. The quality was the best this broken little land could do. But the Welshmen's main interest was alcoholic, the irregular 20 mark handouts soon vanished, and so did the clothes; I heard the word "flog" far more often than "bint." They even flogged some of my clothes.

Before joining the British Army, Stump was a ship's stoker. He was black-haired, roughly good-looking, very strong, liked to laugh but thought slowly, and could drink himself into a growling delirium. When sober he was easy to get along with. Dai (Welsh for David), small, wiry, passionate, spoke and moved drastically, and was suspicious of Germans and most other nationalities. He was deeply proud of Wales, especially his coal-mining Rhondda Valley. The fierce class consciousness of this miner's son did not extend far beyond Rhondda. He drank less than Stump but it was best not to anger him. Jonesy, a handsome and well-groomed blond, was the most intelligent and could hold his liquor, but could push the others into situations he was wily enough to avoid. We two shared a room.

It violated etiquette to ask why they were here. Maybe they had over-stayed their leave while drinking and been picked up by Soviet patrols on the Berlin subway, which still crossed freely between east and west. Perhaps fearing punishment and being single and carefree, they had agreed to move eastward. With my job I saw less of them. While reflecting on this luck I heard loud noises. In the door came hopelessly drunken Stump. "Had an-other hard day at the factory, Victor?" he asked with friendly irony, tossing a pillow playfully at the chandelier, smashing one of the three glass lamp shades. As I dodged the splinters, he aimed a heavy ashtray at the big glass mirror over the sink, a remnant of the hotel's glorious past. I was too flab-bergasted to do anything and more than a little fearful of this powerful mad-man. Just then Jonesy entered. It was impossible to check Stump by force, so Jonesy called out in an authoritative voice: "Remember, Stump! Seven years bad luck if you smash it." "Oh, yes, I almost forgot!" he mumbled, dropping the ashtray, and was led off peacefully to his room.

The Welshmen discovered other foreigners in Bautzen's dives, and one Sunday they took me to visit an American. Freddy's building was only a little less ancient than 1,000-year-old Bautzen. After four rickety flights of stairs I found a small man in a small room who offered to fry us eggs in the smallest frying pan I'd ever seen. Allegedly, this friendly fellow had hit his officer over the head before hurrying eastward. Guesses as to the severity of the blow and what inspired it varied, but we maintained etiquette and asked no questions. We listened to his descriptions of Bautzen and the other for-eigners, especially the crazier ones, evidently the majority. Freddy used "fucking" before every noun: the pan, his shoe, an egg, the army. In his un-tidy little room were an easel and oil paintings with a wide range of themes. I had never heard of a U.S. soldier with such a hobby. (Maybe the influence of socialism, I thought.) Freddie had another pastime which endeared him to the Welshmen; he drank far more than his wiry little body could handle.

Other British and U.S. ex-soldiers I soon met had the same problem. Some were old warhorse types who had stumbled into often alcohol-linked difficulties which made even an East German solution seem preferable to what faced them. Single men, especially if their only German was "Ein Bier und ein Schnapps," usually landed in new misfortune here, financial or otherwise. Those with mates were occasionally kept under partial control, like O'Neill, a puny fellow with a large, stout woman and four kids, one or two of whom might have been his. She was always hunting him in the dives, he was always in flight, casting doubt on the inner value of the partnership. Such relationships, though, seemed preferable than total devotion to the bottle or teaming with a rapidly changing series of women with that same interest.

Two Englishmen loved drinking and had good wives as well. Jim, a clever, witty man, fell for the daughter of a West German professor while a postwar occupation officer. "Fraternization" was forbidden when they married, so they fled to an East German village where she worked as a teacher. They were finally "discovered" and brought to Bautzen, where she raised five children and he did his best — except when lured to the nearest pub by Johnny, quick-witted in a Cockney way, who seemed always to land on his feet even when drinking hard and often. There was no TV then or much else to occupy the men in their free time. Their favorite turf was the railway station bar, open all night, where they found kindred spirits.

Freddy introduced us to Charlie, the first African American in Bautzen and its star athlete. Powerfully built, of middle height, he was a boxer, a true sportsman who didn't smoke or drink, which accounted for his comfortable home. He was a brigadier in the town's main bakery. He sought to master German, but if he didn't know a word he used an English one and often mixed English and German. But what he said was sensible and witty. Charlie loved children, who flocked around him like the Pied Piper. As an established, popular figure he had no enemies, except perhaps a few racist British or Americans. But after a look at his fists and biceps they joined in friendly smiles. A newly arrived young Englishman once insulted this normally good-natured fellow. He apologized after three minutes; after three days he was again fit.

Charlie had problems that could not be diminished by strength and character. Freddy said that Charlie "came east" because the U.S. Army disapprovingly called his woman-friend a prostitute. In those days relationships between black soldiers and German women met with deep hostility from white Americans in uniform. Charlie refused to drop her. The army wanted to transfer him to Korea, and the two landed in Bautzen — with Charlie probably unwilling to put his life on the line for a racist system. But his blonde left him and moved back west. At a local boxing tournament we joined a Bautzen audience wildly cheering Charlie to victory. It was one of his last triumphs; he was growing too old for the ring.

A Californian arrived a few weeks after I did. It was he who had spoken broken Russian with the guards below my milk glass window in the house in Potsdam. Unlike most of us, George had been a civilian when he came across. Unfortunately, he was mistaken for a CIA spy; it seems that, unknown to him, his compartment companion on the train through Europe was indeed a "company man." In the midst of boiling tension in 1952, it took quite some time before this nasty mistake was cleared up. But he wasn't dismayed, and this short, chunky American, with long sideburns, sunny disposition, and similar views to mine immediately became my close friend. We arranged to share a room in the hotel; like me, he was no heavy drinker. There were no broken chandeliers, but much talk of our troubled homeland and much wildly unrealistic hope of radical changes in a few years.

George and I were sipping beer and talking politics in the hotel restaurant when a middle-aged woman and her daughter came in. The daughter was dark-haired, beautiful, well-dressed, faintly mysterious. Like an apparition from another planet, she didn't fit this little town at all. Our discussion switched to a more urgent matter: going over and getting acquainted. My German was better, but George had more nerve and was soon chatting away at their table while I sipped my increasingly bitter beer. He soon had a date with Hella — once a dancer in the local operetta ensemble, she had injured her knee and was now a secretary. Before long, they were a couple. I got over it; after all, he was my best friend.

But my eternal quest went on. I went out with a gentle, intelligent young woman with a major "flaw": she was hostile to the GDR and was a secretary at the Liberal-Democratic Party, whose role in the "National Front" I could not fathom at the time. I argued resolutely but futilely, and our relationship fluttered and faded; I was too much a political animal. My next hope was the barlady's daughter. She was seventeen to my twenty-four, but very pretty, as was "revealed" when she dressed for a costume party as a poppy blossom without many petals. But there were problems again. I ordered a 50-pfennig liqueur, the only drink I could afford, and expected her to choose with similar modesty. But she demanded expensive wine and scolded that I was dubbed a "Casanova" in these parts because I went out with other girls. I countered that I went out with different partners until I found the right one. "We don't do things that way here," she pouted. I soon lost interest and continued my search.

———————

I had been in Bautzen a few weeks without work, was tired of idleness, and increasingly eager for a chance to "build socialism." So I descended on our man at the County Council; my priority was not money, but a job. The next day he took me to the VEB (publicly owned) Railroad Car Company, where I was taken in tow by a union official who led me around the stations establishing me as a worker in a socialist plant. When I addressed him as "Sie," the formal "you," he corrected me: "No, no, here we are all equals. Everyone is just plain *du*!" When to use *du* or *Sie* often seemed an insurmountable problem, so I almost sobbed out my gratitude. But when I happily said "du" to an accountant and to a clerk in the factory store, I received icy stares. My joy waned.

The arena where I was to battle with world capitalism turned out to be the lumberyard, where I loaded heavy planks onto a handtruck and pushed them to where they were cut up for railroad cars for the Berlin elevated system. My brigadier had a friendly way with people and many recollections of the Hungarian homeland he was forced to leave at war's end. A disciplined worker and boss without being a slave-driver, he avoided political discussions: "Let's get the work done first." There was also an older man, skilled and cynical about life in this new republic, but not inclined to argue with an enthusiast from abroad. Rounding out the team was a young man of twenty, always in good spirits, but with squeaky voice and simple mind.

The old brick factory buildings recalled those in Buffalo a few years earlier. We still worked a forty-eight-hour week, till 1 P.M. Saturday (later cut to forty-three and a half hours and five days). In Buffalo it was forty hours but there was pressure to work eight hours on Saturday at time-and-a-half. Here we were paid twice a month, but in cash, with no lunchtime line at the bank or need to take a loss by cashing checks at a bar.

Workers brought sandwiches in briefcases; I kidded them that they looked like American lawyers. But no one knew when the factory store might sell lemons, raisins, or other rarities, and the battered old briefcases held anything short of a watermelon. Another departure from Buffalo was handshaking. I had to shake hands every day with every workmate. One could only imagine what American workers would have thought had I tried that.

I joined the Free German Trade Union Federation and, like most workers, was recruited into the German-Soviet Friendship Society, where I paid small dues without a murmur, unlike some workmates. Under moderate pressure I bought lottery shares to build up Stalin Allee in Berlin. Now a regular member of the workforce, arriving promptly before 7 and leaving at 3.45, a tired "builder of socialism," I netted 340 marks a month, which seemed a lot.

My fellow workers were males except for a sturdy woman in her mid-forties who heated the oven, cooked "house coffee," and cleaned up, happily singing "Oh, the men are all criminals." Everyone used the polite *Sie* with her — yet another exception. Our foreman, dignified but friendly, had deep socialist convictions and relied on our self-discipline. But he was often ill and his deputy was a ratty guy with a rasping voice, whose political "clarifications" were frequent, overbearing, and far less convincing than the occasional comments of the low-key foreman. During a coffee break we were called on to take a position on something or other. One old "re-settler" from Silesia (the word "refugee," used in West Germany, was taboo in the GDR) burst out querulously and naively: "Does that still leave a chance open for regaining the lost areas of Germany?" Silesia had been lost to Poland for good reason and for good. I grasped the old man's bewilderment; he probably never understood what went on beyond his cottage door, noticing only that life was better after Poland was conquered than before. That "improvement" cost six million Polish lives, and the deputy foreman tore into the old man: "You know damned well the Oder-Neisse frontier is our new border and will stay that way. Whining about old borders is Adenauer propaganda straight from RIAS radio!" (RIAS was the acronym for "Radio In the American Sector," the CIA station broadcast into the GDR.) I agreed, but wished the deputy foreman had been cooler and wiser, perhaps opening the old man's mind a bit instead of cowing and antagonizing him.

There was a lot to learn about the varied citizens here. One day when we were alone, Max, a garrulous woodworker, produced a pack of cheap GDR "Salem" cigarettes, urging me to read the letters backwards. He said in an oily voice: "M for Marx, he died long ago, E for Engels, so did he, L for Lenin, he died thirty years ago, and then"—he looked at me searchingly—"then A for Adolf, he died eight years ago". Before I could voice disgust with this grouping, Max reached the punch line: "And S's turn is soon." This man, always a master at grumbling, could not know how soon his "joke" would come true.

A factory-wide announcement made a different impression: "Workers wishing to enter the law field, with the possible goal of judge, should apply for preparatory courses by Tuesday." This didn't pertain to me, a foreigner, but I tried to imagine such an announcement in a Buffalo factory. I was constantly comparing. As in Buffalo, some people worked more, some less; those on piecework ("achievement pay" here) always worked hardest. Weekly hours were longer here but so were vacations, which were granted sooner and not lost when changing jobs. Medical insurance was subtracted from wages, but coverage was total. The buildings were drab, and there was more exhortation, but I found less friction with supervisors (aside from our ratty deputy foreman). The factory had been seized six years before from war criminals who had worked slave laborers till they dropped, then thrown the starved bodies into furnaces. They had fled to West Germany. It was now a "People's-Owned Factory." In Buffalo I had been laid off after six months, with one week's wages. Here all jobs were safe and steady.

The presence of an American hardly went unnoticed, especially after an enthusiastic letter from me was printed in the factory newspaper, naive and in awful German. I joined the FDJ (Free German Youth) and was invited to meet its factory committee, whose members were fervent, but had disturbing methods and ideas: at the meeting I attended a girl of seventeen was raked over the coals for using lipstick, which in 1952 was "unbecoming to an FDJ member." FDJ leaders were evidently unaware of how such petty repressiveness echoed a tortured past, but they were expert at antagonizing young workers.

On the tenth anniversary of the Soviet victory at Stalingrad, work ended early so we could attend a big rally in Bautzen. Stalingrad, one of history's transforming events, meant for me the beginning of the end of fascism. It also meant the wounding, killing, and imprisonment of hundreds of thousands of Germans—some of the survivors now Bautzen residents. I was moved that antifascist Germany marked the event. There were no complaints or sarcastic remarks, but as we ambled toward town I saw many disappear down the garden paths we passed along the way. No more than half reached town; before the end of two long speeches, many more had slipped away. It was perhaps less a rejection of the occasion than a result of many boring rallies and meetings — and a chance to get home earlier.

Work now took up a large amount of my time. George was busy stoking coal in a local factory, and he had his Hella. Life was better than Potsdam and the army, but I was lonely. A few days after a dreary New Year's Eve, which, with Hella away, George and I limply welcomed, the Russians unexpectedly "came to town" again. This time they brought three Scotsmen, members of a "downtrodden nationality" like the Welshmen and therefore to be especially befriended. One evening, one of the downtrodden came in fairly drunk and began needling me. He had learned that I was a "red," supported the GDR, and, to top things off, was Jewish. The Welshmen had grown accustomed to my weird ways, especially my disinterest in heavy drinking. But the Scotsman was new, had a chip on his shoulder, and was increasingly belligerent. We reached the dueling point; I had to challenge an insult or label myself a hopeless coward. But this guy was scarily muscular. We marched to my room, I laid my jacket behind me; before I had completely turned around, the fight ended with three powerful blows. I was down, bleeding, with large cuts between eye and ear and on my chin. He fought dirty, but the outcome would have been much the same in any case. George found me, wiped the blood, put me to bed, and sought vengeance. The Scotsman's door remained stubbornly locked, and the next day he regretted the matter so convincingly that George started no new battle. When the Soviets heard of it (not from me) he disappeared for a few weeks and when he returned the matter was considered closed. But we never became friends.

Unlike Mark Twain's "Connecticut Yankee," I was unconscious for only a second or two and didn't wake up in the England of 400 A.D. I too was thousands of miles from home, but was I in the past or the future? The city was partly medieval; some things recalled the 1920s. There were few cars and not very many commodities. Yet the country was billed as an excursion into the future, not least of all by me. Some things did fit a future we on the left dreamed of: nationalized factories, full medical insurance, no unemployment, the first collective farms ("cooperatives" or "LPG"). Did it add up to more past or more future? I would have to wait and see. For the present, I had to get out of this hotel and find a room closer to the general population.

The Wentschers, with whom I was given a room, were clearly "politically reliable." The husband, who worked for the County Council, wife, and daughter were all friendly and hospitable. The little room was clean, central, yet on a quiet, tree-lined street. But it was not modern — lacking a sink, only a pitcher and basin for washing and shaving. I didn't want to be a spoiled American, but was unhappy that a half flight down was a gravity toilet with a pail of water to ensure cleanliness, but not quite eliminate odors or flies. The bed, with its unwieldy three-part mattress, had a soft goose-down comforter, warm for summer, too short for winter.

After agreeing on 25 marks rent, Frau Wentscher told me that she would leave rolls and chicory ersatz coffee ("muckefuck" in German and tasting that way) at my door every morning. But she had to leave very early for her cook's job, and I would have to fire the tiled "Dutch Oven" which in 1952 heated nearly all homes and provided a pleasant if diminishingly warm temperature. But to fire it up, one needed to erect an artful structure of paper, wood splints, and lignite briquettes — "brown coal," the GDR's main source of heat, power and light. That took an hour (if one evaded explosions), and I lacked both skill and patience. My solution was to do without the damned oven. I paid, though, by freezing bitterly. On some Sundays Frau Wentscher took pity and fired it for me — with a mildly scornful look. Power failures were another problem, occurring almost daily — usually while I was shaving or at an exciting spot in a novel. Like everyone, I got used to lighting candles in the dark.

The factory supplied warm lunches which I supplemented with bread and "Kunsthonig" (artificial honey). On Sundays, in line with working-class tradition, I ate Wiener Schnitzel, cabbage, and boiled potatoes with the family. Sometimes I ate in local restaurants, whose menus stated how many ration coupons were required for each low-priced dish. We foreigners got the highest category of rations, which I was entitled to anyway as a "heavy worker." In state shops (HO) commodities could be bought without coupons but at far higher prices. Textile and shoe rationing ended soon after my arrival.

Life, greatly improved since the first postwar years, was still Spartan, with many working hard to replace possessions lost during or just after the war. No one went hungry, but few people lived really well, and widows and pensioners especially had to count pennies. Supply and variety were limited; I walked all over town to find a washrag and handkerchiefs, and during a razor blade shortage I lined up not to buy blades, but to get old ones resharpened. Supermarkets or elegant shops were unknown.

I had never been spoiled and could adjust fairly easily. Since I sympathized with the GDR, I sought explanations for difficulties and did not complain, even to myself. The self-imposed heating problem and the sanitary facilities were worse than my room in Buffalo, but there my unskilled laborer's wage was very low and no one provided breakfast or lunch. I had feared my landlady's curiosity there, while the Wentschers were antifascists, with the same ideals as mine, so I had no apprehension and nothing to hide.

Wandering through ancient Bautzen was like a history lesson. The palace gate high above the Spree had a stone relief of King Matthew of Hungary and Bohemia who ruled here in the fifteenth century. The cathedral, built about 1300, was divided at the Reformation into Catholic and Protestant halves. Giant fortifications kept the Hussites out in 1429, but the Thirty Years War turned the Nikolai Church into a beautiful ruin. More recent were ruins wrought by retreating SS troops and a monument for Soviet soldiers killed by those same troops. Some street names were medieval, but the main street was now Karl Marx Strasse, and many others bore names of Communist or Sorb victims of the Nazis. Ernst Thälmann, the most prominent victim, was imprisoned in Bautzen's ugly penitentiary before he was murdered in 1944.

Sorb women from nearby villages wore multiple petticoats, printed dresses, and black bonnets with big bows and long black streamers called "butterflies." Older women wearing kerchiefs were often from Hungary, voluntarily or involuntarily sent "home to Germany." I had to get used to some customs, such as elderly men constantly tipping their hats in greeting, or everyone saying "Guten Tag" on entering a shop, and "Auf Wiedersehen" on leaving. Despite much talk of equal rights and many women in "men's jobs," men recoiled from baby carriages as if ashamed of fatherhood, if necessary pushing them absently with one hand.

At restaurants men ordered beer; women and children usually drank brightly colored carbonated "limonade." My pleas for water brought mineral water or seltzer; when I finally learned to demand "Leitungswasser" (tap water), I got a half glass of lukewarm liquid. Handshaking was an astonishing pastime: one shook with workmates on arrival and quitting time; children shook daily with schoolmates. Latecomers at meetings shook all around and disrupted business. But rapping on the table, instead of shaking hands, was permissible only in bars. People doing wet, greasy, or dirty work proffered a forearm or an elbow. Two couples meeting on the street shook hands in strict order: woman to woman, man to woman, woman to man, man to man. Crossing hands was taboo. Farewells meant repeating the whole procedure. In winter, peeling off gloves was mandatory, even when told, "Oh, don't bother."

Certain greetings exist to this day. After Christmas one wishes a "good slide" into the New Year. At a later encounter, even in February, one inquires if the other indeed had a "good slide."

The gender of nouns — masculine, feminine, or neuter — was an eternal mystery. Certain endings require certain genders (making "Mädchen" — girl — and "Fräulein" neuter). Trees are feminine, metals neuter. All alcoholic drinks but beer are masculine. Such rules slightly reduced the chaotic situation which haunted me when speaking or writing. When I knew no rule I closed my eyes and guessed, usually wrong. Aside from grammar and genders, I learned words which amused me, like *Handschuh* (glove), or bothered me, like *Brustwarze* (breast wart = nipple).

I soon bought a typewriter, which served me for twenty-five years. Every evening I pecked out the story about the union contract meetings in Buffalo, hoping to capture some of the tension and excitement, and maybe break out of the honorable but exhausting job of carrying lumber. But my dreams were numbed by the icy winter invading my room. I piled on sweaters, coat, blanket, and comforter. Since I could hardly type with mittens, my hands numbed and I retreated to bed. But I kept at it and finally mailed a forty-page story to British journalist John Peet, who quit as chief Reuters correspondent in West Berlin after distortions of his reports, and Stefan Heym, a German exile who sent his World War II U.S. Army medals back to Eisenhower and came to the GDR.

In March 1953 we heard startling news: Stalin was dead; the country went into mourning. My emotions were mixed: Stalin had been head of the homeland of socialism, the country closest to me after my own. But I worried about the idolatry and had doubts about personal dictatorship, purges, and alleged labor camps. I was unbelieving yet curious about predictions that the USSR would now collapse. With unease mixed with my sadness, I still sincerely supported the condolence note we foreign deserters sent to the local Soviet military community. My planned birthday party was impossible; I went alone to a restaurant, drank bitter beer, and returned to my room disgruntled and lonely.

George and I met weekly at the bathhouse, an important facility, since few homes had bathtubs and none showers. We used the occasion for conversation, although the heat and humidity may have affected my thinking. I said that after our Stalin memorial meeting Americans would consider us traitorous crazies. George responded that most Americans also voted for Eisenhower and Nixon. They couldn't be free of propaganda pressures. "Yes," I answered, "but it can make you feel a little bit lonely." George insisted that ours was the winning side in the long run — "the right side and the good side." That's like one of my father's jokes, I said: "When Jim's family watched him on parade, they said, 'Look, they're all out of step but Jim.'" George advised me that when in the dumps, I should think of the Rosenbergs in Sing-Sing or the CP leaders in jail, and grasp that such persecution was a sign of weakness, not strength. I hoped he was right. "Sure I'm right," was his rejoinder. The real America will assert itself soon enough. People will see through phonies like Ike and Nixon. With that I was invited to face the steam, and admonished that sitting in my cold little room pounding on those keys — or more — was getting me down impermissibly. It was time to meet a friend of Hella's, and dance.

So on Saturday at George's flat I again encountered a young woman who had earlier been introduced to me by Hella. For this shy, pleasant village girl, finding herself with two odd-speaking men from legendary America was a new experience. But she became almost cheeky when more comfortable. George turned on a slow foxtrot. "What are you doing now?" she asked when I tried simple variations, like dancing side-by-side. This impressed her, for it was not done in Bautzen and seemed very modern. When I tried a "dip," she again asked for an explanation for this move, completely unknown; it seemed almost dangerously daring. After a few tries she got it. We danced, chatted, and sipped some poisonous liqueur. While I would meet other women, Renate seemed a pretty, pleasant, uncomplicated person.

In the meantime, big changes were going on. At my factory there were constant appeals to increase and improve production. Since my feet always hurt, I sought to sit down in ways that did not suggest laziness, and my thoughts also turned to improvements. Couldn't we eliminate the heaviest work? Might handcranes and handcars between the lumber piles lighten our job? A campaign also began to change norms, the quotas on which wages were based. Posters praised brigades which altered "soft" norms to "produce more for our socialist republic." I didn't really grasp it. I hadn't paid much attention to the campaign, which had not reached our department. My brigadier brushed my questions aside, looking rather uncertain.

Other things changed too. Cheaper railway tickets for workers, students, and the handicapped had been canceled if income were above a certain level; so were reduced weekend and outing fares; tough measures on unpaid taxes or unfulfilled crop quotas brought confiscation of private farms and small enterprises. Ration cards, based on job status and always a subject of rancor, were heatedly discussed when some categories were downgraded. There were even hitherto unknown price increases involving pastry, sweets, and even my staples, jams and Kunsthonig. What in the world was happening? I read about poor crops and other explanations and watched dissatisfaction grow.

"Is this the socialism they've been raving about?" Max, the Salem joke man, asked maliciously. "Things are getting worse, not better." I was an innocent and ignorant foreigner, but voiced my faith that things would get better. Max responded sarcastically that Father Christmas was coming too, but Easter would come first, and he had to buy eggs for his kids.

I had no answers. The Kunsthonig price increase was not large, nor were my purchases on a large scale. I was still restricted to Bautzen county and did not use the train. Largely unaffected, but puzzled and unhappy, I went about my business; personal matters were still more important. One day I ran into Hella, who wondered if I was interested in her workmate Renate. If so, she cautioned, I would be wise to do something about it, for she was dating a young engineer. I suspected that the two women plotted this advice. Renate later vigorously denied it. But if meant to stir jealousy and action, it succeeded. Renate seemed definitely more attractive and I soon took the bait.

At about this time two Soviet officials visited me. They offered embarrassing praise for not missing work and awarded the handy bonus accompanying such praise. They then spoke of a clubhouse for us foreign ex-soldiers, a better place to gather than bars or the railway station. Cultural activities would also be possible. It seemed a good idea, although I had kept out of the way of all but George, Charlie, and one or two others. Now I was asked: Would I leave my job and become the club's cultural director?

I had no experience in such work and had doubts about getting along with the men and their women: But "When do I begin?" I said. They hoped that everything would be ready by May Day.

On May Day Bautzen was covered with snow. But the sun melted it in time for the parade and celebrations. I watched Renate and her dance group in the main square; women had to dance men's parts and she wore carpenter's bell-bottom trousers, vest, and slouch hat. Then we spent the day together, marking the real start of our friendship. And for me the start of a new job.

[6]

THE CLUBHOUSE & THE LATHE

Though still convinced that those involved in productive labor made history, I was glad to get the new job. No more getting up before dawn to lug lumber with aching feet. The clubhouse was an early twentieth-century *art nouveau* mansion with wrought-iron fence, grottos, and two imposingly decorated floors. The large staff encompassed the janitor, an ardent leftist who spiced his often-stated convictions with jokes and comical Polish curses from his native Silesia (but later hanged himself when it was found he was spying for Western agencies), the zither-playing old doorkeeper who tried to look busy, a secretary, a bookkeeper, and Heinz Schattel, our director who was responsible to the Soviet administration for all that involved us Westerners. Energetic and pleasant even under stress and with strong belief in the young republic, he knew neither French nor English and never quite fathomed the mentalities of the weird jumble of "old soldiers," who drove him to wit's end with demands, transgressions, and departures. I shared an office with a friendly English Communist, Douglas Sharp, who had refused to fight in Korea. In all, a staff of ten served thirty-five men and their families.

The Americans included a Deep South check forger, a Pennsylvania thief, alcoholics from all over, Charlie the boxer, and an innocent Indiana farm boy who insisted on marrying a motherly woman almost twice his age, despite officers' warnings that she came from an East German family of reds. The British claimed as many backgrounds and motivations, but more dialects — from Scottish burr and Irish brogue to London Cockney. I once introduced the Welshman Dai to a newly arrived Alabaman, who responded to the Welshman's greeting with: "Don't talk no Dutch to me. Ah don't know this lingo."

As for the French, one hinted that his parents were top Communists;

why he was in the GDR was a mystery. Another, it was whispered, had been in a Nazi SS division; this too remained a mystery. Lively but dense Henri, it was rumored, had been in the Foreign Legion, but when ordered to kneel all night on hard sticks, he had killed or injured his torturer and escaped. When once asked to repay a debt, Henri noted he had been returned to Bautzen by the Russians who caught him after he fled to Czechoslovakia, declaring him a new man who must start life from scratch. With that injunction in mind, Henri declared that old debts didn't count. Jean, with metal front teeth, threw occasional tantrums, but had leftist views, making him one of the rarities — like Douglas, George, and me. The five Moroccans spoke Arabic, French, and some German, though all were illiterate — a legacy of French colonial policy. They had fled to escape military duty in Vietnam, like scores of Americans years later. The one Algerian had jumped off a French military train and tramped with his German girlfriend night after night to the GDR border, surviving on raw potatoes. Though she may have been a prostitute, like many soldiers' women, he shielded her with inordinate jealousy. Both were intelligent, but denied education. The Algerian even doubted that the world was round. It was whispered that Chaik, an aloof elderly Moroccan, had used a knife in some fight. He lived in a village and seldom visited Bautzen. I found him friendly when convinced he was being treated fairly. Once I arranged an excursion to mountainous "Saxon Switzerland" near Dresden. Everyone signed up. Only Chaik refused; the word "Switzerland" made him suspicious: it bordered France and he would take no chances.

I had to find ways to amuse this odd bunch. One regular duty was to simultaneously translate a weekly GDR film. Some were quite good, but I rarely grasped them adequately; even when I caught the dialogue I knew little about German history and culture. Despite the fact that my skills had lain fallow, I sometimes had to translate into French as well. Less taxing was my organizing of Ping-pong, chess, and billiard competitions, treasure hunts, and improvised auctions. When I launched a Bingo game, Heinz Schattel was puzzled. Wasn't that capitalistic gambling? With support from George and Douglas, I convinced him that it was harmless; our political purity would not be violated. Bingo soon rivaled the films in popularity.

Heinz also had problems with art. Two young gay Dutchmen, both good artists, got apprenticeships with a GDR advertising company and made a striking poster for a dance we were planning. Wasn't it "formalistic?" Heinz asked. It's just a nice sign with lots of motion, I responded innocently, as if I hadn't heard of the Soviet campaign against "formalism." But people don't look like that, Heinz complained. He never knew when some higher-up would raise "principled objections." I think we won, but before long the Dutch artists decided to go home and confront problems there. Formalism was hardly one of them.

The Soviet Army, not art theory, caused another problem. Every month a truck brought each of us a big ration: beef, margarine, macaroni, herring, tins of good cod liver and other fish, even matches and the coarse, pungent makhorka which Soviet soldiers rolled into cigarettes, always with paper from *Pravda*. The ration was especially welcome to family men. Our new clubhouse was given the task of dividing up the food. Douglas was skilled at cutting beef but soon there were complaints that some portions were better than others, or that we gave single men as much as families. So we switched to the Communist principle: "To each according to his needs." But we had neglected moral principles. Legal wives said unwed families should not get more rations and whispered words like "sluts." Douglas decided to ignore moralistic issues, but one man — he claimed to be an IRA member — strained good will by showing up each month with a new woman, who evidently stayed only until the rations were devoured. In late 1953 the rations ceased, either because GDR supplies improved or because our wrangling had killed the golden goose.

We held dances with an elderly three-man band where I joyfully whirled Renate to a polka or waltz. I had to keep eyes and ears open; conflicts arose between nationalities or over women who flirted with the wrong men. But no one tried to steal warm and popular Renate. It had become clear that she was not to be had. We had become a real pair. On my free nights we went to the movies, which Bautzeners analyzed endlessly, whether shallow "oldies," the Swedish *She Only Danced One Summer,* with its then sensational seconds of nebulous semi-nudity, or the powerful, naturalistic Italian *Bicycle Thief.*

Near our club a dormitory for Greek engineering students was opened with a plaque of the murdered Greek partisan hero Beloyannis adorning its entrance. The twenty young men and women were refugees from the civil war, which was lost, they claimed, when weapons and aid were given the Greek government under the Truman Doctrine and when Tito perfidiously sealed off supply and escape routes. Splintered refugee families were scattered across Eastern Europe. Some young Greeks, many still clad in U.S. uniform parts taken from government troops, trained in the GDR in trades and professions ranging from engineering to printing and songwriting. We invited the Greeks to our club, and I went to their parties, recalling Greek dances learned in Boston in my distant past and the Radcliffe beauty I had once loved.

We met Thomas, who had taught fellow Greeks in the GDR but was now a mechanic at a regional Machine and Tractor Station. One warm Saturday George suggested that we hike to Thomas's MTS, sleep in the open, and later visit Renate's village. On a beautiful evening, after hours of walking we settled into what was possibly a potato patch, listening to crickets and peering up at millions of stars. It struck me that the Milky Way and the Dippers up there were the same as at home; I wondered if we'd ever look up at them again from New Jersey or California. Ever confident, George was certain that we would. It might take a long time, but people inevitably find the right road in the end. I hoped so, but why did people here in East Germany flee to the West? George asked me to think about what these people believed in until eight years ago and observed that human beings can't always change quickly. Why not? I responded. They changed quickly enough to back Hitler. George maintained that when the Nazi idol cracked, the people became cynics, refusing to believe anything. Or nearly anything; whatever beliefs they embraced were shaped by the conservative Catholicism that dominated this Sorb region. Since we were restricted to that area, we couldn't compare it with the others. Was this really the worst section? But George no longer answered and I was soon off to a well-aired night's sleep.

In the morning we found the MTS, filled with ancient equipment and a few highly praised new Stalinetz tractors. We chatted with Thomas about the world and its woes, then walked along the railway tracks to Renate's home in Baruth, aware that our accents had never been heard there before. The little main street had four shops, a gas station with a hand pump, and an old church. An ancient castle belonging to a princess had been destroyed after the war by zealous "revolutionaries" revenging "blood of the poor peasants" shed during its long history. Some whispered that the destruction was really a cover for those who stole castle furnishings. On its site was a pleasant new school with a little park and pond. The princess, whose husband was killed conquering Poland, now bred pedigree dogs in West Germany, and the gatekeeper's house was now home to Renate's family.

Renate was slightly flushed at the unannounced American visit. We were fairly grungy by now, but the family welcomed us with dignity and a home-cooked dinner. When George announced in unusual German that "it tasted like crazy" we were joyfully accepted. Our tale of sleeping "in a potato patch" added to the merriment.

Renate's tall, quiet father was friendly but with a Prussian constraint, though he was a Sorb national raised in Saxony. A pre-Hitler Social Democrat, who neither supported the Nazis nor found ways to oppose them, he had been a civilian carpenter for the Wehrmacht. The chaos at war's end enabled him to escape becoming a POW; he sneaked home and became the first village mayor under Soviet rule. Like most villagers, he received a few fields when the estates of the big landowners were broken up.

His wife's parents died in poverty and the many children were farmed out to relatives. Bad luck landed her with an aunt and uncle who worked her hard. Too small for farm work, she became a maid for the princess in Baruth, where she met the carpenter's apprentice, three years her junior, whom she finally agreed to marry. Her refusal to go along with the Nazis had led to threats from neighbors. For needed cash, she did washing for her Storm Trooper brother-in-law, whose brown uniform on her clothesline afforded some protection. But she hung no Hitler pictures, refused the Nazi salute, joined no organizations, and put potatoes outside for hungry slave laborers. It was no great act of resistance, but risky, more than most did, and no small gesture for this diminutive woman with little exposure to political ideas.

Renate's two older sisters lived upstairs with their "new teacher" husbands, recruited after the war when all Nazi teachers were fired and replacements desperately needed. Straitlaced Karl-Heinz, a former Luftwaffe pilot, was married to Renate's eldest sister Ursula. Blond, chubby Hildegart had a golden temperament and a willingness to serve anyone, above all her dark, handsome, and independent husband Werner, who had spent months in a Wehrmacht stockade, been captured in Normandy, and sent as a POW to the United States and Britain. Skilled and witty, he loved machines and soccer, and landed on his feet wherever he fell. On his return, he agreed to teach athletics, but was pressed into geography, science, and history as well, which he crammed just before teaching the students, who admired him more than his stodgier brother-in-law. And then there was Karin, a "furlough child" loved by all, who was ten years younger than Renate.

Discipline was demanded of everyone in this busy household, which raised its own food from a bustling menagerie of animals which had to be fed or shepherded. The new "land reform" fields provided grain and potatoes in a little universe of endless chores.

While George and I were returning by train it dawned on me that a visit to Renate's parents might be viewed as a new stage in our relations. A new stage, indeed, did arrive. Late one balmy evening, after I closed the villa, Renate and I sat alone as the moon poured down its soothing light. The inevitable happened. Even at twenty-four, I had had only bad luck with amorous experiences. This time it was different, and we were grateful, happy, and a bit amazed. We repeated the event often; as the moon changed position many times in ensuing months, so did we. On free evenings, as we strolled arm in arm, I saw no ugly ruins or water damage creeping up old walls, no ancient, noisy vehicles. I marveled at the ancient fortress paths along the cliffs high above the Spree, at little cobblestoned streets winding under archways among ancient churches and towers, rejoiced at graceful Mount Czorneboh and Mount Bieleboh in the distance, and discovered an empty park where we daringly succumbed to romance.

In those pre-pill years I knew only one birth control method and once, in ignorance, flushed away the evidence — only to have it reemerge. André, one of the Frenchmen, indignantly called in Heinz Schattel and me as witnesses to the shameless goings-on in "our clubhouse" and shot an occasional sarcastic glance at me. I tried to look shocked without blushing, and learned a new lesson in applied physics.

During working hours I also ran our small library with books in French and English produced in the USSR, old Tauchnitz paperbacks in English, and what I found in secondhand shops. I was always surprised at the avid reading of men who had read little as soldiers and now seemed glad to find something in their own language. We received the *Daily Worker,* and sad as it was to read about difficult times back home (between unceasingly optimistic lines), it was still a link to my homeland and to old friends and comrades. How heartwarming it was to read the words written on New Year's Eve 1954 by that old scrapper Elizabeth Gurley Flynn: "the frantic and panic-stricken death throes of capitalism we are witnessing today create for me, at least, not pessimism or fear but joy and defiance. It won't be long now till the whole world, including our own country, will belong to the working class. What we suffer temporarily in the process is of no moment compared to the magnitude of the results." A year later she began serving two and a half years in the Federal Prison for Women in Aldersonville, West Virginia.

Framed portraits of two Americans hung in book shops and many offices: the writer Howard Fast and Paul Robeson. Two other American names were everywhere. Julius and Ethel Rosenberg were in a last desperate fight for life that winter and spring. I was moved deeply by painted slogans, even on locomotives: "Freedom for the Rosenbergs!" and wrote this memorandum, perhaps for myself: "In a country where, until eight years ago, anti-Semitism was an official, deadly government policy, now, in the GDR, the opposite is true. Not only are there meetings and demonstrations, petitions and telegrams by the hundreds of thousands, but the German people paint on their trains, which cross every corner of the land, their demand for the freedom of this progressive young Jewish couple, imprisoned and threatened with death in a country five thousand miles away."

I felt no animus toward my country, but believed in the bitter 1950s that it had been usurped by antidemocratic evil. There were moments of homesickness which brought me close to tears. More often I felt guilty at my security here while people I knew and loved back home were under siege.

Dramatic changes soon came. On June 9, 1953, the ruling Socialist Unity Party (SED) decided to halt its severe regulations — dropping ration card limits, rail fare increases, constraints on farmers and craftsmen, and price rises for sugar products. Only the new work rates, or norms, remained unaltered. On June 11th, in what was called the "New Course," the Council of Ministers publicly characterized the unexplainable measures as mistakes; a new, milder breeze was blowing.

I met Salem-joker Max, who now wheeled a big motorcycle, and teased him about his new prosperity. He replied acidly that it was an old model and would not last long. "Come on, Max," I needled, "admit it. Things are looking up at last." Max voiced annoyance at my "looking up" optimism, insisting that things were no better than before. "Just wait," he said, and off he rattled.

Was Max again showing Cassandra qualities? One week later, we heard puzzling reports from Berlin: Stalin Allee construction workers had struck and demonstrated, burning red flags and even buildings. The next day there were similar reports on RIAS from Halle, Leipzig, and other cities, including Görlitz, not far from Bautzen. GDR media said nothing, until a clear announcement: The Soviet Army has moved against the demonstrators and announced a national curfew. No one was allowed out in evening hours.

Poor George, who planned his birthday party on June 17th, believed it was a plot against him. Little occurred in Bautzen; a cluster of youngsters defied the curfew until a truckload of Soviet soldiers called on them to disperse and fired into the air. We heard later that striking workers at LOWA in Görlitz sent a message to LOWA workers in Bautzen (my old plant) urging them to join the strike. Little work was done, but there was no strike; the young teletypist in Bautzen refused to pass on the message.

It was hard to separate fact from fiction. Western radio stations like RIAS, which helped direct the uprising, described it as a defiant demand for freedom by East German workers. The GDR press called it Western-inspired counterrevolution to overthrow socialism which some workers unfortunately fell for. I believe there was truth to both — a Western decision that a planned uprising must be started before corrections and improvements won people to the system. But there was certainly very great dissatisfaction; otherwise the call to rebellion would have fallen on deaf ears. At the time, I could hardly judge; I had never been to Berlin, Leipzig, Halle, or Görlitz.

The traumatic days passed. GDR leaders dropped a few top people (those who understood the workers' demands best, it was said), but seemed determined to press the "New Course." Price cuts were announced, wages and pensions raised, power darkouts in private homes abolished. For most, the atmosphere improved markedly in late 1953 and 1954. During all the upheaval few seemed to notice the executions of the Rosenbergs at Sing-Sing on June 19th.

I finally left Bautzen for the first time to visit a National Art Exhibition in Dresden, where I recall only a West German painting of striking Hamburg dock workers. In those days West Germans were welcome, and it was the GDR which demanded German unity. I will never forget my view of downtown Dresden: desolate lanes led into a vast ocean of rubble — a few lone building skeletons pointing upward accusingly. The Nazis had provoked this by smashing cities and murdering millions. All the same, learning of the needless destruction of a beautiful city and the burning and shooting of thousands of fleeing people just before the war's end made me feel shame at what U.S. and British bombers had done.

New ex-soldiers kept arriving in Bautzen. Some had signed a statement, printed in the GDR press, that they had left the U.S. Army to protest its imperialist policy. But few were really capable of such ideas. One day two Englishmen climbed out of the Russians' big-finned old Tatra, followed by a limping white sheepdog. The naive younger Gold brother was initiated by the old-timers into the joys of alcohol — downing the innocuous-looking vodka and collapsing when he stepped outside. The older brother preached "moral communism," whose main tenet was that God walked the earth in human form to check on how things were going, especially with political leaders (he even sent a warning to Soviet Foreign Minister Molotov). The man produced hundreds of unread pages on a borrowed police typewriter. After a year or so, the Golds returned to Britain and told the press about the terrors they had suffered, including horrific rent, a sum arrived at by multiplying exchange rates and not mentioning the food and lodging for their giant pet.

Piet, a Dutchman, was less naive. Friendly and full of praise for the GDR, he nevertheless organized a petition protesting deficiencies, genuine or exaggerated, but aimed at fueling a minor uprising. The Soviet advisers removed him to Dresden for a few weeks; he returned undamaged, still friendly, but launched no more campaigns. Arthur, an American, was intelligent and vaguely sympathetic with life here, if often sarcastic. He had no left-wing background and like many others had a drinking problem. After weeks of sobriety he would disappear — his German wife scouring every dive until she found him. Rumor had it that he had carried incriminating CIA documents eastward. Madelani from Nigeria was never a soldier. He exuded prosperity, played piano, spoke like a Marxist, and assiduously collected money for various causes. Something about him didn't ring right. But more than that, being black made him the butt of the shrouded racism (forbidden in the GDR) of some Americans and Britons. Madelani stood out more than Charlie the boxer; people stared at him in restaurants and pointed him out on the street. He was their first "real African" and, on May Day, celebrations wilted as villagers followed him, mouths agape.

Some men came, some went back and were imprisoned. Blevins was a tall, scraggly young man with a pretty West Berlin girlfriend. At various times he claimed to be a veterinarian, an adventurous Korean War correspondent, or, he told me, "sort of a helper to the Pope, like a cardinal." Then this strange and funny character disappeared, presumably back to West Berlin. Months later he turned up again; straight-faced as ever, he said he had escaped an army cell with a saw his girlfriend burrowed into a cake. We roared, but someone heard the story on Armed Forces Radio, saw and all. Then he went west again, this time for good.

The club was beneficial in many ways, but problems remained. Some men drank up their wages, skipped work, and sold clothes or furniture to buy alcohol. Under pressure from wives, a few marched into Heinz Schattel's office demanding succor for empty pockets and bare cupboards. Schattel suggested that if they worked, they would have enough. One insisted that even with work his children had no bedding, and the youngest no bed at all. Schattel protested that the man had been given those things less than three months ago. The supplicant replied that it wasn't enough, things had to be sold to feed the kids: "My wife thinks we should really consider going back west again."

Schattel answered that such an action would be a grave mistake. Again the threat: "I really don't think we can hold out much longer." The bargaining began, concluding with some money and hope that the sodden petitioners would work regularly. Everyone knew that Schattel was good-natured but was responsible for our staying in Bautzen. It looked bad if too many went back west, often through an effective underground for getting even the densest to West Berlin. It would be wiser, I suggested, to tell people just to leave if they wished, with no hard feelings. This would improve the atmosphere, ending blackmail tactics and quarrels about "money favoritism." But it seemed impossible to simply say "Go."

In March 1954 the GDR gained sovereignty over its domestic affairs; our connections with the Soviets ended. However, the problems remained.

One night the Welshman Stump stumbled upstairs in the clubhouse. We ran up after the cleaning woman's screams. Stump was asleep on the sofa with a puddle in the middle of the room. I woke him angrily, shouting that the room was not a toilet. "I didn't do that," Stump insisted, despite his wide-open pants, pointing to the puddle. But who could argue with Stump? Nolan, an equally strong American and a hard worker, went on a drinking spree every few months. His gambit was to touch up new arrivals for whatever he could get. His wife also liked a drink or, even more, to flirt with almost any male that arrived. Once a group of drinkers decided to "go west" in Huck Finn fashion on the Spree that flowed north into West Berlin — oblivious to obstacles like dams and the huge Spreewald bayou region. They never got a raft together, but made such a drunken racket it was miraculous that it took a while to pick them up. They spent a few days "drying out."

Douglas and I discovered that the clubhouse canteen where we sold beer, soft drinks and cigarettes was going deeper into the red. Ashamed of our ineptitude, we tossed in our money rather than admit the problem. Later, we learned that "resourceful" Henri collected bottles and their deposits that we never charged, and probably more than just empty bottles. One of our drunks got caught trying to sell the upstairs curtains.

I was in a bind. The GDR paid me to help make the club work. But the men expected me, as a bilingual foreigner, to both translate and support their demands, however preposterous. Rulings from above could also be bureaucratic or worse; when Charlie had asked to become a GDR citizen, he was put off repeatedly and finally rejected. He could only conclude that his color was the reason. Inconsistency in giving financial help, less on merit than aggressiveness, or a wife's weeping ability, or fear of saying "No," made life difficult.

At one party things got nasty. When Nolan's wife started flirting, he blew up. When he also threatened me, George, recalling my run-in with the Scotsman, moved between us and also blew up, hitting him with a billiard cue. Some foreigners became sudden devotees of law and order, demanding that George be punished. That ugliness blew over, but tensions kept rising. One day the Alabaman cornered me with his woes: he had sold everything movable and was still thirsty. Would I translate for him with Schattel so he could get some cash? As he blathered his long list of troubles and injustices things suddenly snapped. I burst out crying, more bitterly than since my childhood; I was having a minor nervous breakdown. George found me leaning against a tree across the street, unable to say much. Wisely, he left me alone and sought out Renate. She sized up the situation and led me to my room where I slowly came to myself.

I felt like a grain of wheat between two millstones. But I had Renate (and two visits to a doctor) to help me overcome my breakdown. In two weeks I was back to normal, though for a long time I found it wise to withdraw from stressful settings — and quit that job. Luckily, a year's job-training course was beginning in our clubhouse; I decided to join it.

First, Renate and I planned a week's vacation in Leipzig. But she over-slept, and we made a frenzied dash for a moving train — only to get her big umbrella stuck in the door with me struggling to get into the car — under the disapproving glances of punctual, law-abiding Germans. In 1953 it was still a no-no for unmarried couples to share hotel rooms. The desk clerk at the elegant Hotel International listened to my clumsy lie, but our papers mercilessly exposed our single status. He insisted on separate rooms but pointed with a wink to their adjacent numbers. The extra cost was an un-mitigated waste. Leipzig, with 600,000 people, was a far cry from Bautzen, and we whirled from zoo to opera to dancing. Renate's low-cut dress brought stares, and I, an "urbane" New Yorker, spoiled Renate's pleasure by cringing from discomfort born of the small-town rube I had become.

The first four months of job-training were in the clubhouse: German, civics, math, and technology. The meek German teacher, not without rea-son, mortally feared these alcoholics and assorted misfits so different from his usual little pupils. The civics teacher, a veteran antifascist, tried to explain what the GDR was about, and even something of Marxism-Leninism, to our weird bunch of runaways. He ran into problems; shortly after his polemics against West German lotteries — "theft from workers aimed also at distracting them from struggle" — a government soccer pool was initiated in the GDR. He was honest and devoted, but a bust with the doubtful or cynical.

Schattel was clubhouse manager, but a separate school director was ap-pointed. He was a respected Communist and anti-Nazi LOWA foreman, but without any experience with schools, languages, or irksome foreigners. Per-haps it was thought that he would be good for occupational training. His pedagogical method was to shut himself into his office, drink tea, and read the official *Neues Deutschland*. When a Briton assaulted Madelani, someone ran to his office, but he just burrowed more deeply into his "*ND.*" He was replaced by a man with more experience and command, but troubled by epilepsy. His occasional grand mal at least defused tense situations.

I learned a bit more German grammar and math, watched with sympa-thy when the civics teacher was baited, and was exposed to technology that was new to me. In the second four-month phase we spent two days in class and four days as apprentices at LOWA, where I had once lugged lumber. The final months were only at LOWA.

Wolfgang, who taught the French and Moroccan groups, was a lively, sophisticated, and effective teacher who spoke perfect French and good English. We became good friends. I had always wondered how to communicate with my parents without compromising them. I asked for a rather thin disguise: could I use his name and address?

My mother soon wrote in October 1953, the first of many letters:

Dearest, dear boy,

Even though I knew by intuition that you were safe, yet I needed the assurance of a message from you to still any doubts. Now I know that you are safe and well, and oh! what a relief.

Both of us old folk are working. I have a very creative and satisfying job. All I needed to give me peace of mind was word from you. Now I feel so close to you. Who knows, perhaps we will see each other some time soon.

I would love to hear all about you, your experiences, adventures and hardships. . . . Please do take care of yourself. Perhaps it would be safer if you were a little further away. Dad & I have little to lose, our house in the country can provide for us and our needs are simple. So far as we are concerned you can write freely. It is your own safety we are concerned about.

Like most GDR people Renate was baptized a Lutheran, though she had hardly attended church since confirmation. But when a hard-working American who avoided Bautzen problems in a nearby village invited us to his church wedding, we went. The pro-GDR father-in-law had helped to found one of the first GDR "cooperative farms," then a source of bitter conflicts in rural areas. Schattel, once active in rural affairs, had even been warned anonymously that it wouldn't be long before he hung from a lantern. The pastor opposed GDR policies, and his hatred intruded into the marriage sermon, whose main tenor was that the couple would find happiness only in Jesus Christ. This message, hardly part of normal GDR weddings, was repeated with variations, making the atmosphere icier than the cold which tormented Renate in her flimsy, diaphanous dress. On the following Monday, Renate went to City Hall and declared her withdrawal from the church, meaning no more church taxes checked off her wages. When we informed her family, they all approved; her father, mother, sisters, and brothers-in-law soon followed Renate's apostasy. Those of the family in the Socialist Unity Party ended a double membership, not uncommon at the time. One sermon had cost the church a lot.

All that was forgotten on Christmas Eve; we ate copiously, sang carols, and welcomed a thinly disguised Saint Nicholas bearing a switch in the old German way. Out of costume, Renate's father recalled the first postwar Christmas, when he was lucky enough to catch a wild rabbit. The hunger years were over and we gorged ourselves on two breakfasts, a huge, delicious goose dinner, afternoon coffee with gooey cake, and a supper of sausage and cheeses. Just eating was a major challenge, and cleanup, though a collective effort, was almost endless.

Back at Bautzen, Renate and I feasted on cheap, wonderful Kamchatka crabmeat, piled high in unbought cans in fish shops, and also on equally inexpensive and unappreciated salmon. We ate quietly at her room, for Renate, no fighter, feared the landlady who nastily tattled to her father. While old-fashioned in some ways, he retorted that his daughter was old enough to know what she was doing.

Although a legal advice item in the newspaper affirmed that boarders could have any guest they desired, Renate had enough of her landlady and found a room not far from mine. In bitter January cold, we moved her possessions to a sublet with a friendly and understanding couple with a three-year-old boy. One evening he looked into the room when the door was ajar and asked why "uncle" was in bed. Kindly Frau Munzig replied that "Maybe he's not well."

Impelled perhaps by my doubts about our cultural differences, Renate took an evening course on painters and began learning guitar. I gave her some books to "improve herself"—first, Engels's "The Origin of the Family"—and was surprised by her lack of enthusiasm. My second attempt, a novel about auto strikes in the United States, had no greater success. My cultural plan also involved exposure to classical music. "Don't go to sleep during the concert," I joked. Of course Renate had to nudge me awake. World events were alien to her then, but I tried not to fall into male chauvinist derision about "women and politics." And, politics or not, she was for me unwaveringly warm, lively, and lovely. Her break with the church did not keep us from the "Christmas Oratorio" in the cathedral, and when power broke down and candles were lit, the music was more beautiful than ever to both of us.

Apprenticeship meant lots of metal filing, a skill I never mastered. I then tackled my selected trade, an ancient lathe. Somehow I fulfilled journeyman requirements, making a steel cone fitting into a steel case; I look at it today in disbelief. Our teacher, a meek man in his fifties with nine children, must have helped greatly. He was a Social Democrat before the Nazi era — and a devotee of nudism, still banned in both Germanys in the 1950s. Our crazy bunch of foreigners developed growing cohesion, even solidarity. Newly arrived Tony, a chubby young Mexican, soon distinguished himself as both craftsman and lover. One day his father showed up and rushed him home, leaving a heartbroken and very pregnant young woman. She had dreamed of a future in "the Golden West" which for her included Mexico. We chipped in for a baby carriage.

A few of us foreigners were invited to the anniversary party of the FDJ, where the young Germans admired the jitterbugging of Charlie and George — for them a rare pleasure. Later I photographed the fireworks with my new camera. A week later the English ex-officer Jim asked me to photograph his big family after work so I took the camera along, not worrying that cameras were forbidden in LOWA. Was it coincidence? For the first time my briefcase was checked at the exit and the camera taken into custody — with those mysterious firework photos. How would they interpret them? A week later I was summoned to police headquarters — and received both camera and negatives without a question.

In a friendly shop climate I got closer to the Moroccans and proudly learned Arabic numbers from one to ten. One day Allal taught me "I like to eat Schnitzel," and sent me to another Moroccan, who burst out laughing. What I said I liked to eat wasn't Schnitzel at all!

In the spring of 1954 there was an "All-German Referendum against Atomic Weapons," official in the GDR and pressed by an unofficial, beleaguered left in West Germany. We foreigners couldn't vote, but decided to join the cause of keeping atomic weapons out. Instead of the unimaginative GDR campaign, with repetitive banners and even duller oration, we sought livelier approaches. We would plant crosses downtown, marked with the years of both world wars and, after giving onlookers a simple leaflet, would briefly address them, urging their support. The FDJ was hesitant, so we went ahead on our own.

At work, George got crosses nailed together. The Nigerian Madelani, a Greek girl, Douglas from England, and a few others would speak. But mimeographs were rare, and those responsible for the one at City Hall were unused to wild Americans (or Germans) coming in to run off leaflets. They insisted on a "responsible" signature. Our pleas, based on the contents — in line with the line but briefer and readable — were futile. On a last-chance Saturday afternoon, George and I blustered into the SED central office, where only the top man was present. He read the leaflet, said, "Of course," signed, and stamped it.

Our crosses attracted fewer people than expected; the campaign had worn many down by then. But the first public speeches by hitherto shy people were salutary in the long run. We then decided to have our own vote. The school management approved until we insisted on a really secret ballot. The idea was mind-boggling for them but they agreed, since no higher-ups needed to know about our vote. So thirty-odd American, French, Moroccan, British, and other foreigners marked ballots secretly. Many "no" votes were expected from those hostile to the GDR. Either there was a secret agreement to avoid controversy or an honest consensus; the vote against atomic weapons was unanimous.

In June 1954 an "All-Germany Meet" of the FDJ was held in East Berlin, with hundreds of thousands from all over the GDR and small, illegal groups from West Germany. Seven Bautzen foreigners from the United States, Britain, France, and Morocco and two GDR teachers also made the trip. For hours in a makeshift freight car we got young Germans to happily sing everything from "Avanti Populo," to "Alouette" as we rolled on to Berlin to march, to sing, to talk, to see the marvelous Soviet dancer Ulanova in scenes from *Romeo and Juliet,* and to again enjoy the Moisseyev dancers whom I had wildly applauded in Prague.

East Berlin, still deeply scarred by war, was jammed with youth. The opening ceremony was joyous, and Charlie as always was a magnet. But the parade through downtown Berlin took us past street after street of ruins, worst of all just before the rococo Stalin Allee, the GDR's first major housing project. In the background, two hills now covered by shrubbery consisted of bombed rubble. Our lusty singing was interrupted when a West Berlin balloon burst overhead, scattering anti-GDR propaganda. Parade marshals tried to gather up the leaflets while paraders scrambled after them. Such actions were frequent, I was told; against the intentions of the festival organizers, many young people were drawn to West Berlin. I was not among them. Partly to discourage such visits we were housed at an idyllic Interior Ministry vacation home and were assigned a group of young men and women as hosts and guides. Their job certainly included keeping an eye on us, but they were pleasant and intelligent. The interior minister himself, once an active anti-Nazi, also paid us a visit. I couldn't find Renate at the festival, but triumphantly brought home half a pineapple from Berlin — the first she ever ate.

The trip was both a break from small-town life and a look into the complications and contradictions of the broader scene. But we had enough problems in Bautzen, and tragedies as well. Seemingly jovial, well-adjusted Charlie became engaged to a German woman from a railroad office. Many foreign and German friends attended the City Hall wedding. All but the bride. I never heard her explanation; some time later Charlie took his life.

There was another tragic death when Coffman, a Jewish-American, died the day after a brawl in a Piglet Market dive. Two Germans were sentenced to nine and seven years, but we wondered about our alleged IRA member, who "went west" the next day. He was in the bar; had he provoked the brawl? Quarrels continued to erupt at times with national or racist roots or caused by alcohol and conflicts over women. At one party, I felt something brewing and insisted upon leaving despite Renate's desire to stay for cake. The next day I heard that before the cake was consumed the chairs had started flying.

Bautzen — and problems with my fellow foreigners — were weighing on me. I had more twinges of homesickness as I thought of dogwood, tanagers, square dances, and the songs I loved. But the United States still faced frightening times. McCarthy remained on the scene; the House Un-American Activities Committee was riding high; Congress, including John F. Kennedy and Hubert Humphrey, piled on anticommunist laws; comrades lost jobs or went to jail. My college classmate Dave Schine was touring army bases to destroy suspect books, some of which I had enjoyed as a GI. Book-burning now scarred my homeland.

Was I, like Don Quixote whose books were burned while he fought windmills, also fighting windmills? I was still searching for new paths. Stefan Heym had given a friendly response to my manuscript on the Buffalo battles. John Peet commented on my piece and urged me to write for his newsletter, *Democratic German Report*. He printed a story I did on improvements at my LOWA plant, and surprisingly sent 120 marks, a large sum for me. Wolfgang, who received my U.S. mail, arranged for me to write for a Dresden paper. Again, I was paid.

George won a chance to study at a technical college and insisted that if he could do it, so could I. With help from club authorities I went to Karl Marx University in Leipzig for an interview, doubtless to check my German, my educational status (I had no school records), and, surely, my political views. I was accepted and expressed interest in American history and literature, a four-year program. The panel noted that the university also had a three-year program in journalism. Thinking of my twenty-six years, and four years of college behind me, I took journalism.

I returned to Bautzen joyfully to break the news to Renate, but got an unpleasant surprise from her: "Do you think I'll sit and wait for you here while you are surrounded by those college girls? I wouldn't think of it!" My shock and resentment made me walk out in a huff, our relationship asunder. I had wondered if we could get along with our different cultural backgrounds and interests. This seemed to settle the question.

In the evenings, I prowled around aimlessly. George was busy with Hella. Movies were no fun alone. I grew more and more miserable. At last I threw in the towel, bought some poisonously green peppermint liqueur, and knocked at Renate's door. "Let's get married," I said, and we sealed our engagement with the green liquid. Renate quit work and found a little room and a secretarial job in Leipzig.

But first, we traveled with a group of Bautzen foreigners to a resort on the Baltic island of Rügen, whose scenery included beautiful chalk cliffs immortalized by the painter Caspar David Friedrich. We again had to have separate rooms, but a handy balcony connected Renate's room with mine and the whole vacation went well. A new phase of life in the GDR was beginning.

[7]

A STUDENT AGAIN

"What American?" boomed an angry voice through the open door. "I don't know about any American!" After hurried whispering, the Journalism College official's voice trailed off. I was ushered into the room by the personnel director who sprang a surprise: the course lasted four, not three years. She looked astonished when I asked about credit for my Harvard years. My next surprise came when she said she hoped I realized that socialist journalism was taught here, with no resemblance to "the wild, hard-drinking kind you may know from Hollywood films." I reassured her, and in later years smiled as I turned down drinks from socialist journalists. I moved into a dormitory for European, African, Asian, Arab, and other foreign students: all friendly, gifted, radical. But when I learned that journalism students had dorms almost allowing them to fall from bed into the classroom, I moved there instead.

The institution, renamed Karl Marx University a year earlier, was founded in 1409, 227 years before Harvard. Unlike Harvard's, its dorms were crowded and lacked private bathrooms. But also unlike my old college, there were no limits on guests of the opposite sex; the problem was "paying off" roommates to take a stroll. Happily, Renate had a room elsewhere.

I got along well with my roommate, especially after I learned that his embroidered nightgown was accepted male sleeping apparel, and that his hands moving rapidly up and down in his lap were honing his razor. A cheap hot lunch was guaranteed everyone in the GDR, costing only 25 marks a month. Breakfasts and suppers were costlier and some students bought only lunch. Room rent was only 10 marks, and I could afford all three meals. Workers' and farmers' children received scholarships of 180 marks monthly, the others 140, barely enough. But many students got

40- to 80-mark monthly bonuses for good grades and extracurricular work. We foreigners received 250 marks.

At the matriculation ceremony, the rector was introduced as "Magnifizenz." It must be a joke, I thought. But his robes and big golden chain proved that I was mistaken. Rector Georg Mayer was famed for speaking extemporaneously in endless sentences — students timed them — but always ending with the right verb. Though his scarred face was not a result of the Spanish War or the Resistance, as I had surmised, he was a wise historian and had been a courageous antifascist.

An anniversary meeting of the university's postwar reopening was addressed by Siegfried Wagner, a top SED cultural official, who gave the usual long-winded pitch about GDR achievements and West German threats. Students in the balcony stretched out to sleep; the *Spektabilitäten*, as university senators were titled, nodded wearily. I berated Wagner afterwards for not talking about the early postwar struggles against cold, hunger, fascists, or aristocrats. The speech was boring, I said, mentioning dozing students and nodding senators. Although surely unused to such criticism, he reacted to my weirdly accented attack in a tolerant, even friendly way. But he apparently didn't understand the point.

Things went better in my courses. In the 1930s our dean, Hermann Budzislawski, "Boodzy," continued the work of jailed Nobel Peace Prize winner Carl von Ossietzky by publishing his legendary magazine *Weltbühne* from Prague. When the Nazis moved in, Budzislawski fled to the United States and worked with the famous columnist Dorothy Thompson. In the GDR he briefly fell afoul of the brass; "western emigration" was a distrusted category in the early 1950s. Then he was asked to head our college. A nervous lecturer, he paced up and down, clearing his throat, changing spectacles, yet was always riveting. From his course on the German press I learned much of German history.

Fiftyish, angular Hedwig Voegt seemed to put stress in all the wrong places; but I soon stopped noticing. She taught German literature with wisdom and love — visiting Büchner and Klopstock, Günther, the great sad Lessing, Goethe, Schiller, and the one closest to my heart, Heinrich Heine. Our most famous lecturer, Wieland Herzfelde, had headed Malik Publishers in the pre-Hitler years and with his brother John Heartfield and George Grosz cofounded German Dadaism. He had subsequently emigrated to the United States. This and his independent ideas caused him problems in the fifties until Boodzy hired this immensely knowledgeable man to teach world literature.

Lenning, the lecturer on Marxism-Leninism, had a dry style which sub-liminally threatened a papal-like ban on anyone not embracing his words as gospel. In the first semester, SED and FDJ leaders sought to convince students to welcome cuts in scholarships to 100 marks in gratitude to "workers whose toil paid for them." They had little success. But Lenning spent ten minutes of every lecture agitating us. As rejection of the cut increased, the GDR press suddenly announced that "rumors of scholarship cuts" were only "RIAS lies." We awaited Herr Lenning's comments, but he stayed silent — without even a self- ironic joke.

All journalism freshmen attended the same lectures and seminars for twenty-five or thirty hours a week. One hundred and twenty-five freshmen were divided into five seminar groups; each seminar formed an FDJ club and a smaller SED unit. Scholastic and cultural life centered on such groups, which made decisions, without or without our tutor, even on granting bonuses. A control function was certainly involved; we discussed the political and moral standing of group members, which probably offended doubters and nonconformists. When we helped a village cooperative during harvesting season, one of our members, confusing harvesting with planting, impregnated the mayor's daughter and was severely chastised by the group. He later married a student and was again sharply criticized by our FDJ group for slapping her. Some may have seen our actions as intolerable meddling in private affairs; we saw them as issues of justice and equal rights. Most students were faithful, even unquestioning in their political attitudes; many had joined the SED during a recruiting drive honoring Stalin after his death. The few who were opposed had a choice between dissimulation, silence, or flight. But there was little opposition in our ranks; our near unanimity stemmed from willing agreement by most students on major issues, which won our journalism school the nickname "Red Cloister."

At cultural gatherings of our equally male and female group, members recited from favorite writers or sang old student songs. A railroad worker's son prodded us to concerts, many for the first time — with the germ spreading to films and plays. At times we jettisoned college lunch and headed for the "pony bar," where big slices of unrationed horse meat were offered to sturdy truckers or hungry students. For the queasy, vegetarian food was served down the block.

Changing roommates, I bunked with Max, whose parents had died in the German flight from East Prussia as the Soviets approached. Trained as a baker, he was sent to one of the GDR's college preparatory "Workers and Farmers' Institutes," where he drew close to some gifted Chinese students and roomed with a young Chinese who later became a leading Brecht expert. I too, remained friendly with foreign students and helped organize a rousing international evening where handsome Albanians sang and captured hearts and shy Chinese were cajoled into a duet. Sadly, we couldn't repeat it, because the Chinese, now a hundred strong, held to their rule: everyone goes — or no one goes. After two small-town years I liked this city of a half-million with its Old Town of countless private and nationalized shops, narrow streets, and passageways displaying porcelain, shoes, books, cutlery, or other goods during the 800-year-old Leipzig Trade Fairs. Renate, whose flair was displayed at Fasching (Mardi Gras) with a dress festooned with foreign headlines, was gladly accepted by my seminar group. I often waited for her near her nationalized wholesale firm in what had been a major fur district until Nazi mobs smashed all Jewish shops in 1938. There was much to see: the Nikolai Church, where Bach played the organ, and the Thomas Church where he was cantor and choir director and is now entombed; his statue with one pocket turned out, symbolizing the miserliness of his bosses; the gracious Renaissance Old City Hall and a huge, hideous memorial to Napoleon's drubbing in the Battle of the Nations. When SS men holed up there in 1945, U.S. artillery shells hardly chipped the heavy granite. Otherwise there were factories, endless blocks of grubby apartment houses, a few parks, and the Pleisse River, which carried almost more reeking phenol than water.

We often marched. May Days, a main occasion, featured loud singing before 6 A.M., a supposedly salutary contribution to local class consciousness. As I sang the leftist songs and chanted slogans against atom bombs and Adenauer, I wondered why we antagonized people so early on a holiday morning. Later in the day things were pleasanter, and Renate joined in. One icy day we marched to mark the fiftieth anniversary of the German youth movement, only to endure the district head's dull polemic. When we students confronted him, demanding to know why this man who suffered years of Nazi confinement offered ill-prepared old slogans, he mumbled fearfully "No time," and ran to his chauffeured car.

There were other disturbing problems. Candidates for the People's Chamber were questioned at neighborhood meetings and occasionally met disapproval. But most voters dutifully deposited in the box their unmarked ballot with the one National Front slate. Only a few brave souls used the tiny voting booth in the rear. Most people feared that it might seem that they were crossing out names, and who wished to risk a possible bonus or promotion just for a secret ballot? When a fellow student found no pencils in the booths, he circulated an angry petition to Premier Grotewohl. For his efforts he was censured by his SED party group. That was his only punishment; he earned no enmity from other students, but the authorities surely had labeled him a potential troublemaker.

My age and experience gave me an edge in classes and on exams. But not in physical education, where in the obligatory rope climb I strained every weak muscle but repeatedly missed the ceiling. Finally, with the entire gym cheering me on, I reached the top and the end of sport classes forever.

In June we had our first *Praktikum,* six weeks in a big newspaper printing plant, learning all aspects of then useful but now obsolete typesetting methods. Most students also spent two summer weeks on the Baltic island of Rügen at "GST camp," the "Association for Sport and Technology," which offered courses in sailing, driving, glider flying, and motorcycling but whose main purpose was a sort of paramilitary training resembling ROTC. I went along and so did Renate; besides the marching and training there was time for bathing on the beautiful beach and even lovemaking in the shrubbery. One thing I hated: the final steps of a march were in goosestep. I had seen a movie theater rock with bitter laughter when uniformed GDR men were first shown doing this ridiculous step with its far from ridiculous memories. I complained to our director, Professor Basil Spiru, who had spent years as an exile in the USSR. He insisted that it was no Nazi step, but had been in use since 1698 and was practiced in the USSR and elsewhere. I got nowhere, refrained from it myself, but reflected that the old hypocrite saw no obscenity in the goose-step but sent a student home in disgrace for playfully covering his girlfriend with sand, exaggerating her figure and adorning it with appropriately placed seaweed. "Pornography," he said.

Renate and I left the camp early and returned to Bautzen. A woman at City Hall married us simply with a little speech about loving and respecting each other on equal terms while recalling our responsibility toward the happiness of other people the world over. We honeymooned in the Elbe Sandstone Mountains, "Saxon Switzerland," climbing around the picturesque region, careful, as warned, not to stray into Czech territory.

Back at college in September 1955, I tackled new courses in dialectical materialism and the Soviet press taught by the same old Professor Spiru. He was insipid and uninspiring, but his thick accent delighted all but me; I missed his boners and struggled with my own accent. Our clever student wall newspaper (a substitute for a printed paper) joked about his errors, while slyly urging more politeness and attentiveness. The humorless Spiru fled to the party secretary to demand "protection from such attacks" and became an even bigger laughing stock. Subsequently, after the old moralist made passes at a woman student, he became universally despised.

Students were expected to volunteer labor for the national economy. During October "potato weeks" the whole school system piled onto trains or trucks and headed for the harvest. It was healthy, fresh air work — but backbreaking. Our male students spent a January vacation week in the lignite mines near Leipzig, which provided heat and power for homes and factories, and the basis for the huge chemical industry. After a commute by train at 3:30 A.M., we sleepily descended into a giant open pit where mammoth excavators scooped away at the pit walls. In pre-dawn darkness, this arid lunar landscape had an eerie, almost beautiful quality. Transporters like Martian monsters carried earth and sand across the pit to dumps, to wait for years till the pit was refilled, while crumbly semi-carbonized coal was loaded into trains to be converted in foul smelling, smoky factories into industrial coal or household briquettes. We helped reinforce makeshift tracks in the soft ground and shared briefly in miners' camaraderie, if not in their impressive wages. I was awed by a tough-talking woman, the driver and team boss of a giant excavator. I tired sooner than my young fellow-students and was barely able to climb the 120 steps out of the pits. At week's end we were "urged" to contribute part of our pay to Algeria or some other solidarity fund. A few complained; most complied.

We sometimes worked a half day clearing the last rubble from the severely bombed city, weeding sugar beets, or building a huge sport stadium. We grumbled and some found excuses to duck out, but I kept telling myself that I was engaged in a just and good cause and that my toil was not enriching any profiteer. Working with the country's backbone, farmers or miners, brought me closer to my second homeland, I decided, wiping my sweaty brow.

A severe housing shortage left Renate and me with only an allotted small room and a half with joint use of a bathroom. The elderly couple whose home we invaded were unfriendly, placing their kitchen off limits and reducing us to a hot plate in our room, refusing their tub and directing us to a public bathhouse "only" ten blocks away, and pressing us for assurances that we did not expect a baby. Skeptical about an American who did not join in their sarcasm about this absurd "socialist republic," the Hankes pegged us as "reds," and unleashed several weapons: haughty politeness; blasting us every evening with BBC radio's rabid anti-GDR newspeak; hinting to me behind Renate's back that she was not my intellectual equal. Those remarks were cleverly barbed. I had worried about my consuming political and intellectual interests joined to a village girl unconcerned with such matters unless they affected her directly. My doubts were overridden by Renate's warmth and goodness, admired by all but the soulless. But I was surrounded by intellectual, politically engaged young women, also generous and attractive.

Coming home tired in those autumn days we often squabbled. Renate was suspicious about "those pretty students" and Frau Hanke made her nervous. We argued about housework: why scrub clothing in a tub on the floor instead of on a table top? Why stand to prepare vegetables when sitting down was more comfortable? "It isn't done that way!" she insisted, as if all else were laziness. I always tried to help, but clumsiness marred my efforts and sharpened conflicts. Had this marriage been a mistake? I never concluded that, but the Hankes might have been subliminally influential. Then Renate discovered that she was pregnant. I learned something: early pregnancy can be a nervous or quarrelsome time. By the third month we were happy again. Marital quarrels were also overcome by the narrow day couch with one down comforter. I could either overcome pride and snuggle up or stay angry and freeze. Not one squabble outlasted the night. Our spats about housework never ceased fully; my clumsiness and distraction by outside events and her keen sense of responsibility always gave her a greater burden. But my commitment to equality stirred me to do my best.

The second year's *Praktikum* focused upon founding "village newspapers" to encourage farm collectivization. After four years, many collectives (LPGs) drew ineffective or unmotivated farmers hoping for group cover, while skilled, energetic farmers tended to stay private. Many students feared primitive conditions; it took arguing, moral pressure, and veiled threats before they acquiesced, ultimately discovering great rewards in starting papers with little help and many obstacles to overcome. My circumstances did not allow me to have that experience. Though my German was fluent, it was too faulty to publish a paper, and with a baby coming, I worked at the Leipzig radio station learning about tapes and recording — with my attention greatly distracted.

Renate was very patient during the last months. She enrolled in the new, somewhat misnamed course in "painless birth method": breathing exercises, gymnastics, and baby care kept her happily busy during the six-week prenatal leave. Finally from a pleasant waiting room I heard the first cry of the overdue baby and saw briefly a little head with a dark curl and button nose. We called him Thomas; he could later choose Paine, Jefferson, Müntzer, or Mann as a role model.

Before eight paid postnatal weeks were over, Renate was forced to return to the clinic with a breast inflammation. But the clinic was unable to care for a healthy six-week-old baby. So was I. In desperation, I found the university weekly nursery for students where the head nurse, who saw that loving care was given to every child, agreed to take him until Renate recovered. With day nurseries hard to find in those days, he was permitted to stay. We had no proper facilities at home; I had my studies, Renate her work, and Tom got on well at the college nursery. We had him weekends. But it hurt when his first recognizable word was his nurse's name.

Chicken pox hit the nursery when Tom was seven months old. Unaffected babies were sent home, and with a college holiday, the task of caring for Tom fell to me. Burping, feeding, and squeezing out carrot juice by twisting pulp in a handkerchief — there were few baby foods then — were my specialties. Beyond that, Renate was the expert. One morning, I suddenly saw a spot on a nether cheek, then pimple after pimple. Tom was afflicted and could go to the nursery — and I to my studies. Health insurance covered fully Renate's training course, ambulance, delivery, and mastitis treatment plus fourteen weeks paid leave and 500 marks for baby expenses: two installments at prenatal checkups, two for postnatal checks, the main sum after delivery and a bonus for breast feeding. Pregnant and nursing women got more ration coupons (the semi-rationing system ended two years later) for milk and other foods.

In late 1956 we were allocated two rooms in a widow's apartment with full use of a bathroom, and a kitchen where we cooked regularly. Most shops had a normal supply of basic items and occasional tinned delicacies from Hungary, Bulgaria, the USSR, or China. Lines were common but usually short — except for oranges, bananas, or other scarce items. With ration coupons covering many needs, groceries were inexpensive. Rent and the nursery were minimal, but our income was limited and we rarely bought major items of clothing or furniture. I made 120 marks working in the mines. We found a stroller — also 120 marks.

I was now integrated into GDR life and we were quite happy. Renate made acquaintances easily and we soon knew all our neighbors. Politics played a role in apartment house affairs; a puppeteering couple was stoutly pro-GDR, so were an elderly woman and daughter, the woman's husband murdered by the Nazis. A man downstairs hated the GDR and attended "homeland" rallies in West Berlin to demand Silesia from Poland. A young pastor and his wife were also opposed, if not so stridently. Their baby was Tom's age and we got along with them, as with virtually everyone.

I now corresponded frequently with my parents and occasionally got packages of cereal, candy, spices, good potato peelers, and once a *Peterson's Guide to European Birds,* filling a gap which had always caused homesick twinges. But I was not only occupied with potato peelers and birds; the world was changing fast. Khrushchev and Bulganin moved to the top in Moscow and steps were taken toward detente — easing tension with the West. France defied its allies, rejecting the European Defense Treaty in 1954; it also agreed to peace in Indochina. The occupation of Austria was ended. But shortly thereafter West Germany joined NATO, changing its Basic Law to permit conscription. The East Bloc countered in May 1955 with the Warsaw Pact. In October the highest West German court ruled that 1937 borders were still valid: the GDR, Silesia, Pomerania, and East Prussia, "belonged" to the Federal Republic. The GDR responded in 1956 by creating the "National People's Army."

Students generally granted the need for an army but complained about uniforms that conjured horrible memories. One tutor, in response, asked sarcastically if they would prefer U.S. or Soviet styles. I wondered if there were no other alternatives. Why must rigidity undermine support for a justifiable measure? This was the same obduracy that brought back the goose-step.

With no transistors yet, students in the dorms, with only GDR radio, learned the inconceivable news quite late: at the Soviets' 20th Party Congress Khrushchev denounced Stalin. For youngsters raised with an almost eerie devotion to Stalin it was akin to American young people being told that George Washington was a thief or child-molester. One puzzled student asked Professor Spiru for an explanation. Spiru got red in the face, blustered that it was all "part of the class struggle," and hastened from the room.

My confusion went beyond Stalin's death. For years I agonized over the contradictions: his leadership in the victory over the Nazis, but the abhorrent hero worship; his buildup of the USSR, but the purges and accounts of postwar injustices in the USSR and East Germany; his pithy interviews and writings, but inexplicable decisions alienating legions of potential supporters. As the report leaked out in the GDR, some of the bloody truths emerged. The students felt an urgent need to discuss this. But the SED decided: "No discussion of mistakes." This slogan, as contrary to Marxist principles as can be, reflected a fear of the consequences of such deliberation. Not surprisingly. Some, like Walter Ulbricht, had been involved themselves and feared upheavals resulting from any revelations — as in Poland, Hungary, and many Western Communist parties.

Since June 1953 the GDR had been on its "New Course," with strenuous efforts to improve living standards, remove restrictive measures, and relax some strictures on criticism and free speech. But at our college we were still badgered by teachers like Spiru and Lenning and students like Gisela Heuch, a zealot who specialized in pressuring those at meetings who voted no or abstained on hard-line motions. Things eased, however, and discussions blossomed, especially after the Stalin revelations.

Some of us decided to augment our limited "wall newspaper" with a printed newspaper. In December 1956 it proclaimed the modest aim of helping us practice journalistic methods. An editorial by the student who had petitioned about missing election pencils complained wittily that GDR media were saying so little about upheavals in Poland and Hungary that people listened to "enemy radio," a fact never officially accepted on high. One article documented the failure of Leipzig's main paper to deal with readers' letters, another ("Class Struggle with a Blindfold") claimed we should know what the other side writes, but didn't study West German media. I wrote a column urging the media to avoid simplistic U.S. coverage and report more, positive and negative, about racism, unions, but also the Salk vaccine, which had hardly been mentioned. Interviews on a planned pension raise revealed the great difficulties older people often faced. None of this was overly abrasive, but our little paper caused alarm at high levels, which feared any spark that might ignite upheavals like in Hungary. Only one more issue appeared — tamer than a blind lapdog.

No one criticized me or my column. My position was rather privileged; I was not in the SED, but was invited to party meetings as a "member-in-exile" of the U.S. Communist Party and treated as a rather exotic, perhaps heroic character. I was generally respected, but there were a few limits. When, during seminars on dialectical materialism, I asked for other examples of "quantitative into qualitative change" than what Harvard Communists used nine years earlier, as well as other questions, the tutor reacted with growing irony. But he could hardly dismiss them as provocations; after all, I was a "persecuted Communist from the imperialist world," The other students kept mum; their only worry seemed to be getting to lunch on time.

There was plenty of talk that season outside classes. We breathlessly followed the British-French-Israeli attack on Suez and the bloody struggle in Hungary, which was far more menacing and confusing. The *Worker,* mailed from the United States, was undergoing amazing changes. A full page was devoted to readers' letters, with no holds barred; it was new for the party paper to print letters bitterly critical of the USSR and its role in Hungary, and critical of the Communist Party. It is not easy to recall; I think my conclusion at the time was that Soviet military intervention was nasty but necessary, seeing that Hungary almost fell to forces opposed to socialism: the landed nobility, church hierarchy demanding a return of church lands, rightist groups, and indirectly, the Western powers, creating a direct threat to Soviet borders. A huge question remained: how could a situation arise in which even coal miners hated the system so violently they lynched its leaders? Things must have been very foul. I had an inkling as to their nature.

When party members in my seminar group discussed Hungary I expressed my doubts and worries. Then I noticed the secretary taking notes on my remarks. I told myself to keep on saying what I thought, but I became distracted, and my remarks grew weaker till I trailed off and ended them. Years later I questioned that student, a good friend who would tell the truth. The notes were routine, not to record differences or make trouble; my statements never went further than her pad. But I did become inhibited publicly in reflecting on basic questions. Later that year the invitations to party meetings ceased.

It was a tense time for anyone with doubts and questions. I have bitter recollections of endless FDJ meetings where someone was raked over the coals for some stupid reason. A student was chastised for using an assumed French name when singing chansons to earn extra money; another student with theater tickets left an interminable meeting without permission and was angrily informed that meetings were more important than the theater. A cynical student joked about GDR elections, and the usually sweet girl in front of him announced this to the meeting. Someone who bought a sweater in West Berlin got an earful; a student was censured because his sacred party membership book disappeared while he napped.

Most students maintained pained silence at such sessions. Some assailants seemed sure they were fighting the class enemy. But whether sincere, rigid, power-hungry, or sadistic, they hurt our cause. We lacked the guts to resist them, but did not abandon our beliefs under their pressure.

The worst case haunted me for years. I was in the beginners' class in Russian. Our teacher, Dorschan, did his best. But he also dismissed the local party newspapers as "wurst sheets," and called Eisenhower a peace-loving president. When he allegedly taped Voice of America broadcasts for use in his lessons, he was hauled before the student body, with Spiru and the sarcastic department head, Herr Simon, as the two Torquemadas. The charge about the Voice of America tape was weak; as with Nixon, "someone had erased it." They quoted his "politically shaky" comments, including a criticism of Mao Zedong, then an official hero, mentioned some old pregnancy, and said he had registered classes he had not given, an unfair charge, we knew. The caustic Simon, and Spiru, sounding like those Soviet prosecutors in the 1930s, alternated the attack. Dorschan was given a brief, hopeless chance at rebuttal. No one, including me, dared protest the witch-hunt atmosphere or the decision demanding his resignation. Dorschan maintained his dignity but instead of seeking "rehabilitation," usually a factory job, he got on a Berlin subway headed westward; the GDR lost a good teacher. Before he left I apologized for my silence; he said he understood.

This episode caused me more nightmares than anything but my own flight eastward. A year later the righteous Simon also went west.

I felt forced to make comparisons with the United States, where Communists were imprisoned, and thousands, including many teachers, lost their jobs. I had feared to speak my mind in Buffalo; even at Harvard fear had been growing. The Rosenbergs, I was sure, were executed for their views. Here, the authorities insisted that these inquisitions were defense of the common people's interests and a response to attempts to undermine the GDR. I remained convinced that the goal here was socialism and resistance to forces that had toppled a popular government in Guatemala to aggrandize United Fruit and overthrew Mossadegh in Iran to protect oil interests. Such events kept me from abandoning my beliefs. But I hated the methods used against Dorschan.

America was always on my mind. *Salt of the Earth,* made under constant attack by blacklisted Hollywood artists, was now in GDR theaters. I watched this story of a New Mexico copper strike winning against odds, thanks to the unity of Mexican and Anglo miners and their wives who, after an injunction, walked the picket line while their husbands overcame macho prejudices and cared for the kids. That was my country. A Paul Robeson film brought back memories of Peekskill and rekindled awareness of his courage, his music, his words about socialism. That magnificent voice from home also boosted my pride and morale.

Back home, Rosa Parks refused to give up a segregated seat in Montgomery, Alabama, and a new young pastor helped galvanize an entire black community to walk rather than ride Jim Crow buses. The Supreme Court struck down segregated schools, and in Little Rock the heroes were high school kids who braved mobs to integrate the school. I looked with growing hope at my homeland, where the civil rights movement was emerging and the McCarthyite nightmare, though not as dead as its namesake, was receding. The little Sputnik alarmed some Americans but made many view the USSR as a land capable of great things. At the same time, the Soviet "thaw" brought a spate of honest films. These developments softened the shock felt about Stalin and Hungarian events.

On an October Sunday in 1957, the radio carried an urgent announcement of a sudden currency exchange; new bills would be given out for paper currency — up to 300 marks outright, the remainder in a week. Amazingly, it worked, in one exciting day. Three groups suffered: Western espionage units holding huge sums of GDR money, West Berlin operatives who exchanged money taken illegally out of the GDR, and GDR citizens with large caches they could not account for. All day West Berliners tried to cross the temporarily sealed borders to smuggle money back into the GDR, while GDR smugglers scurried to trade funds inconspicuously before they became worthless. Some, fearful of questioning, tearfully burned piles of currency. Many in the GDR found pride that this giant, complex action had not leaked to the West, where so many were caught by surprise.

In those years throngs of foreign businessmen visited the Leipzig Trade Fair to connect or deal with the East. Leipzigers earned extra cash servicing visitors; I worked as an interpreter and met a variety of people — a porcelain dealer from New York who sought to make me his agent, a genteel Indian vegetarian who enjoyed the stares at his native dress, an Icelander, a first-time visitor to "the East," who wanted to gaze upon a Russian soldier. They were rare in the cities, but at last I spotted a short lieutenant. The Icelander stared and asked, "Are they all so small?"

After one fair I toured as translator with the Sudanese minister of trade. In Dresden a class of fourth graders crowded around to see "a real Negro." To end an embarrassing moment, I said that if they kept staring we would charge admission. They misunderstood, and thinking this African needed solidarity, tried to give him their small change and apples from their lunch bags. Happily, this wise and gentle man was amused.

For Paul Robeson's sixtieth birthday the central radio station accepted my offer of a musical program. A visit to East Berlin was attractive, but I had heard reports, some credible, that ex-GIs had been forcibly abducted to West Berlin. Whenever I neared the open border I peered over my shoulder — and when a barber, hearing my accent, asked nosily whether to address me as Mister, I shut up and left as fast as I could.

I met Bea Johnson, deported to Poland as an "alien Communist" under the McCarran act, but settling in Berlin as *Daily Worker* correspondent. She led me to David, the son of Stefan Heym's American wife, who worked as a chemist near Leipzig. David and I became friends, providing a fleeting touch of home and allowing me to occasionally speak "American." In Berlin, I also met Werner Händler, who had fled from the Nazis to England and for whom I taped some reports from the Leipzig area for his new English broadcasts. That required return trips to Berlin, where he introduced me to Brecht's renowned Berliner Ensemble. I saw a riotous

Playboy of the Western World, and from then on, whenever in Berlin, I made a beeline there, often sitting in the highest balcony seat of the rococo theater to see the thrilling *Three-Penny Opera* or *Galilei,* the outcry against the misuse of science, or the classic *Mother Courage* with Brecht's wife Helene Weigel in the title role. Some critics griped that the title figure never got the antiwar message. But the audience did. Typical of Brecht, each scene's contents were announced on signs and songs were sung at the audience — devices aimed at getting people to think, not just react emotionally.

In early 1956 Brigitte Klump, a beautiful blond student who had worked briefly at the Berliner Ensemble, offered to take interested students to see a play there and then meet with Brecht. But a day before departure we read on the blackboard: "The Berlin trip is canceled for technical reasons." Despite his quip that the "government should try to find a new population worthy of it" Brecht, always devoted to socialism, stood by the GDR stalwartly during the 1953 uprising. But he never concealed his abhorrence of hypocrites and idiots. It was thanks to just such idiots, no doubt, that the trip was canceled, a great pity, since Brecht died a few months later. Brigitte was soured forever; she left the GDR and became an ardent campaigner against it.

East Berlin had an ample cultural life with the great Comic Opera, the State Opera, and the Deutsches Theater. But swarms of GDR people were drawn to West Berlin by films like *Bridge over the River Kwai* or *On the Waterfront,* by existentialist plays, or by an increasingly wild nightlife. Western attractions at my college were taboo and less obvious, but present nonetheless. I rarely reacted with the anticipated joy when asked about some shoddy U.S. cultural fad. The answer to this politically potent allure, I felt, was not useless taboos, but cultural efforts reaching beyond fans of opera or Brecht, and borrowing, as the United States had done, from the vibrant cultures of Europe, Africa, Asia, and the Americas.

The rapidly growing foreign student body might have helped in this area. Renate and I were enriched by our friendships with foreign students including Nigerians, among them Tunda, a brilliant medical student whose chubby face graced many GDR magazine covers, or the fine, intelligent Iranian refugees from the shah's terror. The gentle, modest Vietnamese also became friends, while the Chinese, after large numbers arrived, often isolated themselves and were harder to get to know.

There were problems. Syrian students, no longer sent by leftist groups but by their government, were wealthier and very critical of the GDR: the prevalence of pork, room sharing, courses in Marxism, even the drinking water. A professor was assigned to make needed changes and provide for airing complaints. For the 1957 May Day parade a Syrian group decorated a float to protest the Suez invasion with an anti-Semitic caricature of a "Jewish tailor" representing Israel. At an Arab meeting my friend Moussa, a Lebanese Communist, and other leftists, argued half the night against this but were outvoted. It took an order by parade directors to remove the figure. Years later I heard that Moussa died during the fighting in Beirut.

In 1957 my *Praktikum* was with a multilingual magazine in Dresden, where I marveled at the superhuman efforts that had been made to rebuild the downtown area. One summer evening as I was strolling with my roommate, we were drawn to a brass quintet playing movingly under a big oak. A pastor then spoke; pointing to a half-moon, he said dramatically that we know the moon is round, though we do not see it: "We have faith. So too, with the Lord." The church youth group then discussed its deeply controversial visits to West Germany. GDR relations with the church were very strained at the time. The pastor asked what we wanted, suspicious of my accent. We left without a quarrel, wondering why pro-GDR groups couldn't present their views in equally moving ways.

In Dresden I visited two Jewish antifascists who emigrated during the Nazi years, the husband a Spanish War veteran. Now, rapidly and profitably, they translated the magazine I worked on into English. When I questioned their sarcastic tone in political matters they told me about Walter Janka, another Spanish Civil War vet imprisoned because of an alleged anti-GDR plot. The story of Janka was disturbing, and media reports of such cases were opaque. I heard little more about it for years and pushed it to the back of my mind. Unable to affect such things, I did my work, hoping that the society's road, despite deep fissures, was toward a higher humanity and justice.

Now that it was possible to take courses in other departments, some of us attended candid, knowledgeable current events lectures at the law school or those by a West German historian, Josef Schleifstein, who detailed the dramatic stories of the Italian, Chinese, French, and Polish Communist Parties. Many of us eagerly read Stefan Heym's *Berliner Zeitung* columns, so lacking in "bagu" clichés and empty polemics. Those bursts of fresh air often cost fights with his editors. When we invited him to speak at our college, however, he displayed surprising arrogance, scolding nastily when a misunderstanding had him waiting a few minutes at the station. But then he gave an incisive, thought-provoking talk.

I worried often about GDR problems, like opportunists and careerists who joined the SED for personal gain. With partial tongue-in-cheek I proposed that, after a set date, party members would receive no privileges and less pay than others in the same job. Whoever wished could quit; only those ready to sacrifice would be welcome. My ideas earned only patronizing smiles.

In my final year a campaign with some moral pressure opened to win all journalism students to the SED, exempting only those in other parties constituting the unified National Front — and me. But I too was convinced. I found two sponsors and tackled the questionnaire: previous jobs; relatives abroad; had I been in Hitler's army, the SS, or the Nazi Party, or positively, in the antifascist resistance, exile, or prison? Problems arose. My tutor heard that I had a few reservations. I told him and the party group that we were not supposed to listen to Western radio, but I wanted to listen to the Armed Forces Network. "You know better than most what poison Western radio spreads to disrupt and slander us," the tutor said. Yes, I replied, but artfully raised a GDR sacred cow — folk music — declaring that only AFN played my homeland's traditional music. The party group agreed that this need be no hindrance. I added that while I grasped the need for discipline, with all having a voice in decisions but abiding by them once they were made lest nothing get done, I could not abdicate the right to think for myself. My tutor asked if I was questioning the collective judgment of experienced Marxist leaders, able to assess factors far better than any individual. Could I be more correct than they were? No, I answered. I only insisted on my personal right to draw my own conclusions, right or wrong. I was responsible to myself even when following collective decisions. No one agreed.

The tutor suggested that I withdraw my application with no prejudice; perhaps I would reapply after settling into a new job. But despite a few invitations in later years, I let things stand. I sometimes felt guilty about not joining the most important organization whose goals of building the GDR and socialism I supported. But I saved myself a lot of stress.

Was it pressures I had witnessed which caused people to "take off for the

West," in a constant hemorrhaging of East Germany? Or was it the dream of making it in the wealthy West, a dream nurtured by Western radio and West Berlin itself, into which billions were poured to create a garish showplace. Both played a role, while the ideological stress achieved the very opposite of its presumed goals. Our college had fewer losses than most; the students were more faithful, and Western firms had less interest in luring leftist journalists than in snagging engineers, scientists, or doctors. But our unpleasant, haranguing administrator "took a powder," as did two of our group, as well as the censured Dorschan and the censuring Simon.

Despite doubts and problems, in 1958 we were occupied with exams, theses, plans, and hopes for the future. My thesis aimed at rousing interest in newspaper columns, which except for Heym's were almost nonexistent at the time. To make the idea digestible, I analyzed a year's columns in the *Daily Worker* on world affairs, sports, humor, and other areas. I ignored the dean's advice and omitted a "class analysis" (I never did find a class angle), but perhaps I contributed toward a slow growth in the genre.

At last I finished my eighth college year—without even a master's degree. I had experienced or heard of nasty events, but they were not restricted to the GDR; indeed, one Harvard comrade had been thrown out of a university and jailed for defying the Un-American Activities Committee. And I recalled that Harvard had sometimes been a lonely place. Despite unhappy episodes, the Leipzig years had not been bad; I had done more laughing than weeping, learned a lot, especially about Germany past and present, and had made many friends. But I was sick of schooling and wanted to see what I could accomplish in the world, or at least this East German corner of it. Harvard, though stimulating, had not prepared me for a job or profession. Here, though my experience was thin, I was certified officially as a journalist, and diplomas were important documents in Germany, East or West.

Renate, two-year-old Tommy, and I vacationed in "Saxon Switzerland," the beautiful area where we had honeymooned. All went well except that Tommy, usually charming and clever, could not adjust and terrorized the dining room. One day he threw a pebble from a terrace which bounced near a startled nun. She could not see little Thomas, but looked at me with the suffering, defiant mien of Saint Barbara, as if to say: "Now you atheists are even stoning us."

I was called to Berlin to discuss a job. I had hoped to work at radio, at the news agency, or at the multilingual magazine in Dresden, but found myself face to face with my friend David's mother, Heym's wife, who wanted me for her English-language publishing venture, Seven Seas Books. I wasn't interested. But what Gertrude wanted she got. I had mixed feelings as I moved to Berlin.

The author (right) with his brother Walt and parents Mitchell and Judith at Free Acres (near Berkeley Heights), New Jersey, c. 1931.

The author with his parents in Karlsruhe, Germany, 1947.

The author's Harvard College yearbook photograph, 1949.

U.S. Army induction company, Fort Devens, Massachusetts, January 1951.
The author is fourth from left in the top row.
The African Americans were later separated from the group.

The author (right) with an English coworker at the clubhouse for foreign ex-soldiers, Bautzen, East Germany, 1953.

The author with his fiancée Renate just before their wedding, Baruth, East Germany, August 1955.

The author lecturing on American folk music at a Sorb Club, Bautzen, East Germany, 1960s.

The author interpreting for Jane Fonda at the International Documentary Film Week, Leipzig, East Germany, 1974. Photograph by Elke Thionke, used with permission.

The author speaking at an Annual Journalists Solidarity Day, East Berlin, 1980s.

*The author on his sixty-fifth birthday with his sons Thomas (left) and Timothy,
Alexanderplatz, Berlin, 1993.*

*The author and his wife Renate in New Mexico
on their first trip to the United States, 1994.*

The author near his home on Karl Marx Allee, Berlin, 1995.

[8]

JOURNALIST IN A DIVIDED CITY

One Saturday afternoon I waited for a crowded train to depart for Leipzig after the obligatory customs check between East Berlin and the rest of the GDR. Nervous passengers hoped the uniformed men would not examine their suitcases, many of which looked suspiciously full. Before the Wall, visitors to East Berlin from all over the GDR nearly always went to West Berlin to buy "better" coffee, cocoa, and whatever was then faddish, to bring home to families or workmates. If customs found such items they could be confiscated. But the officers, concentrating on ferreting out professionals, made only spot checks with few victims. Standing in a full train I was in a bad mood, but smiled to see a kind of purchase impossible to hide in a suitcase — hula hoops. People held them out of windows; customs "overlooked" them. After the Wall was built in 1961 customs checks at borders between the GDR and its own capital were ended.

In 1958, travel between East and West Berlin was still simple. There were spot checks at borders, but their targets were not Western goods brought by Easterners but GDR goods smuggled to the West. Every subway or elevated train waited at the last stop before West Berlin until the customs men walked through, sometimes summoning passengers to the customs room for a check of luggage or clothing.

Tens of thousands of East Berliners worked in West Berlin at well below that sector's average pay. But since each West-mark could be exchanged in West Berlin for four or five East-marks, an untrained Eastern domestic working in West Berlin, by changing her West- for East-marks, could make more than a GDR college graduate. All this was extremely lucrative for such East Berliners and their Western employers. This profit was augmented by smuggling GDR sausage, butter, or eggs and selling them at well below West Berlin prices, but for West-marks. A 10 East-mark sausage could be sold "on the other side" for 5 West-marks, which were then traded for 20 to 25 East-marks — with the CIA-run RIAS broadcasting exchange rates daily and facilitating the prosperity of "frontier-crossers." Many an East Berlin housewife got caught with sausages or packs of butter hidden under a coat or dress. Far more serious was smuggling of GDR cameras, binoculars, or Meissen (Dresden) china.

Two unequal currencies in one city led to constant drainage of East products and escalating annoyances. Every purchase in East Berlin, even ice cream, required the buyer to show an Eastern ID, affirming that a "Wessie" was not using the exchange rate to live cheaply at GDR expense. Only books, records, theater tickets, and barber-type services were exempt. Largely unknown to the outside world, this was a major source of East-West conflict in Berlin.

I fearfully avoided West Berlin and only gradually got used to this crazy city with its open, zigzag borders dividing hostile worlds. On weekends I visited my wife and son in more normal Leipzig and Sunday evenings returned to my little room in East Berlin's outskirts. Seven Seas Books was on legendary Friedrichstrasse where I worked with two bright, sarcastic young fellows who taught me to compare texts with the original by reading aloud with lip noises for punctuation. They enjoyed slyly quoting Heym's wife saying that he was "the greatest living writer."

Despite many odds, Gertrude, with courage and competence, provided a good service. Besides promoting Heym and publishing classics requiring no royalties, Seven Seas printed writers shunned at home: Albert Maltz, Meridel LeSueur, Du Bois, Ring Lardner, Jr. Most books went to English readers in the GDR and Eastern Europe, but also got to Western countries, bringing some income and audience to the authors. Though as politically committed as Heym, Gertrude mistrusted all Germans except close friends, a feeling extending to the language and the two men with whom I worked. She was sure that they were anti-GDR and anti-Socialist. But they were less hostile than cynical, like many young intellectuals; I defended them mildly, which bothered her. Our relations grew frostier whenever I disagreed. By December we hardly spoke to each other. When I heard that the assistant editor of the *Democratic German Report* had taken another job, I hastened to its British editor and asked to work there. I started in January 1959.

John Peet had moved east a year before me and had a two-room office in an old walk-up building on Friedrichstrasse. This tall, spare Briton with a Quaker background was wounded in Spain in 1938, worked for Jerusalem Radio during the war, and was Reuters correspondent in postwar Vienna, Warsaw, and West Berlin. His bi-weekly eight-page newsletter, sent to readers in English-speaking countries, including many journalists and all British Labour MPs, was well written and informative. It was pro-GDR and critical of West German policies, but never preachy or obtusely polemical, preferring good-natured, even ironic reports on the GDR to the usual blather. He never spared his blue pencil with me, slashing clichés or badly written sentences. He might scrawl "ND style" across a page — the jargon of the official party paper *Neues Deutschland*. We never became friendly, or even used first names, but he taught me more about the trade than I had learned in my years at Leipzig. He should have headed a major newspaper, but this cool Englishman's nationality and perhaps his skepticism made that impossible. Peet supported the GDR but, like so many, was critical of its leaders — more forcefully than my fuzzy doubts would allow. He also knew more about the prewar left and the rise of fascism than anyone else I ever met, could read magazines and newspapers at breakneck speed, and condense or translate articles faster, I was sure, than anyone else in Europe. During the June 17, 1953, uprising, while many hid their red flags, literally and figuratively, Peet hung one defiantly onto Friedrichstrasse. Some from the crowd ran up, grappled with him, and burned it. Peet came from home with another flag under his jacket and hung it out again.

In 1959–60 there was still plenty of cold war tension, some of it almost comical. Once I saw a West Berlin sound truck pull up to the border and blare denunciations of the GDR. Soon a GDR truck raced up and blasted music at the other truck, which sped away to a new site. Just inside West Berlin a tower displayed a news zipper in rotating lights offering all the anticommunist news RIAS could dig up. On one corner you could also see the opposite news, offered by the GDR, rotating around Friedrichstrasse station. On the subways, some West Berlin trains stopped at a few East Berlin stations where West passengers rubbed shoulders with East Berliners; the "Wessies" read papers about hunger in the East while "Ossies" read about joblessness and Nazis in the West. Such was life in divided Berlin.

In April 1960, while the Eisenhower-Khrushchev summit was collapsing over the downed U-2 spy plane, the GDR was preoccupied with an agricultural revolution. About 40 percent of the farms had joined cooperatives or "LPGs," and a campaign was launched to complete collectivization. In view of stinging West German commentaries on its involuntary nature, the Foreign Ministry invited foreign reporters to see for themselves. Peet hated travel, so I went. While I was walking through a field with another reporter, a red-faced farmer came up and insisted that the campaign was based on "pure terror." But in Mecklenburg, once Germany's rural poorhouse, we met farmers who spoke differently. A young farm wife told how she and 106 others learned how to set up cooperatives when invited to a brief course, where for the first time since her honeymoon she had a break from drudgery and her first visit to the nearby sea shore. She returned with such enthusiasm that she won over her husband. Tiny, separate fields made big combines inefficient; without an LPG vacations and shorter hours were unthinkable. When the most successful, respected farmer in the village finally joined, 68 others followed, pooling their strips of land and electing an executive committee, including the woman telling us the story.

Ten refused. Her husband said that they were like horses frightened at the sight of a repainted barn. That is when moral and material pressures were exerted; stayouts could not expect the same credit conditions, high crop prices, and low rent for tractors and equipment that farmers had had up to the transition to cooperatives. That usually sufficed, but rougher tactics were used by local officials eager to report 100 percent success, like loudspeakers blaring away at recalcitrant farmers. That was the red-faced farmer's "terror." Some left bitterly for West Germany; some formed paper cooperatives to satisfy higher-ups while continuing to farm privately — for a while. That year's harvest was poor owing to turmoil and drought. In West Germany the drought bankrupted countless families, forcing them to abandon farms. The GDR was hit by shortages, but the farms were given help, no one was bankrupted, and within a few years farmers were so accustomed to working together that nagging problems and blunders did not make them wish to return to private farming. After the GDR's demise, it took as much pressure to get farmers to break up collectives as it had to get them to join. Perhaps the LPGs were not as productive as Western agribusiness, but they yielded big harvests and no one was forced off the land. Despite the early strong-arming, I believed this was a humane solution to time-worn farm problems.

During my *German Report* years, I traveled a lot to cover the GDR. In March 1961 I visited the plant in Zwickau where stubby little Trabant cars were made. When I asked to talk to "a typical worker," the foreman steered me to a woman leader of the Metalworkers Union; "Aha," I thought, and asked to pick someone at random. I chatted with a smiling man in the upholstery department and learned that he was a devout Baptist, uncommon in this land of Lutherans, Catholics, and atheists. I was brazenly nosy but tried to be totally honest. He told of his four coats, three suits, and his wife's three coats and said that his two daughters went to summer camp for 18 marks, but that the family only took a vacation trip every five years. His heart ailment had landed him twice in a sanatorium in the past six years, a month each time, free of charge and with 90 percent sick pay. Since his wife didn't work, his budget was tight. I wrote that income was not high but improving, that health and education costs were fully covered, and that workers laughed at the idea of losing jobs; the incredible waiting list for Trabants never shortened.

Two months later a London bus driver, his young daughter, and pregnant wife turned up in our office. After reading my article, he had quit his job and headed for the GDR. The pleasant, naive young man said he had only one suit and coat, and his wife added wistfully that they never had a vacation. Flabbergasted, I explained the difficult life, the shortages, and the inevitable language problems. Refusing to give up, they found a room in West Berlin and kept trying to immigrate. Later I got a friendly letter; the wife had become ill, their money ran out, and their consul sent them back to England.

Our little office was a useful stop for Western reporters; Art Buchwald became friends with Peet after Peet satirized his column on East Berlin; Anthony Lewis, Daniel Schorr, and the British journalist Sefton Delmer sought tips on GDR doings or on Nazi judges in West Germany. Peet always saved a few scoops for them. And we did our own exposés of Nazis on the loose in West Germany. A 1951 West German statute required that at least 20 percent of public jobs be given to "former employees." Over 150,000 Nazis swarmed back, protected by the anti-red sword that had rent the last shreds of anti-Nazism. Among a thousand ex-Nazis returned to the West German legal system was a Dr. Hallbauer, a former Storm Trooper and judge in Prague who had sentenced Czechs to death for listening to the BBC, trying to escape slave labor, or hiding food. After submerging briefly, he became a Hamburg judge. The Czechs, seeking justice, were told that Hallbauer's sentences were "juristically correct." In 1961, a local Würzburg judge, convicted as a war criminal in Norway, and the district attorney, accused of murders in Poland, were exposed by a Dr. Herterich. As a result, Herterich's house was searched for "Communist literature" and later stoned; he was sued for libel and tried before another ex-Nazi judge; his Jewish wife was told that "we forgot to gas you." When she was arrested for not promptly paying a small bill, they left Germany.

Many West Germans were prosecuted for ties to the outlawed Communist Party or the GDR; former Nazi judges often sentenced former anti-Nazis. When Peter Umland was sentenced for reprinting Soviet peace offers, the judge called him an "old offender" because he was a Nazi concentration camp inmate. He got three years. Five days earlier an ex-Gestapo officer had been convicted for the murder of 827 Jews and immediately paroled. In 1962 the Association of Victims of Nazis (VVN) was to be tried for being "anticonstitutional." Then it was revealed that the three trial judges had been Nazis, and one a Storm Trooper. Further checks found that of forty-nine judges in this third highest chamber, forty had been Nazis, some accused of murder. The British *New Statesman* said having ex-Nazis judge the VVN was "beyond belief."

Neither the police nor the armed forces were any different. Of 160 generals in October 1961, all but one had been a colonel or general in Hitler's Wehrmacht. One top general, Speidel, had deported Jews from Occupied France to Auschwitz. When he became a top NATO officer, *German Report* circulated the facts in Britain, inspiring protests when he visited. Our reporting also had an impact on the British Foreign Office, which pressed Bonn to retire sixty or seventy of the worst murderers among its judges. Our *Report* also published a map with a swastika at every capital from London to Bangkok to Washington where Bonn's ambassador had been a Nazi or a Storm Trooper. Some had been implicated in mass deportations and other crimes. Headlined "The Plague," it was reprinted in newspapers in over twenty countries. The West German press was silent until *Der Spiegel* mentioned the map. A Christian Democratic paper, *Christ und Welt,* then accused our "obscure and clumsy propaganda sheet" of spreading hate against the Federal Republic. We were flattered by the attention, noting that *Christ und Welt* didn't deny the charges. Its editor had been an SS captain and Nazi propagandist. Our exposés were not basely motivated. We were alarmed that so many Nazis who rarely forswore past views dominated a country which was creating a strong army and becoming a pivotal force in

NATO, and whose leading politicians were claiming "lost territories" well beyond the GDR. Of twenty powerful state secretaries, at least thirteen held posts in Nazi Germany and engaged in such crimes as deporting Jews to death camps; one administered the gold and clothes taken from twenty-eight thousand murdered Jews in Latvia; another, Hans Globke, provided the legal basis for the notorious anti-Semitic Nuremberg laws and was deeply implicated in the Holocaust. We agreed sorrowfully with the philosopher Karl Jaspers, no leftist, that this resurfaced Nazi presence was "a fundamental ailment in the Federal Republic's inner constitution."

In 1960 the particularly murderous cabinet minister Theodor Oberländer was sentenced in absentia in East Berlin to life imprisonment. Western media ignored or ridiculed the trial, but Oberländer had to resign a week later, possibly in part because of *German Report*'s influence in Britain. In July 1963 it was Globke's turn. Though he was shown to be one of the worst "swivel-chair murderers," his trial was also played down; indeed, while it went on Globke testified in West Germany as a "character witness" for four SS men charged with killing Jews. But ten weeks later he was finally retired. It was becoming harder to ignore charges emanating from East Germany.

Democratic German Report's exposés created such dismay that Bonn launched an insipid counterbulletin and assigned an anti-GDR organization to prove that the GDR power structure was also riddled with Nazis, and Western media picked this up with relish. But Peet found that the pitiful harvest of 150 were largely unknown men in unimportant jobs. Thirty-five were in local or village councils (out of 80,000). A few held higher positions of no real political importance: a professor of botany, a theologian, a theater director. Some former Nazis were officers who had taken outspoken anti-Nazi positions as prisoners-of-war in the USSR, which required great courage since it was labeled as treachery by their fellow-officers. Such active opposition to Hitler during the war years was considered full atonement. Nazi Party members who went along with Hitler but committed no crimes were excluded from work in courts, police, schools, or administration; the second-class citizen category was relaxed after 1949, but they were kept out of these fields. One single man of importance, an agricultural leader, was indeed exposed — and immediately dropped. Some undoubtedly slipped through, but the list was a nasty deception; the GDR diplomatic corps, senior officer corps, government, and party leadership consisted almost entirely of people who opposed the Nazis, in Germany or in exile. The British *Guardian* pointed out that "the East Germans have done more to eradicate Nazism than has West Germany," and that as victims of Nazi persecution the Communist leaders in the East felt genuinely distant from what Germany did in the name of Nazism.

Most disturbing to me was the return of cartels and monopolies that built up Hitler and made billions in World War II, worst of all the I. G. Farben chemical cartel, comprising Bayer, BASF, and Hoechst, which built the Monowitz factory at Auschwitz, working prisoners to death or killing them with its poison gas. When West Germany became a cold war partner, the few jailed managers were released and regained leadership; one almost got a Federal Cross of Merit before world protests forced cancellation. In 1945 the Kilgore subcommittee of the U.S. Senate reported that the giant combines had financed the Nazi Party, had become Germany's "principal war makers," and were "as responsible for war crimes as the German General Staff and the Nazi Party." It warned of their plans for the future. In the GDR such companies were confiscated, and most owners and managers fled. Top jobs were given to men like the Spanish International Brigade veterans and never, as in West Germany, to men of Hitler's Condor Legion, which had bombed Guernica. Streets, clubs, and schools were named after antifascist martyrs; the heads of theaters, the media, and publishing houses, like party leaders, were usually men and women who opposed the Nazis. Some, unhappily, were inept or dogmatic or misused power. But on comparing the two Germanys, I could see only one possible choice.

One day in 1960 a Canadian folksinger turned up to perform at our publishing firm. Perry Friedman, a big, bluff singer from Vancouver, sang many U.S. songs, bringing twinges of homesickness. When his interpreter stumbled over the lyrics, I offered to help, and was soon involved in a string of concerts, translating everything from "Froggy Went A-Courtin'" to "Joe Hill." Perry and I formed a good team, with my German mistakes getting laughs and encouraging an informal spirit. He decided to stay in Berlin, and in the process of performing met a great number of musicians and theater people. Some of us decided to try a Pete Seeger–style hootenanny. After a youth clubhouse director turned us down (it was all too new and strange for her), we appealed to Hans Modrow, then head of the East Berlin youth organization, who immediately said yes and wondered why we even had to ask. Thirty years later he was the last SED leader to head a

GDR government and, for a few months, one of the most respected and trusted persons in the country.

Three hundred people jammed the small hall to hear Perry, Lin Jaldati, a Dutch singer of Yiddish songs who had survived three concentration camps and was the last person to see Anne Frank alive, and Gisela May, a top actress at the Berliner Ensemble, who sang Brecht songs. Despite dire predictions about German reticence, the crowd was soon singing joyfully — from "Alouette" to the Brecht-Eisler "United Front" song ("So left, two, three . . . to the work that we must do") — including some leather-jacketed youth who came in expecting rock'n'roll. The word "hootenanny" even got into the dictionary. Inspired by that success, Perry and some of the singers continued with hootenannies in other parts of the GDR. I went along until my family joined me in Berlin and Perry no longer needed an interpreter. Later "hoots," run by people less accustomed to spontaneity rarely rose to the first event's level of enthusiasm, but some high school students caught the spirit and became the core of a new GDR "song movement."

As the sixties dawned, I became excited over the wave of student sit-ins at home and was reminded of our modest battles for equality at Harvard and Buffalo. I only wished that there were greater interest among GDR youth in sit-ins than in images of American affluence. While Kennedy's election did not make me euphoric, I was glad that Nixon was beaten.

I was finally able to get a Berlin apartment, ending my weekend commute. The three rooms, kitchen, and bath were tiny and far from downtown. Heating was by tiled oven, which I still had trouble igniting. A boiler shortage forced us to install a coal oven in the bathroom in the space for the sink. We could hear every cough or every flush of our neighbors' toilet. But it was all ours.

A year later I idly read a notice tacked on a tree. It offered three rooms plus kitchen and bath with central heating in a new building on Stalin Allee — in exchange for an apartment like ours. After the usual bureaucratic tangle, we moved happily into the top floor of our new building — roomier, more modern, centrally located — and heated. We still live there.

Shortly thereafter, an acquaintance from the GDR Peace Council invited me to join the San Francisco–Moscow Peace March, organized by longtime pacifist A. J. Muste, for the stretch through the GDR. Any decrease in world tension was needed, and any tie with my homeland would be cause for rejoicing. When I saw the name of a former Harvard comrade on the list of participants I was even more eager. John Peet gave me two days off and together with my folksinger friend Perry, we drove 120 miles to meet them at the border.

Many of the mainly American group of thirty-six actually walked from San Francisco to New York, with others from Britain, Belgium, and West Germany joining the European trek. They had been received icily at times, calling as they did for draft refusal and nonpayment of taxes for military spending. France refused entry even when a few marchers jumped into Calais harbor in protest. Now they were crossing the storied Iron Curtain. When the straggly group approached I ran to welcome them and, quickly spotting my old Harvard comrade, called out, "Solly, Solly!" He didn't recognize me despite knowing me well years ago. I feared explaining who I was because of my name change, unknown in the GDR. Solly was now a pacifist and an ardent Zionist. Did he fear revealing to fellow marchers that he was a former Communist with an East German friend? We both kept our distance.

Unfortunately, distrust was mirrored in the whole encounter. The group handed pacifist leaflets to as many GDR and Soviet soldiers as it could find. GDR authorities routed it through country roads and small towns. This sparked conflict, as did the authorities' insistence that the group set foot first in the GDR's capital, East Berlin, then go to West Berlin, if it wanted to. The marchers wished to trek directly from West Berlin through the Brandenburg Gate to East Berlin and on to Poland. It seemed petty to me — but not to those involved. Some GDR marchers did not help matters. A Quaker family from Dresden made no secret of its hostility to the GDR. About a dozen young male "peace enthusiasts" also marched, so obviously acting as guards that it was embarrassing. A few even wore army boots.

I tried to overcome the marchers' prejudices, seeking to balance the shabbiness of many villages by pointing out new day care centers, libraries, clinics, and schools. Deeply sympathetic with their motives, but contesting the staunch anticommunists, I nevertheless became friendly with a range of marchers. Among them was Reggie Fischer, a devoted peace advocate who spoke German, was a nurse who ministered to blisters, cuts, and bruises, and was chess champion Bobby Fischer's mother. Despite pride in her son, she acknowledged his legendary arrogance (he arrived in Moscow at fourteen, demanding to play world champion Mikhail Botvinnik) and felt that most chess champions were self-seeking and a bit crazy.

After two days with the marchers, I left them to plod on without me. Later I learned of trouble; the authorities had insisted they bypass Berlin altogether. All but Reggie Fischer and two others refused — and were carried onto a bus headed to the West German border. A compromise finally got them to the Polish border by bus. The explanation came soon; by weird coincidence, the day they were to march into Berlin, handing out antimilitary leaflets, was the very edgy, precarious day that the Wall went up. In the end the group reached Moscow and demonstrated in Red Square. Reggie Fischer married a British plumber, Cyril Pustan, who drove the luggage truck. Though over forty, Reggie went to medical school in the GDR and remained active as pediatrician and peacenik. Cyril joined her, working in various jobs until his death.

On a sunny August Sunday, our family heard the news about the Wall while at the East Berlin Zoo gazing at gibbons and okapi. I was neither surprised nor shaken — which turned out to be a great misjudgment. The move had long been gestating; tension had grown swiftly all year. Kennedy promised more intellect than Eisenhower, but did not promise more peace. An uneasy summit meeting in Vienna had followed the CIA-aided murder of Congolese leader Patrice Lumumba and the abortive Bay of Pigs Cuban invasion. After the meeting Khrushchev stepped up demands for a German peace conference and treaty establishing GDR sovereignty and making West Berlin neutral and independent. The Soviets and the East Germans saw this as a way to end pressure on the GDR and reduce the danger of conflict over West Berlin. But Bonn called it a threat to West Berlin's freedom and refused to discuss a treaty or recognize the GDR in any form. Khrushchev said he was not issuing threats, but the USSR, GDR, and others would, if necessary, sign a treaty, just as Washington did in consummating a U.S.-Japanese treaty without the Soviets.

Such a compact would mean GDR control of access between West Berlin and West Germany (which was agreed upon in 1970). Many in the GDR, panicked by Western media and fearing sealed borders, fled the country. Stores began to close for lack of personnel; some factories were immobilized by departures. Though most people went on with their lives, there was a foreboding mood. At stations on the route to Potsdam I watched security men checking people, presumably to hinder them from leaving the country. Others, with hand luggage, tearfully kissing relatives and surely heading west, were not questioned. I never knew why, but I did believe the GDR was unraveling. As with the 1957 currency change, closing of borders seemed inevitable.

With no relatives in West Germany, with no urge to cross over, and with constant if decreasing fear of being spirited across an open border, I was not alarmed by a stable frontier. But thousands of East Berliners, visiting the West as usual, faced the choice of going home or staying where they were. Other thousands wondered whether to race across to West Berlin while gaps in the frontier still existed. These were fateful decisions in many lives. As for me, while the Wall went up and people were deciding, I watched gibbons and okapi.

The next day I got a tongue-lashing from John Peet, who demanded to know why I hadn't reported in to help with a special edition. I had no adequate answer, only my involvement with family without grasping the seriousness of the situation. That cooled my chilly relationship with Peet even further. Though few imagined that the Wall would stand for decades, many GDR people with relatives in the West were desperate. My brother-in-law Werner's sister had married a West Berliner years before; Werner only saw her again years later in Czechoslovakia, a new meeting-place for Germans. Foreigners and West Germans were soon able to visit the GDR, but since West Berlin would not recognize East Berlin authorities, West Berliners could not visit until Christmas 1963, after long, complicated negotiations and a slight thaw in relations.

Like Helmut Kohl twenty-eight years later, Adenauer and his government had been striving for the collapse of the still unrecognized GDR. Berlin's open frontier was a key element: in 1950 the mayor of West Berlin said it must be "a thorn in the flesh" of the GDR. Now with that ambition stymied, Bonn stressed its deep humanitarian concerns, encouraging people to cross under, over, or through the Wall, risking or losing their lives — but creating headlines, tears, and sympathy. Countless tragedies did occur, but for Adenauer's government, with ex-Nazis at all levels, tears and anger were pure hypocrisy. Theirs was the fury of a carnivore losing its prey. But Bonn won the media battle hands down.

GDR leaders (and their Soviet backers) claimed that if the GDR went under, West Germany with its many pro-Nazis would press demands for the return of "lost territories" and would rupture the delicate postwar stalemate which had survived as long as no one rocked boats. Germany was the biggest boat of all, and the GDR insisted the Wall was necessary to save peace and the lives of millions. It also enabled the GDR economy to stanch losses in smuggled goods and the more serious hemorrhaging of skilled labor and professionals who received GDR tuition-free scholarships for years, then left for jobs in the West.

Stories have circulated for years that Washington knew of plans for the Wall beforehand. It made strong, shocked noises but did little else until late October, when U.S. soldiers with fixed bayonets rushed across the border at what was becoming known as Checkpoint Charlie, presumably to rescue U.S. military men in civilian clothes who refused to show their documents to GDR controllers. U.S. tanks moved to within an inch of the border. From our office balcony I looked right into the dark muzzles. Suddenly I heard a loud clanking; Soviet tanks lumbered around a nearby corner and moved down Friedrichstrasse till they nearly touched the muzzles across the line. One spark could have started World War III, with us in the first line of fire. As usual under such circumstances we joked nervously. Then tensions eased and the tanks withdrew.

The GDR media, trying ceaselessly to justify the Wall, had more success in other parts of the GDR, where East Berliners were always envied for their easy access to the West. For many in East Berlin, a way of life was sundered; not only did they lose contact with relatives but they lost access to Western amenities and entertainment. East Berliners and many others felt locked in. The matter became far worse when escapees were killed — with, at times, border guards also dying.

Cruel and summary actions occurred for evident reasons, though the authorities never uttered them: all successful escape routes had to be closed to prevent repetition and copying. This meant stopping people floating along the coast in sailboats or on air mattresses, cutting holidays in Yugoslavia, ferry trips to Sweden, or Mediterranean cruises, and checking Western cars for concealed escapees. A noxious competition developed between the authorities and people who gambled on leaving, and with it a new industry in West Berlin: "escape assistants," who demanded large sums to smuggle people out. The would-be escapees varied greatly: criminals and ne'er-do-wells, youths who chafed at prescribed school and job paths, political or religious dissenters, and those who dreamed of freedom or success in the West. Aside from those concealed in cars or jumping barriers, some artists, scientists, and athletes used visits to Western events to defect. Most with such opportunities did not seize them, but enough did to affect the entire consciousness of the GDR. West Germany publicized every case and offered jobs and homes to those who bolted, far more than ordinary West Germans received. Especially favored were those who embellished or invented stories of repression, or who provided leads to new targets for blackmail or enticement. Sensational escapes were widely publicized in Western media. Some were obviously coordinated by West Germans with easy access to East Berlin, and often occurred just before GDR anniversaries or similar events, intended to upstage them.

I estimated that 10–15 percent of the population passionately defended the GDR and socialism, especially those who had resisted the Nazis. About 10–15 percent, I guessed, were passionately opposed, dreaming of reunification and an end to the socialist experiment. The views of the remaining 70–80 percent were mixed. Many envied relatives "over there," with unlimited consumer goods and unrestricted travel. But they tended to accept the GDR as home, if only because destiny had placed them here. When they got a raise, a new apartment, or a new car they felt more positive; when they fought with their boss, or couldn't find a flat, or if things just went bad, they cursed the party and the system. In the GDR, blame could not be scattered, U.S.-style, among politicians, races, or genders. Here responsibility was centralized and easily located. Many simply said "Damned GDR," or "Damned socialism." But this vacillating middle group also knew, though it rarely said so, that the GDR social system provided solid security. Free medical care, childcare, and education, guaranteed jobs, very cheap holidays, rents, and food staples were taken for granted. Deep down, however, many knew their value, and hardly yearned for enterprises to revert to private owners or for farm cooperatives to be redivided into small strips. Many endured the clichés and boring propaganda in order to advance in the hierarchy, get an award or a bonus, or simply be left alone.

In general people visited friends, attended concerts, cooked out at their summer "dachas," vacationed at a lake or the seaside, hoped to buy an occasional "Western" product, and led quite normal lives. Those who went to the West were viewed by some as lucky. Others saw them as renegades or fools beguiled by consumerism. There were countless tales of those who "made it" in the West—or fell to the bottom. Few returned; to do so was to admit personal failure and bad judgment.

Polls showed that in the seventies, well over half the population was more or less pro-GDR. Thus there was approval, fervent or opportunist, and much simple accommodation, plus an undercurrent of dissatisfaction whose extremes were all-out dissidence or "jumping the Wall." Top GDR leaders reacted with bragging or paranoia instead of the modesty, self-criticism, trust, and democratic dialogue that might have offered better chances of success. Many socialist partisans felt the Wall was sad but necessary and dreamed of the day it could be "sold to West Germany," as Stefan Heym put it. Dogmatists didn't give a damn. The majority felt the Wall should be removed and permission granted to anyone wishing to leave. But with the West's magnetic attraction and propaganda, the fears of a government lacking the qualities mentioned above were not unfounded; open frontiers could lead, as they nearly did in 1961, and finally did in 1989, to collapse. And I yearned for change to end both this threat and the tragedies.

The Wall did not diminish my fragile contacts with home. One day John Peet got a call asking if he knew an American named Steve Wechsler. He was about to say no when I shouted "That's me" to a nonplussed Peet. It was Katherine Blohm, the old devoted Communist from Free Acres, bringing news of events at home. There was also an exciting visit from Jack Royce, my charismatic high school friend who won me to the Young Communist League. Jack spoke good German and got along wonderfully with Renate, as with most women. He soon captivated Tommy, with whom he marched and sang, and whom he lifted to see Titov, the Soviet astronaut, being driven slowly through East Berlin. Jack was a successful psychotherapist, but divorced and unhappy. He had always been a symbol of success to me; now I measured that success in broader terms, and made comparisons with my own very different life.

At home I was soon getting acquainted with a new family member. Late on February 1, 1962, Renate decided it was time. In a clinic hit by the splitting of the city, with many former staff members in West Berlin, the treatment did not compare with the Leipzig facility. Renate was so angry she returned home. The next night we went back, and my accent, plus a word about being a journalist, did wonders. Renate got excellent care, with a doctor always present. Timothy had passed up Groundhog Day and looked a bit disheveled but soon became as adorable a curly-haired baby as his brother.

My mother had already visited us in Leipzig, without my father, who was already too ill to travel. Now she visited again, no longer with the old dress and frumpy hat she had worn so as "not to be conspicuous in the

East," disappointing Renate, who expected an elegant lady. She admired Timothy, but then asked me to accompany her to Czechoslovakia, Hungary, and Poland. I had not left the GDR since my arrival and quickly rationalized that I would be leaving the family only for a few weeks.

With Peet's help I got a special passport in only three days. Budapest, despite lingering signs of fighting six years earlier, was a handsome city with beautiful bridges connecting hilly Buda on one side of my broad Danube with flat, busy Pest on the other. I was impressed with piles of oranges on sale and an ample supply of opulent Western goods not found in the GDR. The items were expensive and the general living standards visibly lower than those of my adopted country, but people could savor the goods, perhaps save for a fancy outfit or at least dream of buying it. Was this wiser than in the GDR, where most people had money enough and income differences were relatively small, but quality goods rarer? Both systems had advantages and disadvantages, I decided. Budapest, with its attractions that ran from fine museums and opera to strip shows, seemed somehow relaxed with amazingly little bitterness about the events of 1956.

We found J. Peters, who told us of Hungarian developments with the honesty and frankness that marked his class in 1949 for those going into industry. We also visited Erszy Szekely, the widow of Janos Szekely (John Pen), author of the powerful autobiographical novel *Temptation*. He had died in Berlin, delayed on his way to Hungary by the 1956 uprising. His widow, whom I knew from Berlin, was a famous Hungarian actress who with her husband had fled the fascists before World War II. She introduced us to a pleasant young man who showed us around the city and later asked if we had seen a single party slogan or picture of Hungarian leader Janos Kadar. He knew that pictures of Ulbricht and slogans were legion in the GDR.

We spent a week in beautiful Prague, navigating the quaint, crooked streets, enjoying the theater life, visiting the ancient Jewish synagogue and cemetery, and seeing *Don Giovanni* in the theater where Mozart attended its premiere exactly 175 years earlier. But my mother tired and flew home, sending me alone on to Warsaw. The first evening I came upon a Jewish restaurant, and two jolly strangers joined me at my table. I was surprised they were not Jewish, but we chatted and they treated me to a drink. I ordered a bottle to reciprocate, and the waiter brought his best cognac, costing me almost all my expense money for the rest of my stay. The two men no longer seemed so jolly.

I visited the office of an anti-Nazi news bulletin, a sister of *Democratic German Report,* and was taken in tow by the editor, who spoke fluent German and English. The office was in the Palace of Culture skyscraper, a Soviet gift whose Stalinesque gingerbread architecture inspired the joke that the best view of Warsaw was from its observation roof—the only place where you couldn't see the Palace of Culture.

The extremely intelligent, though somewhat cynical editor was completely at one with me in despising the fascists who destroyed three million Polish Jews and three million Polish Catholics. He was enthusiastic about Wladyslaw Gomulka and Jozef Cyrankiewicz, who had regained power in 1956, showing me Gomulka's modest little house on an ordinary block with "only one guard." Gomulka rejected privileges, and when his daughter-in-law had to rush to the maternity ward he would not use his official car, insisting that she manage "like all Polish women."

Caught up in the editor's enthusiasm, and glad to hear that Gomulka's wife was Jewish and that Premier Cyrankiewicz had survived Auschwitz, I was a bit jealous about the rapport which seemed to exist between Polish leaders and their countrymen, as with Kadar in Hungary but much less in the GDR. This rapport did not last forever, however. And I found no pleasure in listening to a taxi driver who was both acrid and anti-Semitic, with a soft spot only for Britain, perhaps because the right-wing Polish government-in-exile had been there.

There was no mistaking the omnipresence of religion in Poland. I visited two Canadian Communists who were attending the party college. They had a souvenir totem pole in the window to remind them of home, but the janitor asked them to remove it because its silhouette formed a cross and most passers-by crossed themselves—in front of a party building, no less. They took me to see Fred Rose, a former Canadian MP who, accused in an early cold war spy case, was jailed for years. He now edited an English magazine about Poland. He complained acidly about noisy church processions constantly passing his apartment in beautifully restored Market Square. And this in a Communist country.

I looked up Dora, the Czech doctor and volunteer in the Spanish Civil War who had survived Auschwitz and whom I met on the ship to Europe in 1947. During the wave of repression connected with the execution of Rudolf Slansky and other Jewish antifascists in 1952, she was imprisoned, with barely time to leave her small child with a friend. After she was freed a year or two later, innocent but without compensation or a word of regret, she joined her husband in Warsaw. GDR doctors were among the most prosperous citizens; by contrast, Dora and her family lived in a small, shabby flat, faced a daily struggle with jammed buses to get to work — and were often ill. What happened to these two courageous, decent human beings did not make for a joyous reunion.

Once again I learned how dissimilar the countries of the "monolithic Eastern Bloc" really were. Poland seemed most contradictory. There was more freedom for divergent views in Warsaw than in the GDR, especially Roman Catholic or "pro-Western" ones. I saw two famous films by Wajda, highly controversial in their treatment of the past, some bold short films, and art work of a kind still largely taboo in the GDR. A wide assortment of Western paperbacks was on sale. Political leeway had been part of life since the 1956 antigovernment uprising and Gomulka's rule, but was also part of a national character formed in centuries of struggle against occupation by Orthodox Russians and Protestant Prussians, with the Catholic Church the main bastion. Independence was even displayed in ignoring traffic lights, so unlike Germany. Yes, there was more freedom in Warsaw. But somehow this freedom provided no uplift and seemed almost as dispiriting as restrictions in the GDR. What did freedom really mean? Must it necessarily be both liberation to think freely and to live without economic want? I wondered about the true meaning of freedom from new angles but drew no new conclusions. Perhaps it was homesickness, heightened by the flu, which made me glad to leave. I was bumped from my flight and had to take the long train trip back to Berlin and my very worried wife.

[9]

RADIO, ROBESON, &
THE PRAGUE SPRING

My days at *Democratic German Report* were ending. John Peet was critical of my slowness and perhaps distrusted me as an overly avid GDR booster, without noticing that I too had reservations. At a propitious moment in 1963, Oliver Harrington visited me. Ollie, with light-brown complexion and professorial sagacity, was widely known to readers of the African American press for his ironic cartoon character "Bootsie." Besides his fine work as cartoonist, he was public relations head of the NAACP after World War II. But when McCarthyite clouds thickened, he received a warning from a black friend in government intelligence and left for Paris's Left Bank, where he enjoyed a close friendship with the expatriate writer Richard Wright. Wright had quit the Communist Party but, in supporting colonial freedom movements, was moving leftward again. He died suddenly and mysteriously in 1960, perhaps a victim, Ollie thought, of hostile agents. Soon after, when U.S. pressure on France increased, Ollie moved to the GDR. Now he asked if I wished to work for Radio Berlin International. Glad of the chance, and greatly impressed by his charisma, I quickly said yes.

My first job was to translate GDR news supplied by the central office, add items from the Associated Press and Reuters, get approval from the editor in charge, and then speak the news. The editor's signature was normally a perfunctory matter, especially if he was weak in English. But one, who had learned perfect English as a refugee in England, was a narrow-minded pedant and bristled at liberties I took with central office material.

When Radio Berlin International started a North American department, with half-hour programs of music, news, commentary, and dialogue about varied aspects of GDR life, my work became more demanding. At that time the GDR was recognized only by the Eastern Bloc, while Bonn used its big economic stick to prevent other countries from following suit, and Western media reported only about the Wall. Despite all the country's sins and problems, the GDR deserved fairer treatment, which we tried to provide. Our department head Paul was a wartime resistance hero (he parachuted into Nazi Germany for the OSS) and a dedicated Communist, but neither a journalist nor an independent thinker. He resented my efforts to avoid material which might antagonize Americans. When De Gaulle, Nasser of Egypt, and Sukarno of Indonesia all affirmed GDR legitimacy, East Berlin played that for all it was worth. But all three were anathema to Americans, and I downplayed the story. Paul was incensed. We took the matter to GDR radio and TV chief Gerhart Eisler (whom I met when he spoke at Harvard). When he expressed himself discreetly for "the listeners" Paul never forgave me — but kept quiet, since I was his most prolific program writer.

I was on duty almost alone when John F. Kennedy was murdered. I rushed to alter our program, offering the latest news and my own quick obituary backed up by Beethoven's Seventh Symphony. In my weariness I left my text locked up in our sound studio, now closed for the night. I was about to go home when Paul walked in with Hugh, a militant African American who had also lived in Paris. He was a good friend and taught me a lot about the great jazz musicians — Parker, Mingus, Monk, Coltrane, Davis and "Lady Day," Billie Holiday. But now he and Paul were in their cups; neither of them saw Kennedy's death as a big loss. Paul asked for my manuscript in an aggressively tipsy tone: if I didn't give it to him, I needn't return to the job. But I had no copy and resented his innuendos. I wasn't fired and the matter was buried for the time being.

With the civil rights struggle accelerating back home, I eagerly dragged our clunky old tape recorder to interview Martin Luther King when he spoke in East Berlin. But when I said it was for an East Berlin broadcast to North America, his escorting West Berlin church officials snapped, "There's no time for that." Almost regretfully, King turned me down. A better journalist would have fired questions without permission. Out of reticence or stupidity, I blew my chance. At least I was not alone in committing untimely gaffes. Louis Armstrong came to East Berlin, and his manager granted an interview as long as there were "no politics." Ollie drafted some light questions for a woman on our staff, such as: what did Armstrong think of East Berlin women? In her excitement, her English faltered and Armstrong thought she was doubting his virility. In that unmistakable voice he replied scornfully that he was still interested in women, that his young wife proved that, and to top it off, "I sleep with her every night." We never aired the scoop.

Meanwhile, issues of race and racism were tangible and inescapable. Hugh complained that no one joined his table at the Press Club and the waiter delayed serving him. On the subways, he was confronted with unfriendly stares; Paris was friendlier and far less tainted by racism, he claimed. I assured him that Press Club waiters made everyone wait, and that most people preferred empty tables to joining ones partly occupied. Someone suggested he try smiling on the subways, which did yield some results. But there was no denying manifestations of racism in the GDR. It was constitutionally forbidden, and children from kindergarten on were taught to befriend everyone of every country, race, and color. This influenced many. But relatively homogenous Germany had no great antiracist traditions, to say the least. Where teachers were unconvincing, or unconvinced, or where there was resentment of everything taught (a not uncommon problem), remnants of racist ideology and the effects of Western stereotypes gained ground. Officially, there simply could be no such thing as racism in the socialist GDR, which meant no open discussions on the subject. Without discussion racism could fester and spread. Since only those affected really felt it, others could deny its existence. This would boomerang — after the Wall came down, latent racism, held in check by GDR law, culture, books, and films, boiled to the surface.

In 1964 I took another trip with my mother, this time to Leningrad, Moscow, Tashkent, and Samarkand. We saw much that was fascinating, heartwarming, or impressive, as well as some disturbing things. The guides were friendly and intelligent, candid about both the good and bad in their country. The food was adequate, the ice cream wonderful, Moscow was more cosmopolitan than East Berlin, and the Central Asian cities were fascinating. Tashkent seemed happier than Leningrad, where the worn looks on the faces of those old enough to have lived through the terrible wartime blockade had not faded. At the ballet we were surprised when a young man responded to our question about Khrushchev by saying quietly: "We don't need any more Great Fathers." We could not know that Khrushchev would soon be removed from office.

During the trip my mother revealed that the family had made some informal inquiries about my possible return. Winding its way back from sources close to the CIA was a suggestion that I could return if I was willing to make a media splash about my suffering under communism. My mother added that she did not expect me to accept those terms. Years later my brother said that my mother omitted another condition: that I must agree to stay for a time in the GDR and work for U.S. intelligence. I went back to East Berlin knowing that my stay there would be for a long time — or forever.

Some time after I returned, a new opportunity arose. Frank Löser had been an anti-Nazi refugee in the United States and later in Britain, where he was active in the global campaign to win back Paul Robeson's right to travel, denied him from 1949 to 1958. When Löser became a professor at the GDR's Humboldt University he founded a Robeson Committee; in 1965 he asked me to set up a Robeson Archive at the Academy of Arts. I jumped at the chance, which came at the right moment: my relations with my boss at Radio Berlin were at a low ebb. For me Robeson was one of the century's greatest men. But I warned Löser I had no archival experience and was not a good manager. "That will come," he was sure.

After a month of learning archive methods, I was given a big office at the Academy of Arts, whose roots went back to Friedrich the Great and which included countless celebrities among its members. I was responsible to Löser of the Committee, to the Academy's director, and, indirectly, to its president, the great film director Konrad Wolf. This unusual archive, approved by Paul and Eslanda Robeson, resonated politically as well as artistically; the Robesons had been targeted by cold war hatred and racism in the United States, and this archive was meant as a rejoinder. I collected all I could, from Robeson's New Jersey childhood to his triumphs as an All-American football player to his singing and acting career. I searched for old phonograph records, photos, articles, programs, reviews, and books, and wrote people in many countries for reminiscences. It seemed he knew almost every prominent person in the arts and on the political left. So many of them admired this giant of a man with a rare fusion of talent and courage who demanded equal rights, fought for an antilynch law, laid the case of racial discrimination in the United States before the UN, and led the fight for black players in major league baseball — all before such efforts became "acceptable." My job seemed endless.

The famous British defense lawyer D. N. Pritt told of joining Robeson in a live broadcast to Nazi Germany on Moscow Radio. The Dutch filmmaker Joris Ivens missed meeting Robeson in Spain but had him defy city noises to record a song in Harlem for a documentary. The journalist Cedric Belfrage told of the fight for Robeson's right to travel. Leo Hurwitz and Paul Strand spoke of Robeson's contributions to their classic labor film, *Native Land*. The jazz trumpeter "Cootie" Williams told me that he always admired Paul and would do anything to support him. Letters from President Modeiba Keita of Mali and President Kenneth Kaunda of Zambia sang Robeson's praises. Labor councillor Peggy Middleton, Robeson's secretary in London, brought his Othello costume from the 1959 Stratford production, as well as photos and documents from Paul's son in the United States.

In 1967 I raced around Moscow to gather material. At times I was abandoned by my irresponsible interpreter, and had to fumble my way into the Conservatory, which had once given Robeson a prize, and to grapple alone at the giant Lenin Library with the Cyrillic catalogs. While the interpreter was using my ticket to see the Bolshoi and the great Plisetskaya, I was turned away from the film and photo archive in Krasnogorsk outside Moscow because it was closed on Saturday. But I struck a rich vein in my encounter with Robeson's interpreter during Paul's 1958 visit. He had piles of documents, photos, and hundreds of heartfelt letters from Soviet citizens, often inviting the Robesons to dine with them or gather mushrooms in the woods. I could borrow some of these treasures, he said, but kept me on tenterhooks as to which ones, and even borrowed money from me, knowing that I was dependent on him. In the end he loaned me lots of material.

Despite lingering effects of the hepatitis I had had a few months earlier, I moved around a lot and got views of Soviet life not visible to tourists. I visited Harry Eisman, a New Yorker who jumped bail at age fifteen in 1930 after being sentenced for joining in a demonstration. He had a Russian wife and daughter and told me a lot about changes for better or worse in the USSR. Reports in the United States about Soviet anti-Semitism, he said, were exaggerated, but added that the prewar policy of discussing every case of anti-Semitism in the party had been abandoned. Most disturbing in Moscow was the fear of taking responsibility, even in minor matters. But despite problems and difficulties, life seemed more normal — and human — than indicated in most Western press reports.

Back in Berlin, my frenetic quest for material took on urgency as Robeson's seventieth birthday in April 1968 approached. My illness made a projected illustrated biography impossible, but we pushed ahead with an exhibition on his life, and asked John Heartfield to design the catalog. Johnny, who took an English name to defy anti-British propaganda in the First World War, was a great graphic artist whose bitingly ironic anti-Nazi photomontages brought him fame between the wars. After a narrow escape from the Nazis he worked in Czech exile, then got to Britain with the help of Ernest Hemingway's wife Martha Gellhorn. Returning to East Berlin in 1950, he was regarded with skepticism by stupid SED bureaucrats, as was his brother Wieland Herzfelde, my literature teacher, but was finally accorded respect. I was fearfully cautious of Johnny's legendary volcanic temper, but he remained friendly. A month or so later he had a fatal heart attack, so I was the last person to work with this legendary artist.

Our inaugural event, a large meeting at the State Opera House, was addressed by Albert Norden, a wartime emigrant in the United States, a Robeson Committee member, and most important, a Politburo member. We had sought a leading African American as a speaker, like Stokely Carmichael, or a Black Panther representative, but the GDR could not accept the required armed bodyguards. Robeson himself was too ill to travel in his last years. Another superb singer did appear: Bernice Reagon, later head of the quintet "Sweet Honey in the Rock." She did not get a sufficient chance to demonstrate her great talent, yet created an amusing stir on TV by slamming the Olympics. That was the year of raised black fists — but also the year a euphoric GDR got its first chance to participate.

Meanwhile, I raced to get our exhibition finished on time. A skilled designer did a fine job despite photographic bows to Walter Ulbricht, Albert Norden, and Frank Löser, with whom my relations had become increasingly strained. I never became a good administrator and did make errors, but his resentment was driven mainly because I as Archive director inevitably got as much publicity as he did as head of the honorary committee. When I signed my name under his on a telegram to a Robeson Committee in England he became incensed, and thanks to my frayed nerves, my response was not conciliatory. He had me summoned before the Academy director and demanded an apology or my resignation. I explained my position and resigned. When I saw the snide official evaluation of my work at the Academy I insisted it be altered, but accepted a compromise formulation that I had been "individualistic."

Years later Löser was found to have made unpleasant mistakes in his books. He was pensioned off from his job as professor "due to poor health." So he tried to make a big splash by "choosing freedom" during a contrived lecture tour to the United States. The splash lasted two minutes on CBS news and brought no contracts; he returned sheepishly to West Germany and wrote scathing attacks on the GDR. Some points were certainly valid, but descriptions of his own active "resistance" made all who knew him laugh. As for me, in 1968 I suddenly belonged to an almost nonexistent category in the GDR. I was unemployed.

While at the Archive, I had also created a bi-weekly radio program based on U.S. history, weaving narrative with recorded songs I had grown up with, now provided by friends and relatives. That allowed me in the sixties to introduce GDR listeners to Leadbelly, Woody Guthrie, Pete Seeger, and younger singers Phil Ochs, Tom Paxton, Joan Baez, Bob Dylan. Almost no one in the GDR knew them at the time: One program began, for example: "Those were the days of hobos who traveled in empty boxcars, or under them, dodging tough railroad cops, stewing an unlucky rabbit in hobo jungles before jumping another boxcar, looking for work as lumberjacks, dockers, or whatever they could find. Here's a song they sang, a hobo's dream of a land where hens lay soft-boiled eggs, cigarettes grow on trees, and the cops have wooden legs, like the Schlaraffenland of old German stories." Then came "Big Rock Candy Mountain," "Hallelujah, I'm a Bum," and a song or two by Joe Hill.

I was rewarded by more letters expressing love for the songs than I could answer. Many requested texts, a tape, or historical information on a theme covered in school. Sometimes they asked me to come and lecture — with my LPs. A Lutheran pastor in Thuringia, a Seeger fan, invited me to his small town; we are still friends. I worked with a radio man who advised me, corrected my faulty German, but rarely questioned my texts. However, when I quoted Pete Seeger's remark, after being sentenced to a year in jail: "If they really want to punish me they would put Toshi in jail and leave me alone with the kids," he rebelled. He just couldn't see the humor in that.

Besides the stories and songs of pioneers, cowboys, or the Wobblies, I commented on current events and told of living singers. During my first years in Berlin I needed special permission to receive records. Now LPs, books, and periodicals came without difficulty, but the border watchdogs drew the line at tapes, especially unmarked ones in a foreign language. A tape sent by Pete Seeger was returned to him. On tour in Moscow, Pete gave the tape to the musicologist Grigori Schneerson, who gave it to Ernst

Busch, who passed it on to me. I was grateful to meet the legendary Busch, whose Spanish War songs had moved me deeply and whose Berliner Ensemble roles were magnificent. He was known as a grump but I was pleasantly surprised to find him playing happily with a little son, caroling from room to room.

Seeger and his wife Toshi overcame inner reservations about visiting Germany and gave concerts in West and East Berlin in January 1967. I was interpreter in East Berlin. A small concert with the Hootenanny Klub was a great success; its members rejoiced to sing "Wimoweh," and "Guantanamera" with the man who made them famous. The next day we were to do a film for TV. But the director, knowing neither Seeger nor what he stood for, asked Pete to walk down a long carpet past potted palms strumming his banjo to a playback. After a long wait for some cable to be repaired, Pete was uncharacteristically terse, asking me to tell the director that he didn't sing strolling on red carpets, that he never used playbacks, and that his contract included only one hour for TV. The show never panned out. But on his last night his big Volksbühne concert sold out. There was even a scuffle between people with "can you sell a ticket?" signs. At a restaurant before we went to the theater, an apprentice waiter placed a card on a silver tray and an artistically folded napkin in front of Pete. The card said: "Dear Mr. Seeger, I love your music. Is there any way to get into the concert?" The tour manager nearly shouted, "Impossible. They say the President of the People's Chamber can't even get a ticket." Pete responded that the young waiter would get in even if he had to carry Pete's banjo. He did — and sat in the wings.

Pete wondered nervously how East Germans would respond to his music. He played "Shtill di Nacht," a song by a young Jewish partisan murdered by the Nazis; all were deeply moved. He sang the words of Lisa Kalvelage, a German woman married to an American and arrested when she held up a shipment of napalm for Vietnam. I translated her words about how she learned from the Nuremberg Trials that everyone has a duty to resist killing. When he sang "Peat Bog Soldiers," a song of the Nazi concentration camp prisoners, everyone "sang out like nowhere else," Pete wrote. He found an antifascist, antiracist audience at perhaps one of his most emotionally charged concerts. At the airport eight youngsters played him a grateful farewell serenade.

The euphoria did not last; it gave way to the heavy hand of dogmatic stupidity. Someone must have whispered to some clueless big shot that

American songs were playing too big a part in young people's lives. A spate of articles, especially in the party organ *Neues Deutschland,* warned of the suffocating expansion of American culture around the world, including even the Bach Swingle Singers. The Hootenanny Klub changed its name to Oktober Klub — for the Russian Revolution — and the radio station ended my series so suddenly I could not tape an Abe Lincoln program I had already prepared. My programs were only a side job and my hepatitis would have ended the project anyway. But Perry Friedman lost his living when club directors and concert managers played it safe.

When the articles in *Neues Deutschland* reached a peak of stupidity I got mad enough to write a letter to the head of its Culture Section, who had been my teacher in Leipzig. Should progressive artists like Seeger and Robeson be rejected? Songs like "The Marseillaise," "Avanti Populo," the Spanish Civil War songs — even "The Internationale" — were from the capitalist world. Should they be spurned? Renate brought the response to my hospital bed. "Yes, I must agree with you," the editor wrote, "I'm afraid we shot well beyond the mark." Something had changed up on top. The radio station wrote to apologize for the abrupt end to my series, praising it and thanking me. But I never did a radio program again.

Some years later Joan Baez gave a concert in East Berlin. After ducking out of the welcome reception she showed up at rehearsal arm in arm with a young man. At the concert she dedicated one song, "Oh Freedom," to a Herr B——. I did not catch the name and wondered if it were Willy Brandt. Perry enlightened me: it was the man she had been with, the dissident singer Wolf Biermann, anathema in official eyes. The man translating her remarks between songs tried to mute their critical tone, no easy job since half the audience knew some English. When he stalked out before the press conference, I filled in. The press still described Baez as a courageous opponent of the Vietnam War. But when she answered the first questions in an unfriendly tone, with harsh words about the Wall, the People's Army, and anything else she could jab, the GDR journalists put pads and pencils away. Some debated her: "Do you know about the threats against the GDR by West German politicians and generals with their huge armed forces over the past twenty years?" To answer their questions, Baez turned more and more to a bearded man next to her, her manager or guru. My impression was: she was very committed, but grasped little of the complex cold war situation. Somehow she did not seem all too bright.

A different kind of musical adventure unfolded in 1973 — a tour with

Earl Robinson, singer and composer of "Joe Hill" and "Ballad for Americans," and young accompanists Mike Martin and Jeffrey Landau. The GDR did not yet have enough modern equipment, so makeshift arrangements were required for almost every concert. Robinson, at sixty-five, took this in stride; he sang, played piano, and with a little help from my U.S.-style explanations, struck up easy-going relationships with his audience. One audience member, a short, squat man, came backstage during intermission at a Berlin concert to thank Earl modestly for his singing. He was Hermann Axen, a Jewish Politburo member who had barely survived Auschwitz. The other two performers, sound-oriented perfectionists, griped incessantly about inadequate equipment, once nearly walking off in mid-concert. But the problems were compensated for by their successes with not a few young GDR females. A more earnest compensation was their reverence for the many musical shrines in the GDR. Michael often shamed me with his knowledge of the comings and goings in eastern Germany of Brahms, Schumann, Wagner, and Mendelssohn. Earl was an old leftist with rather curious new theories and therapies. I recall that at Bach's grave in the Thomas Church in Leipzig he suddenly dropped to his knees and kissed the flat stone.

The "song movement" was growing steadily in those years; there were scores of groups in offices, schools, and factories — some were good and most were simply fun. In 1970 the Oktober Klub organized the first of its annual Festivals of Political Songs, inviting singers from six countries. Later, as many as fifty singers or groups came from thirty countries. Nonpolitical songs were also sung, but a left trend was dominant, though GDR groups were often torn between the upbeat songs expected by official sponsors and the independent, questioning, usually far better songs from some young composers. There was consensus on themes like Vietnam, Chile, Nicaragua, racism and fascism, past or present. Concerts might offer the melancholy Angolese Santocas, the stirring Chilean Quilapayún singers, Cuban Silvio Rodriguez, or one or more widely known artists like Miriam Makeba, Mikos Theodorakis, Mercedes Sosa, Billy Bragg, Ewan MacColl and Peggy Seeger, Bruce Cockburn, Sweet Honey in the Rock, Guy Carawan, and the San Francisco Mime Troupe. There were brilliant musical statements by the Uruguayan Daniel Viglietti, a Hungarian rock group, and singers from the GDR mining town of Hoyerswerda. Musicians from all continents traded songs and ideas and performed in East Berlin theaters and concert halls for sixty or seventy thousand young people, some of whom waited all night for tickets. A Danish newspaper called it the "best annual gathering of progressive singers in the world." For young people (and older ones like me) it was a breath of action-filled air which in the GDR, sadly, was far too rare.

In 1972 Barbara Dane and Irwin Silber took part. I recalled Silber from the Folksay Club in Manhattan and had heard of Barbara Dane's singing, so I asked to be their interpreter. I was surprised to find that Barbara, under an earlier name, had been at the Prague Youth Festival in 1947, then a slim, beautiful blonde on whom I had had a crush. Both were militant leftists, leaning toward Maoism or anarchism and viewing the GDR as revisionist. They scorned pedestrians who waited for green lights even when no cars were visible and loved a bit of provocation. Barbara prefaced each song with a speech, and listened intently to see if I were bowdlerizing it, politically or otherwise. She sang "FTA" and wanted to hear the similar German word. I used it, but explained to her that "Fuck The Army " meant nothing in German, since the equivalent word was used only literally. At the final big concert, with Honecker and other top brass present, she made sure to sing "Insubordination" with a lengthy explanation. I did my best to present her reasons for never conforming to the powers-that-be, a precept not too popular officially. But no one objected, and she made a big hit by singing a favorite song of Vietnam. A chorus of young Vietnamese studying or working in the GDR suddenly realized this big American was singing their song and rushed forward to embrace her in one of the festival's most moving moments.

The sixties were filled with both highs and lows. A friend's heart trouble got us talking. When I told him that I too had problems climbing stairs, he arranged for me to see his doctor. My heart was fine, but I had to be hospitalized immediately with hepatitis. It took nine weeks for my bilirubin and transaminase counts to behave, and four more weeks at a convalescent home near Potsdam, a former estate of the Siemens electronics billionaires — and war criminals. We lived in a beautiful park in wonderful May. The *Kur* involved daily mudpacks, medicinal baths, and pleasant massages. There was no physical or financial pain — everything was free and I got my full salary (I still worked at the Robeson Archive). A year later I was sent to the famed Czech spa Karlovy Vary (Karlsbad), staying at a bright, small hotel high above the town where a small river flows, warmed by curative springs. The treatment included two daily trips to the Colonnades where a few hundred people, from Bostonians to Mongolians, strolled to the music of a small band and used porcelain cups with nozzles to sip warm mineral waters bubbling into little fountains.

I was busy with treatments, voracious reading, and wanderings through the hilly pine or beech woods, with little contact with local people. But breezes of the "Prague Spring" were noticeable. At the hotel where I waited, usually vainly, to telephone Renate, the German cloakroom attendant complained bitterly about her husband's low pension, but was happy that with new leader Alexander Dubcek she could finally speak her native German openly. Her hopes ran beyond linguistic concerns: "The new rulers in Prague are learned people; they must mean well. As for the old ones. . . ." She shrugged, intimating disdain for the old working-class leaders who were not "learned." She also foresaw financial credits from West Germany; Western visitors always bought the expensive cigarettes, not like the Russians who smoked the cheapest brands, she scornfully noted. But any trouble with the Russians could mean world war, she added pensively.

Knowing something of the strong Czech folk tradition, I spoke with members of a music group. But they were more influenced by the folk scene in the United States, which I had propagated in the GDR. Yet, while most U.S. folkies opposed the Vietnam war, they seemed uncritically pro-Western. This was a tourist center, I knew, influenced by Western spa guests and with more West Germans than I expected. But typical or not, most people were enthusiastic about Dubcek. The Prague *Volkszeitung*, a German-language weekly, helped me follow events. It was strongly pro-Dubcek and differed from any East Bloc newspaper I had ever seen—friendly to West Germany and mocking the GDR. This reflected the way the media in the two German states treated current Czech leaders, but it shook me nonetheless (if the paper mirrored official views). Sudeten German groups with Bonn's financial support played an important role in West German politics; even cabinet ministers demanded Czech territory, dismissing Nazi terror during the long occupation. The GDR rigorously opposed such claims and catchwords. The paper lampooned GDR press reports on caches of Western weapons under a Czech bridge: they did sound flimsy. But such pro–West German leanings made me nervous. I understood the enthusiasm for the "Prague Spring" (the name came from a music festival) with its feeling of new freedom after years of phrasemongering and restrictions like those in the GDR. Even Dubcek's interviews were different; his spontaneity and joking responses to reporters' questions were refreshing. Kadar in Hungary, Gomulka in Poland, and Khrushchev had almost been human. Dubcek went further, and people loved it.

But where was the country moving? Important Americans like National Security Adviser Zbigniew Brzezinski lectured semi-officially in Prague, getting applause for statements which virtually called for ending the whole system. The Czechoslovak border with the USSR was short, but it existed, and I could no more imagine the USSR tolerating a U.S. ally on its border, splitting Poland and the GDR from Hungary and the Balkans in the south, than I could the United States tolerating a Communist Mexico. The atmosphere was heating up rapidly; Czechoslovak meetings with Warsaw Pact countries led nowhere.

This hardly affected us. One day German-speaking patients (east and west) were driven along a magnificent valley route to the other famous spa, Mariansky Lazny (Marienbad), with impressive buildings, but less charm than Karlovy Vary. We visited the residence of Metternich, the most reactionary post-Napoleonic European leader; I was surprised that the elderly guide spoke almost lovingly of him. Another excursion took us past a monument to U.S pilots shot down by the Nazis, and then on to Cheb, a beautifully restored little town where the cold war was also visible. From a West German mountain just over the border a giant tower broadcast U.S.-financed RIAS programs into the southern GDR. Things seemed almost normal — but a climax was near. On August 13th, I waited at a crowded corner to see Dubcek and his guest Walter Ulbricht drive past after a key meeting. I overheard a German woman gripe to a visiting Austrian about life here. A Czech gallery director complained bitterly about waiting five years for his Simca car. The convoy passed; Dubcek waved happily while Ulbricht looked tense and pale. Was the absence of GDR flags only a protocol triviality?

A week later I went contentedly to bed after a concert of Bach, Handel. and Mozart. At 3 A.M. I was awakened by heavy tanks clanking swiftly down the steep road near our hotel; the noise lasted twenty minutes. I cursed, wondering why they had to hold their damned maneuvers in a spa at this hour, and went back to sleep. At breakfast I learned of the occupation. Though not totally unexpected it was a terrible shock. The first thing I noticed in town were the many crying women. A few Soviet armored vehicles drove by, jeered by the crowd. Traces of nighttime tank damage at corners and curbstones were visible. There were crowds at all food stores; some shops were closed — and the Western patients' cars had left town.

I saw no GDR forces (none were sent in) and most traces of Soviet troops soon disappeared, while Czech soldiers on military trucks raced through town, waving and shouting anti-Soviet slurs. Their vehicles and many walls were marked: "Dubcek and Svoboda." Svoboda was both president and the Czech word for freedom. At the "Red Army Liberation" monument an angry crowd battered the bronze Soviet soldier.

I was amazed at how quickly resistance was organized: the national colors were in many lapels; clever slogans were everywhere. Graffiti on the buses said: "Occupiers Go Home — Moscow 4000 kilometers." Street signs were blacked out to confuse strangers. When I next passed the Soviet monument the bronze soldier was torn down; a sign "1938–1968" likened current events to the Nazi invasion of 1938. The young crowd was extremely agitated; there were menacing shouts when two civilian Bulgarian cars passed by. I spoke only English.

Suddenly I heard German and was surprised to see the flushed face of Siegfried Wagner, the cultural official I had attacked years ago for his boring speech at the university. He was loudly explaining to a Czech colleague why this unavoidable step was to "to save Czechoslovakia, not enslave it." He was almost taking his life in his hands saying such things in a language understood but despised by many. I wondered whether to shake my head at his foolishness, admire his courage, or reject him altogether. I did not call out to him; he would hardly have recognized me — and I was in no heroic mood.

No telephone calls to home were getting through. GDR patients split into loose factions; one, led by a GDR railroad functionary, hotly defended the intervention, tried to rally others behind them, and explained to any Czechs in sight that it was all to protect them. Another group clearly opposed the move, sympathized with the Czechs, but remained fairly quiet, recalling that they would soon be returning home. A third group, which included me, was confused and uncertain. The patient who impressed me most with his quiet analyses was Herr Kluge, chief accountant at a huge East Berlin factory; he was neither dogmatic, uncritical, nor unprincipled. But he was very ill; his skin and eyes had an almost greenish color. A young woman had fallen in love with him here; she was now frantic.

Things grew even more tense the next day; fewer Czech military vehicles raced through town, Soviet troops were not visible, but potatoes were unavailable and rationing began for staples. Radio and TV "freedom" stations which began broadcasting almost immediately after the intervention were now in full swing, allegedly from Prague, Brno, and Pilsen, but reportedly from West Germany (perhaps from that huge tower across the border from Cheb). Russian hotel names like Stalingrad or Yalta were altered, road signs blacked out, and posters called for a one-hour general strike at noon.

The waitresses in our hotel battled with tears on the first day, then became taciturn. During the strike they sat in the clubroom, watching the "freedom" TV program. When sirens marked the end of the strike at 1 P.M., they served lunch, with no aprons, pointedly hasty and unfriendly, spilling soup onto one patient. The doctors behaved correctly; we remained patients, regardless of what they thought of the GDR.

The Colonnades where we took the waters were renamed after that early anti-Communist president Tomás Masaryk. An orchestra played Smetana's patriotic "Ma Vlast" to an emotional, almost entirely Czech crowd. The omnipresent graffiti were increasingly aggressive. I deciphered a verse giving every Warsaw Pact country (except Rumania, which did not intervene) an unfriendly attribute: the Hungarians as paprika-gorgers, the Bulgarians as primitive corn-eaters, the GDR represented by the Wall linked to Hitler. Resistance was well organized: the posters, graffiti, radio, TV — all were engineered swiftly, efficiently, and doubtlessly centrally. GDR motorcyclists arriving from a camping area near the border said Czech units had been pulled back from the border before Soviet troops marched in, thus buttressing my feeling that everything was prepared in advance, including the resistance.

With health improvements impossible, staff rebellious, and the atmosphere worsening, we had to leave. But rail connections were interrupted. The dogmatic man from the GDR railroad authority now proved valuable: at the transportation office he insisted on an ambulance for Herr Kluge and a bus for the rest. When we arrived late that evening at the GDR border, another bus awaited to crisscross the country, taking every patient home — ending in early morning in Berlin.

My final recollections of Karlovy Vary are of the big red star and USSR-CSSR slogan from the Imperial Hotel lying broken in the river. Also torn down was the "Moskva" sign, restoring the spa's best hotel to its glorious old private name of Pupp.

Back in the GDR, I realized why telephone contact with Renate had been impossible. The whole country, especially its southern half, was almost hysterical watching Soviet troop movements. Many GDR students, often pro-socialist, were so shocked and alienated by events that they distributed handmade leaflets; some who were caught were given jail sentences.

While the whole nasty business was clearly against the will of most Czechoslovaks, I was torn back and forth. "Socialism with a human face" was a beautiful idea, we urgently needed something similar in the GDR. But behind the smiles, Czechoslovakia had been moving sharply to the right. One indication was the way some groups opposing the trend were ostracized or threatened. I feared a giant step backwards, not only endangering social benefits and threatening the USSR, but threatening the survival of socialism in Eastern Europe. I was haunted by John F. Kennedy's words written years earlier (in his *Strategy of Peace*): "The West can create an advanced bridgehead in Central Europe which will undermine the military and political position of Soviet Communism in Poland, Czechoslovakia and Hungary." To many, liberty clearly meant a return to capitalism and to the Western fold, as had been offered just before my 1947 visit to Prague, rejected then and again in February 1948, prevented in the spring of 1968, but achieved in 1990, with the resulting breakup of Czechoslovakia.

Echoing its conclusions after the Hungarian uprising of 1956, the GDR's ruling SED felt that to permit political control to slip from the ruling party's grasp was like skating on a ramp or running up a down escalator. I saw the truth in this for any country, east, west, north or south, but felt an equally important conclusion was again ignored. Leaders must never permit a gap in trust and confidence to grow between them and the majority. There must be dialogue and participation in the media, in personal encounters, in every way. If too many lose confidence every state is endangered; only force and violence remain.

The patients at that tragic cure were surely left with mental scars. For many in the GDR, especially students and intellectuals, the state's authority was damaged in ways which never fully healed. Herr Kluge died a few weeks later.

[10]

FREELANCING IN EAST GERMANY

After losing my Robeson Archive job — unemployed for the first time since 1950 — I sat almost paralyzed on the sofa, leafing vacantly through the newspapers with a degrading feeling of being unwanted. I knew there was work, but where and when?

I called my old friend Douglas Sharp, who had worked with me in the Bautzen clubhouse and was now an editor of the Dresden magazine where I had done a brief stint as a student. Yes, he needed translations. So I translated four or five articles a month for that magazine, which plugged the GDR in six languages. The work paid well, saving me at a rough moment. Translators into German were not rare, but only a few former refugees to English-speaking countries could translate into English. A foreign affairs magazine asked me to translate and other customers came along. Much of it involved rose-colored glasses, a far cry from John Peet's irony which I admired.

I started writing on my own. Many former fellow students were established in the media, so I would call and ask if they needed articles on hot issues in the United States, where life was full of drama: black liberation, Native American struggles, elections, the murder of mine union leader Jock Yablonski, labor strikes, women's liberation, and the anti–Vietnam War movement. The Hallstein Doctrine of Bonn's foreign minister forbade nations outside the East Bloc from recognizing the GDR at peril of losing crucial trade. Its overall aim was to deepen the GDR's isolation, especially in terms of travel. East Germany had little Western currency; even worse, travelers going west needed special West Berlin papers, which basically denied their GDR citizenship. To get a U.S. visa they had to swear they were not "mentally incapacitated, suffering a venereal disease, or a member of a Communist organization." Most journalists were at least in the last category. So the GDR got few direct reports from the United States.

I did not rejoice at this nastiness — but benefited from it. After my name was known a bit, I might get a call: "What's the story on this 'GOP' Convention? Can you tell our readers what it's all about?" So I switched from translations to articles. My income was less regular and my account dipped into the red during vacations, but I was soon back in my bank's good graces (and being a publicly owned bank it didn't charge for overdrafts).

Most satisfying was my work for *Junge Welt,* a daily youth newspaper. Obligatory news and reports were on the front pages, but the inside had good international coverage, lively sports, youth fashions, culture, and a regular column on sexual matters, including homosexuality, equal rights in sex, masturbation, contraception, abortion, and, later on, AIDS. Circulation was over a million, including not a few grandmas and grandpas. My column on the United States never outdid sex, but I tried to make it light and free of jargon and simplistic reporting. I couldn't be impartial, but avoided polemics and offered all the information I could on conflicts involving real people trying to achieve a better life and a better country.

I rarely strayed from U.S. themes. But my first column explained Valentine's Day, then unknown in the GDR, and dedicated a few "valentines" to admirable women like Beate Klarsfeld, an antifascist who publicly slapped West German Chancellor Kiesinger to remind the world that he had held a key job with Hitler's Propaganda Minister Goebbels. I joked in rhyme that it might have been better if the women's shotput champion had done the slapping!

Some editors straightened out more than my halting grammar; they felt that "you just don't say things that way." Thus I sometimes found my best gags, metaphors, and attempts at originality ground back into the old jargon. If I complained loudly or insisted on seeing all changes in advance, I might be tagged by humorless or fearful editors as an unwanted troublemaker. But by and large I got along, lucky not to be writing about the GDR, criticism of which was limited to homeopathic doses, making honest journalism a nervewracking affair.

But I too had "bonehead" problems. At times I was asked to do television commentary. I jumped at such chances. Many people watched West German news or none at all, but enough recognized my face to massage my ego, and TV paid well. The woman who corrected my grammar on a Vietnam piece liked the piece, but her boss bluepenciled a third of it, substituting stale jargon. While I insisted on arguing the matter, I realized that if I was "difficult" I might not only lose the commentary but jeopardize future TV work. But I just couldn't read that crap. Luckily, her boss was out of the room, and the chief editor, a good, intelligent fellow, though often weak-kneed under daily pressures, read it, smiled, and told the now-returned pencil-wielder that it was unusual, "but as a foreigner he has his own way of speaking. Leave it as it is."

My near monopoly withered when in 1972 the GDR was recognized by the United States. Regular correspondents now covered Washington, and a reporter on the scene looked better on TV than I did in the studio. While my phone rang less often, my American upbringing generated enough salable ideas. Also, speakers with American accents were sometimes needed for films — and I was the "genuine article." Almost every Briton or American around — there were a dozen or two — was invited to play such parts. Once I played a sinister role with a paste-on mustache which looked so good to my wife that I grew a real one. For one true-to-life film about the daring sabotage of Nazi V-2 rocket production by Communist concentration camp inmates, all available Britons and Americans were taxied to the huge DEFA film studio. Cyril Pustan, the husband of Bobby Fischer's mother, was driven 140 miles from Jena, only to find that he didn't have a word of dialogue. We prevailed upon the director to give him at least one line.

I also did some dubbing; German audiences, east and west, balked at reading subtitles. In one Rossellini film I spoke the part of an American pilot shot down over Italy. (Years later, dozing over TV, I was suddenly awakened by my own voice.) But when GDR films were entered in international competitions, English subtitles were required. I was one of just two people who learned to squeeze colloquial English dialogue into two-liners, up to thirty-two letters each, which could be read easily. This job, which usually came up about once a year, enabled me to work on fine films like Konrad Wolf's *Goya.*

I also began writing my own books, starting with a bedtime story I had once made up for Thomas, *The Hippo and the Stork.* Then came a history of the United States, stressing in a popular vein the roles of blacks, women, unions, and peace movements. *Hitchhiking through the USA* was based on my trip as an eighteen-year-old, enlarged with chapters on current subjects. Some liked it, others, who expected a manual on hitchhiking, were less rhapsodic. I followed with my own story, up to my arrival in the GDR in 1952. The publishers insisted on calling it *The Way across the Border,* which suggested to some a book on how to jump the Wall. Finally, I wrote a history of American songs and singers, from Yankee Doodle to Bruce Springsteen. Books took years of pre-computer research and writing, but voracious GDR readers usually guaranteed 10,000-copy first printings and often equally large second and third printings. Losing my job had proved to be a lucky turn. The freedom to choose my work and to write without the pressure to please a boss was priceless. I did have to hustle to earn a living; no one paid for holidays, vacations, or research time. But it may have added ten years to my life.

One morning in 1961, four months after we joyfully moved to our new apartment on Stalin Allee, I woke up and found that I now lived on Karl Marx Allee. A few blocks away residents looked in vain for the big Stalin statue in front of their house, and a town on the Oder River suddenly was no longer Stalinstadt. While changing our street name to Marx overnight didn't reflect too much respect for the German thinker, we were relieved at the overdue change of our address.

Though born a week after the official deadline for entering, Thomas was admitted to the first grade. The school was in easy walking distance, part of our neighborhood complex, a mix of varied five-to-eleven story buildings, stores, playground, nursery, and preschool kindergarten. Our windows on Karl Marx Allee gave us front seats for parades — a dubious advantage during nocturnal rehearsals of the annual brassy military procession.

When Timothy was born, Renate stayed home for three years, savoring the opportunity to watch the baby grow. She also had time to meet the challenge of shopping, exulting in the arrival of fresh tomatoes or Christmas oranges. On the prowl for scarce fruit or delicacies, Renate, like others, joined lines first and then asked what was being sold. But three years of talk about shopping, baby teeth, or the neighbors began to bore me — and her. Renate's financial dependence on me did not help our relationship either, but childcare was not always available in the sixties. When a social worker offered her a place in the nearest kindergarten if she took on work as a school secretary, Renate grabbed it. Timothy became a member of the parklike new kindergarten across the street, part of a group of exuberant preschoolers who kept pets, learned to help younger children, and ran wildly (and naked) into the wading pool, dispelling stereotypes of a regimented social order.

In 1967, Renate left the school and became a librarian in the hospital where I recovered from hepatitis. She had only a village grade school diploma and a limited reading background but had sympathy for everyone, listened to problems the busy doctors or nurses had no time for, and gave a smile or comforting word to all. Her boss and some of the personnel were snappy with foreign patients whose German was weak or nonexistent. Renate gave them special attention, finding Portuguese newspapers for a Mozambiquan, helping a Chilean exile who spoke little English, and chatting at length with the South African singer Miriam Makeba. A gallant young man from Mali was confined for a year with severe kidney trouble. Feeling stronger one day, he was taken by Renate to do some shopping. When he tired, she invited him to rest at our apartment where, nearby, neighbors chatted—and raised eyebrows. Upon my return two days later from a trip, one woman asked sly questions. Renate and I laughed at the innuendo and became lifelong friends with Boubakar and his French wife. We also befriended a Congolese educator who delighted Timothy's class with "medicine man secrets" like rubbing lion fat on shoes to send dogs away whimpering. Renate's new friends and fascinating stories of the events within hospital walls were far more absorbing than tales about teething and shopping.

But we still had to shop with less time for it, and Renate's job ended any excuse for her doing most of the housework. I shouldered my share, especially with children and meals, though I still wrestled clumsily with laundry at the nearby "washhouse," inducing her icy comment that "men are just no good at such things." Renate never considered herself a feminist, but insists on her rights in the household. She may have been meek with bosses, but not with me. Once in a while angry fists pounded my back, usually after arguments on raising the boys.

No arguments ever lasted long, however, and our lives were quite peaceful on the whole. Our building had parties, travel lectures, card games, and excursions to local lakes, also twice-a-year cleanups of lawns, shrubs, and trees. We sometimes went to the remarkably inexpensive State Opera or the rival Comic Opera, which combined great singing and design with wonderful acting. For plays we had the Volksbühne, Deutsches Theater, Gorki Theater, and the Berliner Ensemble, our legendary "Brecht Theater," which had unfortunately declined over the years. The kids had the

"Tierpark" zoo, almost free summer camp, family travel, especially to the Baltic, and a children's chorus. They also played guitars — forming a nice but short-lived duo.

I remained a rare species — an American with no driving license — until 1963, when I bought a little Trabant. Offered in a state of sweaty dissolution, my wild guess on the license exam that a tow rope should be over thirty meters long(over ninety feet) got only a tired shrug from the examiner and an admonition to drive carefully. I did, and our radius expanded to the many lakes surrounding Berlin and in winter to the sledding slopes.

People in the United States imagined all kinds of privations in East Germany — mostly fantasies based on ignorant or prejudiced reports. Today, with the victim dead, this disparagement is stronger than ever. Actually, life went on normally. We lived modestly compared to middle-class standards but better than I had generally lived in the United States. I never was much for consumerism; by and large we had all we needed.

My American relatives were impressed by the ordinary rhythms of our lives, despite the lack of washer-dryers, stereos, or fancier cars. A cousin who was a filmmaker even drooled over the beat-up old buildings in working-class Prenzlauer Berg — perhaps dreaming of replicating the legendary *M* which captured the mood of old Berlin. A house nestled in woods with studios and canteen belonging to one of the GDR's many documentary film teams captured his admiration — and envy. When my brother visited he already had a daring plan for my escape "when anti-Semitism increases." My reassurances did not quell his talk about sailboat landings in the Baltic. But he loved old Bautzen, the village of Baruth where he met my in-laws, and the magnificent art works in Dresden, risen from the ruins of war. His escape plans soon faded from consciousness.

My father was unable to visit before he died. My mother's last trip was in the early 1970s; I think she knew of her fatal illness. We strolled through Friedrichshain Park not far from our home, enjoying the sunshine and the Fairytale Fountains. After her usual admonitions to be more ambitious and write more, she said: "Who knows what would have happened to you back home? Perhaps you were lucky to land here after all."

In June 1969 I interpreted for a U.S. delegation to an international peace congress in East Berlin, meeting an interesting and sometimes eccentric group of passionate activists. One young woman visiting "the East" for the first time spotted some people playing tennis, and asked with consummate naiveté why they weren't out working for peace. The comedian-activist Dick Gregory, at the height of the "black consciousness" era, occasionally baited white congress delegates in retribution for remarks he considered racist, and spoke jokingly of a future "Black House" in Washington. Then he decided to go on one of his fasts for peace, consuming only distilled water. On the opposite culinary pole Carl Braden, the Kentucky civil rights fighter, had a meal with us and declared: "I don't know when I last ate grapes or lettuce! And now both at one time." After I assured him that the grapes were from Bulgaria and the lettuce from Hungary, he ate with relish. GDR youth were surprised to hear me tell of boycotts and voluntary abstention from commodities for political reasons. Doing without for them meant that an item was not available—nothing more.

Such interaction with visitors helped me enliven lectures and articles and see the GDR from an outsider's perspective—both that of the hostile visitor who found nothing good, not even the weather, and those who expected a wonderful Utopia and then found one. I tried to moderate both extremes.

This proved amusing in connection with a huge, heroic statue of Lenin by the Soviet sculptor Tomsky (next to a new 25-story apartment building, which people soon labeled "Uncle Tomsky's Cabin"). When the statue was unveiled in 1970, live on national TV, the band played, big shots orated—but only half the draping fell, a mishap recalling an unveiling in Chaplin's *City Lights*. At last someone found a ladder and ended the misery. Years later I filled in as a Berlin guide for some elderly American leftists. I had just begun to tell this amusing tale when the statue came into view. They all burst into applause. I swallowed my irony and decided: this was probably the first such statue they had ever seen.

So much depends on one's preconceptions. During a chat with three American feminists at an international women's congress in East Berlin, the abortion question came up. I mentioned proudly that abortions had been legal and free of charge in the GDR since 1972, but added that after the first trimester a medical commission was consulted. One woman asserted indignantly that "no man should ever make decisions about a woman's body". Flabbergasted, I did not even mention that many gynecologists were women, and that a woman's health seemed more important to me than a doctor's gender.

On another plane of GDR life, there were scores of "Indian Clubs" reflecting a strong and romantic fascination with Native Americans tracing back to the German writer Karl May. The clubs made "genuine" Indian clothing, tepees, and tomahawks, sometimes wore long-haired dark wigs — and a politically inclined segment supported jailed Native Americans like Leonard Peltier. Since genuine artifacts were nearly unobtainable, an arrowhead or a "real porcupine quill" was a treasure. A young fellow I knew had inherited a beautiful Native American pouch with beaded decorations and showed it proudly to Russell Means, a leader of the Native American Movement. Means studied it and said weightily: "This is a sacred Indian object which belongs with us,"—and, to the young man's almost tearful chagrin, commandeered it.

Dr. Ralph Abernathy had recently succeeded Martin Luther King as head of the Southern Christian Leadership Council when he visited the GDR. At Berlin's Humboldt University a student choir waited to greet him with a few songs. At the last minute I was able to prevent them from singing that "good old spiritual"—"Way down upon the S'wanee River." Evidently none of them understood its meaning. At Abernathy's final press conference, an official of the sponsoring Peace Council pressed me to ask Abernathy about his impressions of the GDR, a standard way of angling for flattering quotes. I disliked such assigned and unconvincing questions and answers so I asked him instead about developments in the United States. It was years before I was again invited to Peace Council gatherings.

Ben Chavis, long before he briefly headed the NAACP, had been arrested with eight young African Americans and a white woman in Wilmington, North Carolina, after defending themselves against the local Klan. I had helped gather signatures for them at the annual "International Solidarity Day," run by GDR journalists, when tens of thousands jammed Alexander Platz. Countless American GIs, impelled by curiosity or wanting to buy merchandise for almost nothing, used to visit East Berlin. Four of them must have been surprised to hear my oration in good American. They signed, even letting GDR-TV film them in the act. I met Chavis briefly when he visited to thank the GDR for its support. I also got to know his sister, who received a scholarship to study medicine at Humboldt University. She was first in her class and one of the finest persons I ever met.

Far better known in the GDR than Chavis or Abernathy was Angela Davis. When she was arrested after the courthouse tragedy involving her bodyguard Jonathan Jackson, the GDR media, but especially *Junge Welt*, swung into action. With the gas chamber threatening this attractive black Communist, it was a story to move people. "Free Angela" buttons and T-shirts soon abounded, and literally sackloads of letters, cards, and petitions from the GDR were lugged into the California courthouse. A far larger number of young people joined in such causes than in most East Bloc countries. The way such cases were officially encouraged to make political points has been disparaged or ridiculed, but it seemed to me no less legitimate than Western campaigns for some Eastern dissidents like Andrei Sakharov.

At the World Youth Festival in East Berlin in the summer of 1973 Angela Davis, as an honored guest, thanked GDR people for their support.

The festival was quite an event. Crowds of young people from the GDR and twenty-five thousand from other countries sang, danced, played music, competed in sports, paraded, and collected addresses and autographs. At Alexander Platz and along the main boulevards knots of people exchanged ideas and often debated. A few West Germans sought to inflame tensions, but exchanges, though sometimes loud, remained civil. Only once, when West Germans became very provocative, did I see obviously organized young "participants" tactfully and politely urge them to move on. Though most GDR youth delegated to the festival were doubtlessly "reliable," a large number of "uninstructed" East Berliners took part as well in a vast sprawl of debates in which most young people surprised Western media by defending the GDR.

The American group was multiracial, with several young Native Americans fresh from the recent siege at Wounded Knee. Some Americans were so enamored of the GDR that they inquired about remaining. I tried to provide a realistic picture of problems here: the inability to travel westward, the scarcity of new cars, stuffy limitations on criticism or independent ideas, discontent with a largely predetermined course: kindergarten, school, apprenticeship, military service for males, a job, or college and a job. But a young black woman journalist from Harlem heard me, then answered: "Don't you understand, man? With us it's a question of survival!"

On September 11th, shortly after the festival, Augusto Pinochet and other officers seized power in Chile, dissolving the democratically elected socialist government. An amazing number of people gathered for a makeshift protest on Unter den Linden. No one had been pressured to come, but half of East Berlin seemed to be there. I felt a powerful spirit of solidarity uniting people, due partly to the impact of the youth festival. The tragic death of President Salvador Allende, the murder of the great singer Victor Jara, the months and years when thousands were tortured, killed, or sent fleeing abroad brought recollections of Hitler's seizure of power forty years earlier. I think more people identified themselves with the GDR then than ever before or since.

In the midst of these tumultuous events, I neglected to book a summer vacation trip. At the last minute we found a big room on a run-down farm near a beach on Poland's Baltic coast. We had been warned about Polish antipathy toward Germans, and my license-plates were German. As we entered the village a crowd of youngsters ominously blocked the road. Then we saw that they were in costume, waving and joking. One youth grinned, turned, and pulled a string on his hat, dropping the seat of his pants. We wound up with them around the campfire, eating candy and swatting mosquitoes. They were among the nicest young people we ever met.

Polish living standards were generally lower than those in the GDR, and no matter what meat we ordered we got hamburger. But people were so friendly we were ashamed of the prejudices of some East Germans, generated in part by resentment toward Polish traders who sometimes cornered scarce GDR goods. Of course, East Germans also engaged in buying sprees when they traveled. Americans too, could be anti-Polish. I recalled hearing a left-wing American explain "Polish" jokes — by implying that "Polish intellectual" was an oxymoron. My shocked look made him grasp what he had said — about a country where the Nazis virtually wiped out two generations of intellectuals.

Our first international family vacation had been in 1962 at a Journalists' Home in Hungary on the fifty-mile-long Lake Balaton. The rooms were luxurious by GDR standards, as were the meals, and thanks to our little Timothy we made friends with journalist families from all over Eastern Europe. Indeed, being limited to the East Bloc was by no means smothering for our family. Each country had its own cuisines, customs, religions, and problems. We visited Hungary again, took a fascinating train trip to Moscow, climbed the snowy Tatra Mountains in Slovakia, and vacationed in the Giant Mountains of Czechoslovakia. We often traveled to Bulgaria, where another journalist hotel was on the Black Sea. That was our Riviera or Caribbean.

I also got to see the world in another way — every November at the International Documentary Film Week in Leipzig. About a thousand others were also there: filmmakers, critics, buyers, and TV people, from both Germanys and countries east and west. The atmosphere attracted mostly leftist films, and certain themes were the heart of the festival: Vietnam, Nicaragua, struggles in Cuba, Grenada, El Salvador, Chile, strike battles in northern countries, films on fascism, tragic ones about the past or warnings about the future. The festival also provided a forum and testing ground for young African, Arab, Asian, and Latin American filmmakers. Some films were brilliant: one about women construction workers in India, and another about Vietnamese women bringing supplies to the fighters on heavily-laden bicycles; *Brickyard Workers* and *Boys in the Street* about appalling conditions in Colombia; and *The Battle for Chile*, Patricio Guzmán's tragic documentation of the destruction of the Allende government. I will never forget seeing marauding soldiers after the putsch, one of whom waves his rifle — and then a blackout marking the death of the cameraman.

Warsaw Pact countries sometimes sent the "optimistic," happy worker films we despised (unless they were so weak as to be comical). But many were honest and searching, increasingly grappling with real-life problems. They reflected bad conditions, as was their duty, but sometimes seemed to generalize the worst possible situations. Films from Poland especially were often deeply depressing. It was the old question of a half-empty and half-full beer glass, but sometimes suggested a yearning for a bottle of Coca-Cola. Not all films were earnest; especially the animated shorts were deliciously satirical. Cartoons and documentaries lasting from two minutes to four hours played almost uninterruptedly from 9 A.M. to past midnight. With a separate video competition thrown in, the strain on the eyes and rears became severe. Most films were not masterworks, of course, but even some weak films were worth seeing because they portrayed fascinating people and events in far-off places. And every year there were always three or four masterpieces.

GDR films were characteristically contradictory—honestly critical or dishonest and shallow. Winfried Junge turned out a revealing film every few years set in a village near Berlin, tracing the lives of children from their first school day to adulthood. Thirty years later, he is still following their successes, failures, loves, and tragedies—a concept used elsewhere but never for so many years. Gitta Nickel made a film about the problems of shipyard workers in Stralsund: their conflicts with bureaucracy, their hunt for decent homes. Later a British filmmaker showed her documentary about Glasgow workers fighting desperately simply to save their shipyards and their jobs. The men from Stralsund were deeply moved by the contrast — and so was the British filmmaker when she visited the House of Culture of a GDR shipyard, with its amateur film and theater clubs, its music and dance and other hobby groups, all free of charge and managed by a staff of over thirty professionals.

There were always good U.S. films at Leipzig, many of them prize-winners: *Harlan County, USA,* the riveting documentary about mine workers' struggles, *Union Maids,* about women workers in the thirties, Michael Moore's *Roger and Me,* about the abandonment by General Motors of its home plant in Flint, Michigan, and many poignant films against the Vietnam War. There were bitter and sweet U.S. films about legendary musical artists Malvina Reynolds and the Weavers, about jazz and blues musicians, about radical broadcaster Studs Terkel, about subway graffiti, and about "donor firms" collecting blood from the poor on the Mexican border. How often I was moved to tears, anger, or nostalgia — and twinges of homesickness.

The festival star in 1974 was a big American with leonine mane and streaked beard, Californian Abe Osheroff. His film *Dreams and Nightmares* told how he left his fiancée to fight the fascists in Spain, and then thirty-five years later went back with a video camera to battlefields where he had fought. It was the personal, heartfelt nature of the film, free of all posturing, which caused a thousand people in the theater to stand for a long ovation — and potential purchasers from as far away as Japan to besiege him.

Ten years later another U.S. film, *The Good Cause,* also told of Abraham Lincoln Brigade volunteers in Spain, their courage and their losses, and their ongoing commitment against the war in Vietnam or for the revolution in Nicaragua. The individual portraits were moving and vivid: a little woman who defied male opposition and drove an ambulance truck in Spain; Bill Bailey, a Lincoln vet for whom I translated in 1961, who told witty but meaningful anecdotes about the volunteers' resistance to military discipline and pompous lectures by political leaders who paid short visits; and an American who sang "Freiheit" in German, a song known to every GDR citizen, playing the piano with the one hand that remained after Spain — engendering a deep, moving silence.

Some fascinating Americans came to Leipzig, often extending a cultural lifeline helping connect me to home. The left-wing screenwriters Alvah

Bessie and Lester Cole were both members of the "Hollywood Ten" who in 1947 defied the House Un-American Activities Committee and later spent a year in jail. Mark Lane, the controversial lawyer who was among the first to challenge the official version of the John F. Kennedy assassination, also attended, as did Emile de Antonio, the brilliant documentary filmmaker who was honored with a retrospective of his many films on Kennedy's murder, the "Weather" underground of the sixties, Vietnam, and Watergate. De Antonio once warned me that another American was asking too many questions about me and my story; perhaps not every visitor to Leipzig was a film buff.

The most famous American visitor was Jane Fonda, who brought a film she made in Vietnam in 1974. At her press conference a colleague nudged me to ask a question. Surely Fonda would be curious about an American here; then a private interview could be sought. It worked. We met in her hotel and talked about Vietnam, women's rights, and her film *Nora,* based on Ibsen's *A Doll's House.* She was a fervent, committed artist and activist in those days. The next day I interpreted her viewing of a film by Gitta Nickel about a woman mayor in a North Vietnamese village. Fonda then asked me to chair and translate for her meeting with festival-goers in the big theater. My usual Leipzig flu, a result of switching from stuffy theater air inside to damp, smelly air outside, had gotten worse, but I couldn't turn down this invitation. It went well until a Palestinian woman, a good director and ardent defender of her cause, asked a question which turned into an impassioned speech. Things began to get out of hand; so did my flu. I was more relieved than offended when an experienced TV speaker took my mike and saved the situation.

In earlier years few Leipzigers took note of the festival. More and more they began to wait patiently on line for tickets and often wound up standing or sitting on the floor during screenings. Many hoped for "dissident" films from the East, rock star portraits from the West, or humorous ones from all over; but they watched radical political documentaries as well. I often wished GDR schools could show how Scottish shipyard workers struggled, how school-age kids in Nicaragua fought and died to overthrow the dictator Somoza, or the desperation of U.S. ghetto youngsters. GDR-TV showed only a few such films, mostly at late hours. I kept asking about ways to get a youthful audience for them, so urgent in those last GDR years, but never found them.

The problems grew visibly and tensions increased, generated in part by the pressures of *glasnost'* emanating from the Soviet Union and by the halting and at times frightened response of GDR leaders to those pressures. A few Soviet films were even barred; that would once have been unthinkable. Film discussions in the ancient, vaunted student clubs grew unrestrained; when some GDR students supported critical Western voices the discussions were dropped.

In 1988 some young people held candles in protest at the entrance of the main theater. The action was organized in the Nikolai Church, once the scene of Bach's greatest organ performances but already a main center of opposition. GDR authorities never tolerated public opposition, most certainly not at an international event with Western journalists present. Some demonstrators were arrested, making things far worse, and a largely American-initiated petition soon circulated among festival delegates, which began to split the entire festival between GDR opponents and supporters. A year later, the whole GDR would see a massive replication of the Nikolai Church initiatives.

In 1990, after the demise of the GDR, the festival changed its character. It also became very expensive and I stopped attending. But for over two decades I had seen the many peoples of this earth trying desperately to eke out a living for themselves and their children, to find peace and a bit of decency against terrible odds. I saw men and women sacrifice comfort, liberty, even their lives to make the world a bit more human. This moral jolt, stimulating and deeply moving, made me question my own life, not luxurious but more than comfortable, and become wary of symptoms of smugness. It also made me impatient, even angry at colleagues and officials unwilling to jeopardize safe jobs, promotions, or even a bonus for the causes they so loudly praised. For me the festival was always a trenchant draft of pure oxygen.

[11]

TREMORS

In 1971 a cowboy from Denver, Colorado, named Dean Reed brought his film about Chile to the Documentary Festival at Leipzig. This guitar-playing singer and actor with a model physique and long blond hair had scrubbed the U.S. flag in a pail near the U.S. embassy in Santiago to protest the Vietnam War. That got him arrested, made headlines, and, he was sure, helped the Socialist Allende win the close 1970 election.

The film made less impact than Dean himself. He also sang at the "Anti-Imperialist Film Evening," and was soon invited to sing elsewhere, with me often interpreting for the enthusiastic crowds. A persistent fan was gorgeous Wiebke — once a teacher but now a successful model. The attraction was mutual. GDR-TV offered him a guest show, then came a big concert in Potsdam, after which over a hundred women and girls rushed him. "Let's get out," I pleaded, but Dean insisted that signing autographs was an artist's duty. He had become a celebrity.

Dean quit college in 1958, drove to Hollywood, and got lucky. Trained in acting by Warner Brothers starmaker Paton Price, a pacifist who influenced his embryonic politics, Dean also launched a singing career. Somehow South America loved his songs, and Capitol Records had him tour Chile and Argentina, where he was greeted like a conquering hero. But this son of a conservative teacher was confronted by Latin America's rural and urban slum misery. He opposed nuclear testing, had a run-in with the U.S. embassy, and met a Soviet soccer star who altered his stereotypical notions about Russians. In Argentina, he got his own TV show, planted a big on-air kiss on Soviet Valentina Tereshkova, the first woman in space, and had his house raked with gunfire by government goons who didn't care for his increasingly warm embrace of Soviets.

But the Argentine Peace Council liked his show and delegated him to a peace congress in Finland, where he diverted a split between Chinese and other delegates by singing "We Shall Overcome." From there he was warmly welcomed in the USSR, moved to Italy with his American wife to make swashbuckling films with Anita Ekberg and Yul Brynner, went back to Chile to make his film, got divorced, and landed in the GDR.

Dean got the title role in a film based on the German classic *The Life of a Good-for-Nothing,* and asked me to interpret. Most scenes were filmed in a baroque chateau near Dresden, where Dean enlivened the filming by walking on his hands or juggling tomatoes. He bonded with the crew and noted happily that workers on the set got the same food ration as the stars. We moved on to a wonderfully romantic castle in Romania. Dean got along well with people there, speaking in Italian. He protected an adoring little ten-year-old Gypsy girl who followed her "Prince Charming" wherever she could, but punished a snobbish Romanian chauffeur who wanted to drive "only Americans" in the Chrysler assigned to us. Dean took with him, on the front seat, a one-legged extra, unshaven, costumed in rags and a horrible scar. The chauffeur drove in angry silence. After finishing the film, Dean and Wiebke got married and bought a small lakeside home on Berlin's outskirts.

I also joined the crew for Dean's second GDR movie, based on Jack London's Klondike stories and filmed in the Slovakian Tatra Mountains and in snowy, beautiful Soviet Karelia. In Leningrad, on our way to Karelia, we visited the Hermitage with its great collection of French Impressionists and Expressionists tucked away on an upper floor, reflecting long-standing Soviet discomfort over such works. Dean, it turned out, shared that discomfort about art that did not "look real." He wondered aloud why Matisse or Braque didn't first learn to paint and added that "anyone can smear up a canvas like that." When the sophisticated Wiebke scoffed at his backwardness he sought support from me, his pal. But it was the provincial Rockies versus Manhattan; I tried to mediate — but couldn't support him. After this double betrayal, he stormed out. In his rage he walked a mile, coatless, through the bitter cold. Yet at breakfast the two were as lovey-dovey as ever.

I got to know Dean better on the frozen Karelian lakes that were our "Yukon." His political passions were stronger than those in official circles. Once on a TV show he held up the clenched fist popular with Western leftists — only to have GDR-TV cut the scene. The censors judged audience sentiments better than Dean, an irony in view of claims that he was misused for his leftist image. Clenched fists, real or verbal, didn't go over well with most GDR and East Bloc audiences, which knew little of the militant American or West European left of the sixties and seventies.

Dean was his own man who believed in socialism but was always skeptical about hypocrites. He was rarely naive — except about himself. When people heard self-seekers mouthing official clichés they came to reject not just the hypocrites, but those like Dean who were very sincere. He lost popularity with rock'n'roll fans who gazed enviously westward and with intellectuals for whom he was not highbrow enough. The GDR, despite being falsely described as "cut off" from Western culture, was inundated by Western fashions, pop or high-brow. Many distrusted an American who wanted to live here. Unless they could dismiss him as a U.S. failure, he upset their image of a Western paradise.

Dean wasn't a pharisee or a failure, but his showmanship made many question his sincerity. The revolution he yearned for, above all in Latin America, was linked in his fantasy to himself on a white steed, charging over barricades. I couldn't imagine him being content with humdrum labors without applause. But many celebrities seek the limelight with no principles or dreams except personal fortune. At least he sacrificed for genuine ideals, which involved some egoism but no selfishness.

As Dean's German improved we saw less of each other. He continued to make films with the DEFA studios, playing the white "blood brother" of a Cheyenne without racism or condescension and making *Sing, Cowboy, Sing,* a slapstick western with a bit of class consciousness and gentle digs at the GDR's weaknesses. Intellectuals sniffed, but the kids flocked in. In 1977, he made *El Cantor,* about Chilean singer Victor Jara, Dean's model for his image of a singer for freedom and revolution, who was murdered by Pinochet's executioners. But *El Cantor* could not match up to the great Hollywood film *Missing.*

Dean's travels took him in 1977 to the front lines in Lebanon with Yasser Arafat. Some Americans viewed his association with Arafat, the archvillain of the day, and his support for the Palestinians as anti-Semitic. He was anything but that. At a big Moscow concert he insisted on singing his standby song, "Yiddishe Momma," and the Israeli "Hava Nageela," both seen as part of the troubled "Jewish question," hence taboo. Those two songs or none, he insisted. The culture minister herself finally acquiesced and he sang them to sustained applause.

On a 1978 trip to the United States he joined a farmers' protest in Minnesota against a company stringing power lines through their fields. He and nine others were arrested. The GDR press pounced on this like a lion on a gnu: "Our Dean" arrested by the oppressors. There were protests and petitions, Dean got the other prisoners to join in a hunger strike. When I heard the charge was "trespassing," I thought: My God! The *worst* he can get is a fine or a day or so in the slammer. When the romantic fighter against oppression was acquitted, his ratings with GDR skeptics did not rise. But Dean courageously spited the dictators of Chile and Argentina and was briefly arrested there too.

The quarrels with Wiebke worsened; despite their little daughter they were divorced. In 1981 Dean married his third wife, the beautiful, dark-haired actress Renate Blume.

As the 1980s wore on, Dean's doubts increased. We discussed them when we met, questioning not the merits of socialism but the way it was applied. With popular opposition growing, more people turned from Dean, without knowing or caring much about his doubts and questions. His days as a juvenile hero were numbered, and his fan base in the small GDR was tapping out. There was still magic, if you were ready to like him. If not, his best material couldn't win you.

In 1985 Dean visited his Colorado home for the first time since his youth. Always torn between illusion and reality, he hoped a documentary film about his life would help him homeward. It didn't. Few Americans rushed to an hour-long film about someone they never heard of who was supposedly loved by Russia and Arafat.

When *60 Minutes* came to the GDR to interview East Berlin Americans, my vanity drove me to say yes, despite Mike Wallace's reputation as a tough interrogator. Dean's vanity was hardly weaker. That popular program offered new hope for a comeback in the face of fading popularity and uncertainty over a new film on Wounded Knee. A woman from GDR-TV told me that Wallace had tears in his eyes when Dean sang "Yiddishe Momma." But the tears had dried when he hammered Dean with everything from Afghanistan to the Wall. I worried about how to be credible with rough questions before a huge audience while smiling and avoiding a grim mien.

With my workroom jammed with lights and cameras, Wallace asked about my past, but then no Afghanistan, no Wall, just queries about Dean Reed and the GDR's alleged misuse of "a blond rock'n'roll" star. Wallace jumped on my comment that not everyone liked Dean's music or acting. But I'd be damned if I'd bash my friend for him—and mentioned that most people in Germany were blond. Luckily, he did not use the interview with me.

An American friend copied and sent me Dean's interview. It was a disaster—fully out of touch with U.S. sensibilities. When he jestingly spoke of Gary Hart's empty Senate seat if Hart got to the White House, I nearly collapsed. His self-appointed U.S. "manager," a Colorado woman named Dixie, forwarded to Dean copies of letters to CBS condemning it for airing the interview. Worse yet, some said his singing was terrible. One man wrote that he should be shot. Dixie said this was the end—and Dean spent hours in bed, despondently rereading those appalling letters. His dream was over.

While Renate and I vacationed at the Baltic a few weeks later, we heard the news: Dean's body, after "a tragic accident," was found in a lake near his home. I knew it was suicide. Countless friends from the arts and politics attended the funeral. Dean's mother spoke movingly, but refused to believe it was suicide or an accident, especially since the police behaved so strangely. Evidently, the SED leaders could not admit that this heroic friend of the GDR could take his life.

Their silence worsened things and stoked rumors: he had been drunk or drugged; the CIA killed him, or the Israeli Mossad. Encouraged by a letter from Dixie, Western media implicated the Stasi. That was absurd. If Dean wished to spill dreadful GDR secrets, as the tabloid press hinted, why did he pass up the chance on *60 Minutes*? Did the Stasi kill him for wanting to leave? He could go to West Berlin or the United States whenever he wanted, and often did. Many artists like Wolf Biermann or the actor Manfred Krug left with or without permission, and with no fear of retribution.

I had witnessed Dean's depressed moods and impulsiveness. Years later I read the long note he left in his car; he had been angry with Renate (I knew Dean's quarrels). He also wrote: "My greetings to Erich [Honecker]—I am not in agreement with everything, but socialism has not grown up yet. It is the only solution for the main problems in most of the world." After farewells to his daughters and adopted son, he added: "I love you and so many in Chile, Argentina, Uruguay, Palestine, the USSR, Czechoslovakia and the GDR, which became my second homeland for a short time. May all progressive people join hands and together create a better, just and peaceful world. . . ."

When his ashes were interred I spoke at the brief ceremony and compared him not to his hero, El Cid, on a white steed, but rather to Don Quixote, who dreamed of changing the world but was destroyed pursuing his dream. I had liked this difficult man, sometimes despite myself; for fifteen years we shared common ideals and common quandaries as Americans in the GDR. His background was like a layer cake: a rodeo-like childhood, Hollywood glitz and a love for showbiz gimmicks, treasured ideals learned from Paton Price, a macho-tinged Latin American revolutionary impulse with anger at poverty and "Gringo imperialist" aid for dictators, and finally the GDR and his readings in Marxism. His star had risen, but shifts in entertainment styles and the inevitability of aging combined against him. Ultimately, he was a victim of the East Bloc's disintegration, which crushed far more than one lone cowboy singer and actor.

For me, life went on. I was constantly invited to lecture to youth groups, schools, teachers' clubs, and factories, and this took me to all corners of the GDR with its historic sites, ancient towns, and beautiful scenery: Romanesque churches from the tenth and twelfth centuries in the Harz foothills, or Tangermünde's squares and alleyways where one can imagine princesses and knights in armor, or Königstein castle in "Saxon Switzerland," or the Saale valley near Jena with blossoming orchards and fairytale houses, or the white cliffs on the Baltic. Those sights, untouched by growing ferment, compensated for hours in my two-stroke Trabant or sooty railroad coaches and nights in seedy hotel rooms. Incredible as it may sound, I grew to love the place.

My lectures dealt with the United States. To allay skepticism, I admitted my long absence, joking ruefully: "In the country of the blind the one-eyed man is king." Everyone has an opinion about the United States, I noted, based either on dismal GDR media or on the popular TV fare *Dallas* and *Dynasty*. Being a foreign freelancer gave me some "jester's license" which I used for digs at the GDR's failings. When I ridiculed the deadly boredom of GDR-TV, most applauded. I remarked that if I said only bad things about my country, no one would believe me and if I said only good things, I would not get invited again. All but sleepier audiences loved that gag.

I described the United States not as a badlands of rampant unemployment, poverty, and crime, as some dutifully expected, but a country with a much higher standard of living than the GDR's. Yet it was not the syrupy land of boundless wealth and elegance portrayed on TV, but a land of conflicts and contradictions, of good and bad. I noted skeptical looks; illusions were being battered.

To rouse audiences not accustomed to disrespect for authority, even on the "other side," I culled jokes and anecdotes heard from Americans about Nixon's mendacity, Gerald Ford's pratfalls, Carter's bout with the swimming rabbit, and Reagan's denseness (like one about Reagan's ranch burning down, both books with it, and one not yet colored). In the GDR, deflating big shots as fallible was infrequent, but I considered it wholesome. Reactions to my talks were livelier and discussion less inhibited if no teachers, managers, or party secretaries were present. When a seventh grader asked my views of the USSR, I spoke of its heroism in destroying fascism and its support for freedom in Chile, Vietnam, and Angola. But I added that it was a complicated country with ups and downs and I wished the schools taught about controversial periods like those under Stalin or Khrushchev. The teacher broke in: "Oh, we discuss Stalin's cult of the personality." But before I answered a boy piped up: "Who was Khrushchev?"

Even when I skated on thinner ice it was difficult for hard liners to attack me because of my support for the GDR and socialism, with a quotation from Marx or Lenin thrown in. One quote caused problems in 1977. Speaking at a high school in Lübben, south of Berlin, I answered a question by advising skepticism about Western radio and TV programs, and broadened this with a maxim quoted by Marx: "Everything must be doubted." The teacher wrote me wondering if youngsters should be advised to doubt everything when it was so difficult to get them to believe anything. I sent a long reply saying that having pupils echo teachers was useless; the only way to help them attain genuine convictions was to debate frankly with no inhibitions, encouraging them to draw their own conclusions. She responded that after much reflection she tended to agree and confided that her invitation to a dubious writer like myself had led to difficulties with her principal. She soon left for another school.

I could not ignore examples of GDR stupidity and mismanagement; unexpected critical remarks about the GDR won me easy guffaws. But I did not engage in cheap tricks or betray my principles. When laughter subsided I often recalled the other side of a complex picture — relativizing GDR evils to poverty, violence, and environmental sins in the West. I tried to avoid worn clichés, but spoke of the GDR's role in pulling itself up from the ruins of war and blocking the ambitions of West German reactionaries. But the chronic inferiority complex of GDR citizens made them doubtful about my love for their country. When I told apprentices in Tangermünde how thrilled Americans would be to see their beautiful town, I faced the disbelief that a tourist from Paris might receive when enthusing about Newark.

In earlier years older people often said that if Americans knew war as they did, they would not support billions for armaments and military pacts to encircle socialist countries. Later there were questions about the black freedom movement and the Ku Klux Klan, about the Kennedy family, always about Indians — and about what Americans thought of the GDR. I responded that I had been away a long time, but was sure that Americans had as many different opinions as people here (the latter another rarely uttered truism). But I quoted a U.S. friend that little was known about the GDR — except the Wall. For that matter, some Americans didn't realize there were two Germanys, and knew little about West Germany or even Europe.

As the 1980s progressed there were fewer questions about the United States. Discussions involved a single vital issue: which was really better, socialism or capitalism? Answers became increasingly difficult. After a speech and a few questions before students at Köthen who then happily turned to the disco that followed, I was attacked almost physically by an angry youth with a big blond beard and mane. I had avoided oversimplification, I thought, but he lumped me with an "establishment" he opposed with every golden hair. A zealous Green, he and his friends had built an "ecological" house in Thuringia (with two-phase flush toilets). He related how one ecology event by churches and other groups was stopped by Stasi and police suspicious of actions not officially sanctioned. Our voices defied the blaring disco for an hour: I advised him to try to win changes without beating his head uselessly against the wall, but not to give up principles or beliefs either. GDR leaders, though rigid and often wrong, were not his main foes. We didn't agree fully, but did come closer, and parted on good terms.

I wondered if my advice was correct in view of an intractable leadership and asked myself why youthful enthusiasm could not be used to improve the country instead of being forced, for no good reason, into opposition? Did that young man want to be rebellious at least as much as he wanted a

better environment? If so, was that abnormal or undesirable? Before a lecture at the Technical University in Dresden, a worried youth leader said
that he hoped there would be no hostile questions. I surprised him by saying I hoped there would be.

I sometimes traveled with Werner Sellhorn, a complicated, well-read
lecturer on jazz, Woodstock, rock, and rap. His LPs, unavailable in the
GDR, brought eager student audiences but occasional problems with authorities, partly because he promoted those genres before they became acceptable, and partly because he was a friend of Manfred Krug, Wolf Biermann and other dissidents. When his audiences expressed interest in the
United States, he invited me.

On the road he hit me with the latest GDR dirt; knowing many dissidents he heard the worst. When it rang true I agreed with his condemnation — but clung to general support of the GDR or, falling back on my last
defenses, said that things might be worse with a government like Bonn.
There we agreed. He too hated right-wing nationalists and fascists (which
may shed light on why his son became a top non-Jewish interpreter of Yiddish songs).

My audiences, though getting smaller, were mostly pro-GDR. Sellhorn's audiences — and mine when I traveled with him — were usually not.
I often faced hot barrages, with one East Berlin youth club debate lasting
till midnight. In such circles it took more courage to defend the GDR than
to attack it.

Even with my usual audiences, any acceptance I found on Western
problems was only because I also listened, spoke of GDR difficulties, and
condemned what I found bad. I also noted that if the GDR were lost there
would be travel and commodities galore, but unemployment and poverty
too. Yet my talk of Western problems was only half-believed, and no solace
for people's difficulties. Increasingly I was met with skepticism when I
pleaded the overall advantages of socialism. The growing disbelief and cynicism were echoes of the Western media, though their path was eased by a
Stalinist legacy of discouraging debate or individual efforts to improve the
economy, ecology, education, and social life. There had been improvements, overlooked by many, and an ongoing conflict between good and
bad influences. But with the growing orientation of GDR citizens to West
Germany, why were party leaders still filling the media with boring eco-

nomic success statistics which no one believed, clichés no one listened to, long meetings and speeches no one paid attention to, while explosive problems waited for a spark?

Despite a gathering storm our family was busy with everyday problems like getting the kids to school with clean fingernails, combed hair, and completed homework. Once when I was away, Renate checked Tim's second grade homework, an essay on "Where My Parents Work." He wrote that his mother was a hospital librarian and his father "works in the bedroom." "You can't write that, Timothy," Renate exclaimed to a confused child who only knew that, with no study, I wrote in the bedroom.

GDR schools taught a great deal, especially in math and the sciences. There were good sports programs which contributed to GDR successes in international competition (those successes due not only to drugs as later claimed). Students were introduced to great German and some foreign writers, if not always in a way conducive to true love when, for example, poems were analyzed to the point of blurring their beauty.

Some teaching had unintended consequences. In Timothy's music class the kids heard Robeson songs and the teacher spoke of U.S. segregation in trains and buses. But it was 1971; Timothy knew from me about the victories of Martin Luther King and others — and corrected her. She didn't appreciate that — and a hostile schoolmate told the teacher in the next class that Timothy had made "racist remarks." I had to visit and clear things up.

Antifascist, antiracist, and internationalist sentiments were almost always stressed. But their force depended on the effectiveness of teachers. The occasional appearance of swastika graffiti engendered paroxysms of near hysteria. Police were even summoned but culprits rarely apprehended. And what could be done with kids whose main intent was to shock adults?

So much depended on adults. A teacher I knew ran a rest home in conifer-covered mountains for children from unhealthy mining and chemical plant areas. Once he took them to the grave of an unknown black soldier from a French colony or the United States, who at war's end, ill and exhausted, fled a prisoners' death march. Despite villagers' attempts to help, the Nazis found and killed him. The teacher told the story in simple words, the children laid flowers on the grave, and the little ceremony had a deeper impact than pompous, routine antifascist rites in many schools.

Joining the Young Pioneers was part of growing up for all but those whose parents were very religious, very anti-GDR, or both. Pioneer clubhouses in every town and borough, sometimes quite palatial, offered everything from story time to chess, from art and music to bird watching to astronomy. In big cities children could be engineers, conductors, or telegraphers on little Pioneer Railways. Tom took recorder and guitar lessons in such a club, far more sophisticated than school musical activities, which often centered around the *Schalmei,* a sort of multiple bugle. It was fun to play but too easy to learn — and ghastly for the neighbors.

For me the Young Pioneers had enriching activities but too many hands-over-head salutes and "be prepared" responses. Official ceremonies, like Lenin and Thälmann birthdays, were often deadly. They were like those overanalyzed poems; after a few years the children would never want to hear those names again. As so often, I liked the good and disliked the bad, recalling that the Young Pioneers, set up by most Communist Parties in the 1920s, were based on the Boy Scouts, which they resembled in many ways. Too many for me.

Parents elected a school advisory council, like the PTA, and met with teachers to discuss progress and problems. Perhaps the major problem for teachers was to remain credible to pupils caught up daily in the East-West conflict. Attempts to portray everything in the GDR as good and everything in the capitalist West as bad worked to an extent in the youngest grades but soon misfired; felt-point pencils from the West were nice for little ones, jeans sent by aunts and uncles in the West were nice for big kids. Since local problems were common knowledge, teachers were increasingly on the defensive, with Western media spreading the word on every GDR blunder or shortage. If teachers pressed the "black and white" categories expected of them, many students lost interest, others became adept hypocrites, and some chose total rejection, elevating to principle a belief in the opposite of what was taught. Those from pro-GDR homes supported the teacher, boycotted Western TV, and became isolated or bitterly depressed when incapable teachers attacked honest questions as provocations.

In the early years, many people watched GDR-TV programs and avidly discussed good dramatic shows and reportage. But after the 11th plenum of the SED in 1965, which castigated all Western influences, GDR programs became dull and lost popularity while West Germany stepped up football, sex, suspense, U.S. serials — and aggressive politics. The GDR waged endless campaigns against "West TV." Attempts to bulldoze people to avoid those channels succeeded only with the staunchest SED adherents (or in a few areas not reached by Western TV), so teachers were told to pressure parents to keep at least the kids from watching them. This also proved ineffectual. Parents warned children "not to let on," spreading to the kids the hypocrisy of saying one thing in school and another everywhere else.

At a parents' meeting, a school councillor zeroed in on keeping kids from Western TV. I interjected that I watched some Western programs with my sons so we could discuss them critically, adding that when our children are exposed to Western influences they should be able to recognize half-truths or lies. Some agreed, others did not. One father said passionately that he would not expose his children to poisoned food or poisoned TV. It was a fair discussion, I thought, but later realized that the councillor must have fumed at the dissipation of her efforts while she had to remain polite because of my accent and my past. Thomas once begged to see a West German sci-fi film series which came on at a late hour. We relented when he pleaded that all his classmates talked about it. He had seen one episode when the class went on a weekend excursion where the teacher eavesdropped a bit. I was not at the PTA meeting when Herr Knoppik said that the excursion went well "although the boys talked long and loud about Western TV. And who spoke longest and loudest? Thomas Grossman." Another father added sarcastically: "But then his father is an American." Renate, who they didn't know was present, complained bitterly to Knoppik and invited him to talk things over. He was less rabid than expected and said he understood our views but did not share them. Knoppik never watched Western TV, quoting Heine that he didn't want to "preach water and secretly drink wine." I wondered how teachers could respond to students' doubts and problems if they never saw the programs which had led to them.

Both Thomas and Timothy were accepted to an "Extended High School" for college preparation, open to the best students at age sixteen after the tenth grade. This dispersal into "tracks" had formerly taken place after the eighth grade, far too young, I believed, although there were alternate ways to get to college. But West German systems introduced after reunification separated children as early at the fourth grade at age ten.

After high school and eighteen months in the army, Thomas chose the Journalism College I had attended. Timothy, excused from the draft owing to a medical problem, worked in a factory for a year, then studied dramaturgy at the Film College in Potsdam.

While they were being educated, I constantly had to combat political apathy, caused by the schools' well-meaning but heavy-handed teaching. Thomas once asked me why the 1920s were so boring. "Boring?" I asked. "Were the Sacco and Vanzetti case, the British general strike, Mussolini, struggles in China and India, and the Nazi emergence here boring?" "OK, OK," he broke in. The schools left out seminal events; even the Nazi period, taught at great length, was often conveyed in a numbing way.

I wrote a long letter to Minister of Education Margot Honecker (the wife of Erich Honecker) urging an overhaul of dry, theoretical teaching of history, stress in geography on learning about many countries, and an analytical course on film and TV, encouraging skepticism as a shield against reactionary influences, including camouflaged pro-Nazi themes and violent, kitschy, or sensational films people were often hooked on. I also suggested a course on marriage and marital relations aimed in part at changing the consciousness of young males so they might share responsibilities and not push all the burdens on future wives. I received only a cool thank you note.

I was always a bit of a Don Quixote myself in the GDR—hatching ideas, some illusory, others upsetting to those who disliked boat rocking. Some things never got off the ground, including my plan of throwing an Adenauer effigy from the high dive into a swimming pool to condemn his atomic weapons strategy, or a 1955 scheme to have Leipzig students wear gags to protest a "Gag Law" against West German progressives. The authorities probably feared that people might mistake the aim of the action.

I hated *Verboten* rulings, which were the only antidotes the authorities could conjure to deal with the purposeful flood of music, clothing, dance, and hairdo fads from the West. I once proposed, partly in jest, that experts be put in a room to hatch new GDR fads in music and fashion. Our stores still offered only chess and dated kids' games in the face of the growing popularity of Monopoly and Scrabble games. If only an occasional GDR fashion caught on, it would be a big gain.

In Berlin, I suggested to the heads of publicly owned restaurants (whose acronym in neon lights read "HOG") that they brighten monotonous fare with "chicken in the basket" restaurants, spaghetti diners with moving belts from the kitchen, and seafood barges. They were polite, and a "rooster bar" was later opened — no baskets but an expensive mural. It didn't last long; people did not easily grasp novelties, nor was the supply of chicken and seafood dependable. Years later, the GDR set up broiler and seafood chains, less frightening than the McDonald's now inundating us in hamburger fat.

The ungodly 6 A.M., 2 P.M., 10 P.M. hours for shift work chopped up days and evenings, and I proposed to substitute the friendlier U.S. 8 A.M., 4 P.M., and midnight shift schedule. That would have made it easier to win GDR workers to shift work. But traditions were stubborn, and my letters didn't get a single bite.

Bonuses were another problem. When we once moved our office at *Democratic German Report,* the seventy-two-year-old cleaning woman worked very hard. I proposed a substantial 300-mark bonus at semi-annual bonus time. But bonuses could not exceed a certain percentage of one's salary, it seemed, and she got a small one. The rule was well intentioned; but here it was discriminatory. Differentiated bonuses caused more envy and quarrels than the efforts they ostensibly promoted. Regarding wages, I once was asked to choose a topic for discussion at our publishing house, and selected a segment from Lenin's *State and Revolution* where he advocated reduction of top officials' pay to "working men's wages" as "self-evident democratic measures." I wondered if such disturbingly relevant words could be discussed openly. They could; everyone agreed with Lenin.

Why couldn't numbing May Day parades be like the port town of Wismar's 750th anniversary celebration with colorful costumes, witty floats, candy thrown to the crowd, and not a single tired slogan or Politburo photo? In our annual May Day parade, factories, boroughs, or schools carried their flags and slogans a few blocks past reviewing stands, waved to big shots, and dispersed. Few watched; everyone was on parade or gratefully at their dachas. A once genuinely popular May Day afternoon fair with artists and writers chatting with fans, book sales, music, and dancing grew feebler over the years. But my May Day ideas never found the right ear.

The site of the Nazi book burning, I felt, cried out for a big statue, perhaps a phoenix. Some influential people had the same idea — and got a plaque. Western tourist buses stopped regularly to stare at Hitler's suicide locale. I thought there should be an antifascist monument there. But the official view was that Nazi pilgrimages were undesirable. Now a big Holocaust Memorial is planned for that site.

I wrote Hermann Axen in 1986 suggesting that a GDR delegation place a centennial wreath at the Chicago graves of the Haymarket Martyrs, five of whom were German-born and whose trial and execution gave birth to May Day. Stamps with their pictures could be issued, streets named after them. Axen's assistant said it would wait till 1990, the one-hundredth anniversary of the official start of May Day. That chance never came. I had crazier schemes — deluging the U.S. Senate with salt to protest its resistance to ratifying the Strategic Arms Limitation Treaty (SALT); having Honecker speak from a mountain top near the West German border to plead on TV against Euromissile deployment and for a ban of all nuclear missiles on German soil. To the Russians, I suggested that a Soviet Moslem and a Soviet Jew be sent into space to demonstrate how well they could get along if given the chance. My message did not find the correct address. Less zany was a proposal to offer apprenticeships to young West Germans, who faced a shortage of such chances in the Federal Republic. That act of solidarity would show both sides that the GDR, though poorer, guaranteed its youth jobs and job training. I was told it was not feasible. A British coal strike during the Thatcher years energized me to meet with someone at the SED Central Committee to urge that more be done than inviting miners' children to the GDR. I proposed to use union contacts to declare a worldwide day of support and, as with SALT, to swamp Thatcher with pieces of coal. But he showed little interest.

Many ideas were unrealistic; some failed because of my innate flaws: not fighting to "sell" them, giving up too easily, having too many irons in the fire. But I always deplored the stuffy nature of GDR politics — never proactive, with no ear for lively ideas. Too many were imbued less with belief in a cause than with the desire to climb a ladder which they would not shake for fear of falling. But without boldness and, above all, close ties with the people, the East could never overcome its weaker economic state.

Then there was my need to make a living. The Academy of Sciences, founded in 1700 by the mathematician and philosopher Leibniz, used a small resort hotel on a beautiful lake for training courses, and I drove there every fall and winter, one of the teachers hired to improve the scientists' English. Fortified by good food, good company, and a substantial honorarium, I had the job of getting groups arguing, and keeping them from slipping into German in their excitement. My battle cry was "Not in German! Back to English, please." I tried to increase general vocabularies, improve pronunciation, overcome speech inhibitions, and foster quick comprehension.

As the only American, I was in great demand. GDR schools taught British English, but one scientist explained that scientific congresses used two main languages: good American and bad American. I spent time on the differences between American and British pronunciation and meaning, warning them about tricky ambiguities like "bum" or "knock up" and telling them about trucks, baby carriages, subways, and busy signals (not lorries, prams, undergrounds, and "engaged"). I explained the title Ms., which none had heard of, words like chairperson and spokesperson (superfluous in German), and the fact that a letter was never signed Professor Doctor Schmidt.

A meteorologist said my class enabled him to understand from the start what transpired at a Washington meeting. That was good to hear; there was plenty that I didn't understand after weeks at the resort. My students, mostly doctors or professors, talked about their work in fields ranging from astrophysics to cancer research, DNA, higher mathematics, and zoology. I had to follow all that with my 1945 high school science base. I also taught a biannual course for the Meteorological Service, where I expected forecasters but found physicists, engineers, and stratospheric specialists. They warned me to trust only three weather rules: "If the cock crows on the dunghill top/the barometer rises or it might just drop"; "thunderstorms in May mean April is passé"; and "in the later evening hours we can expect increasing darkness."

I made some good friends strolling around the lake or playing Scrabble and discovered a fascinating array of occupations — a zoologist expert on wolves, archaeologists, computer scientists, from whom I got a whiff of emerging computer technology known to but a few in the GDR, and, in the social sciences, a Middle East authority, a specialist on German exile literature during the Nazi years, historians, and linguists. Most kept their noses to the English grindstone, but some found time for jogging, windsurfing, beer drinking, and even boar hunting.

One friend had done research at Harvard and described how it differed from his GDR laboratory, where he had an 8 to 5 workday. At Harvard, scientists came and went when they wished but usually worked late evenings, even weekends; most were single or divorced. He soon learned the reason for this intense work. If they did not produce during their two- or three-year contracts, their scientific careers might end, except perhaps for teaching. This powerful motivation, plus access to modern apparatus (difficult or nearly impossible in the GDR), brought results, if not the happiest of lives. In his GDR institute, tucked away in a small town, he and his scientist wife had time for chamber music, a cinema club, and even birding. But travel was a dilemma. He was in the limited, privileged group able to visit Western countries. His wife was not; such discrimination caused constant bitterness.

Then there was the rare watchdog over political correctness who undermined my task of getting students to argue freely enough to overcome language inhibitions. But I encouraged debate on issues like women's rights, and the women were ready to fight — or laugh. Especially when one scientist boasted that he cared for car and garage while his wife took care of meals, children, and laundry. We argued about education. Surprisingly, these scientists felt that the schools taught too much science; they should teach fewer facts but more independent thinking and put more stress on literature, languages, and the arts. I asked what party they would support in West Germany. Few liked the Christian Democrats, but few were for the Communists. Contesting about nationalist pride in German traditions, one woman surprisingly praised her Prussian background, obviously aware of its militarist aspects. I asked: should GDR citizens cheer for a West German team? Some said they should not, some were quiet. One man would back West Germany against all except the GDR. He was German, after all. I asked him if he would have supported Germany during the 1936 Olympics. He didn't answer. Ecological questions were heatedly debated. An expert described the dangers to the vulnerable Baltic sea and blamed both East and West. A specialist on atomic power insisted on its reliability. He was hotly disputed well before Three Mile Island and Chernobyl.

They traveled more than most GDR citizens, though not without worries. A meteorologist was so alarmed by stories about U.S. crime that in two weeks in the nation's capital he never left the Hilton. Another, taking a cab with a colleague from Kennedy Airport to Manhattan, worried about the speeding meter and asked if the fare, now about $40, was for both passengers or one. No need to mention the answer! I asked a group what they would do if their U.S. hotel were blocked by a strike. Would they go in anyway? Few had seen or even visualized a picket line and their answers were often naive; one student said that he would explain to the strikers that he was from the GDR and did not know his way around.

I learned a lot, including some unwelcome wisdom. An expert on nuclear power, an assistant to Klaus Fuchs, the scientist jailed for passing atomic secrets to the Soviets in the 1940s, told how long he thought it would take for the socialist countries to catch up with the major capitalist ones. His pessimistic assessment was a shock — a salutary one, I know now. But that was in the 1970s, when the GDR media loudly sang another tune.

There was an interesting mix of teachers: a refugee from the Nazis who grew up in Shanghai and came to the GDR to marry a German who fought with the Greek partisans, an Iraqi woman who fled Saddam Hussein, a South African threatened with prison for fighting apartheid, a Jewish emigrant who had married a German veteran of the Spanish Civil War. One teacher, whose family fled from the Nazis to Australia, became an ardent feminist, then an ardent Zionist, and lectured the scientists on both subjects. That didn't bother them, but a few were annoyed by her nude bathing; she was too easy to spot because of the autumn season, when no one else tried nude bathing — and because of her not inconsiderable girth.

For years we had parties to close each course, with students singing or playing instruments. We had limerick contests, the linguists once organized skits poking fun at the teachers, and a mathematician fashioned riddles based on "wanted" posters for fairytale or mythological characters. A young atomic scientist sang songs learned from a Pete Seeger record. His guitar was way out of tune, but he kept playing despite all our hints. Several years later I told this anecdote at the scientists' course and we all laughed. One man slowly stopped laughing; I had failed to recognize the guitarist of an earlier year. I slunk away and did not betray him, but he offered no songs that year.

By 1988 Western cultural influences were so strong that energy to contest them became spent — no longer were useless prohibitions and polemics issued, nor, except for a few GDR rock bands, were serious efforts made to fashion alternatives. This near-capitulation was symbolized by a GDR-TV concert for youth with a U.S. band playing country-western music, which was sweeping Europe, West and East, replete with phony cowboy regalia and caricatured square dancing. This group was competent or clever enough to work the audience into a frenzy. I enjoy good country myself if sprinkled with a touch of self-irony, which here was in short supply. The Marlboro logos on their shirts riled me too; cigarette ads were forbidden in the GDR. I was pondering the merits of giving youth something to get excited about when the final insult came. In the middle of the wildly applauding audience, someone waved a huge Confederate flag while the camera zoomed in for a long closeup as the show came to a tumultuous end.

That did it. I wrote GDR-TV a letter: I might understand such music if nothing equally popular were available, but I could not understand the Marlboro ads or the Confederate symbol of slavery. West German TV showed a film with the same flag buried in mud — and the GDR raised it on high. An editor answered, agreeing with me, but adding that the Marlboro logos were a contractual condition about which nothing could be done. She forwarded my letter to the Rostock studio that filmed the concert. Their response was apologetic, but probably a concession to pressure from Berlin superiors. This was the opposite extreme of the SED dictat of 1965.

The Confederate symbol came up again in the GDR's final year. An American teacher visiting East Berlin asked a youth on a local train if he knew that the rebel flag on his jacket was used by the Ku Klux Klan. Was he also against black people? He did know, and he was a racist. She wrote down the exchange before leaving for home. I gave it to the *Junge Welt*, adding an explanation about the flag, mentioning Alabama black legislators who faced charges for removing the flag from the State House, and warning about growing racism in the GDR. I rejected an editor's rewrite of my comments. A compromise was reached, with the very worst remarks of the young man expunged under the ridiculous old motto: "what must not be there is not there."

Efforts were always made to mold an internationalist consciousness in children and youth. Children's books, children's theater, children's films, and the one and only authorized comic book series all stressed friendship among nationalities with varying degrees of skill and subtlety. Books about African, Asian, and Gypsy children were classics. But such works did not reach all homes. Many youngsters became so Western oriented that they automatically rejected GDR culture. Some hooked onto rock idols, others onto racism. This reflected a rebellious search for alternative models to those preached — valid or not.

A lack of visible "class struggle" in the GDR made hatred of the "capitalists" unreal and unconvincing. What target was there for young people's rebellious feelings? Sometimes, teachers and all "authorities" were targeted — and what such people taught (or were supposed to teach), including their proclaimed internationalism. Also, racism found a response among some youth, as in every society, partly because "different" people —

others — are met with misunderstanding and rejection. Too few grasp that a person of another sex, age, or dialect, and especially with another language, nationality, culture, religion, or skin color, is as human as they are. Too many are mired in provincial chauvinism: my street, my team, my language, my culture are better than yours.

When strangers stayed in the background (like the thousands of Vietnamese in the GDR), providing neither problems nor competition, they were tolerated. But when foreign males looked for GDR girlfriends, maintained their own cultures, and sometimes flashed highly desired Western currency, hatred could grow unless something were done to oppose it, working consciously to forge respect for both nationalities and individuals. Bringing people together in mutual respect is not easy and must be done constantly, accompanied by frank discussion and enlightenment about problems, difficulties, other ways of seeing things. Good examples of this were too rare.

There is another factor. Germany had conquered its colonies late in its history and had less contact with Asian or African peoples than France, Britain, or other nations. The GDR had less contact than West Germany, friendly or unfriendly, with immigrants. Foreign workers in the GDR often lived in special dorms with little mixing except at some colleges. There was less deep-rooted bigotry perhaps, but a greater chance of friction when contacts increased. I was glad when the *Junge Welt* helped me break the ice on this subject, so often avoided in the media. But instead of promoting a readers' discussion it let the matter drop. This could partly — only partly — be blamed on the rapidly growing crisis in the country, with all its fatal, but not totally unrelated issues. It was far too little and far too late.

[12]
DEATH OF A NATION

Life in the GDR began to feel less like isolated Pitcairn's Island and more like Mt. Etna. The official attitude, "there can be no eruptions here," seemed blind and unworthy of anyone seeking a better world. Had we learned nothing from Pompeii?

The rise of Lech Walesa and Solidarity in Poland elated some and worried others. To its shame, the SED, fearing contagion, tacitly downgraded its traditional "everlasting friendship with the Polish people," and chauvinist drivel about "lazy Polish workers" bubbled from mudholes. Tension also rose when NATO stationed Pershing missiles in West Germany despite protests by 400,000 West Germans. The Soviets responded with nuclear missiles in the GDR despite the SED's displeasure — which was never publicly stated.

Education and propaganda in the GDR were riven with contradictions. Peace was stressed in every school and factory. But preparedness was also emphasized: the need for young men to do "honorable" military service. Civil defense programs, a weekly "defense hour" in school curricula, but above all the draft were hated by pacifists, who moved increasingly into opposition and were given sanctuary and support by churches. The Evangelical (Lutheran) Church enjoyed special status. For years the government sought a modus vivendi based on laissez-faire. The church held a trump card; it could call for help from its West German sister church. The GDR, seeking foreign recognition and trade, hoped to avoid bad press from religious institutions. But GDR leaders had alienated churchgoers by raising college entrance hurdles for active worshippers and made things tough for conscientious objectors, especially those rejecting even nonmilitary service.

Disarmament groups in the churches (and many an atheist) created a network to oppose the missiles, the draft, the school curriculum, and toy weapons, which were fewer than in the West but still too numerous. Their line was "a plague on both your military and nuclear houses," but the main targets were East Berlin and Moscow. Church leaders distributed shoulder patches with the swords-into-plowshares Soviet statue at the UN coupled with the slogan "make peace without weapons." Asinine authorities fell for this clever jab and had teachers and cops insist on removing the patches, antagonizing thousands of students.

In 1985 the Gorbachev era began. The USSR now had a leader urging new thinking about freedom and socialism, just as many of us had dreamed. We rejoiced at his courageous quest for disarmament; peace seemed closer and we loved Gorby for it. Youngsters wore picture buttons, birthmark and all (official portraits erased it; Soviet leaders were unblemished). Gorbachev's calls for ending nuclear tests, for arms cuts, and billions for the Third World threw not only Ronald Reagan off balance, but also the opposition in the GDR. Some lost interest in disarmament.

They found other issues, like human rights. Some demands were indisputably sound, but the enterprise was ideologically driven and advanced selectively with a blind eye to human rights violations in the West. I was friendly with some dissidents and could sympathize with many who were sincerely devoted to peace, human rights, or the environment. Yet the anti-GDR hostility of many blinded them to the country's support for freedom in South Africa, Chile, and Central America, in marked contrast to West Germany, where they lacked interest in freedom for Nelson Mandela or Leonard Peltier. Every easing of GDR restrictions brought new demands — calling into question whether they really wanted greater freedoms or the end of the GDR.

Ecological issues also moved into the spotlight. The GDR was one of the worst sinners, owing to its compelled reliance on smelly, sulphurous lignite, its tight budget, and rising pressure for energy-expending growth in housing and advanced technology. Remarkable results were achieved with recycling, but when opponents increased attacks, for ecological or political reasons, a lid was clamped on most actions not initiated from above, making things worse.

Homosexuality was another opposition issue, though not all church officials were happy to have gay and Lesbian groups under their roofs. The FDJ, realizing at last that it was wrong to ignore the issue, sponsored open discussions; relevant GDR laws were very good compared to those in West

Germany or the United States, but people's thinking, and some actions, often lagged behind.

Vera Lengsfeld, an important opposition figure, later summed up the situation leading up to 1989: the ferment was preceded by a decade "of building an opposition movement for peace, human rights, and the environment under the protection of the Lutheran Church," which itself enjoyed a relationship to the state that was unique in the East. Opposition activities — seminars, conferences, exhibitions, independent newspapers, libraries with Western materials — were developed on church premises, with church representatives often participating actively as organizers and advisers. By the mid-1980s the independent groups were firmly linked, with annual meetings attracting thousands. Defense of the opposition earned for the church "much moral credit," making it "a significant political factor in the country." Three years before it fell, the government could not make a decision without considering the church's response.

Berlin's 750th anniversary was meant to improve the atmosphere, but the celebration became a one-upmanship race with West Berlin that had people bored before 1987. There were fine concerts, more quality goods, a big fair and parade, even a Miss Berlin, the first GDR Miss anything. Berlin was again overly favored. When humorless cops had sarcastic Saxons remove bumper stickers saying "Dresden: 771 Years" or "Leipzig: 831 Years," they soured even more people. Some remarked: "Marx tried to build socialism in the world, Lenin in one country, and Honecker in one city." In Leipzig in July 1987 for an English course, I found bitterness about downtown and neighborhood decay, despite new housing and the beautiful new concert hall. After returning to my run-down hotel I understood anger at neglect of Saxony's largest city in favor of rival Berlin.

Restrictions on Western travel were a major source of unrest and envy. After the erection of the Wall, it was long limited to top athletes, trusted scientists, writers and artists, politicians, journalists, truckers, machine experts, fishermen, and seamen. Some youngsters planned whole careers that made "going West" possible. Security officials trembled because promotions depended on how many of those they granted West-visas also returned.

It was a harsh game: Western agencies did everything to get GDR visitors to stay. A journalist friend was treated roughly in the United States when he rejected repeated offers to defect. A GDR orchestra was followed the length of its West German tour by men trying to bribe two bassoonists to remain. I knew firsthand of organized attempts to get doctors to "flee." Western media directly subsidized some escapes at crucial times.

Pressured by the GDR population and West Germany, the government relaxed travel restrictions. Men over sixty-five and women over sixty had long been permitted to visit the West for one month each year. Groups of young people, sifted to exclude possible defectors but growing in number, toured Western Europe, Algeria, Mexico, even the United States. Suddenly people not in "sensitive jobs" could visit Western relatives for family gatherings. The rules eased more and more: the sixty-second birthday of a great-aunt twice removed seemed to suffice. A joke explained an alleged shortage of shovels: everyone was trying to dig up forgotten relatives. In 1987, the numbers of nonretirees visiting the West nearly doubled in one year to 1.2 million. Even legal emigration, though slowed by red tape and often meanness, grew easier. Barriers were clearly falling.

At the huge Buna chemical plant I had a "friendship contract," a common practice in which writers paid annual visits to read or speak. Buna had been part of the Farben cartel, which ran the main factory at Auschwitz and produced death gas. It had been confiscated after the war and placed under public ownership; despite its big clubhouse, its library, and an "artotheque" which lent reproductions of great art, it wasn't pretty in looks or odor — but was rid of its Nazi past. During one of my visits there was a "lingerie fashion show," actually a mild peep show, unthinkable two years earlier. As we waited for the models, talk turned to travel to the West. Legions of GDR citizens were returning from West Germany with complaints of too little travel money and worn-out welcomes, but starry-eyed about a modern consumer paradise. Few knew or cared about problems there. In an increasingly permissive climate, T-shirts picturing everything from Donald Duck to U.S. bases sprouted everywhere — while one could not escape getting an earful of anti-GDR invective from perfect strangers.

In the winter of 1987, I too embarked on travels. The Iraqi exile who had taught English with me for the Academy of Sciences was now at Oran University in Algeria, and asked me to lecture there. I prepared eight classes on American themes and in May crossed the Mediterranean to a land of palms and minarets — my first destination outside the East Bloc since 1952.

At beautiful but run-down Oran University I faced about a hundred mostly female students, many with their hair piously covered. The young

Moslem women reacted well to my antiracist subject matter and my lectures on trade union history from the Molly Maguires to the Harlan County coal strikes. We canvassed a wide literary and cultural horizon from Mark Twain to Woody Guthrie to Bruce Springsteen. They asked about Harriet Tubman, were eager to learn more of Martin Luther King, Malcolm X, and Du Bois, and were receptive to my remarks about racism, women's rights, even anti-Semitism. I felt almost at home.

In Algeria I saw handsome streets, well-ordered villages, and frightening poverty. Street life was animated and markets in Algiers were awash in products. This contrasted with the GDR—but so did the beggars and the destitution. Algeria was fascinating despite its daunting problems. But surprisingly I found that I was glad to return to quieter East Berlin which, despite dogma and decay, had after all become my home.

I had hardly returned when a new salvo was fired across the GDR bow. Just across the Wall, huge concerts were to feature David Bowie and other artists with irresistible appeal to GDR youth bitter at being barred from such live events. Love of music or altruism for deprived young people hardly inspired the concerts on June 6–8, 1987. Western media plugged them so thoroughly I half expected a pilgrimage to the Wall rivaling Mecca. In 1974 RIAS had hinted that the Rolling Stones might perform from a rooftop near the border. They would not have been visible—but crowds of youngsters showed up, the cops lost their heads, and the resulting riot pushed the GDR's twenty-fifth anniversary out of the news. Now concert organizers knew that crowds of fans would draw less musically interested police and security. If thousands came and stormed the Wall, would there be nightstick assaults, tear gas, and worse?

The concert could be heard a mile away; a decibel deluge buried the nearby Charité Hospital. There were scuffles the first evenings as young East Berliners moved closer to the Wall than allowed. On the third evening, crowds pushed harder toward it, throwing bottles and firecrackers. Cops and Stasi men, clearly under orders to avoid violence, linked arms to hold the line. Some in the crowd were arrested, including two or three West German newsmen. Deluded as this was, West-TV hysteria about police violence was based on a bruise on one leg. More was needed. Some GDR kids looked sheepishly into the camera, calling out weakly at first, "Down with the Wall" and "Gorbachev." But they were clearly directed by some maestro off camera. Western media erupted in an enraged outcry; one paper recalled the GDR revolt of June 17, 1953, and added hopefully: "That day is no longer distant."

Three days later Ronald Reagan arrived in West Berlin and at the Brandenburg Gate called on Gorbachev to "tear down this Wall!" The concerts and possible attacks on the Wall were surely provoked to prepare for Reagan's demands — while smothering Gorbachev's peace proposals and threatening a new Berlin crisis. But it all misfired when vehement protests in West Berlin answered Reagan's rejection of the peace proposals; 360 protesters were arrested, bystanders (including journalists) severely beaten, bus and subway lines halted. The West Berlin events made East Berlin look like a kindergarten tiff. Yet media reports of the anti-Reagan protest were so muted, in contrast to blaring the "passionate demands" of East Berliners, that few in the West were aware of the bloodshed on their side of the Wall.

The irony of Reagan's injunction to Gorbachev was that relations between the GDR and Soviets had cooled greatly. GDR leaders, who for years trumpeted the universal validity of the Soviet model, now feared Gorbachev's changes. "Perestroika" was brushed aside as irrelevant to the GDR's economy, and "glasnost'" was rejected in favor of continuing media controls. Increases in the price of Soviet oil further exacerbated relations. Gorbachev's speeches were printed in the SED paper, but so was veiled criticism, with Politburo member Kurt Hager saying: "You need not renovate your house when your neighbor repapers his walls." "Gorby" buttons quickly multiplied.

Soviet leaders feared that the GDR might sign agreements with West Germany behind their backs, although (or because) they were probably negotiating their own changes in relations with Bonn at GDR expense. In July 1987 the GDR moved to improve ties with Bonn. Anticipating Honecker's West German trip in September, which went ahead without Gorbachev's blessing, the GDR abolished the death penalty and freed most nonviolent prisoners. In September, Honecker negotiated accords on trade and travel and expressed the hope "that the GDR-FRG border would soon resemble the GDR-Polish border [which had no wall]." A joint statement by the SED and the West German Social Democrats agreed to differ but to respect the other's views. Bavarian leader Franz Josef Strauss arranged a billion mark credit for the GDR. Things began to look peaceful.

Elements of the West German right became alarmed by the warming atmosphere. Helmut Kohl recalled that "Germany must be reunified" and "The German question is still open." Soon after Honecker's successful visit, programs aimed eastward became icier, turning small GDR stumbles into big events. The annual January march that honored Karl Liebknecht and Rosa Luxemburg, who founded the German Communist Party in 1919 and were then murdered, was used by dissidents who sought to wave "unauthorized" banners, the shrewdest a Luxemburg quotation: "True freedom means respecting the freedom of those who think differently." They were quickly arrested, while West-TV filmed the melee, which was known about in advance by both West German media and the Stasi. Equally orchestrated, I suspect, were immediate candlelight protests in GDR churches. Luxemburg was a sudden heroine of a West German press which rarely mentioned that this Polish-Jewish Communist had had her head bashed in by people claiming to save Western freedom from Bolshevism.

Some demonstrators hoped to be expelled from the GDR, which obliged. Others, a director, a singer, and an artist, were banished temporarily to the West. Hitherto little known, they had been built up after the Honecker visit by Western media as leading dissidents. The government had again been baited into a trap with its breathless arrests. The opposition gained the initiative: repression enhanced its stature; toleration gave it victories and further growth.

The blunders continued. The price of GDR-made cars was suddenly raised. *Sputnik,* a Soviet magazine exported especially to the GDR, published an article blaming Hitler's rise to power largely on the German Communists. I felt it was distorted; Honecker, who spent ten years in jail for fighting Hitler, evidently found it far worse. *Sputnik* was banned, alienating subscribers. Some asked why there had not been open debate about the article. That, sadly, was a method never learned by East German leaders.

Critical supporters of the GDR faced growing isolation both from pro-Westerners and from officials, either "true-blue" or hypocrites who removed party buttons after work. Many deplored the stupidity and occasional brutality of GDR leaders but could hardly support the Adenauers and Kohls. Especially for those who had suffered under the Nazis, "over there" seemed a diluted continuation of the tragic German past. Many of us hoped for change when the old-timers left the scene. But they clung to power, believing that only they could be keepers of the flame. And what would come next? Would a principled leader like Hans Modrow emerge, or would the country inherit a fresh crop of incompetent careerists?

At a lecture in an East Berlin library, I was critical of the GDR but defended its positive achievements. Later a writer friend said wryly: "You're the last of the Mohicans."

The United States was always on my mind. Jimmy Carter had announced a conditional amnesty for deserters, but it applied only to Vietnam-era servicemen, not to the sparse few from earlier conflicts. In 1977, I got a letter from the U.S. embassy, which had opened in East Berlin three years earlier when the United States recognized the GDR. It asked if I had given up my citizenship (I had not) and what status I considered for my sons, and invited me to come in and talk things over. Although I was in the telephone book, they sent the letter to my publisher, using both names. I had confided my real name only to my family, but they had finally ferreted it out!.

Summoning up all my courage, I walked into the embassy and met with a courteous consul who asked why I didn't go home and assured me that nothing serious would happen. I agreed to have him cable the Pentagon, and a few days later he called to say that I would face a charge of going AWOL, not desertion, since intent must be proved in those cases. That probably meant a general discharge.

Yet I had not only deserted but had written and spoken in ways which I felt were completely loyal but which few U.S. Army officers would see that way. In the following months I spoke with consuls or vice-consuls several times. All were encouraging, but one told me that if I met a member of the armed services, he would be obliged to return me to my last army station. That was hardly reassuring. When I next visited, his successor invited me to come along with him to West Berlin and check on my status at the Judge Advocate's office. That did it. Wouldn't the first soldier with whom I came in contact be obliged to nab me? I was still frightened and stopped visiting, though I never gave up completely.

In 1987, I came across the address of an old Harvard leftist pal in a magazine. We corresponded fairly often, and when he included a copy of our class bulletin, *The Forty-Niner,* I wondered why I should keep my existence a secret. I wrote an account of my adventures and sent it in. It was printed in 1989.

I received a letter from a professor who had held important positions in the Nixon and Reagan administrations and who invited Renate and me to the fortieth class reunion. What exciting news! With help from a prominent alumnus with government experience, the great leap might be possible. I wrote him about my concerns, asking discreetly if Harvard would back me.

Time was too short to await an answer. I gave the new U.S. consul my two names, mentioned the invitation, and asked about my prospects. She seemed confident and gave me questionnaires to fill out supporting my claim to citizenship and a passport. I left the embassy with a thumping heart and filled out the papers as soon as I got home. I booked last-minute flights for Renate and myself, and then rushed to the police to ask permission for Renate to accompany me—which was granted after I explained that she also wished to see relatives, the reason for millions of permitted Western visits.

But when I returned to the consul she told me that my case was not as simple as she had thought, and advised me against a trip: "The army has a long memory." I walked out dazed, but convinced that despite my disappointment, I damned well better let the trip go. The flights were canceled. I had managed so long without returning; I must accept this and get on with my life. My alumnus contact later informed me that Harvard would welcome me but take no responsibility toward the government or army.

We had decided to take an earlier planned vacation. When we returned to Berlin in August, letters in response to a *Harvard Magazine* reprint of my account began to arrive, sixty in all, mostly from people I never knew, but also from an old Bronx Science classmate, from two Harvard Party comrades, and, amazingly, from two very elderly former Fieldston teachers, including my brilliant literature teacher, who though past ninety recalled my 1945 essays—even a lousy one.

The Harvard exchanges led to some interviews, including one with the *Washington Post*. My attempt to go home had failed, yet I was in closer contact with the United States than ever before. Some letter writers visited, including a linguist who had a theory that Yiddish was not based primarily on early German, but, as evidenced by synoptic and grammatical elements, on Sorbish, my father-in-law's language. Correct or not, this bore an interesting connection to my life and marriage. That contact, along with a letter from a Harvard alumnus who asked how I felt about living in the country that his parents had had to flee, renewed my thoughts about my American and Jewish background.

I understood the mistrust toward Germany, East or West. Any thought that anti-Semitic feelings had disappeared almost anywhere — especially here — was nonsense. Yet I was convinced that there were basic differences between East and West Germany, and not because West Germany paid compensation to some Jewish survivors and had relations with Israel, while the GDR had almost no contact with it.

In 1948 the USSR and Eastern Europe supported Israeli independence far more than the West. But Soviet-Israeli relations soon deteriorated. Stalin turned fiercely anti-Semitic and incited "anti-Zionist" campaigns in Eastern Europe. The new GDR as a German state was very sensitive on the issue, and was spared most of this. But a mistrust emerged, stupid as it was vicious, toward returned antifascists, many of them Jewish, who had survived in the United States, Britain, and elsewhere. Such painful signals caused part of the small Jewish population to move westward. This ended with Stalin's death and the so-called thaw under Khrushchev.

I knew nothing of such developments until years after my arrival in 1952. The havoc wrought was nasty but patchy, and Jewish Germans, mostly with leftist roots, were always important to the GDR and to me personally. My Journalism College was headed by Hermann Budzislavski, a Jewish emigrant to the United States. Gertrude Heym, a Jewish-American, was my first boss after school; her husband Stefan Heym, also Jewish, was for years an honored popular author. My next boss, John Peet, was not Jewish but knew far more about Judaism than I (he even read Yiddish). His wife had survived the death camps. The head of our publishing house had been a Jewish refugee in Shanghai. At Radio Berlin International two successive party secretaries had been Jewish refugees in Britain and the head of GDR radio, Gerhart Eisler, was a Jewish refugee in the United States. The honorary president (Politburo member Albert Norden), the chair, and most members of the Robeson Committee where I was archive director had been Jewish refugees in the United States. The president of the Academy of Arts, the archive's "home," was film director Konrad Wolf, once a Jewish refugee in the USSR. The Writers' Association I joined in 1980 was headed by the renowned Jewish writer Anna Seghers, whose wartime refuge was Mexico. The artists' and composers' associations also had Jewish presidents, and major theaters were headed for years by Jewish men or women. One minister of culture, Klaus Gysi, was Jewish, as were leaders in the arts, the press, and politics. Few, if any, were practicing Jews, but the number in leading positions (with Jews constituting less than 0.4 percent of the population) was without parallel in West Germany. Nearly all leading figures had fought the Nazis, were imprisoned, or fled into exile.

Because I had accepted the name Grossman, I was constantly asked if I were of German descent, thus giving me an opportunity to check attitudes. I replied that it was "a Jewish name" and watched for reactions. Invariably, the responses were indifferent, as if I had said "Danish" or "Welsh." Occasionally I was asked my grandparents' homeland, or a rare few told me some ancestor was Jewish. I never once felt threatened, disadvantaged, or out of place because of my ethnicity.

The large number of returning Jewish and anti-Nazi intellectuals spawned countless plays, films, and books that were strongly antifascist. This also reflected the efforts of early Soviet occupation administrators (like Alexander Dymschitz, also of Jewish descent), who encouraged such works. Although some were later recalled by Stalin, they had already helped create a long-lasting foundation. Not accidentally, the first play in East Berlin after the war was Gotthold Lessing's *Nathan the Wise*, with a Jewish philosopher hero, and the first film, the powerfully anti-Nazi *The Murderers Are amongst Us*, was followed by films assaulting anti-Semitism, *The Blum Affair* and *Marriage in the Shadows*. The latter, the most moving condemnation of Nazi racism I have ever seen, was viewed by ten million East Germans, of a total eighteen million.

As Israeli–East Bloc relations worsened, especially after the 1956 and 1967 wars, there was a tendency to downgrade the "Jewish question." But it was never obliterated, nor was anti-Nazism forgotten. The GDR's all-time best-seller, read by nearly every schoolchild and countless adults, was *Naked among Wolves*, a stirring book about the rescue of a Jewish child by inmates in Buchenwald who then found courage to hold out. This true story was filmed three times over the years, twice for TV. Attempts to find the child finally succeeded; an Israeli athlete, he was welcomed in the GDR with immense publicity, to the joy of all the book's fans.

Essential to all this was the removal of Nazis from the educational, legal, and administrative systems from the start. The worst of them "fled west," but a few Nazis in the GDR were later caught and convicted, and received severe sentences, including life if their crimes warranted it. A Western media cliché was that the GDR, unlike West Germany, denied the past Nazism of its citizens, proclaiming them "partners in anti-Nazi resistance."

This is untrue. President Wilhelm Pieck in his first speech demanded that the country be cleansed of rubble in the streets and the rubble in people's minds — a constantly recurring theme. West Germany, not the GDR, claimed to be "the legal successor of the Third Reich," kept many old laws, and allowed Nazis to glorify Hitler's armies in magazines and pulp novels that sold in the millions. Jewish culture in the West was undoubtedly richer, with larger congregations and closer ties to Israel. But Holocaust deniers and Nazi apologists were also common. Though Nazi annihilation of European Jews was badly underemphasized in GDR schoolbooks, a terrible mistake, the Nazi past was never denied in the East and any trace of sympathy for it was stigmatized.

In the GDR's final years there was growing attention to Judaism, partly sparked by the fiftieth anniversary of Kristallnacht, the 1938 Nazi pogrom, and partly by gradual normalization of relations with Israel. Performances of Yiddish music were often sold out; new surveys of Jewish art, culture, and religion — and their repression under the Nazis — proliferated in the West and East, including a large East Berlin exhibition. A West Berlin cantor visited the GDR to sing in Hebrew with the Lutheran cathedral choir of Magdeburg and the equally non-Jewish Leipzig Synagogal Choir. The head of the GDR's small Jewish synagogues gave the keynote address at the Parliament's memorial; the parallel ceremony in Bonn featured Bundestag President Phillipp Jenninger, whose attempts to "explain" Nazi anti-Semitism were so questionable that he was forced to resign.

Life in general in the GDR was becoming more modestly comfortable. In 1952, I couldn't find a washrag or razor blades; TVs, washing machines, and refrigerators were hardly known. But by the 1980s nearly everyone had those appliances. New generations took them for granted, as they did full employment and an absence of poverty. A big high-tech program had begun: district capitals were rejuvenated; historic concert and opera houses were beautifully restored; new high-rise projects were built. Many picturesque half-timbered houses were deserted by grown children who preferred flush toilets and central heating in low-rent apartments. But state budgets could be stretched only so far, and the fastest construction could not catch up with the huge demand. Many fumed at shortages of oranges and bananas and at long searches for fashionable clothing or tiles for "dachas." VCRs or computers were rarities and there were incredible waiting lists for not-so-modern cars, but since wages rose more quickly than production or imports, supply always lagged behind demand and shortages were part of life.

By the mid-eighties the race to catch up was faltering. The economy stopped improving as it had for decades; even common items were not always available and industries were plagued by missing machine parts and down time, though the GDR media cheered about our scientific-technological revolution, replete with thousands of industrial robots. A scientist I questioned smiled ironically; robots could be counted in many ways; we're lagging behind.

Rent, fuel, most food, carfare, childcare, utilities and services kept the same low price levels as in 1958. But the cost of cars, books, and imported movies (mostly U.S.), shoes, textiles, and some toys edged upward. A public accustomed to prices going down complained bitterly. Many railed about Intershops, where better Western goods were sold for Western money to the detriment of those without access to magical hard currency. A social divide was emerging with Western money as the fault line. New chains of shops offered desirable goods for GDR money, but their high prices only raised hackles.

Dissatisfaction continued to be fanned by West German TV, which effectively played up GDR problems while displaying alluring Western life styles. The two GDR channels, though sometimes excellent, rarely matched the visual aromas wafting into our more Spartan society, while our authorities kept stuffing news reports with boring statistics claiming successes which no one believed, and making speeches no one listened to.

People like myself feared such rigidity, but also dreaded nervous overreaction which might ignite a disaster. Also, it seemed that a new offensive was emerging aimed at ending the "socialist threat" once and for all. It included B-2 stealth bombers and MX missiles around the whole East Bloc. The densest concentration of missiles in the world was in West Germany. On the carrot side, Deputy Secretary of State John Whitehead said during an East European tour that "positive movement toward political and economic pluralism" in the region could lead to better relations with the United States. He stressed that U.S. policy was "activist, not passive," in seeking to advance "positive change in Eastern Europe." Even the carrot had an "or else" flavor.

The offensive showed results. In Poland and Hungary more and more power was transferred to foreign investors and local people whose main interest, despite resounding words about democracy, lay in getting rich. When Polish and Hungarian workers wildly cheered Bush or Thatcher, who loved strikers and unions only in Eastern Europe, their political leaders seemed unable to muster the conviction and moral authority to counter such responses. When religion or nationalism were invoked they floundered badly. The GDR, bordering Poland, but once so politically correct, was now edging toward the same slope.

As tension grew, I wrote about the growing danger to Horst Sindermann, a Politburo member who had spent twelve years in a Nazi prison. I proposed an urgent series of well-crafted TV addresses, patterned on Roosevelt's "fireside chats," speaking truthfully about the housing problem — impossible to solve by 1990 as promised — about rising prices, the auto shortage, travel, and exchange rates. If these were discussed honestly, credibility might gradually be rebuilt. I learned later that Sindermann read the letter and put it in his pocket.

In the summer of 1989 we spent three weeks at Usedom, an island off the Baltic coast, at a thatched house surrounded by fruit trees and gardens overflowing with roses and dahlias. Renate preferred "FKK" ("Freie Körperkultur") or nudism, which covered (or uncovered) at least a third of GDR beaches and was expanding into "textile beach" areas. I preferred an adjustable wicker beach chair where, enveloped in my textiles, I could read and fight off an invasion of ladybugs. While we enjoyed flowers and fought bugs, the situation kept deteriorating. In August, 130 GDR citizens holed up at the West German mission in East Berlin, demanding exit visas. Crowds of East Germans soon camped at West German embassies in Budapest, Prague, and Warsaw, while Bonn reiterated its claim to be responsible for "all Germans."

While beaches and lakes were packed with vacationers, others gathered in Hungary to await a chance to cross to Austria. Like all GDR supporters, I felt helpless and frustrated. In late August, I wrote Berlin's party secretary, Günther Schabowski, imploring that at September's annual Memorial Day for the Victims of Fascism, attended by tens of thousands of Berliners, the usual boilerplate be replaced by an honest, dramatic speech that discussed not only shortages, but the whole question of socialism versus capitalism. Schabowski invited me to a discussion, but called my idea unattainable. The speech was written, the speaker chosen: the uncharismatic Hermann Axen. At the once meaningful ceremony, people strolled, chatted — and paid no attention.

On September 10, the Hungarian government agreed to let GDR citizens cross into Austria. While Kohl piously advised them to stay in the GDR, journalists from Springer's ill-reputed *Bildzeitung* rushed to urge GDR vacationers in Hungary to seize the chance. Thousands did — with chartered buses taking them to a royal welcome in West German reception camps. Years later we learned that Hungarian Premier Karoly Nemeth had secretly agreed with an "eternally grateful" Chancellor Kohl on opening his border. U.S. Ambassador (and old CIA hand) Vernon Walters, with a long record of bringing down "unfriendly" governments, most likely played a role in those arrangements.

Most of those who departed were young couples and singles, especially from Dresden where, ironically, the absence of West-TV sealed them from the few programs for Western audiences that discussed West German problems. Disbelieving GDR polemics, they imagined a snakeless West German Garden of Eden. Mecklenburg in the north was once Germany's feudal poorhouse; now with industry and prosperous farming, very few left.

But disaffection was widespread. Some sincerely spoke of freedom from repression and yearned to travel. Others were gripped by dreams of VCRs and fine cars. When a teacher in one of my dwindling lecture audiences said that she might go west, I was amazed; teachers were among the staunchest pro-GDR groups. Later I scribbled an emotional memorandum pleading that we not be ruled by the attractions of Coca-Cola, Levi jeans, or planting one's ass on the seat of a Mercedes: "We must remind our ass: 'Be careful, my lad! You must never rule over my head or I might end up with it planted upside down in the ground like an onion in the Jewish curse'." Our heads should tell us to "forget neither the union organizers murdered by Coca-Cola in Guatemala nor the connections between Mercedes and gold teeth broken from Auschwitz corpses." The siren song of reunification made my Trabant, my free sanitorium, and the GDR's beauty dearer to me. I convinced myself — but didn't reach too many others.

As September rolled on, GDR media finally uttered belated, miserable responses, typified by "good riddance to bad rubbish." Honecker, seventy-seven, was recovering from surgery, and the others seemed to fear moving without his orders, or perhaps were jockeying for the expected succession. I decided to again play "Don Quixote" and managed to have a talk with a party media boss, Dieter Langguth, whom I had known when he edited *Junge Welt*. I begged for attempts to reach GDR people in Hungary to warn them against the *Bildzeitung* and urge their return. Couldn't the media try reaching minds and hearts? Langguth answered that people were enticed to the West by commodities. More and better products were needed here, which the media must encourage with livelier reports on good production and good results. My God! that was the same journalism which helped create this mess.

Protest was gathering force in Leipzig, the angriest city, under the protection of the Lutheran Church. On September 4, several hundred demonstrated for "Freedom to Travel, not Emigration." This was repeated after a Nikolai Church "prayer meeting" a week later, then every Monday, despite desperate Stasi efforts to discourage it. Soon, excited riots took place in other cities.

We were headed for a long-planned Bulgarian vacation. Just before leaving I wrote about the mood of doubt, even resignation, among faithful comrades, and my fear that a violent response to a West German provocation could spark a big rebellion, most likely in connection with the October 7 anniversary celebration of the GDR's founding. Nonetheless, it was a shock to hear that fear confirmed by telephone. On October 7 the lid did indeed blow. Several thousand left an East Berlin church and sat down on a major avenue, peaceful for the most part but blocking traffic. Hundreds were arrested, including passersby, locked in overcrowded cells, insulted, and sometimes beaten. East Berliners were outraged. Similar scenes occurred elsewhere. The provocation and the overreaction took place almost as I predicted. There may have been some truth in the security force's view that many protesters wanted to end the GDR, but that did not excuse violent overreaction. The country fearfully awaited the Monday demonstration in Leipzig two days later. Honecker allegedly ordered the army and security forces to carry loaded weapons, which could have meant disaster. Before services in the Nikolai Church, in a gesture of conciliation, a few hundred SED members joined in and an agreement was worked out by SED leaders, orchestra conductor Kurt Masur, and others, to assure a peaceful, undisturbed march of about seventy thousand people. It appeared that party leader Egon Krenz prevented armed force and bloodshed on this night. The Monday marches in Leipzig continued and grew bigger and bigger.

Party leaders took belated action. On October 18 the Politburo fired Honecker, economics boss Günter Mittag, and media head Joachim Herrmann. Egon Krenz, young at fifty-two, became party leader, and a week later the

People's Chamber elected him head of state, though with an unprecedented twenty-six "No" votes.

Within days more hoary heads and wrinkled faces disappeared from the Politburo. The whole country was seized by a fever of change as Krenz announced a new program, including opening the Czech border, which had been closed to block the exodus to the West German embassy in Prague. A new flood of motorized emigrants ensued. Gaps created by workforce losses widened in every factory and office. The loss of doctors was especially disturbing. Enticed away by salaries two to five times higher than those in the GDR, some left their patients in the lurch and drove off.

The new leaders finally began "dialogues" to answer questions or criticism and promise action. On October 29, twenty-two thousand gathered for a heated debate with the Berlin mayor. A day later the media suddenly discovered *glasnost'*, launching frank, open discussion of any issue along with exposés of corruption. Three days later the unloved trade union federation leader was replaced by the first woman in that job, while the unpopular minister of education, Erich Honecker's wife, resigned in a huff. Was there still time to build the country we had yearned for? Or was it too late?

On November 4, well-known East Berlin actors and directors sought permission for a big march. It was to test civil rights guaranteed in the constitution but never respected. I had mixed feelings; some organizers were overflowing with vitriol for the GDR, but I hoped that this would be a constructive step for new freedoms and long-needed democracy. Huge crowds held signs backing New Forum, a critical organization founded two months earlier. It had been denied official recognition but was seeking to overturn this decision legally, an unprecedented procedure.

As tens of thousands marched, I walked along the sidewalk, reading clever oppositional signs such as none I had ever seen. The main targets were Honecker and the old Politburo, but also the entire SED and new top man Egon Krenz. The rhymes, puns, and cartoons that I had missed at official events were skillfully employed to demand clean air, or the right to travel, or simply democracy. Police were rare or reticent as the theater people provided marshals with sashes saying "No violence."

I should have rejoiced; most slogans were justified, God knows. I was moved when a former neighbor, totally deaf, pointed proudly to a sign carried by his organization of the deaf: "We want at least to SEE the world!" But despite the joy and energy on this sunny day, I was gripped by icy fear, comparable only to my flight in 1952. Those thirty-seven years had meant much to me, and despite the painful blunders, this had been my second home. I had hardly a last tatter of respect for the old guard and little enthusiasm for the ambitious Krenz, whose big teeth and frozen smile were being gleefully lampooned. But the new leaders deserved a chance; in two weeks a lot had changed.

Almost no signs opposed socialism or demanded a "market economy"; not one favored German unification. But I sensed that such relentless attacks, justified or not, could bring the GDR crashing down. Was New Forum's immense organization of the parade really aimed at a better socialist society?

I met a journalist friend and said: "This looks like counterrevolution." He eyed me strangely, but avoided an answer. I walked on, feeling more lonely and despairing, and met another journalist who was enthusiastic and rejected my fears. Did no one see where this was leading?

Walking alone beside the ambling thousands back to Alexander Platz, where a huge meeting was underway, I had to admit a sense of relief to see banners reflecting what people thought or said privately but never in "official places," where they spoke like editorials or kept their mouths shut. As an American, I knew as well as any what needed changing. My homeland had suppressed freedom of thought and I never liked the same thing here.

I had often spoken critically in lectures and discussions. But with more "jester's license" to speak out than most people, perhaps I had not done enough. Were my compromises justified? I had always made clear that I was against the boils and carbuncles, but wanted to cure, not kill the patient. Was my socialist dream of a society free of corporate greed and exploitation false?

There were reasons to rejoice if hypocrisy and sycophancy were evaporating. It seemed wrong to bemoan the giant crowd listening intently. I should rejoice at the boos, formerly so rare, and the applause that came spontaneously and not on a signal. Like so many others I wondered: What does this speaker really mean, what can we believe? Some were good, especially the writer Christa Wolf, the lawyer Gregor Gysi — an SED member who had fought for New Forum's legality — and Stefan Heym, who was strongly applauded when he called for a new democratic socialism as a model for all Germany.

When Berlin party head Schabowski spoke in the face of boos and whistling, I wondered if SED leaders could learn from events. Was it new thinking or pressure, or both, that had recently brought change? Clearly, if new leadership wanted to win trust, it must learn to listen and speak honestly, abandon old habits or lose everything. New Forum's Jens Reich said: "This dialogue is just the appetizer!" and promised "pepper and cayenne for the main dish!" Sharp spices yes, but what kind of dish would it be? One offering the improvements I had yearned for since my arrival as a young man? Or a mess of overcooked pottage? We needed to be skeptical — both about cooks with tired old recipes and about those with stews delicious for the lucky ones, but with only bare bones for the others.

The meeting ended peacefully, and I relaxed a bit. But I could not sleep; was the GDR's end close at hand? On November 7 the cabinet resigned, opening the way for a new government. New organizations formed right and left; teachers finally won a five-day week, and the nagging issue of freedom to travel boiled to a head when a provisional minister offered a law allowing free travel for thirty days a year. It was too little and too late. On November 8 the SED Central Committee fired more of the "old guard," called for an end to mismanagement and dictatorial rule, and picked the uncorrupted Hans Modrow as candidate for prime minister, to be chosen by the People's Chamber in five days. Thousands gathered at SED headquarters, successfully demanding a party congress; four districts rejected their own representatives to the Politburo, forcing them to resign.

On November 9, at the end of an unprecedented press conference, Schabowski nonchalantly, as if in an afterthought, mentioned that all travel barriers were lifted. Where the announcement came from remains a mystery. Perhaps SED leaders hoped that unrestricted travel might stop the hemorrhage of those leaving for good. Thousands immediately surged into West Berlin, where they picked up 100 West-marks in "welcome money" offered by Bonn. Hundreds of thousands followed, then millions, in fantastic scenes of joy and relief. Most of those going across returned the same day.

Renate went over the next day without telling me. So did Thomas, then Timothy. Renate spent most of the 100 marks on presents for the grandchildren, Thomas bought Bob Dylan records and exotic foods, and was given a pound of coffee beans. I didn't dare to go, and resented the money given as alms even to unborn babies. This new "gold rush" was not always euphoric; Leipzig crowds rushing a Berlin train to get their 100 marks pushed one woman to her death. Two billion marks were handed out, meaning twenty million claimants in a country of sixteen million where four million did not cross over. In one cartoon, a man whispers to five kids: "Don't tell them you were here with your mother!" He holds a big tom-cat — in baby clothes.

Despite the elation, some feared that drugs, AIDs, and crime, absent or far less frequent than in the West, would no longer be largely sealed off by the Wall. Would kitschy pseudoculture begin to flood the GDR? Would the small number of antiforeign, anti-Semitic skinheads and "Republikan-ers" (West German neo-Nazis) grow with the barriers down? Also, with one West-mark fetching ten or more East-marks, would open borders mean financial disaster?

Not many were disturbed by such matters. Nearly everyone crossed the borders, avidly read the press, and even watched GDR-TV news, suddenly grown interesting. We saw vigorous debates and suspenseful votes in the People's Chamber, which narrowly elected Modrow prime minister while Stasi boss Erich Mielke cried "I love you all" to his many accusers. A new cabinet was formed, a committee was created to investigate previous "mis-use of office," and the SED recommended a "Round Table" of all parties and organizations. The Krenz leadership, along with bosses of the labor, youth, and "bloc parties," were all ousted. This was a tragic end for many who had fought in Spain or spent years in Nazi prisons. But absolute power had again corrupted absolutely.

Many who wished to stay wondered if the GDR could end its economic tailspin with genuine workers' participation in production decisions and removal of bureaucratic roadblocks. For its part, West Germany condi-tioned financial aid on steps toward the "free market," a euphemism for capitalism, and toward "reunification." Social Democrats, recognizing that even the loudest opposition in the GDR did not demand those goals, toned down their rhetoric. But Kohl took a tough line. It was an old tac-tic: with each concession from the GDR, raise the stakes, keep the pot boil-ing, and keep the opponent off balance. For the GDR, failure could deeply affect Germany, Europe, and the world. Success could mean new life for socialism built on broad democratic support, consolidating what social guarantees were already won plus new gains in political and economic life. That could be a model for others.

The chance faded rapidly. At our semi-annual English course in mid-November, the TV room was uncharacteristically packed because of the impending collapse of the Czech regime. The scientists were split, with a majority cheering every step toward the dissolution of the Czech government. I never cared for that oppressive, wooden regime, which seemed much worse than the GDR. But theirs too was a form of socialism with hope of democratization and a better life. The ascendancy of Volkswagen and Coca-Cola would dash that hope. Not many saw it that way—for Prague or the GDR—while I wondered if all the rapid changes in different countries within two years were coincidental and caused only by righteous hunger for freedom.

That was the last English course. After seeing the scientists cheer collapse in Prague, I was not surprised that some were active in dismantling the GDR. I wonder how they felt after their time-honored Academy was disbanded, forcing them into a mad race for jobs where some survived, but many, especially women, the young, and social scientists, did not.

After a sharply divisive meeting of the Writers' Association, I headed again to Leipzig for the documentary film festival. Among many soul-stirring films, the best was Michael Moore's *Roger and Me,* which documented GM's layoff of thirty thousand workers and its ruination of Flint, Michigan. Its humor, irony, and controlled anger made me wish that more than this handful could see it, especially workers in Eisenach in East Germany joyfully awaiting GM's Opel subsidiary.

On Monday night most of us skipped the films to witness the now famous Leipzig demonstrations. What a shock! Dominating the huge rally were groups yelling not "we are the people," but "we are one people," or "Germany, united fatherland," waving West German flags, and shouting down any alternative view, including a West German speaker who warned against blindly accepting the Bonn model. No one dared challenge the fascistoid types. Unlike the Alexander Platz gathering in Berlin, most of the hundred thousand people listened silently. The Leipzig demonstrations, so highly praised in early fall as democratic outpourings, had changed by November. "Republikaners" mingled with local skinheads; the meetings were now distribution points for neo-Nazi posters and swastikas. A week later, when students waved GDR flags, a mob chanted "Throw the reds out" and ran to attack them until a clergyman interceded. A few weeks later a mob invaded a Leipzig dorm and attacked an African woman student. Slogans against Poles, Jews, Vietnamese, Turks, or other "non-Germans" reflected new trends, with abuse of foreigners, the defacing of Soviet memorials,

and bomb scares at hospitals, schools, and public buildings all contributing to destabilization. On November 28, Chancellor Kohl announced a
ten-point unification plan. Also on that day, Christa Wolf and Stefan Heym
advanced a petition, "For Our Country," pleading against the absorption
of the GDR. But the tide continued to turn. The ousted old guard's special
stores, hunting lodges, and other privileges came to light — minuscule
compared to Western sleaze, but devastating in view of its claims to socialist equality.

On December 7, "round table talks" among all parties and political
groups produced agreement to write a new constitution and hold elections.
On December 8, over 2,700 SED delegates, chosen at the grass roots, met
in East Berlin while speculation raged about whether the party would survive or die. After a seventeen-hour session there was no split; the party
would not disband. It apologized for past failures and misdeeds, vowing
to democratize its structures while fighting to preserve the GDR and socialism until the elections and beyond. A totally new executive was chosen,
headed by the energetic, bright, and witty Gregor Gysi, little known before
his speech on November 4. What a contrast with the old dimwits!

The temporarily named Socialist Unity Party/Party of Democratic Socialism (a sudden, total change would appear dishonest) was heavily burdened by its past. Many of its more than two million members left owing
to exposés of old practices; many more, perk-seeking careerists, tore up
their party cards as soon as the winds changed. Chances of survival depended on isolating dogmatic deadwood, sticking to ideals, and learning
from the past. Perhaps voters would recall that, despite corruption and
phony optimism, a society had been created with economic security for all.
Polls (something new here) showed from 20 to 34 percent for the SED-
PDS, while the population was evenly divided on unification. Only if this
new-old party got at least a slim plurality could the GDR be saved and unification blocked.

Calls from the West for pluralism and free elections were coupled with
millions of marks and huge media coverage for new parties like the new
"Democratic Renewal" Party and two old "bloc parties," the GDR Christian Democrats and the Liberal Democrats, which decided to "reject socialism." Some intellectuals swallowed the truly desirable bait of pluralist
democracy but did not see the hook inside — the "free market economy."
Others, especially old antifascists, feared resurgent nationalism and control

by West German big business. I too feared this danger, which could even end in personal catastrophe. Gysi and other new leaders provided some hope. My feelings shuttled between "up" and "down."

Fear kept me from West Berlin and Renate was too busy to go there often. In the midst of all the excitement, Timothy's second child, Gregor, was born, keeping his family busy. The open border spun off some consequences. Half of East Berlin seemed to be in West Berlin and half West Berlin here. I saw the first beggars in decades, and became a bit worried walking around downtown with my wife.

Just when democratic socialism seemed possible, Western leaders and opposition forces called louder for unification. Attacks on the Stasi and other evils drowned out even timid mention of past achievements. The trend became clearer on December 18, when Kohl visited Dresden with Modrow. The welcome turned into a wild demonstration, with thousands shouting "Helmut, Helmut" in the city where Modrow had led the party with unusual modesty for so many years. Careful organization by Kohl forces was obvious, while pro-GDR groups chose not to attend. Courageous exceptions were pushed aside.

Encouraged by unceasing media exposés of the old guard and a deepening witch-hunt climate, the anticommunists in the Writers' Association took over. I understood their anger and frustration at years of official pressures and expulsions. But their vengefulness and antagonism to socialism were disquieting; their hostility seemed to extend beyond "apparatchiks" and officially approved writers to officers who had tried to help or protect members and books discriminated against from "on high." Hermann Kant had once presided when nine writers were expelled, but I also knew of people he had helped to escape political difficulties. He was hounded from office.

Sometimes the anticommunists resorted to blackmail: "support our resolutions or face a split." Of course it was sweet revenge against those who had misused their power, but it was often equally unjust and irrational. I thought again of evil times in the United States and spoke at one meeting of the growing threat of McCarthyism, xenophobia, and anti-Semitism, urging that we avoid splitting the forces opposing such dangers. One writer called out: "Stalinists always view their opponents as splitters." That hurt. During the GDR years, I had asked critical questions and had neither crawled nor shouted hurrah. I'm still angry at that man's words.

A day after Kohl's Dresden triumph, about ten thousand mostly young people with varied views but all against "annexation" demonstrated in East Berlin, waving GDR flags and chanting "Down with the Nazis!" and "We want no Kohl plantation" (Kohl means cabbage). In the midst of some altercations, I responded to a bus driver who shouted nasty words about the GDR that at least it gave him work. He yelled: "I'll take unemployment!" Within a year or so he probably did — as millions lost their jobs.

Nineteen-ninety began with a giant New Year's celebration at the Brandenburg Gate, featuring a unification frenzy fueled by hectoliters of alcohol. The famous victory statue on top of the arch was wrecked so badly by the all-German fans it had to be hoisted down and rebuilt, this time with the Prussian eagle and Iron Cross the GDR government had removed after the war.

Parties and organizations mushroomed, framing demands and maneuvering for slices of power. Despite their lofty names — "New Forum," "Democracy Now," and "Democratic Revival" — I was skeptical. The biggest, New Forum, was a mix of honest democrats and careerists angling to "change everything." The cabinet still spoke of saving the GDR, but more and more Western aid was given to groups opposing the GDR and socialism. The Social Democrats (East) decided to support unification; Kohl's CDU told its "sister," CDU-East, it would get no aid unless it quit the cabinet. After coy resistance it obeyed orders. Petitions for "immediate reunification" began circulating while visits by Western politicians multiplied, despite pleas from the government and the "Round Table" to desist. The Social Democratic Party (West) sent leaders like Willy Brandt to campaign, the largest Bavarian right-wing party met in Leipzig as if it were on home turf, and West-TV aired even more frenzied "GDR exposés," aimed at crushing the SED-PDS.

Two contrasting events took place in mid-January. I attended the annual Liebknecht-Luxemburg march with a veteran American radical, Bill Reuben — warning him that only a few old-timers might show up. After experiencing crowds chanting "Helmut, Helmut," shouting for unification, and preparing to destroy good things because bad things were done, I felt increasingly pessimistic and alone. But as we squeezed out of the subway, sandwiched between old folks, students, and parents with baby carriages, it was clear that we were not alone. One hundred thousand people, perhaps more, marched without authorized banners or a reviewing stand where wise leaders graciously waved to us. This time people carried self-made slogans and banners, varied, original, humorous, but determined to prevent a swing to the right and hoping to save the flawed and tragic little republic from a greater tragedy. The marchers, many with SED-PDS signs, exuded solidarity and quiet resolve. The camera crews left early. There was not a single fair TV report about this huge wave of people affirming its belief in the dreams of Rosa Luxemburg and Karl Liebknecht and in its own dreams of a better, free republic—in the spirit of Karl's defiant: "In spite of everything!"

The following day, another hundred thousand showed up at the State Security Building, urged by New Forum to come with spray paint and "symbolic" bricks, while it cynically advised against violence. Fueled in part by free drinks, the crowd broke into offices, spray painting or demolishing whatever it found while mysterious trucks in back loaded up tons of tapes and records, documents which were later to play a huge role in ending many careers.

Anger against the Stasi was extended to the SED-PDS, and much of the media clamored for disbanding the party. As pressure grew, more members quit or urged dissolution, but Gysi insisted that the party must keep fighting out of responsibility to future German and European generations. If it could withstand attacks until elections, it might at least establish a minority opposition. While the union federation also fought for survival, wildcat "warning strikes" of building workers, taxi drivers, medical personnel, factory teams, salespeople, even milk drivers, were organized to show rage at the Stasi or just to disrupt life—making unrealistic demands upon a perilously floundering system.

In an attempt to achieve some stability the economy was opened to private investment by local small business or West German big business. When Christa Luft, the responsible minister, authorized shares up to 49 percent, the West Germans grew more aggressive: "Either open up altogether, or we won't invest." Modrow, after visiting Moscow in February, announced that he, too, saw unification as inevitable. This was an almost paralyzing blow to those hoping to save the GDR. I recall my sadness on a trip to Thuringia at seeing state-owned factories, once confiscated from Nazi war criminals or newly built by the GDR, now adorned with West German flags. But as revelations of corrupt practices filled the media, many rejected everything from those "forty years of deception."

The Writers' Association atmosphere improved slightly because vigorous exponents on both sides dropped out, but also because publishing houses were folding or being sold to Western companies, worrying authors for good reason. Despite quarrels with GDR publishers or censors, authors usually had steady incomes that ranged from modest to very high, depending on genre and popularity, and were supplemented by readings at clubs and libraries. The GDR was proud of being a "readers' land." Now all this was endangered. Western authors rarely lived from their writings; instead of the 12 percent of sales guaranteed GDR writers, they rarely got 5 percent, while some resorted to vanity publishers. Such knowledge eased our conflicts. A proposal to bar meeting rooms to SED members was superseded by a near unanimous vote to open the rooms to all groups. A special Writers' Congress held in early March was also quite peaceful. It reinstated nine writers thrown out in 1979 and turned out to be the last congress of an organization which had included greats like Brecht, Seghers, and Arnold Zweig. We soon lost our meeting place, then our writers' vacation home, and finally joined the West German association.

As the crucial March 18 GDR election approached, the atmosphere grew tenser. My sister-in-law reported from her village that people were receiving ominous calls asking if they intended to vote for the SED-PDS— "against reunification." Kohl spoke in Leipzig, Erfurt, and other cities to huge audiences attracted by giveaways of Western junk food and his glittering promises that in a unified Germany they would soon have Westmarks, Western commodities, and Western glamour with "blossoming landscapes" where "almost everyone will have a better life; no one will have a worse one."

While all parties, even the neo-Nazi Republicans, claimed to be "social and environmental," most openly demanded capitalism and unification, their priority being to beat the SED-PDS. Thomas and I watched the returns in SED-PDS headquarters, now opened to the public. There was no joy. The CDU and its allies got almost half the votes; many had expected a Social Democratic majority, but it got barely a quarter of the vote. The right-wing victory reflected a massive repudiation of the entire past, good, bad, or indifferent. Lavish promises and ceaseless muckraking paid off (while huge scandals lay ahead in West Germany). The innocents of Saxony and Thuringia voted heavily for Kohl, far more than northern Brandenburg and Mecklenburg. East Berlin was furthest left. The SED-PDS total vote at 16– 17 percent meant third place and a significant opposition role. The new parties that got the ball of change rolling did poorly; getting even less support were small parties with big consciences like the Greens and the Women's Federation. The SPD agreed to join the CDU in a coalition, typically grasping "compromise" and retreating from its promise to defy the right. It would join a CDU government "to slow its rightward turn and work to protect people's rights." Again the tail wanted to wag the dog. Not until shortly before the end of the GDR did it withdraw from this fatal misalliance.

Hints abounded of what lay ahead. Factory directors began trimming libraries, clubhouses, polyclinics, vacation homes, sport, and cultural activity. In East Berlin endlessly dancing Hare Krishnas and "reborn Christians" who lay crumpled on dirty sidewalks became first-time attractions, while the city was flooded with enticing if expensive foods and a virtual tsunami of advertising, a blessing spared us in the past. Buses and streetcars were painted over with logos and slogans. Huge new billboards, neon lights, even sidewalk café parasols pushed Camels or Marlboros, now in vending machines available to any eight-year-old. Cheesy newspapers like the soft-porn *Bildzeitung* appeared, with explicit anatomy-describing ads by prostitutes as well as invitations to pretty girls to work as photo models and erotic dancers, both transparent euphemisms, and a daily assortment of political lies like: "Leipzig Doctors Sell Children's Organs for Transplantation!"

The People's Chamber was a mélange of anti-GDR characters like "Wendehals," a pun for turncoats, or "Blockflöten," a pun ridiculing GDR loyalists in the "bloc" parties who suddenly recalled that they had been resistance fighters against red oppression. Many "victims" turned up after years of well-paid professional or administrative work, now emoting about being passed over for a promotion or a trip abroad "for political reasons." An unknown lung specialist was elected chairperson and thus became provisional head of state. Both jobs entitled her to a state limo, and she took both on official visits.

The majority of legislators agreed on harassing one-sixth of their members from the renamed Party of Democratic Socialism, and rushing toward unification. While a few good things were achieved, their bumbling behavior was hardly more meaningful than the rubber-stamp activities of the People's Chamber in the past. With street vendors already hawking wares for West-marks before they were legal tender, most people were mainly interested in the impending currency reform — above all the rate of exchange. Would we get half a West-mark for each East-mark, a full 1:1 conversion, or some mixed rate, and if so, on what basis? With each rumor people sought a favorable position by transferring money from one account to another. The writers decided to join in protests against the 2:1 rate. I recall the strong, emotional voice of actress Käthe Reichel: "The GDR is an immense stable of calves, all going joyously to the slaughter because they will be slain by a West German knife made of Krupp steel. . . . Yet our revolution cannot be bought out. We are the people!" But most people savored West-marks on any basis, an opulent symbol of desirable goods in unlimited quantity and a source of prestige even in East European countries where West-mark Germans were treated with courtesy and privilege.

The final decision came: people over sixty could exchange up to 6,000 East-marks at a rate of 1:1, other adults up to 4,000, and children up to 2,000. The rest would be halved: two East-marks for one West-mark. People scurried to find accounts of seniors or children to rescue some of their savings. We found no one. Since many had to go to the bank repeatedly to make complicated transactions, the lines were endless as money became a relentless obsession.

At midnight on July 1, 1990, we got our first West-marks. Hundreds crowded around a former GDR ministry on Alexander Platz, now housing the Deutsche Bank. The first man to reach the teller nearly got his ribs crushed while cars raced up and down Karl Marx Allee, waving West German flags and honking like mad. Renate got 4,000 and I got 6,000 marks at the 1:1 rate; the remainder, about 50,000 saved up for our old age, was halved overnight like the money paid me for the one-third-completed sale of my book *If I Had a Song.* The rest, and the publisher as well, went down the drain. The next working day store windows and interiors were totally redecorated. Almost all "eastern products" were replaced by abundant Western household appliances, fashionable clothing, exotic foods. The bookshops stocked formerly taboo books by GDR foes and anti-Stalinists of every shade — Trotsky, Koestler, Orwell, Solzhenitsyn, and all the others. There were dozens of new "do-it-yourself" books, Dale Carnegie advice books and travel guides to every corner of the world, and a plethora of West German or American bestsellers featuring sex, horror, violence, or kitsch in all combinations. Almost everything by GDR authors, along with other GDR-published books, unless available in West German covers, was gone: from Sholem Aleichem to Tennessee Williams to Yevtushenko and Zola. Millions of German and world classics were tossed into the garbage to meet a West German condition for doing business. A West German Protestant minister, angered by such desecration, salvaged over a million of the dumped books and later offered them free to anyone contributing to the UN's children's fund.

Most people were so elated to receive the new money that they failed to grasp that West-marks were great for travel, but at home it all depended on how many of them you earned and how much things cost. Gradually, they caught on.

In May, voters elected town and county officials, and the north-left, south-right trend was unchanged, with Christian Democrats remaining the strongest party. The second man in the East-CDU, a gimlet-eyed wheeler-dealer named Krause, worked out with the second man in the West-CDU a giant nine hundred-page agreement on the rules of unification. It was so one-sided that Krause was later rewarded with a lucrative ministry in the new all-German government — until scandals proved him too sleazy even for Kohl. But before being sacked, he sold out vital interests, like land and property ownership or job protection — while the Round Table's democratic constitution was shoved under the table.

In the third election of 1990, the GDR's geography was emasculated when five traditional provinces that had been broken into fifteen GDR districts in 1952 were now restored. County boundaries were redrawn, encouraging a scramble by some counties to try to change provinces. Old prejudices, reduced by the GDR district system, were revived between Saxons and Prussians or Prussians and "fishheads" from coastal Mecklenburg. There were conflicts about capitals: would Rostock or Schwerin be the capital of Mecklenburg-Pomerania, and Halle or Magdeburg that of Saxony-Anhalt? Each had many reasons — and hopes for positions, prestige, and funds.

In August the People's Chamber voted to dissolve itself and unite the redrawn provinces with the "old provinces" in the West. Only the PDS voted no. Ceremonies at the Reichstag building near Brandenburg Gate on October 3 ended the GDR experiment forever — with solemn speeches, a fireworks display, and the crowd singing a moving rendition of "Deutschland über alles," now the national anthem in east and west.

13

A NEW LIFE IN UNITED GERMANY

Where can I flee if necessary? I wondered as the GDR neared its end. I had no idea how Bonn would regard me; the United States seemed impossible, no socialist states remained in Europe, Cuba looked shaky, and a friend in Austria offered no hope.

Only after a year did I risk stepping gingerly into West Berlin at Checkpoint Charlie, the famous border crossing now full of peddlers selling dubious pieces of the Wall and memorabilia from a collapsed society—GDR and Soviet flags, and fur caps with the red star that had stirred me when I first looked upon it thirty-eight years earlier. I finally saw downtown West Berlin with the famous Memorial Church ruin, and the Kurfürstendamm, the garish shopping avenue with its unfamiliar blaze of neon lights.

With the new, united Germany requiring identification papers, I urgently had to clarify my status and name. The U.S. embassy in East Berlin closed after the GDR's demise; the consulate was in a western suburb menacingly next to U.S. Military Headquarters. I finally risked the trip, flanked by my sons, but called the woman I was slated to see from the subway station. When informed that she was out, I decided not to again enter the lion's den, opting instead for a series of calls which finally elicited from her an offer of an identity card which she would bring to an East Berlin hotel for a $20 fee. But when we met, she informed me that such cards were no longer issued; I could get only a one-way pass from the army (very interested in me, she confided) to the United States, an ID card, a uniform, and a flight home. She did provide an informal affidavit on official stationery confirming my citizenship.

After repeated visits with that document and other materials to the alien registration office, I received a German residency permit and alien's passport with a note prohibiting me from earning money. More tedious visits — with additional proof of my years in the GDR, my German wife, college degree, home, and bank account — finally yielded a better, unrestricted document in the name of Grossman.

I got used to visiting West Berlin with its impressive new or renovated buildings, the payoff for billions poured into this "showplace of the West." As an ex–New Yorker, I enjoyed the mixture of nationalities, colors, and languages, with Turkish predominant, much more varied than in East Berlin. Yet differences between East and West Berlin diminished as commercialism swept into the East, where neon lights and shop displays had heretofore been far fewer and more restrained. Now gaudy decoration of every store, café, or kiosk enlivened drab streets. But I could not rejoice; I had liked the paucity of advertising in the GDR and its total absence in the media. The new torrent of ads on TV, radio, even movie screens trying to be shocking, witty, or sexy with puckering lips around phallic symbols to sell candy or cars stupefied and angered me — especially the ubiquitous American cigarette ads. I had quit smoking in 1968 and seethed at each billboard.

Countless porn magazines elicited a similar reaction. True, no one had to buy them, or patronize the new peep shows on Rosa Luxemburg Strasse, or the chain of sex shops owned by Beate Uhse, a "heroic" Nazi aviatrix, now a talk show heroine. I never saw a single peep show, brothel, or street walker in the GDR, but seashore and lake nudist beaches belied stereotypes of East German prudery. Not until the *Wende* (the turn to reunification) did West German tourist pressure result in restricting untroubled nudism.

West Germans quickly took advantage of eastern hunger for Toyotas and Volkswagens, even BMWs and Mercedes, and eastern naiveté about sales methods (GDR cars were not sold on credit), often joking: "beginnt's zu rosten, verkauf's im Osten" (when it starts to rust, sell it in the east). Every East German who could beg or borrow bought a car. Soon seven million jammed streets and highways, multiplied the accident rates, and taught us about gridlock. I gave up my old Trabant and was conned into a painted-over, gas-guzzling, rusty Opel.

Renate got a "free trial subscription" to a West Berlin paper — and we soon learned how hard it was to get rid of it. Other slippery blessings were door-to-door insurance salesmen offering "better than you've ever seen" coverage for helicopter rescues in case of heart attack. There was a mad onset of "absolutely no risk" get-rich-quick schemes; endless junk mail congratulating us for winning millions if we paid 100 marks monthly to some lottery; offers of almost free travel to the West and lovely gifts, conditioned on long pitches for household products at rip-off prices. "High pay" job ads duped those who fell for them. Soon Ossies were slamming doors on most con men.

In January 1991, Year One in unified Germany, we again honored Luxemburg and Liebknecht. Events had taken a toll. Some were frightened by rightist pressures, others apathetic or too burdened with personal problems for "one more demo." Yet 50,000 to 80,000 showed up; they had worked all their lives for a cause and would not now capitulate. Most handmade signs opposed the impending Gulf War, which had been protested at a march of 150,000 the previous day in West Berlin. Many East Berliners had been drawn there, an unexpected yield of unification. Kohl, once enthusiastic about marches, now spoke of "despicable loud-mouthed groups" of ungrateful "anti-Americans."

At our once publicly owned supermarket, now part of a giant West German retail chain, we faced commodities undreamed of in the GDR. The pudgy woman at the cheese counter always advised us about what was tasty or a good bargain. One day she was tearful: the new manager insisted she take her vacation in winter, something unknown to her, then added that she would soon be fired because they wanted young women. Where would she go at fifty-one? Crying, she said: "That's not what we expected, is it?"

Some in expanding fields like communications and transportation were luckier, like a young accountant neighbor whose gasoline firm was bought up by the French cartel Elf. But in East Berlin's industrial heart in Schoeneweide, where thirty thousand people once built giant transformers and a variety of electrical products, a workforce that had shrunk to two thousand in two years fearfully awaited layoffs, dooming them to early pensions if over fifty-five, or joblessness if they were not. Typically, Daimler-Benz bought the transformer plant, then shut it down.

The GDR's economy had compared favorably with those of many states, but not with that of West Germany, its main rival and Europe's richest country. East Germans produced a wide range of products (too many, in fact), and the GDR was a major exporter of cranes, machine tools, fishing boats, textiles, printing and farm machinery, Zeiss optical equipment, furniture, even plush animals and glass eyes. Collective farms produced dairy surpluses and potatoes, grain, meat, sugar, honey, apples. But paltry natural resources made the GDR rely heavily on trade, where it faced immense competition and severe discrimination. High tech imports were embargoed by NATO; under pressure from Bonn, the United States denied the GDR "most favored nation" status. It relied most on Soviet and East Bloc markets which vanished with the hasty *Wende* when they were unable to pay hard currency for goods previously available for "transferable rubles." Domestic markets collapsed when East Germans rushed to buy western products stuffed into supermarkets that had been grabbed up by western giants. Before the "Ossies" realized that many GDR products, from butter to beer to sausage, were as good as or better than merchandise whose packaging was adorned with pictures of happy cows, most firms went bankrupt. Once-normal credits from GDR ministries suddenly became high interest debts to private banks, while overall the decks were stacked against GDR firms by established giants with unlimited resources.

Instrumental in bludgeoning GDR firms into bankruptcy was the Treuhand (Trusteeship), a giant organization run by the Finance Ministry in Bonn and charged with liquidating publicly owned industry and agriculture. In 1984 I lectured at a mainstay of Thuringia, a big computer plant where 13,500 workers turned out quality products. In 1990, 9,000 remained; in 1994 a twelve-minute Treuhand meeting shut it down forever. Buna, my "partnership" plant, jettisoned its "frills": day care, vacation homes, sports, a library—and 20,000 jobs. This became standard procedure. Factories built with the sweat, muscle, and taxes of the people went for a song to operators looking for a killing. Plants were sold "for an apple and an egg," as the Germans say, to western rivals which let them go bankrupt, thus eliminating competition, to speculators wanting only real estate and knowing which palms to grease, or to incompetents who worked them hard, made a quick buck, and sold the best machinery before absconding. Even western-equipped state-of-the-art factories went belly up. Some firms used GDR plants as "extended work benches" with small, fearful, low-wage and no-benefits workforces. Underpaid foreign workers were hired illegally. Sometimes desperate workers and managers developed daring new products. Few survived long.

With two-thirds of GDR manufacturing shut down, whole regions anchored on production of textiles, mining, machinery, or agricultural products were swept clean of jobs. A friend told me in 1995 that every man and woman in her building worked in 1989; "Now not a single family has more than one breadwinner, and when Daimler-Benz shuts down the transformer plant four families will have none."

The end of four thousand collective farms cost the jobs of two-thirds of all GDR farmers. Some returned to toilsome family farming; others "privatized" collective farms to save them, but ran into all kinds of economic and legal pressure. Lower payments for farm produce than in West Germany played havoc; huge orchards were axed while apples were imported from Tirol or New Zealand. Whole villages were ruined, and almost forgotten earls and barons sought ways to return after fifty years.

When Thomas first visited an employment office soon after reunification he found very few people there. The second time there was a crowd. By his third visit it wound down the stairs. The jobless rate, near zero in 1989, soared: a year after the currency reform it hit a million; after two years experts estimated that 4 million of 9.4 million GDR jobs were lost. The rate settled at about 16 to 20 percent; far higher if temporary measures and euphemisms were discounted. And West Germany was hit hard too.

In 1996 a professor friend at my old journalism school asked me to speak there. In response to my inquiry, I was told that another friend had been fired and that he himself was the "only one left from GDR days—the 'token Ossie'." I also talked with the head of the school, now the "Institute for Communication and Media Science," who returned to his Hamburg home each weekend. He laughed when I mentioned the nickname "DIMIDOS"— for administrators who work in the East on Tuesday (DIenstag), Wednesday (MIttwoch), and Thursday (DOnnerstag), then go home to the West. While he seemed to be tolerated, most Wessies running almost everything in East Germany were bitterly resented. Many men (very few were women) got what was cynically called a "bush bonus" plus higher pay than experienced local staffs, which were often viewed as ignorant, helpless provincials and had to constantly face job loss for "inadequacy" or redundancy. In Saxony-Anhalt, with the worst jobless rate in Germany, a "Wessie" minister grabbed so much for himself and his buddies that he had to resign when the facts surfaced.

College teachers in "unreliable" fields — economics, history, law, philosophy, pedagogy, journalism—were *abgewickelt* ("wound down," fired). Often over fifty, they had little chance for new jobs, especially if they were former SED members. Some were narrow dogmatists, disciplinarians, or worse; many were respected scholars. Even professors in nonpolitical fields had to face West German "expert" panels which "tested their competence and moral record." Professional jealousy, political views, or theoretical disagreements could trigger firings. I met a couple who were Sanskrit and ancient India specialists at East Berlin's Humboldt University, both facing degrading cross-examination and job loss. Student protests against the whole humiliating business of destroying careers and savaging self-esteem had little effect. Top doctors, many women among them, were also sacked. Accusations of Stasi contacts were a frequent justification, often based on unavoidable dealings with an agency that controlled access to special foreign equipment, medicines, and travel permits. A world-renowned transplant specialist and a leading neurosurgeon for children were among the victims, the latter supported by vainly demonstrating parents at the famous Charité clinic.

Not only did bureaucrats and academic types swarm into the East, but businessmen, sniffing big money, jammed hotels and expensive restaurants, snaring the prostitutes now lining Oranienburger Strasse in East Berlin's fabled old ghetto. I could not help thinking about how the North would have felt had the South won the Civil War and had replaced the Stars-and-Stripes, changed the names of schools, streets, and towns, and moved southerners into all key jobs. True, the GDR died from an election, but I doubt many expected colonization instead of unification. And, as with other colonies, it was crucial to destroy all remnants of the old culture and stamp out the memory of positive social achievements which contradicted an unrelieved portrait of totalitarian repression.

Soon after unification, three West Germans alighted from limos and marched into East Berlin's broadcasting center, wiping out the lively, democratically determined TV and radio programs that had emerged in the fall of 1989. A hectic scramble to save jobs ensued, even at the expense of friends and principles, as good people who had often worked well for decades were thrown out. By December 31, 1991, fifteen thousand employees had been sacked. Battles to save popular programs failed; all that remained was *The Sandman,* a goodnight show for toddlers. As some new stations sprouted in the provinces, some of the staff found work under strict West German supervision.

The press landscape was also bulldozed with the aid of the Treuhand, which sold local papers to powerful West German publishers able to swallow the greatest number and staff them with new personnel. Attempts at independent critical journalism were killed as rapidly as in radio and TV. All but a few magazines also landed in the hands of western syndicates which strangled them, including one whose 450,000 circulation was deemed "unprofitable." Still around with fractions of their old circulation are the now erratically left-wing *Junge Welt* and *Neues Deutschland*, friendly to the PDS. With eradication of the socialist vision a high priority, the latter paper was subjected to relentless efforts to destroy it — including being forced out of its building and temporary seizure in a dubious debt quarrel.

Streets and squares were renamed all over East Germany. Our Karl Marx Allee was spared, perhaps because West Berlin had a Karl Marx Strasse. But in Gera, a Karl Marx Allee was returned to a Prussian kaiser's name; avenues no longer bore the Dimitrov name honoring the Bulgarian who turned accuser in the famous 1933 trial, proving that the Nazis torched the Reichstag; an East Berlin street named for great feminist and anti-Nazi Clara Zetkin now again salutes some Prussian ruler's wife; many streets lost Ernst Thälmann, the Communist leader killed by the Nazis. Lenin Allee, near our home, was renamed Landsberger Allee in 1991 (a graffito asked "Who Was Landsberger?") while a huge Lenin statue was removed at great cost. I never liked the statue's heroic pose, but its removal was not for aesthetic reasons; it was aimed at showing who was boss. All this happened while West Berlin kept the names of warrior kings, queens, kaisers, even pro-Nazi "war heroes," like Spanische Allee which honors Nazi "Legion Condor" airmen who bombed Madrid and destroyed Guernica in 1937.

Many East Berliners were riled over the fate of the "Palace of the Republic," shut down in 1990 because of its asbestos fireproofing; its ultimate disposition is still debated and still unsettled. West German leaders abhor this site of the old People's Chamber. But it also had a 5,000-seat concert hall, inexpensive restaurants, little theaters, a disco and bowling alley, and welcoming lobbies. Even such East Germans who disliked its great cost and overdone incandescence (its nickname was "Honecker's Lampshop") now rallied to clean it but save it — far cheaper than destroying the building. When a West Berlin congress center was found to be asbestos-ridden they asked sarcastically: what was the difference between asbestos and asbestos? Despite pleas and petitions, hope is fading.

The drive to wipe out symbols of the GDR grinds on, prompting the famed West German writer Günter Grass to note that many East Germans

wanted to join the West, but not obliterate their own identities and experiences. "But the West came in like colonial masters," shockingly treating
East Germans like children and dividing Germany into first- and second-
class tiers. "I'm afraid this will take longer than the Wall to fix," he sadly
concluded.

In the meantime, those in East Germany who clung to their jobs or
found new ones can now happily buy cars, Cokes, household gadgets,
VCRs, and flights from Tenerife to Thailand, and sate the old GDR yearning for tropical fruit. Many older people get good pensions with new benefits for veterans and widows. A new stability is sought as people shop,
stroll, or drive to the weekend bungalow — if it was not reclaimed by some
Wessie. McDonald's and Burger King have arrived, and Chinese and Italian restaurants come and go in a birth-and-death cycle quite new to us.
Banks and travel agencies are everywhere. Workers, often imported from
Britain or Eastern Europe, build modern, if still unrented office and apartment buildings. Old restrictions and petty tyrants are gone while elections
are free and many Ossies are optimistic about their new world.

But new problems have replaced the old ones. We shed the sodden GDR
red tape and fell under a wildly more expansive bureaucracy. Worst were
tax returns, with the convoluted Value Added Tax and the task of saving
restaurant, gas, and post office bills by those who schemed for deductions.
In the first year I spent weeks on tax returns, made repeated revenue office
visits — and paid far more than in the GDR. I had to restructure social security and all my insurance. Innocent Ossies like myself switched money
from one bank to another seeking the best of confusing offers. How easy
it was in the old GDR: 3.5 percent interest for everyone in a single savings
and checking account. Health care insurance, formerly uncomplicated,
now required hard decisions as to which company offered more or cheated
less. Should I buy my apartment (if possible) or keep paying fast-rising
rents? Even after we became familiar with the complicated regimes im-
posed upon us, the bureaucracy, we found, was intractable and permanent.

Homelessness was a new and growing phenomenon. Among the first
homeless were those who left via Hungary in 1989, never made it in the
West, and returned without jobs, homes, or sympathy. Many slept in trains
parked at Leipzig's main station. Some are forlorn winos, but with rents rising from 50–120 marks to 600–1,500 and evictions legal, it is easy to become
homeless — without addictions. Some were broken when their work places

closed or laid them off before retirement. And some still with housing can no longer pay for commodities bought on credit during the first euphoria.

As usual, women were hit hardest. Over 90 percent worked in the GDR; today less than 50 percent have jobs. That is particularly catastrophic for single mothers. For them, jobs are becoming impossible with day care centers costing more, limiting hours, and dwindling in number. I was shocked when a TV show told of single jobless mothers in Leipzig who became prostitutes, subject to sickening violence from West German pimps. Women and girls are lured or kidnapped from Eastern Europe and the Far East for streetwalking and new brothels. Despite claims that porno and prostitution are safety valves to prevent rape, there has been no decline in that crime. Abortion, legal on demand in the GDR since 1972, was permitted in West Germany only after doctors and social workers confirmed the need — no easy matter in the Catholic south. Both systems remained after unification, but when West German women began getting abortions in East Berlin, Kohl and his allies mobilized their righteous minions in defense of the unborn. The SPD abandoned a vigorous fight, and a weak compromise was reached: abortions would not be penalized if women first submitted to "advisory consultations," often urging them to have the baby. Paying for abortions remains a serious problem for many. The *Wende* brought a one-half reduction in East German marriages and a two-thirds dip in the birth rate. Whole villages and towns registered few or no births. Maternity wards were reduced and more day care centers closed in a vicious circle.

The GDR provided apprenticeship training for all but collegiates; this is now a dream, despite the fact that apprenticeships are needed for nearly all jobs in Germany. Young Ossies now leave for better chances in West Germany or hang around street corners while scores of GDR youth clubs are closed for lack of funds or are now centers for neo-Nazi gangs.

An American friend wrote about her fears of the "big, nationalized, depersonalized structures of a Communist state." But in the GDR there were private shops, membership-owned "co-op" groceries, and nationally owned retail shops where neighbors and salespeople chatted. Thousands now drive to warehouse-like supermarkets or malls, jamming roads, spreading pollution, and dooming small shops. Gathering places like village post offices are shutting down, factory clubhouses are boarded up, as are sport clubs once financed by now defunct factories or collective farms. Scores of inexpensive trade union vacation homes were shut or privatized, costing 13,500 jobs. With hand weapons for sale (unknown in the GDR) fear of crime has become immense. Streets and parks empty before dusk; locksmiths have a heyday.

When luxuries beckon, ways of thinking change; the differences between Wessies and Ossies diminish as hard work and striving for money prevail — and relationships cool. People push each other out of jobs; stress and insecurity grow apace. The alienation and isolation feared by my friend has deepened since the *Wende*.

"Which matchbox has the marble?" is now heard around Alexander Platz as the lure of easy money attracts abysmal yokels to floating shell games run by sleight-of-hand experts, often from Kosovo, abetted by shills and cop spotters. Once I witnessed a raid where ten hustlers were frisked, beaten, and insulted by police who usually ignored skinhead violence. To my surprise most of the crowd approved, with one man demanding that while so many were jobless, the foreigners be thrown out. Antiforeign hatred grew quickly after unification. Political confusion, economic collapse, and widespread hopelessness help explain why western neo-Nazis found fertile soil in the East, especially with the demoralized state of anti-Nazi forces. In this xenophobic upsurge, Jewish and Soviet graveyards were desecrated as fascists marched and chanted "Throw foreigners out." Dresden neo-Nazis threw one Mozambiquan from a streetcar to his death, and another was fatally trampled. Fire bombs were hurled into foreigners' homes, injuring and killing women and children.

Such hostility is often actively or passively supported by the police who, for example, did not lift a finger as they watched the murder of one of the Mozambiquans and routinely protected neo-Nazis while ignoring right-wing attacks on antifascists. Harassment of foreigners, especially Africans and Asians, is ongoing. Those seeking political asylum, even children, are often treated like criminals, while the courts routinely grant neo-Nazis ridiculous leniency.

In eastern Rostock in 1992, local authorities assigned Gypsy refugees to an overcrowded, filthy building and cut their paltry allowance, triggering minor shoplifting. Predictably, many of the local citizens applauded when out-of-town neo-Nazis attacked. The police had left by the time the mob set adjacent Vietnamese homes ablaze. Telephoned pleas were ignored;

families escaped over a roof while two hundred cops kept their distance as the rioting went on for days. When young leftists arrived to protect the foreigners they were stopped, frisked, and some arrested.

Bonn's interior minister was in Rostock when the riots began, suggesting that they were allowed to escalate to spark a perception of asylum-seekers as dirty freeloaders, thus winning votes for Bonn's anti-immigrant legislation. Sadly most Social Democratic deputies succumbed to CDU pressure and voted for the new law. Indeed, the spread of racism was abetted by mainline political demagoguery. CDU party manager Volker Rühe urged his candidates to use the "foreigner issue"; Helmut Kohl refused to attend funerals for murdered Turkish and Lebanese women, but warned of a "national state of emergency" due to immigration, a toxin echoed by an SPD leader who spoke of "a basic threat to German democracy." Most people of foreign descent, even those with parents of German birth, remain aliens, including a few million Turks who are not allowed to vote.

When the assaults and murders undermined tourism and sparked internal outrage, a few neo-Nazi groups were banned and the government toned down its xenophobic rhetoric. But it did not let up on Kurdish refugees — outlawing the leftist Kurdish Workers' Party, raiding Kurdish clubs, threatening many with deportation and certain torture or death in Turkey. Bonn also gave Turkey ex-GDR weapons to kill and torture Kurds, destroy villages, and pursue them outside Turkish borders, casting new doubt on the sincerity of politicians who invoked human rights to discredit the GDR.

Germany's 1949 constitution included asylum for refugees. But when the flow of white-skinned exiles fleeing Eastern Europe abated, so did the fervor. Welcome mats were pulled and the constitution altered, echoing the lack of U.S. enthusiasm for Haitians compared to the ardor for Cubans and others fleeing communism. Refugee crises have been manipulated in the United States and virtually all developed states. For Germany, however, memories of the "final solution" for non-Aryans always hovered menacingly. The question lingered: could joblessness and social dislocation again lead to tragedy?

The *Wende* inflicted no wounds on us two. Renate kept her job; her non-membership in the SED and lack of political activity spared her problems with snoopy questionnaires which reminded me of the fifties, including the fateful one I had signed. But with a hemorrhaging of staff, East Berlin hospitals had to give doctors and nurses higher pay. Renate benefited as well.

As a freelancer, I couldn't be fired. But lecture invitations dwindled to zero; outfits that formerly invited me were broke or dead, and people could see the United States for themselves if they had the money, or had other worries if they didn't. Demand for my articles also sank. But some TV films still needed subtitles or help for translators having problems with unfamiliar spoken text like Clint Eastwood's old *Rawhide* series on West German cable. Transforming "Texan to English" for thirty episodes gave me a nest egg. But the last episode marked "The End" for the whole studio; most had to switch from cattle rustling to job hustling.

With Renate's salary we got along well until she reached sixty in 1992 and was obliged to go on a small pension. In 1993 I started my pension and, despite complicated taxes, I could keep part of my additional income. Those reaching retirement age, men at sixty-five, women at sixty, even early retirees at fifty-five, are often the luckiest ones around—better off than our sons, who have not had an easy time. Thomas, who studied journalism, lost his job, his woman partner, and his little son. Of thirteen thousand GDR journalists only four thousand were spared; he took a retraining course in public relations but found it just as hard to find jobs in that field. Next was a subsidized job like the New Deal's WPA, but limited to two years. Now he is mailing out dozens of applications again. Timothy lost his job when the DEFA studios shut down. Dramaturgy—finding ideas, working with writers, making manuscripts filmable—was hardly known in the West. After a subsidized movie house job, he joined with three others to start a little art cinema. The others left, but he made it a success in all but profits. Like tens of thousands of new entrepreneurs in the ex-GDR, he finds rent, taxes, and other expenses almost suffocating. His marriage dissolved after almost fifteen years, but he remains friendly with his ex-wife, a physicist who married a "full" American and moved to Arizona.

Occasionally we go to West Berlin for a concert or exhibition, or for meetings of the media labor union I joined when the GDR Writers' Association folded. I chomped on my first Big Mac in West Berlin, but now fast food is available all over East Berlin, where, like most Ossies who do not work in the west, we spend most of our time. But our horizons did widen—a trip to Hamburg, then to beautiful Prague, then Vienna with its imperial edifices but less charm than Prague; and then further afield to Denmark, Sweden, and Paris.

The invitation to the forty-fifth reunion of my class of 1949 included an offer of some support from Harvard. On May 24, 1994, with time running out on a decision to go or not, a lawyer in the United States assured me that my return would be safe. It was now or never. I spent three mornings obtaining a once-only entry document from the U.S. consulate. At the airport I was questioned about this unknown credential; a phone call was reassuring, and we were off!

The day arrived that I had long dreamed of and feared. Was I swapping "Man without a Country" for "Prisoner of Zenda"? Or was it "Rip Van Winkle?" I was trusting a lawyer I had never met. When Long Island loomed my stomach felt queasy and my mouth dry — from angst, not airsickness. Renate and I walked down a long, menacing corridor to encounter five army men in civilian clothes who the lawyer said would meet us. Assuring us that all would be well, they guided us to a waiting van led by a squad car.

The skies were wonderfully blue, and we caught a moving glimpse of the Statue of Liberty. The New Jersey Turnpike was seedier than I expected, but the scenery improved as we neared Fort Dix. My heart jumped when I saw robins hopping over the lawns, and then a blue jay, a cardinal, a mockingbird, all unknown in Europe. I knew I was home.

Getting discharged from the army after forty-two years lasted not the expected weekend in a stockade, but a painless two hours. Asked to waive my right to dispute my final discharge status, and told not to expect an honorable discharge, I smiled and said that I didn't expect one after deserting. They smiled too. A pretty black lieutenant, with her little daughter nearby, said the McCarthy years were before her time but she heard they were rough. I signed a statement forgoing physical and mental checkups and a right to sue for damages. A brief meeting with two gentlemen from Army Intelligence was not quite so smiley, but also passed harmlessly. The four-decade nightmare affecting my life, my actions, and my fears was suddenly over.

After snacking at a fried chicken drive-in (my first), then on to an army hotel, we were in a mood of pure euphoria. It was "Rip Van Winkle" after all, waking to a very different army from the one I fled. The next morning I got a hernia hoisting a heavy suitcase past a bus driver too lazy to open the baggage compartment. But when we saw the New York skyline, even a hernia could not get me down. As we crossed the Hudson to reach the city I had hardly hoped to see again, I mused about rivers in my life, and of course the wide Danube came to mind.

Passing the porn movies and run-down sights of Hell's Kitchen on the way to the fancier West End Avenue where we would stay, I recalled that in my youth the Upper West Side was predominantly Jewish. Now along Broadway I heard Jamaican or Trinidadian lilts, Spanish and languages of the Far East, and saw a multiplicity of ethnic shops and restaurants. But it was unsettling to see homeless people on Broadway and on almost every bench along Central Park West. It was so easy to become indifferent, even callous toward fellow humans, a response I tried to repress.

We encountered a buoyant African American saleswoman in an apparel shop on Broadway. Before fumbling for travelers' checks, I mumbled that I had no cash or credit cards. The woman boomed that I must be a stranger because anyone familiar with New York knows that one must have money to survive. I told her that I was impressed with the city that I had not seen in over forty years, but it was hard to get used to beggars and homeless; there had been no such things where I came from. She was sincerely amazed at that, and said that it was hard to get away from New York; she was stuck, but we could travel wherever we wanted. I smiled at the unintended irony.

In the midst of dealing with all manner of new things from subway tokens to shower taps to linguini, I noticed that the building where my American Youth for Democracy club met was gone. That had been the place of adolescent fumblings and political awakenings. I recalled our arguments about bombing Germany. I had never dreamed I would be helping to clear wartime rubble left by the Leipzig and Berlin bombings.

The Harvard reunion began in Newport. My message to the fortieth reunion five years earlier meant that most of the two hundred alumni present knew my story. If there were ill feelings, they were muted. I was treated like the Prodigal Son and only one person, the wife of an old friend, seemed to avoid Renate. She was Jewish and came from a country that had been occupied by the Nazis. I told my friend that Renate's parents had not been Nazis and she, twelve at war's end, could not be responsible for the hateful years of her childhood. She still trembles at anything recalling ranting fascists. The fortune that brought us together saved me from sadness, bitterness, homesickness, or frustration; Renate was a protecting angel who made possible a happy life in that little land. And yet — we could understand, and disregard, a snub by a woman we had never met before.

Though my closer college friends did not attend, everyone acted if they had been just that. Each day seemed better than the last, finally inspiring me to jitterbug on a terrace overlooking the Atlantic, amazing Renate and myself. At a Quincy House dinner someone called: "Sit here, Steve!" and we found ourselves next to a retired *Time* editor and an ex-congressman who heads a quasi-governmental institute devoted to defeating communism. We chatted amiably at what seemed to be the "VIP Table." At the next day's gathering featuring Al Gore, one woman assured me that she never regretted joining the John Reed Society. Another, accompanying a well-known anticommunist-writer, corralled Renate to find a cool spot on a torrid day. We two men tagged along chummily. What a weird thing, I thought; surely I was the only person who had attended both Harvard and Karl Marx University. My mind drifted to the alumni of that other alma mater, journalists now mostly jobless, dismayed, or disillusioned. But that was worlds away.

Perhaps by implicit assent, we avoided politics. But when someone rambled about "socialized medicine" in the East Bloc during a symposium on Clinton's health plan, I could not resist showing my old GDR social insurance book and explaining how it covered all medical expenses without limiting choice of a doctor. There was a friendly comment, but no arguments — which was just as well.

I paid the hotel bill by signing travelers checks as Victor Grossman. The cashier pointed to the name on my lapel and asked who was Stephen Wechsler? "A phantom," I grinned, almost a bit confused myself.

A classmate and his wife invited us to their home in beautiful, mountainous Vermont. He, an erudite retired professor, and she, equally cultivated and pleasant, share a solid eighteenth-century farmhouse with tasteful furnishings and vegetarian meals. On Sunday we joined them in a white New England church where my friend, substituting for the minister, pleaded for tolerance and mutual understanding. But I later blundered into an intolerant debate with my hostess, shocking her with views on politics and religion which were truisms in my circles, but extreme in this gentle world of friendly churches and liberal sensibilities. How I regretted my tactlessness.

As if to punish me, we were back in loud, sweaty New York City. We loved it all the same, especially when NBC's *Today Show* interviewed us — at the top of the Empire State Building, in Central Park, at Battery Park with the Statue of Liberty in the background. Then on to Free Acres, about which I had often spun images for Renate of my Huck Finn life there. It was now a prosperous, conventional suburb. My brother railed at our idyll's downfall, but I was still thrilled to see my childhood house where our thin saplings were now tall, thick-trunked trees. I was also moved by a visit to a gentle, intelligent woman I knew from childhood. She wistfully said that with rising taxes and a small pension she would not be able to keep her house for more than a year or so. A week before, my old childhood friend Don deKoven, a freelance medical journalist, said the same: with journals folding and taxes rising, he could not hold on much longer.

We reached Washington by train, riding past lush estuary landscapes and trackside ghettos. My cousin, a retired lawyer, greeted us warmly, and we soon joined his wife, a Quaker converted to Judaism (now more devout than he) for their Friday evening ceremony enriched by her singing in Hebrew. Roaming around Washington, we were moved by the Lincoln and Jefferson monuments and the immortal words enshrined in them. I knew that Jefferson owned slaves to the end, and Lincoln was often inconsistent. And yet their core principles were deeply embedded in my background and makeup. The Vietnam monument caused mixed emotions. Seen from East Berlin, Vietnam was among the worst chapters in U.S. history, and attempts to counteract the "Vietnam Syndrome" were aimed at smoothing the road for new interventions. Wasn't the monument such an effort? But the long wall, the endless list, the families weeping at finding the names of loved ones, were far more mourning than glorification.

On July 4, we joined a half million at the Capitol to watch fireworks, settling down in an immense sea of flags. I couldn't help thinking about patriotism. If flag-waving meant "my country, right or wrong," looking down on other cultures and nationalities in Mexico, Congo, Fiji, or Gaza, justifying hatred and war, it wasn't for me. I loved my own history, culture, and language only because I knew them best, grew up with them, and I cherished the quest to make things better — embodied in John Brown defying slavery, Sacco and Vanzetti, Harriet Tubman, the slave rebel Denmark Vesey, the Wobbly Joe Hill, Sitting Bull, Mother Jones, and yes, Jefferson, Lincoln, George Washington for their rebellious association with the dreams of common people. This stayed with me always.

As for Germany, the majority born since the Nazi era, though not guilty, had a responsibility to know its unspeakable crimes, and to fight their recurrence. Some on the left deprecated everything German. Yet histories of bending to all above and mercilessly trampling all below could be found elsewhere, if not on Germany's horrific scale. I opposed inferiority feelings or total rejection of one's country; that only nurtured despair and paralysis, robbing new generations of awareness of their own history and culture needed to sustain the struggle for a better life.

To my own surprise, I could not get my second homeland out of my mind. The next day at the Hirshhorn Museum we found sculptures by Käthe Kollwitz and Ernst Barlach, defamed and isolated by the Nazis until their death, but greatly loved, especially in the GDR. Elsewhere were odious reminders of things German: the letters BASF on a large factory and the logo of Bayer, another I. G. Farben offspring. Why was there such excitement about Austrian President Kurt Waldheim, a tiny link in the Nazi chain, while BASF and Bayer, which had served Nazism on a grand scale, brazenly rebuilt their empires in West Germany, in the United States, and in East Germany, where they had been thrown out in 1945?

In San Francisco we met two old Harvard comrades. Neither was the dedicated radical of the past. Much had happened and the ranks had thinned greatly. One of them said my talk echoed the sixties. I tried to explain that the sharp divide in Germany, marked by the Wall, made political issues more immediate. Socialism and capitalism were not abstractions; they affected every family. Even today, East Germans of all views tend to be more politically minded. My old friends were good guys, doing good things, but I was saddened — perhaps at the loss of our fiery youth.

There was another side of the coin. We were put up by a trade unionist I knew from a GDR visit, who picked us up in a battered old car festooned with stickers against the Gulf War and for single-payer health care. Later she took us on the Shore Point Walk, a mustering of veterans of waterfront strikes and the Lincoln Brigade. There was Bill Bailey, fragile at eighty-five but still with the vigor and humor I first encountered when he came to the GDR in 1961. This legendary guy who cut the swastika from the big SS *Bremen* in New York in 1935 and threw it into the Hudson was the hub of old activists still fighting the good fight. Our union hostess described recent strike struggles. But the climate for wage earners seemed even less favorable than in Europe. Were the days of union militancy forgotten? If so, how would workers fare, not just a few leftover steel workers, but computer employees, city workers, nurses, and hamburger flippers from Frisco to Leipzig?

We pushed on to Santa Fe, where my niece and her British husband lived in a modest house with an informal, almost happy-go-lucky atmosphere. The city with its ritzy art galleries, adobe-style buildings, and blazing sun was hard to manage without a car. We trudged around, heat, hernia, and all.

I had other worries. Eight weeks had passed since I applied for my passport in Stamford, Connecticut. It hadn't arrived, but a mysterious message told me to call a New York number; an Army Intelligence man wanted help in clearing up the fate of ex-GIs in the GDR and insisted on a rendezvous in New Mexico. Was the visit connected in some way with my passport, which the Stamford office kept stalling? I could not understand why he would want to travel so far to learn about a few men long since dead or back in the United States. "There are other questions," he answered.

We met two men in a Hilton hotel room. They asked me to sign a paper affirming that they had read me my "Miranda rights." But that applied to offenses and arrests; I refused. After a tense standoff, I called my lawyer in Washington who said I might sign but not talk without counsel. The men no longer insisted, and we talked about my past: how had I got to the GDR, where had I worked, had I taken part in espionage or known of anyone who did? We parted after three hours in a more relaxed state. Three days later my nephew called; my passport had arrived, dated the same day as the meeting in the Hilton.

I was no longer a nonperson, a deadly status for so many during the Nazi years and still nearly fatal for thousands of today's asylum seekers. Admittedly my only disadvantage had been being barred from countries like Greece and Egypt and delays at every border. But I was relieved to be rid of a life in limbo.

After those glorious visits with my brother's children and their families, we spent our last week in New York. On a Lexington Avenue bench I chatted with an elderly window-cleaner with a Yiddish accent. After I told him that I lived in Berlin, he said: "I know Berlin. I fought there." How could that be? The U.S. Army didn't get there until two months after the war. He responded that he was a Soviet soldier whose Ukrainian town and all its Jews were destroyed by the Germans. With no place to go, he landed in a Displaced Person camp near Munich. A Ukrainian woman seeking her husband came to him; he had the same name. The husband was dead and she married him. They wound up in New York and managed. His story, the opposite of mine, allowed no judgments. We both found *nestwärme*. We were both lucky.

Renate and I lunched in Greenwich Village with an old classmate who had put poker and folksongs ahead of studies and meetings. Knowing how clever he was, we'd all refrained from playing poker. When he was drafted he simply refused to answer any questions about his politics. I should have done the same, he said. I replied that no one gave me advice. He spoke angrily of the party, but who in those years could know the consequences of anything we did? The army shoved him from one job to another and finally gave him a less-than-honorable discharge. In the icy fifties this former *Harvard Crimson* editor had found no better job than messenger boy. His attempts to become a "worker" were even briefer than mine when his politics were exposed. Setting out on his own, this math and computer whiz created the mother of all scratch sheets, a bulletin which compared the speed of every race horse on every track. He made a pile, but clung to his views. When he sang an old radical song the stares didn't bother him. His brassy self-confidence made me feel happier than I had with others I had met.

Riding the Staten Island ferry to escape stifling heat, we found New York's diversity, from well-dressed white men with briefcases to a variety of poor dark-skinned families, always visible. Also striking were unhinged human beings, black and white, shouting on the ferry to win people for Jesus. Had illness made them fanatics, or had religion made them ill? Far quieter, but also disconcerting, were the Chassidic Jews. I could not relate to public displays of intense religiosity, especially in light of the tortuous religious conflicts of recent years from the Middle East to Ireland to Bosnia to abortion clinics. I felt melancholy and uneasy about extremes, but wondered if I was perhaps being intolerant.

A more mundane issue was obesity, still rare in Europe. Surely the abundance of pungent specialties from all over the world was tempting to the palate. If Renate had not monitored my waist and our pocketbook, I would have overindulged. The poor consumed mounds of junk food, but obesity, spurred by relentless hawking of overflowing surpluses, seemed to afflict all classes. The GDR had overweight problems, but temptations to "nosh" were far fewer. Now with an influx of ethnic food stands, Ossies face similar dangers.

Many African Americans, we observed, had broken out of the ghetto. But the ratio of blacks on park benches and begging in subways confirmed the ongoing burdens of poverty and discrimination. In Buffalo I had learned of the heart-breaking problems, untapped talents, and cultural heritage of people of color and how whites were led to view drugs, crime, or welfare as causes rather than results of poverty, just as German frustration is directed against Turks, Vietnamese, Jews—even Ossies, who are now blamed for high taxes, unemployment, and social benefits cuts.

Recalling Buffalo, I thought of my old bed-sharing comrade, Bill Nuchow. When I called the listing I had looked up, a young girl informed me that Bill, her grandfather, had died a few months earlier.

My childhood pal Allen Abrahams, who taught me stamp collecting, had stumbled into Free Acres many years earlier and was told that I had emigrated to Moscow. He went there in 1993, and of course could not find me. But viewing CNN in his hotel room he suddenly saw an interview with me, made in Berlin, replete with photos and both my names. Contact was established, and I looked forward to seeing him if I ever returned home. But when I called him from New York, his wife said that Allen had died five months ago. I had stayed away a little too long, it seemed.

After finally coming home, would I return to Germany? How pleasant it was to be surrounded by my own language! American informality impressed Renate greatly, and, if no racial barriers intruded, so did its generosity. There was joy in revisiting the culture I grew up with: Pete and Toshi Seeger's folk festival, Mark Twain's Hartford home, my old music school, the New School for Social Research where I saw my first film; even Macy's department store evoked memories. That softened what was unpleasant, such as superhighways and parking lots gutting downtown areas to aggrandize the automobile, or sophomoric television, with little news.

Could I start over at my age? I had missed the good fight in the United States. If I moved back, could I now get involved in a plethora of causes from the Cuban embargo to Palestine to abortion rights? Would I enjoy life in this amazing land of magnificent scenery, tall buildings, and unnumbered conflicts? Few Americans could imagine living outside the United States . What drew me back to East Berlin? I didn't admit it even to Renate: I was a bit homesick. My books, papers, and an accumulation of forty years were in Berlin, also our sons, and my wife's family which had been mine for years. Health care was still more humane (a *New York Times* article said hernia surgery might cost up to $14,000. In Berlin I paid about $50). I knew my way around what had been home turf for years. I had come to love the writings of Lessing, Goethe, Schiller, Mann, Brecht—and Heine, who especially touched my heart. I loved the works of artists, architects, and workmen who built old Romanesque churches and the modern Bauhaus. All this still held me, even after the loss of the sense of ownership that I had in the GDR.

Renate and I gaped at the white stretch limousine which came to take us to the airport. Through the blue-tinted glass we watched the run-down sections of the city roll by, then the sunny beaches of the Rockaways. For now, at least, we were going home.

14

THE BIG ROCK
CANDY MOUNTAIN?

They poured through the Wall, embraced, and cried: "Wahnsinn!" (Crazy!). The GDR and the whole East Bloc would soon have democracy—and a market economy. A GDR majority yearned for an end to pressures and propaganda and to missing the cornucopia of consumer goods so close by. Many expected "Schlaraffenland," the Big Rock Candy Mountain, where roast pigeons fly into your mouth and grilled piglets stand ready for slicing. The West and its West-marks were wealth. So they pledged allegiance to Bonn.

Not a few have some of the candy. Looking around East Germany I see renovated facades and malls with succulent fruits, computers, home tools, cellular phones, dishwashers. Best of all, cars of every make, and travel everywhere.

Too much was wrong in the GDR; besides the flagging economy and the stuffy repetition of official lines, there was a narrowness of spirit and an intolerance of other beliefs. With the twentieth century's bloodletting, which took a horrible toll, there had been none of the rare leaders like Liebknecht and Luxemburg. The men who survived were bound by old habits, hardened by suffering while fighting the Nazis, and pressured by the USSR, which struggled with its own legacy of revolution, civil war, invasion, massive destruction, and three decades of Stalin.

Many who led the GDR into a fatal quagmire toiled sincerely by their own lights to make it succeed. But belief in their own infallibility and a readiness to accept rewards and honors incompatible with accomplishment and the principles of socialist equality put them out of touch. The more they succumbed to flattery, the deafer they became to the problems of ordinary people, not trusting them and preventing them from sharing in decisions. That made it much harder to overcome economic troubles, and easier for those eager to wreck the GDR. The lack of critical media encouraged hypocrisy and aided careerists, caring less about building socialism than protecting jobs and perks. Like the dogmatists, they smothered critics as being "under Western influence."

This created a serious dilemma; should those who held to a vision of socialism embedded in democracy withdraw into niches of passivity? Or escape, or risk opposition and face hardship, even prison, or become unwitting accomplices of those who wished to end socialism altogether? Every choice was painful.

Though hardly tempted to "go west," I could not ignore the state security or Stasi (a word now used to disqualify GDR history in its entirety) and its repressive methods. In my experience the Stasi was unpleasant but less frightening than now portrayed—except for active dissidents, or those planning to flee, or suspected of being in either category. It was hard not to have Stasi contacts. I got along well with my college roommate who lost his parents in the war, grew up in an orphanage, and before college was a baker. When I met him three times in later years, he brushed past with a brief "Hello, how's things?" I met him again after 1990, and he told me of his state security job, which sounded more prosaic than menacing. My GDR niece married four times; the third was a sometimes heavy-handed Stasi officer charged with monitoring Leipzig's neo-Nazis. When the apparatus was dissolved after the *Wende* so was the control. In our building we gradually realized that a stiff-necked fellow whom we rarely saw and a friendlier one who helped with our regular voluntary cleanup were both Stasi men. Hearing that Stasi families lived in a high-rise nearby, my son asked a boy on a tricycle where his daddy worked. "I'm not allowed to thay," the boy lisped. People often joked about the Stasi, especially its unsubtle visibility and clumsiness.

I always assumed some form of surveillance, and probably lost at least one assignment because of impolitic statements. Three times over the years I was approached with requests for aid in finding new contacts in the United States. While a friendly mien cloaked my worry, I always managed to convince the two-man teams that I was not able to help in their search.

I do not wish to make them seem harmless; some could be ruthless, like people of their trade everywhere. FBI informers filed 1,100 pages of reports on me, though my ideas and actions were motivated only by worthy ideals. In the GDR, I contended more with problems of censorship, a constant tug of war for creators of books, films, and theater on what was permissible and what wasn't, with ever-changing boundaries. An unexpected spinoff was rich, often first-rate literature, full of allusions, riddles, and depth based on conflicts between conditioned support, constructive criticism, and opposition. This was rough on creators' nerves, but rewarded avid readers.

Those offering critical support felt that the supreme question of war or peace and world problems like food, housing, and medical care were so central that they eclipsed all else. Intellectuals with that conviction apprehensively accepted restrictions on free speech, press, and democratic choice, hoping they were transient limits, made necessary by unceasing external attempts to destroy the entire experiment.

Such acquiescence can become a very bad habit. But the charge that it is evil ever to justify unpleasant means with desirable ends, frequently aimed at those fighting for social change, is hypocritical nonsense. Many who throw those stones have justified waging war in Vietnam, killing civilians in bombing raids, invading Grenada, blockading Cuba, inflicting pain and death upon children through sanctions on Iraq. And what of the World War II bombing of Hiroshima, Dresden, Nagasaki, Berlin? Were such bombings always justified? The answers are not always simple. Insisting that ends can never justify painful and controversial means would prevent most action. Nearly every step hurts someone; even surgical operations are painful. The real question is: are intended ends so compelling that they justify unpleasant means? Or must certain ends be reevaluated and alternatives sought? All this can require agonizingly difficult decisions, especially since the final consequences of any given act are unknown.

When dismayed or shaken by failures, disappointments, and terrible revelations, we recalled that the devastating cruelty of the Crusades or Reformation moved few Christians to forsake their faith. Nor did the Reign of Terror repel all supporters of the French Revolution into abandoning it. The actions of Begin or Sharon kept few Jewish Americans from supporting Israel; the evils of a McCarthy or Nixon made few Americans lose faith in the entire democratic process. The evils we faced in the GDR, we hoped, were phases to be combated and overcome—but not by forswearing all hope for a just society.

———————

In the 1960s I often passed a square with two cathedrals and Karl Friedrich Schinkel's beautiful Schauspielhaus of 1821, all bombed near the end of the war. Little remained but walls and roofs, from which birch trees were growing. On one occasion I ignored warning signs to slip into the empty building and reflect in the half-darkness near the once famous stage when a sound startled me: a rat, a thug, an angry cop? No, an elderly Italian who told sadly in broken German how he once played violin here. But by 1984 it was a magnificent concert hall again, every statue and column lovingly restored. Then after 1990 I watched Helmut Kohl and his buddies act as if they had rebuilt it, another temple to freedom, denouncing the GDR as a "land of injustice" like Nazi Germany. It has become a cliché for media and politicians to link communism with fascism as two sides of the same "totalitarian" coin and the opposite of triumphant free enterprise, democracy, human rights.

No matter how often this Siamese twin equation of democracy and a free market economy is repeated, it is flawed from the start. They are neither siblings nor wedded to each other. Nazi Germany had a capitalist economy and many a free market ally of the West was, or is, far more repressive than the GDR — Pinochet's Chile, Somoza's Nicaragua, apartheid South Africa, Mobuto's Zaire, Saudi Arabia, Turkey, Indonesia. There is no necessary link between freedom and capitalism. Some free market nations are freer and more democratic, others less so — or not at all.

But are socialism and communism (for me both mean nationalized ownership of major industries and banks) inseparably mated to repression and dictatorship? Must they preclude freedom and democracy? Too often they have. But Chile's government under Salvador Allende was not dictatorial or undemocratic when it tried to introduce socialism; his "free enterprise" enemies were. Cuba and Nicaragua abolished brutal free market dictatorships, establishing elements of equality and participation rare in Latin America. Their stress on freedom from want and hunger differed from views in established northern democracies but was closer to the urgent needs of Third World people for food, housing, medical treatment for devastating diseases, and a chance for their children to read, write, and perhaps climb out of poverty and ignorance. This in no way rules out the need for an unfettered press and free elections, but reflects different priorities at specific historic moments for those who learned bitterly that freedom to speak and vote did not itself solve basic problems in developing countries and in impoverished areas of richer ones.

———

While I recognize the disastrous results of limiting freedoms, I do not consider a secret ballot and a privately run press the final goals of democracy, but possible means of nearing ultimate aims like eliminating poverty and preserving our earth. How wonderful, we dreamed, if we could take a fully democratic path to these goals. But we saw attempts to combine greater democracy with socialism foundering not on any basic contradictions, but because of external attacks — and the rationale these provided for internal authoritarianism.

Economically stable countries with satisfied majorities and few internal or external threats are often tolerant, especially those with long libertarian traditions. Leaders may think: "With no real danger why fuss when isolated radicals shoot off their mouths or issue unread, jargon-filled gazettes? Leave them their soapboxes! Perhaps even let them run unknown candidates and get a few votes! Repression would only give them publicity!" Even where leftist parties can get onto ballots and defy hostile media, one main party is often so far to the right that many choose lesser evils like the Democratic, Labour, or Social Democratic parties, which rarely make real changes when elected. And since poor people vote least, they are always underrepresented. Their abstention stems from less education, from poverty — with many fully occupied trying to feed their families — and because politicians' broken promises breed cynicism and apathy, especially among minorities.

When hardships produce a rebelliousness from which people are no longer distracted by football, scandals, or gory crime stories, leaders' worries about managing elections almost automatically lead to methods like the ancient "divide and rule" based on region, language, religion, race, or emotional issues like abortion, which has a long tradition in Ireland, India, Cyprus, and many other countries. George Bush used racism to win the presidency in 1988, Helmut Kohl used xenophobia in German elections. If dissent continues to grow, harder tactics often emerge: provocations, arrests, deportations, even assassination. U.S. history is filled with examples of such repression: the Haymarket victims of 1886, mass arrests of Wobblies in the early twentieth century, the 1919–1920 Palmer Raids on immigrants, violence against strikers in the 1930s, against anti–Vietnam War demonstrators, against black and Native American militants, and perhaps Malcolm X and Martin Luther King.

Leaders who fear their system's collapse may sacrifice democracy altogether. The terrible depression of the early 1930s led to a rapid rise of left-wing parties in Germany. Those in control of the economy ditched a democratic constitution and helped the Nazis seize power. Similar events occurred at that time in Italy, Spain, Portugal, and most of Eastern Europe. Today, decisions to crush democracy caused by the fears of whoever is in power are unnecessary in countries where most citizens have homes, a car or two, vacation trips, and many a modern toy and gadget. But how are such levels achieved?

How many people in Germany knew or cared that pretty Mother's Day flowers came from Kenya or Colombia, where pesticides poison the health of the pickers and ruin the environment? Cheap tea and coffee, bananas and pineapples require miserably paid workers. By paying low wages for a ten-hour day in Brazil, Volkswagen could agree to better wages and benefits in West Germany. The same applied to Mercedes in South Africa and BASF in Louisiana. And such benefits kept West German workers from peering eastward to the GDR, while causing East Germans to look enviously westward. None cared much about Brazil.

Even so-called foreign aid was flawed — described as "money taken from poor people in wealthy countries to give to wealthy people in poor countries," who bought mansions and Porsches. But it is the poor people in the poor countries who must repay the wealthy people in the wealthy countries, with high interest rates. And their children perish!

Much of the prosperity permitting higher satisfaction, hence more democracy, in developed nations results from Third World poverty, with globalizing capital hunting cheap labor and few environmental rules. Britain, where many democratic traditions matured, profited from the vast wealth of India and Africa. If the United States had not imported oil, ores, fruits, and petroleum so cheaply over the years, would its prosperity have been so great — and dissatisfaction so low?

For thirty years the GDR managed amazingly to pull itself up by its thin bootstraps. But with no colonies, tough trade embargoes, and few natural resources it could hardly compete with the other Germany. It was forced to compete, however, by economic and ideological pressure intentionally encouraging the dissatisfaction which endangered its system. Self-preservation, the rule of all states, dictated the use of extreme, even desperate measures, like the Wall in 1961. As protest grew in the 1980s, GDR leaders allowed millions to visit the West, but kept trying to ferret out presumed or real conspiracies in every nook and cranny. That finally backfired. But it was not alone in such methods. West Germany, which never faced any real threat, banned the Communist Party and most radical organizations by 1956, jailed dissidents in the fifties and sixties, and later instituted *Berufsverbote*, the firing of leftist sports teachers, railroad engineers, or mailmen.

Capitalism and socialism are economic systems, dictatorship and democracy are political systems, and any combination is possible. While fascism copied some trappings of German communism because they were familiar and effective, fascism, always based on private property and profits, is closely related to capitalism, not socialism. That is why free enterprise enthusiasts prefer the right to the left as allies and why fascists see Communists as their sworn enemies. The Nazi-Soviet Pact was a short-lived tactic for both sides and cannot erase the confrontation of the many years from Madrid to Stalingrad.

A system not based on private profit, it is often claimed, is unrealistic because of the frailty of human nature, amply demonstrated by the East Bloc's collapse. It seems undeniable that capitalism provides greater impulses to produce and sell. Those involved, often driven by fear for survival, invest their last sweat and savings. Under socialism there was little chance of either bankruptcy or immense wealth; intense personal efforts and sacrifices were rarer, and the results less fulsome.

The standard socialist response was that worker participation in management would overcome alienation, increase feelings of common ownership, and thus spur productivity. But workers' control is not simple. Modern production requires specialized knowledge not available on a mass scale; the desire of a lathe worker to remain after a long workday for technical meetings is not inexhaustible. Not only women workers want to get home, do the chores, and relax. Nor is it easy to look beyond one's department to the needs of the entire economy. Those willing to sacrifice without recompense decrease in number with the years.

Yet, in the long run, are societies erected on foundations of private enterprise and profit really so efficient and viable? In the early 1990s no chance was missed to blame East German economic failures on socialism — with repetitious pejoratives like "forty years' mismanagement," "decrepit economy," and of course, "Stasi." As its economy slipped, many GDR factories indeed became decrepit and unproductive, especially light industry. Customarily ignored is the fact that workers, with no fear of losing jobs, did not feel driven to work harder and faster. Second, social and cultural benefits were very costly. But aren't such factors morally defensible? Are we here to toil away to fulfill each whim created by advertising, only to discard it for a new whim? Is that humane, ethical, or ecologically justified? Was the GDR wrong to make refrigerators and washing machines less elegant, but to last over twenty years? And is a more relaxed, less productive pace really bad?

Polls have revealed that although most GDR women had jobs, parents (compared to West Germany) let children get closer, helped them more, punished them less, and did not pressure them with ambitious demands. East Germans were more social, caring, and considerate while West Germans were more egocentric and thought less of others.

The overcentralization of socialist or Communist systems is normally condemned as a fatal flaw. But isn't the control of industries and banks in fewer and fewer hands also "centralization"? Who can claim that centralized global capital and monopolies over products ranging from weapons of mass destruction to medicines benefit the public? Centralized planning and control in the GDR decreased flexibility and hindered the rapid opening or closing of industrial facilities. But it also yielded a planned buildup of industrial and cultural centers in backward areas like Mecklenburg which had suffered deprivation for centuries.

I fear a long, severe depression in eastern Germany, with high unemployment in western Germany as well, and when I read that Siemens is moving a West Berlin factory to where wages and benefits are lower, for example, I wonder if it is moral for immensely wealthy men in their skyscrapers to hire and fire thousands at will in pursuit of maximum profits. Is it moral for them to produce and push cigarettes, junk food and beverages, to strip forests, to sell firearms — with no regard for public health, nationally and globally? What is democratic about that?

The idea of public ownership was so frightening to those who stood to lose property and power that they bitterly fought even timid excursions in that direction long before the Russian Revolution and the Paris Commune. We should recall the fate of the German pastor Thomas Müntzer in the Peasant Wars of 1525, of John Ball and Wat Tyler in medieval England, of the slave Spartacus in ancient Rome, and of the carpenter and agitator who drove the money changers from the temple.

Those supporting such ideas in Germany today are vilified and denounced. Even mild questioning of current reality may mean being called a naive idealist, Utopian, or dupe by those who loudly proclaim Christian virtue but sneer at the Sermon on the Mount.

A free market economy aims to produce cheaply and sell dearly, using machines, robotics or humans to keep wages as low as possible. Downsizing of old industries and elimination of union-wage labor further reduces purchasing power, exacerbating unemployment. The search for new solutions remains urgent.

The defeat of socialism seemed to prove the pragmatic wisdom of those Ossies who dropped any search for solutions and moved on to making a pile — or simply surviving. Yet some of us kept asking if our lifetime efforts were flawed from the start, perhaps even criminal, and why it all went down the drain.

Asking if defeat was caused by the losers' defects is like asking if a football team lost because of its own weaknesses or because of the strength of its opponent. Both are usually involved. In addition to its countless internal problems, the GDR faced a far bigger and richer West Germany with ample resources, a giant industrial foundation, and all the engineers and scientists who went west in 1945. It got billions in Marshall Plan aid from the United States while East Germany paid about 95 percent of German war reparations, much of it in desperately needed equipment.

A major element in the GDR's collapse, I'm convinced, was an external well-organized and finally successful campaign. The GDR was barred for decades from world affairs as West German threats prevented its diplomatic recognition, and was subjected to the most refined propaganda imaginable, often by Hitlerites in Bonn who metamorphosed into "democrats." Most damaging was the arms race, forcing the East to massively commit scarce resources to military spending, meaning, among other things, fewer consumer goods. GDR armed forces were far bigger than the small country could afford, but Bonn, which always claimed the GDR, had a much larger military. Meanwhile, both major powers, facing each other, did all they could to prevent even a single country in their orbit from breaking out and influencing others. If that meant tanks in Hungary and Czechoslovakia, it also meant U.S. invasions of Guatemala and Cuba in its own sphere, as well as numerous interventions and provocations from Chile to Vietnam.

Adenauer's strangulation strategy — enticing enough people away to undermine the GDR economy — had to be modified in 1961 when John F. Kennedy rejected storming the new Wall. Foreign Minister Willy Brandt (who became chancellor in 1969) and his aide Egon Bahr substituted a softer, more nuanced Eastern policy. Concessions to satisfy the yearning of GDR leaders for diplomatic recognition and a UN seat were swapped for opening the door to Western media, culture, and travel. The 1975 Helsinki Agreement supported eastern borders and freer trade, as the East demanded, but lowered so many barriers between a magnetic West and a poorer East that extensive penetration resulted. Tighter constraints on freedom in the GDR, Czechoslovakia, and the USSR than in Poland and Hungary offered a wedge to split and undermine them all. Bahr said later: "It was our intent and duty to make the GDR disappear."

The cultural offensive, with luxurious life styles on display from *Dallas* to *Dynasty,* was influential, as were catchy music, svelte clothing, stiletto heels, and fancy hairdos. GDR citizens, in exchange for even grudging support, demanded "modernity," from the latest jeans to VCRs, overtaxing industrial and import capacity. Constant fads require countless do-or-die entrepreneurs, risking everything. France or Italy might accept this; the GDR could not. It tried to meet demands with "Intershops" selling Western clothes, foods, even auto parts for Western money, contributing to the growing divide between those with access to hard currency and those without—making hypocrisy of oft-repeated ideals.

But successful responses to strong foes are not easy. Western culture is like a baby hawk pushing weaker siblings out of the aerie, provoking backlash reactions like Iran's mullahs. How could Honecker or "culture czar" Kurt Hager, with narrowed vision and prudish taste, find answers to Donald Duck and "coca-colonization"—answers which are vainly sought by ancient cultures in China and India?

Culture was by no means the only cold war battlefront. Carl Bernstein reported the collusion between the pope, Ronald Reagan, and Lech Walesa to overturn the Polish government as a first step toward achieving victory in all Eastern Europe. Less enthusiastic about changes in Poland and other Warsaw Pact countries, I wrote a U.S. friend in May 1989 that while freedom and democracy were strong motivating elements, "the old question arises, democracy for whom? If it's the World Bank, the IMF, multinationals, and the Vatican . . . it won't be all too democratic."

Adding to external pressures, relations between the USSR and the GDR were worsening from 1986, with signs that the Soviets were preparing to leave the Eastern European states to their own devices. (In light of

Polish events, I wonder what Gorbachev was thinking when he wrote enthusiastically in 1992, "all that occurred in recent years in Eastern Europe would have been impossible without this Pope, without the important . . . political role he was able to play on the international stage. . . .") With weakening Soviet support, and with Poland, Czechoslovakia, Hungary, Romania, and Bulgaria changing colors in amazing unanimity from June to December 1989, the little GDR could hardly go it alone.

———————

Free parties and elections in united Germany are far more satisfying than the voting rituals of the past (although East German cynics noted that "in the GDR we didn't criticize Honecker but cursed the foreman all we wanted. Now we call Kohl anything we want, but never risk a word against the boss"). For West German leaders one calculation went awry: some voters kept choosing the Party of Democratic Socialism, electing thirty members to the Bundestag in 1994, though it was constantly pummeled as undemocratic and always tag-lined as "successor-party of the SED." Even young PDS deputies were heckled about their presumed GDR or SED misdeeds. Kohl denounced PDS members as "red-lacquered fascists"; ironically, Gregor Gysi was one of the scant few Jewish Bundestag members and most PDS leaders had been active (often Jewish) anti-Nazis. CDU politicians refused to stand up when the oldest deputy, Jewish antifascist Stefan Heym, elected for the PDS though not a member, opened the 1994 Bundestag session. Attacking the PDS as totalitarian rang false from West German parties which insisted that government must be able to read private mail, tap phones, and bug homes, not to speak of CDU-CSU opposition to a Munich exhibition of Nazi atrocities as "defaming German soldiers" who fought honorably and fairly.

Whenever the PDS got the floor for a few rare minutes, it berated bans on refugees, attacked neo-Nazis, opposed military expansion and cuts in social welfare, backed women's rights, and fought for better education and for saving the environment. The Greens agreed on many issues, and when Social Democrats concurred, all three came close to a majority. But pressured by Christian Democrats the other two kept their distance from the pariah PDS. Short speeches by master orator Gysi were ignored by TV, voters were warned that the Verfassungsschutz, an FBI equivalent, was monitoring the PDS, and Gysi was regularly denounced with accusations about alleged Stasi ties. All this hurt the party's growth in western Germany.

I had never joined the SED but finally decided to become a PDS member. It seemed a party with an ever-broadening range of views and a pivotal role to play. A voice for the weak seemed urgent in cowed and tired eastern Germany.

In 1990 Helmut Kohl sought West German votes by promising that unification would be financed with no new taxes, recalling George Bush's "read my lips" (aptly translated to "lies meine Lippen"). Honestly, but unwisely, the Social Democrats called this impossible and lost the election.

Not only taxes rose. For twenty-eight years we paid a monthly rent of 114 marks for three rooms, kitchen, and bath (with monthly earnings of over 2,000 marks). Heavily subsidized rent meant delays of modernization and partially explained the shabby exteriors of many buildings, but also facilitated personal economic security. Since 1990 our rent has soared to 950 marks with no end in sight, while gas and electricity rates have tripled and heating, water, and garbage removal are now exactly measured and billed. From 1945 to 1990 East Berlin transport cost 20 pfennigs on an honor system (where not all were honorable). That was a fifth of a mark; by 1999 fares were still rising at 3.90 marks, nineteen times the old rate! Such fares encourage pollution and driving on jammed, increasingly dangerous roads despite steep auto taxes and insurance. Almost everything is more costly: haircuts, books, movies, and milk shakes.

As we grow older, doctors prescribe more pills; all were free in the GDR. Now every pill has its price and we must also pay for dentures, hearing aids, spas, sanatoria, and the first two weeks of hospitalization, while paying higher health insurance fees. Paid days off to care for ill children were reduced sharply while nursing home charges skyrocketed. Dental care and shots for children and adult checkups were better organized and more thorough in the GDR. Before 1990 only 300 were HIV-infected and 60 had AIDS, while 80,000 West Germans were HIV-infected and 7,200 had AIDS. The lack of a GDR drug scene made the difference, just as the unavailability of firearms made the difference in making gun wounds unknown.

For decades billions were poured into West Berlin to make it a fancy showplace in contrast to the East. Now it has been almost fully left to its own meager resources. Without subsidies and tax breaks, its industry is fleeing to cheaper wage areas; large budget deficits have brought sharp cuts in housing, youth programs, education, culture, even women's shelters. Classes are bigger, outings fewer, even fountains have dried up, and sport and swimming facilities are privatized as are utilities, meaning higher prices but not better service.

Since 1990 economists and politicians have been predicting that an all-German upswing was "just around the corner." The GDR taught us to be skeptical. By 1997 unemployment reached Alpine proportions, with over four million jobless and two or three million not counted. East Germany was hit doubly hard, meaning more alcoholism, suicide, and crime, fewer babies — and doubts about change for the better.

In the current climate it's viewed as reprehensible to defend the GDR. Vituperative media tell us daily how we once suffered. The little country is gone but like the amputee whose lost limb still itches, the winners keep scratching, and continue to put people on trial to keep memories fresh.

I disliked oversimplification before 1989. I still do. To me the GDR never meant only Stasi or the Wall any more than the United States meant only Nixon and Vietnam.

GDR people enviously compared their society with one of the world's wealthiest states seen through cathode-ray prisms or during brief visits where life appeared free of difficulties, while home problems seemed incurable and unbearable. But despite major deficits in the economic and political spheres, life for most people was not rough at all. I recall many gatherings with Renate's family, surrounded by flowers, blossoming trees, and their little swimming pool. Half of the urbanites spent weekends or vacations on their "dachas" or bungalows near lakes, woods, or in garden colonies. City outskirts in the warm months smelled of grills, with unlimited food and drink. Family and neighbors listened untroubled to the latest Western hits; the younger set motorcycled off to a disco.

Like other working people Renate and I went on office and factory team outings and got free or cheap tickets to drama, concerts, opera, or musicals. Like every workplace, Renate's hospital offered employees low-priced vacation resorts and sent kids almost free to summer camps.

The Thälmann Engineering Works in Magdeburg, once the GDR's largest machinery plant, was recently in the news. I recalled visiting in

1960, when I noted problems but was impressed by its ten thousand work-ers and by free kindergartens with two hundred toddlers, its free clinic with thirty rooms (one for surgery) and a staff of ninety-three, compared with the one room and a nurse grudged by the same plant when owned by mu-nitions billionaire Krupp. Women, 18 percent of the work force, earned equal wages for equal work. Big handmade signs read: "Our factory library has thousands of books. How many have you already read?" and: "Our team saw Brecht's 'Mother Courage' and enjoyed Gerhart Hauptmann's 'The Beaver Coat.' When were you last in the theater?"

I visited a crane-producing work team's "brigade evening." Once a month, with spouses or friends, they went to the theater, had picnics, heard lectures, played ball with kids who worked four hours weekly to gain ex-perience, or just met to chat, dance, and get acquainted over wine or beer. They complained about the quality of products in the shops and raw ma-terial bottlenecks at work but were proud of what they made ("as good as any cranes in the world") and sure they could never be laid off. That was 1960. Now the last four hundred employees have been split into five com-panies, hoping for buyers but certainly doomed. It was an open secret: the giant firm's shutdown was not due to backwardness but to its own com-petitive power.

GDR schools had no corporal punishment; differences in quality and standards between urban and rural schools were largely eliminated; college was free, with scholarships for all students; every college or apprenticeship graduate, nearly 98 percent of young people, was guaranteed full pay in his or her trade. Mobility between social strata was high. No one feared get-ting a pink slip; if a factory was closed, every worker was assured a new job with free retraining and guaranteed average pay. Formerly feudal or pau-perized regions (like Eichsfeld, whose oompah music–playing inhabitants begged for pennies) were consciously built up. Then there were acts of international solidarity like the building of the Carlo Marx Hospital in Nicaragua, political and material support for Chile and South Africa, and free job and academic training for Third World youngsters.

The GDR was a complex blend of stupid, sometimes malign people, very many ordinary citizens, and not a few dreamers, many of whom suffered under the Nazis or in exile, and then toiled to create a haven of an-tifascism, culture, and economic security from the ashes of a Nazi past. Blunders and oppression pained us as distortions of socialism's democratic and humanist essence. But renewed hope and rejoicing came with every good crop, every new theater, shop, or building (except the ugliest). They belonged to us all; even in ultimate failure after far too many perversions of ideals and morals, there was never a time when less than 5 percent of the population owned over 40 percent of the wealth while millions of others lived in poverty. Some sleazy big shots amassed too much, but they had only pittances compared to those like Friedrich Flick, who gained immense profits form wartime slave labor and retired with 7 billion marks.

Very few wish a return to the GDR, but not a few are rethinking the abandonment of everything they once achieved. Most people rejoiced when the Wall came down, as in the days of Joshua. But not everyone in Jericho stayed happy about those trumpet calls — which spelled destruction for so many. The whore who helped Joshua conquer the town certainly rejoiced; others wished him back in biblical Shittim where he came from!

———————

Before 1989 West Germany assiduously sought to avoid unfavorable comparisons with GDR workers, so big business was more generous with social payments than in most countries. As one union leader said: "The GDR sat at the bargaining table with us."

It sits there no longer; such pampering is "gone with the Wende." Free weekends, long vacations, full sick pay and substantial medical coverage, winter allowances for building workers, early retirement, jobless benefits, and welfare standards are being dismantled as rapidly as union resistance allows.

Now the big boys cry about cutting expenses to meet foreign competitors and demand "restraint" from labor. Of course, they are doing the same in France, Spain, Italy, and elsewhere. They can now threaten with low-paid East Europeans or Third World women who make clothing, car parts, or electronics for $5 a day or less with no unions, no environmental protection, and repressive regimes to keep them in line. While transnational corporations tell workers benignly to "work harder for less" for their own sake, they don't mention their own shares in Asian factories. There, dollar-a-day wages are used to cut Spanish or Italian pay and hopeless sweatshops are an excuse for less safety or medical insurance on the Rhine or Seine. Mining consortia like Amoco, Broken Hill, and German Degussa in Papua New Guinea work miners long hours for low pay while firing miners in their home countries.

For many Third World nations the disappearance of the East Bloc was a distinct loss: it voted for Third World interests in the UN and supported anticolonial movements and newly independent nations — enabling them to extract concessions from the West by dangling the prospect of turning eastward.

When poor people move north to escape war or poverty, they often are forced to work illegally and for low wages, involuntarily undercutting the wages of others and weakening efforts to maintain decent conditions. Demagogues like Jean La Pen in France and Pat Buchanan in the United States scapegoat them and fan xenophobia. East Germans moving west sometimes serve the same purpose. Wessies are encouraged to blame their high taxes on lazy, pampered Ossies — who are told to stop griping. Helmut Kohl sang this tune by warning that equal wages in East Germany increased unemployment.

Many good people in Germany oppose Ossie-Wessie conflicts or attempts to sow hatred of Third World people. But more years of unemployment and tension could easily spark an explosion. Referring to Nazism, Brecht warned: "The loins from which that crept are fertile still."

My adrenaline level always rose when I saw a new East German outlet of the Deutsche Bank, Commerz Bank, Dresdner Bank, or a branch of Krupp, Thyssen, or I. G. Farben. I recalled William L. Shirer's words that the Nazis needed large sums and got the largest from "I. G. Farben, the chemical cartel . . . the Deutsche Bank, the Commerz Bank, the Dresdner Bank. . . ."

Real estate values jumped and residents rejoiced when Daimler-Benz planned a giant truck plant in Ludwigsfelde near Berlin. How many recalled that over half the 17,000 Daimler "employees" who produced 35,000 warplane motors here for the Nazis were starving war prisoners or male and female slave laborers? The criminal individuals at Daimler-Benz and the other companies are gone. But I worry about their successors. The auto giant has now joined with Messerschmitt-Bolke-Blohm to form Europe's major military conglomerate, boasting of its long-range bombers whose range can be extended indefinitely with air refueling. Such conglomerates still give huge sums to the conservative parties and even to the SPD.

The often-lauded free social market is dominated by such immense banks and transnationals. With Germany again the richest, strongest country in Europe, these institutions praise freedom but look further afield. Even before digesting the GDR they were expanding into Eastern Europe.

Volkswagen is now boss of Czech Skoda auto works, and a Bavarian syndicate grabbed up local newspapers in the Czech Republic and Poland. For years Bonn cultivated exiled puppet leaders of Nazi Croatia, and it still sponsors that now-independent country. Hans-Dieter Genscher, then German foreign minister, blackmailed the European Union into recognizing Slovenia, Croatia, and Bosnia-Herzegovina before protection of minorities was arranged. How much misery might have been averted by striving for other solutions?

Germany's expansion might be considered an economic power's normal growth if there were not such a rapid rise in military activity — and the lessons of history. The West German constitution prohibited all but purely defensive activity. This ban has been eroding for years and is now virtually dead as the SPD and even some Green deputies approved sending troops to Asia, Africa, or the Balkans. First it was "humanitarian" army medics in Cambodia, then blocking unauthorized shipping in the Adriatic, patrolling Bosnian skies, and then a "humanitarian" Somali fiasco. When the Balkans erupted again, one German general eerily complained about American, British, and French soldiers coming home in body bags while the German military had to sit on the sidelines. Before long German ground troops were being prepared to return to a region devastated by the Nazis. The German camp where soldiers trained for Bosnia was hurriedly renamed; until then it had borne the name of a notorious Nazi general and war criminal.

One excuse for sending troops around the globe was the need to "shoulder responsibilities"—and acquire a permanent Security Council seat, a major power symbol. Also a European "Crisis Reaction Force," 53,600 men with the latest weapons for swift "out of area" actions, is being prepared for the role of military cop in the global economy. An official military publication stated the goals: "maintaining free world trade and unhindered access to markets and raw materials everywhere. . . ." In March 1995 German President Roman Herzog said "Checkbooks are not always sufficient" to achieve our "national interests . . . sometimes committing our persons and our lives may be required."

Germany's current aspirations are economic or political, not territorial. But with a GDR barrier against expansion gone, plans for road and rail connections to Kaliningrad — once Königsberg — are linked to irredentist dreams. A column in the influential *Die Welt* on August 6, 1997, stated: "Stability in the region can only be achieved when Russia gives up this

World War II booty." Talk of "regaining" Silesia lost ground when even Kohl noticed how explosive this was in Poland, but territorial demands, outlawed in the GDR, now play a role again, and German Landsmannschaften from the "lost provinces" still get government aid.

Although forceful movements are needed to combat the spread of hatred and expansionism, the German left has rarely reached any unity. The left wing of the Social Democrats, once fairly strong, has largely withered, and the once militantly antiwar, anti-establishment Greens have moved further and further to the right — where their positions contrast less and less with most other major parties. A small, militant, often extremist wing of the left is active but isolated from nearly all of the population. As for the PDS, strong in the former GDR areas, its main problem remains breaking through in West Germany where forty-year-old prejudices make progress difficult. And it, too, is torn between those rejecting accommodation with the ruling economic and political system, those nostalgic for GDR years, and more pragmatic elements seeking positions — and perhaps perks, some believe — within the ruling framework. Its main unifying element is an opposition to German military expansion or adventures, past or present. As for the former dissidents of the GDR, most have either found good jobs in the old parties or continue to pout in their private corners.

The defeat of major twentieth-century experiments from East Berlin to Vladivostok, whether due to inner faults or opponents' power, has set back for years the search for solutions now more nebulous than ever. If such an experiment had first been tried in the larger, richer, unthreatened part of Germany, Europe, or the world, might it have succeeded? That involves many "ifs." An absence of outside threats might remove any rationale for centralized power with its limits on criticism and discouragement of original ideas.

The search goes on for a system which prevents human frailties like greed or hunger for power from holding sway over the lives of millions. No one should live luxuriously off the sweat of others. Without demanding Spartan abstinence the system must guarantee a sufficient, humane standard of living and equal chances for everyone. And now the threat of ecological disaster compels us to hasten the quest.

As for me, my life has somersaulted. From hard early years as an isolated leftist, to the long search for answers in the GDR, I am now back in the system I swam away from in 1952. I am reminded of this full circle by a neon message across the street where once a quiet little light signaled a children's store. Now a huge sign hectically flashes into my room, red and white: "Coca-Cola!" I think of the saying: "You can run but you can't hide."

But I am not a pessimist. I look for encouragement to my American heroes: writers like Thoreau, Whitman, Melville, Twain; singers like Woody Guthrie and Paul Robeson; rebels like Paine, Tubman, John Brown, Debs, Joe Hill, Sacco and Vanzetti, Mother Jones, Malcolm X, Martin Luther King. Those are the symbols to which I owe allegiance. I can add German names or those of people in all countries. In attempts to make the world a little better, I believe, it hardly matters where one lives. I think of my FBI dossier and wonder; was that a funny click in my telephone? Who knows? Who cares? As I have always said (or almost always): to hell with them, I'll always remain a rebel!

[EPILOGUE]
EAU DE COLOGNE

In February 1952, I took a weekend pass to see more of Germany. After Hamburg, Dusseldorf, and Bonn, my stamina flagged, but Cologne woke me up. I was in my required uniform, carrying a small flight bag with several visible cigarette cartons, the illegal, universal trading item for soldiers when German cigarettes were far more expensive.

In the third-class waiting hall I was soon surrounded by several beggars and amputees, probably war veterans. Others with shrill voices may have been overaged prostitutes. They were all friendly, a bit too friendly, pointing at the cartons with crooked smiles and asking me to give or sell them some. The ring grew tighter, their hands were grasping, and I could hardly defend my bag, or myself, against ten or fifteen of them. They kept grinning, but the demands grew louder. Finally, as agreeably as I was able, I said NEIN and made a dash for the main section of the giant station, recalling the 1931 German film *M* with its tribunal of beggars and other denizens of Berlin's lower depths seeking revenge against a terror-stricken Peter Lorre. Did I, like Lorre, symbolize a crime against them or their city? Outside I saw the broad, quiet Rhine, with the remains of a big bridge. The city was a sea of dark ruins, and I remembered communiqués about planes and artillery pounding Cologne to destruction, sparing only the giant cathedral whose two towering spires now punctuated the night sky. Oblivious to the grim scene, a small, makeshift amusement park was open for Karneval, the Mardi Gras celebrated in Catholic regions. A meager crowd of loud youngsters and unsteady drinkers rode the ferris wheel and roller coaster, seeking enjoyment in this gloomy world.

Some bars had survived the destruction or had been rebuilt. Tired and lonely after two nights with hardly any sleep, I went into one — and was immediately invited to a table. This was the British Zone; everyone was friendly

but curious about what brought a GI to their celebration of "Rosenmon-
tag," the night before Tuesday's climax, followed by Ash Wednesday and
Lent. But I was taught appropriate drinking songs of the "Rhine-wine" variety like the "The Best Place Is Always at the Bar," and "Auf Wiedersehen,"
which would later become a hit in the United States.

Once again I faced the perennial question: what had the man next to me
been doing in the Nazi years? One rarely learned the answer, certainly not
that evening with the songs and my tired mind. A half-year later destiny
took me in very different directions with new problems.

I did not revisit Cologne until December 1993. With free time before my
train left, I recalled very little from 1952. The repaired bridge arched over
the Rhine, whose silent waters sped beneath huge statues of two dead
kaisers, and there was the cathedral, larger than I remembered. I walked
down a broad stone staircase and along streets lined with expensive restaurants, then turned into a wide pedestrian zone, with one elegant shop after
another displaying an overflowing array of goods in brilliantly lighted windows. It was late and I was almost alone to admire innumerable appliances,
joyful Santa Clauses, and sparkling, overwhelming Christmas lights. How
magnetic all this had been for people in the republic I had lived in. Only
one item attracted me, exotic Italian ice cream, barred by doctor's orders.
Tired of carrying my small suitcase (no cigarettes this time), I headed toward the station.

A museum exhibiting some Gothic painter was open, but the steep admission price quenched my curiosity. I came to a covered structure, open
and evidently free of charge, a long hall with pillars and replicas of Roman
times, all covered with new graffiti. Cologne — the Roman Colonia — was
truly ancient. In front of one stone replica a young man with a guitar
played "Jesu, Joy of Man's Desiring." He played so well I was about to give
him some change when my attention was distracted to one side of the hall
behind him. There were six people in sleeping bags, rags, and cardboard on
the cement floor. Outside the hall, partly protected from rain by the eaves,
were four more, including a woman who greeted every passerby with a
hoarse but cheerful "Good evening." I saw no one give her any money.

I boarded my train and thought of the ruined city and shabby station
people in 1952, and of today's contrasts — quite normal for Cologne's
people, but not for me.

Within three days Cologne was in the headlines. The worst flood of the century inundated many areas and all the shopping streets I had passed. The TV news just before Christmas showed people wading or paddling through the city, trying to save their homes or livelihoods. I saw no reference to the homeless, who must also have had to find new refuges. Even Noah crossed my mind.

(November 1996)

AFTERWORD
Mark Solomon

When Stephen Wechsler went off to Buffalo in 1949 to join the working class after four years at Harvard, he was not aware that transforming events in Central Europe at that time would deeply affect his already rapidly changing life. In October of that year, the German Democratic Republic came into existence, and three years later that small socialist country carved out of greater Germany would become his home for nearly a half-century.

Wechsler's fateful plunge into the Danube and ultimately to refuge in the German Democratic Republic was a product of his own distinct personality and temperament. But his generational experience also played a role. Little is known of the young leftists and Communists who were nestled between the highly visible Depression and World War II radical generations and the new left boomers of the sixties. Wechsler's generational trajectory formed an arc from the heady Popular Front days of important Communist and left influence to the near annihilation of the left in the fifties. Some aspects of his youth were exceptional, especially his elite education. But the vibrant cultural and political scene in the Communist orbit, especially in New York, was a standard part of life for radical youth who came to maturity in the forties. Both the extraordinary and ordinary aspects of Wechsler's growing up provide a rare window for understanding the wellspring of political consciousness which drove some of that generation to embrace communism and allowed a smaller number to withstand both the buffeting of McCarthyism and the dispiriting revelations of Stalin-era crimes.

Wechsler was literally a child of the Popular Front who ingested through a child's eyes the images of desolate men on breadlines at home and the struggle to defeat Franco's fascists abroad. That gestating awareness of human suffering created by what appeared to be an irrational and unjust social system grew into hardened anticapitalist conviction while Spain, the "good fight," came to symbolize and validate a sacred obligation to defeat the bad guys known as fascists. An art dealer's son embraced the working class and the international antifascist struggle as a vast cultural value manifested in a variety of spiritual and material goods — ideas, songs, relationships — all seeping into a child's consciousness as indisputably just, right, good — and never to be abandoned.

While the potential existed for such ideas to become insulating dogma, the Popular Front itself meant unity around minimally common aims in a spirit of inclusiveness and tolerance. Life at Free Acres, the family retreat full of eccentrics of various political faiths, encouraged a sometimes precarious balance between rigid belief and receptivity to others' ideas. For the precocious Wechsler kid, the Communists seemed to have the franchise on steadfastness and internationalism. He was hooked — soldiering on unsteadily at age twelve, at the fancy Dalton School no less, against hostility to Stalin's nonaggression pact with the Nazis, then basking in renewed liberal approval for Communists with the outbreak of World War II and emergence of the Soviet-Western alliance. Along the way, he immersed himself in the rich community of culture that was still the hallmark of the Communist-led left. He had become a devoted member of the last generation of youth to be part of a substantial, influential radicalism within the Communist orbit.

With all that, Wechsler's fervent communism was never a barrier to a rounded, lively childhood and adolescence. He wasn't much for sports, but his young life was filled with music, zoology, Sherlock Holmes, Irish poetry, classic literature, and the romance of the Mexican revolution — all nurtured by elite schooling, courtesy of a determined mother. If ideology didn't turn him into a stereotyped zealot, Dalton and Fieldston didn't lay waste to his growing proletarian loyalty. Ultimately, embryonic Marxism, elite schooling, and radical culture converged and nourished one another. As young Wechsler maneuvered through Dalton, Fieldston, the Young Communist League, and its successor American Youth for Democracy, he thrived on brainy debate, discovered folk music which provided a spiritual community and anchor for his beliefs — and occasionally succumbed to adolescent romantic longing. Life was not always an idyll; there was a teen's distress over sexual inadequacy and worry about exposure of his family's shabby gentility before his upper-crust schoolmates. But running from downtown Folksay dances to midtown AYD meetings to the uptown Museum of Natural History, Wechsler wasn't encumbered much by worry and contradiction. He was the anti–Holden Caulfield, a red antithesis of J. D. Salinger's lonely, alienated teen traveler in Manhattan.

A heroic aura left by the Allied anti-Nazi struggle spurred pride and international solidarity in Wechsler's leftist generation. There was comfort in identifying with the Soviet Union, admired by a broad public for its incalculable sacrifice in the battle to defeat fascism, and with Italian partisans, Greek guerrillas, and Tito's fighters—all part of a vast liberating current. With the war's end, the quickened pace of colonial liberation struggles, the advancing Chinese revolution, and more, strengthened Wechsler's and his leftist peers' belief they were part of a global tide that would sweep in a genuinely human epoch. Within the context of those events, one can grasp why those young people ignored or dismissed signs of dark, repressive currents in the Soviet Union and Eastern Europe. Soviet Russia was the primary star in a growing socialist and national liberation firmament, but it was also viewed as the flagship for new, transforming possibilities in every corner of the globe, especially "New China" and Vietnam. Such an international framework lessened the chances of obsessive devotion to the USSR and authenticated the commitments of that generation coming to maturity in the early postwar years.

Wechsler discovered a vigorous Communist presence at, of all places, Harvard University. There the political values accumulated since childhood—embodied in Spanish resistance to fascism, the Communist record of battle against racial injustice, the Soviet wartime sacrifice, and left-wing culture—brought him to cofound the postwar branch of the campus Communist Party club. That step came at an exceptional though neglected moment in the history of student radicalism. Like other universities, Harvard absorbed significant numbers of returning servicemen. The ex-GIs were joined by an influx of urban lower-middle-class youth, including Jewish students, admitted under postwar pressures to democratize higher education. The club reflected a potent mix of combat experience and city smarts, drawing together a remarkable group attracted to the yet undamaged vision of radical democracy and socialism. Wechsler, despite having to endure smug displays of alleged expertise in Marxist theory, nevertheless found the young Harvard Communists to be an accomplished array, ranging from a teenage Joyce scholar to prodigiously well-read working-class ex-GIs. In a party that hovered between Popular Front flexibility and a coming political hardening, the Harvard club engaged in imaginative demonstrative activities against racial discrimination and the emerging cold war, and in defense of labor's interests. Its educational and cultural efforts, in tandem with the overlapping AYD, provoked unfettered inner debate and brought outstanding leftist artists and political activists from all over the world to the Cambridge campus, enabling the club to grow even as the CP nationally was declining.

Decline, nevertheless, was the dominant trend. As the cold war intensified, Communists and their allies were subjected to harassment and jailing. Henry Wallace's Progressive Party in 1948 bravely challenged the cold war and racial injustice. Harry Truman adroitly exploited fear of resurgent Republican conservatism and blended red-baiting with theft of elements of Wallace's domestic program. That ended in the Progressive presidential vote falling far short of expectations. Hope for a mass left-of-center third party was crushed in what turned out to be a watershed in the decline of the postwar left. Wechsler's enthusiastic efforts to build the youth arm of the Wallace campaign, the Young Progressives, in Boston's predominantly black Roxbury neighborhood, yielded a small breakthrough in overcoming the estrangement of a few African American teenagers. Slender gains in Roxbury and other locations in Boston, Lynn, Lawrence, and New Bedford stirred optimism. But the losses were far greater. With the arrest and trial of ever-deeper echelons of CP activists under the Smith Act (for "teaching and advocating" the overthrow of the government), the party, with a "two-minutes-to-midnight" estimate of a fascist threat, lost or expelled scores of marginal members, created a semi-underground apparatus, and in response to an increasingly repressive climate hardened its inner ideological life. Faced with growing external opposition, the Harvard club, by and large after Wechsler had left the university, slipped into internecine quarrels over such matters as the party's hostility to psychoanalysis. Whether such disputes were inventions to justify withdrawal, whether they were symptomatic of the independent intellectual life of the Harvard reds, or whether they were some combination of both, the seepage of membership foretold an end to the organized Communist presence at the university. For Wechsler and others of his generation, the well-being derived from membership in a reasonably viable party with connections to the liberal and progressive mainstreams began to evaporate. Now affiliation, if revealed, engendered potential job loss, forced isolation from the larger community, even jailing.

Wechsler, who had determined his political fate and never looked back, had a jumble of contradictory responses to a new situation. He hunkered down, prepared to gut out the repressive period with faith in the party's theoretical foundation, its program, and its right to speak. But such convictions would be at war with nagging fear — an incipient condition that would develop in coming days and months. When he graduated from Harvard without a career plan, he was a logical candidate for "industrial concentration," which required a steely adjustment to new surroundings. The party in 1949 turned with renewed determination to the industrial workforce, which at that time appeared to be the largest, most unionized, and most politically engaged segment of the working class. In the face of a darkening political climate, the CP felt a greater urgency to cast some of its most devoted members into the industrial heartland factories to connect with the workers. Even those of academic bent with little background or facility for manual labor were asked to "colonize" industrial areas and toil in factories with the objective of influencing and reinvigorating that class which remained in the party's view the essential agency of change.

A "colonizer" with little mechanical skill or talent for elbow-bending with fellow workers, Wechsler survived long stretches of isolation and loneliness on the strength of his convictions, his lack of great need for material comfort, and his admirable absence of snobbery. But Buffalo was light years from the culture that had nourished him — and most workers in the city's grimy factories were the antithesis of idealized or romanticized notions about the working class. Wechsler encountered chronic racism, sexism, and crassly individualist ways of retrieving stolen labor value — behavior indicative of misplaced class consciousness. Yet he hung on, vindicated in part by the gut-level militancy of fellow workers who responded positively to his timorous challenge to a corrupt union leadership and who angrily fought against a sell-out contract. Workers may be afflicted with a false consciousness foisted on them by the dominant society, but unlike those not of their class, they must inevitably confront and overturn the system whose essence was their exploitation. That was enough to keep him going. But "industrial concentration" was a drop in a vast industrial ocean, which provokes questions about the wisdom of the policy and whether young intellectuals would have had more impact had they contributed in areas that were consonant with their training and cultural circumstances. As the fifties ground on and the party-led left became increasingly ener-

vated, most "colonizers" drifted back into universities and professions although a few like Wechsler's bed-hogging roommate, Bill Nuchow, went
on to long careers in the labor movement.

Wechsler also drew sustenance from the "Timpkens" (a pseudonymous
legendary black Communist family) within Buffalo's African American
community. Here he found security and a bond of trust between black and
white which had been built in large measure upon the party's long record
of struggle for racial equality. He also found a sliver of connection with the
little-known Labor Youth League, which was launched in Chicago on
Memorial Day weekend in 1949, shortly after Wechsler finished his Harvard education. The LYL replaced the moribund AYD, which had virtually
disappeared within the Wallace movement's Young Progressives of America. An echo of the Young Communist League, the LYL defiantly announced its "fraternal" relations with the Communist Party and sympathy
with the CP's ideological outlook. Leon Wofsy, the LYL chair (later to become a prominent scientist at the University of California) told the founding conference that the new organization will fight for every need of youth
and will educate young people in Marxism in "a spirit of devotion to the
working class and its historic goal of socialism."

The youth organization's apex was at its beginning when it enrolled
about seven thousand members; it was never again to approach that number. While many LYL members were not Communists, the organization
adopted parallel and intersecting "colonizing" with the CP, bringing LYL
youth into factories and into industrial communities. The appearance of
some of Wechsler's generation in Buffalo allowed him to recapture a bit of
the community that he experienced in former days and provided a sounding board to vent his frustration over the dull, rigid, and lockstep mentality of his industrial party club. At this point Wechsler felt growing tension
between independent thinking and obeisance to discipline and collective
decision-making. He struggled with a dilemma that would dog him for
most of his adult life: how to avoid the pitfalls of "robots and lemmings"
who would blindly follow any dotty leader over a precipice or the opposite
extreme of chaotic individualism which negated disciplined and decisive
action. With tightening external repression, internal tolerance for unfettered individual thinking (which often became dissent) evaporated as the
demand intensified for unquestioning support for the line. Wechsler would
become nostalgic over his Harvard club, which was both disciplined and

intellectually free-wheeling. But he had to confess that many of those bright middle-class students who insisted on the sanctity of their own thoughts had fallen by the wayside. Wechsler concluded that indivisible commitment to class struggle, something that many Harvard comrades finally could not accept, required a willingness to subjugate individual doubts to collective action. Yet he never did find a satisfactory solution for a problem that would sunder many minds and movements — and plague him in exile. Wechsler could only agree that in an imperfect world one could not easily become a perfect Communist.

With a few young activists filtering into Buffalo, it was possible to organize an LYL club. But the shards of race cut deeply, making it difficult to attract white working-class youth. Drawing upon the "Timpkens" and the larger black community, the club became an ungainly fusion of African American teens and white college-trained colonizers. Yet it worked, to a degree. Like much of the LYL nationally, the club fought racial discrimination in the cloudy years before the Supreme Court ruled against school segregation in 1954. In the process, Wechsler gained insight into a deep well of resistance in black life to oppression, and again, as with most LYL activists, the struggle for racial justice became a centerpiece of his leftist commitment.

Through the fifties, while Wechsler was in self-imposed exile, the LYL was increasingly forced on the defensive, fending off prolonged harassment from the Internal Revenue Service, nearly abandoning all other activities in trying to save the lives of Ethel and Julius Rosenberg, sending a segment of its leadership underground into "unavailable" status. The meeting at Geneva in the late spring of 1955 of President Dwight D. Eisenhower and Soviet leaders Bulganin and Khrushchev seemed to signal an easing of the cold war and McCarthyism, opening some space for the left. But months later, Khrushchev's report on the crimes of the Stalin era hit much of the LYL generation with crushing force. Having been weaned on the democratic and humanist aspirations of the Popular Front and World War II, and having defended the Soviet Union as an embodiment of a promised better world, a good part of the LYL drifted away with broken hearts or anger or both. The organization quietly disbanded in 1958 although some former LYL activists later sought to bridge their experiences with the emerging radicals of the sixties.

Wechsler's generation had borne three intersecting phenomena: McCarthyism, disillusionment, and a relatively protracted fifties' prosperity which pulled some away from direct political engagement. But many talented people initially spawned by the LYL were destined to have a major impact on the country's academic, artistic, and professional life such as Lorraine Hansberry, the noted playwright, Douglass Turner Ward (Roosevelt Ward, Jr.), founder of the Negro Ensemble Company, and even Robert Fogel, who in later years would discover Protestant virtue in slavery and win a Nobel Prize.

The draft would remove Stephen Wechsler from that milieu. Inducted into the army, he was obliged to reveal civilian associations. Without guidance from the unprepared CP (membership was furloughed upon induction) Wechsler cringed at the prospect of being cast into an ugly spotlight should he refuse to comply. So he slunk into anonymity by simply doing what those around him did: he declared that he had not joined any of the scores of groups on the attorney general's list of "subversive organizations." Only after months of a relatively relaxed army experience where his high score on the Morse code aptitude test got him into specialized training and service as a radio man in Bavaria, did the military catch up with him. During the Korean War, military policy toward "subversives" was to release them after investigation with a "general discharge under honorable conditions." Although there is some question about how scrupulously the "honorable" designation was observed, that mild category was supposed to allow for various benefits, including schooling under the GI Bill of Rights. If Wechsler had simply appeared before a military court, he likely would have been cashiered out of the army with that discharge. But in his isolated state, how could he know? He read and reread the threatened punishment for his false statement: "$10,000 and/or five years in prison." In a period reeking with spy scares and spiraling anticommunist hysteria, he panicked, especially when he sensed that he had drifted into a sensitive classification that could leave him vulnerable to a frame-up. In retrospect, his decision to desert seems irrational. But his desperate plunge into the Danube needs to be understood within the context of that threatening, unpredictable time. In 1954, while Wechsler was settling into life in East Germany, the army, under relentless attack by Senator Joseph McCarthy, shifted political discharges to a damaging "undesirable" category that denied its recipients all postservice pay and benefits, including the GI Bill. The military then caught up with leftists who had earlier been honorably separated from active duty, now bestowing on scores of veterans, including some who served with distinction in Korea, the heinous "undesirable" discharge. In March 1958, the U.S. Supreme Court reversed a decision by the District Court in Washington, D.C. and declared that discharges must be based solely on military service and nothing more. Soon thereafter, the military was obliged to give honorable discharges to all who were punished for their activities as civilians.

––––––––––

By that time Wechsler had long been integrated into East German society which, it turned out, was a refuge in the early cold war for defectors from Allied armed forces as well as a for a few Western political exiles. Shipping Wechsler there, the Russians perhaps also reasoned that he would adapt more easily to the socialist bloc state whose cultural texture came closest to the West. But life in the GDR during the early years of cold war was harshly burdened by the struggle for the heart of Europe.

Ironically, Winston Churchill's obsessive fear of a Red Army march through Germany may have helped give birth to the GDR. In 1943 he pressed for a strong German buffer state against Soviet westward expansion. But with Stalin's opposition and Roosevelt's cool response, the three wartime leaders agreed to defer the German question to a newly established European Advisory Commission. When the Big Three met again at Yalta in early 1945, the Red Army had reached the Oder River while U.S. and British forces were still west of the Rhine. Now thoroughly haunted by fear that the Soviets would themselves end the war and absorb much of Germany, Churchill agreed to the Advisory Commission's proposal to create occupation zones, giving the Soviets a zone in eastern Germany. A new deadlock over reparations ensued when Western leaders balked at Soviet demands for massive restitution, claiming concern over a revanchist upsurge, but, more important, dreading a weak German bulwark against communism. At Potsdam in 1945, with Harry Truman now president, lip service was paid to treating Germany as a single economic unit, but Soviet access to desperately needed restitution was largely confined to its zone except for a limited exchange of raw materials for capital goods from the West. This fell far short of Soviet expectations, which were based on a Yalta accord that the partner who bore the greatest burden of combat and destruction would receive from all of Germany the largest share of reparations. Both sides had reversed positions on a united Germany. Stalin's support for an economic entity, which was to evolve by 1948 into support for a united, neutral Germany, was now viewed by the West as a Soviet plot to absorb the entire prostrate country. With neither side able to control the whole of Germany — which would allow domination of Europe, if not the world — the United States and Britain now cleaved the defeated Nazi regime deeply into zones, pinning the Russians into their largely agricultural enclave. In May 1946, shipment of capital goods from the western zones to the east was halted, and on New Year's Day in 1947 the U.S. and British zones were fused administratively into "Bizonia." With a potential economic entity ruptured, the foundation was now in place for the creation of a West German state.

While Wechsler was getting a joyful taste of internationalism and early cold war hardball at the Prague World Youth Festival in 1947, the Soviets in their zone in Germany had been seeking to expunge Nazis and force restitution. Nazi teachers, judges, and officials were purged while liberated concentration camps and pockets of Nazi-era noncooperation were hastily scoured for replacements (including some of Wechsler's in-laws-to-be); Junker estates, the historic nest of German militarism, were broken up; a few industries were nationalized with part of their production delivered to the USSR as reparations; trolley tracks and other resources of value were ripped out and sent to Russia. A largely hungry, fearful public likely harbored a fluctuating animus toward the Red Army and returning native Communists whom the Soviets sought to install in leadership. The toughness of Soviet rule in their zone stiffened U.S. and British resistance to incorporating that region into a united Germany.

Rapid movement toward the creation of a West German state was facilitated in 1948 by a unilateral bizonal currency reform, which, while preparing the way for huge Marshall Plan infusions of capital that would later fuel West Germany's "economic miracle," threatened to wreck the financial system of the East. With the West formally splitting Germany, the Soviets challenged Western entitlement to an artificial outpost in Berlin, 125 miles deep into their zone. The Russians cut off surface access (to which the Western powers had no legal right) to the divided city after the United States moved to enact a West German constitution. To counter the Berlin blockade, Washington launched a massive airlift that supplied West Berlin and yielded a huge propaganda dividend for the West. The blockade came to an end in

May 1949 when a punishing counterblockade was lifted. A West German state was then established based upon a federal system fashioned by the United States ostensibly to discourage the revival of a dangerously powerful Germany. But that system gave disproportionate strength to rural conservatives, including ex-Nazis, at the expense of the left. In October 1949, the Soviets and their allies in the East established the German Democratic Republic. The division of Europe was now sealed by the division of Germany.

By 1952, the country that sheltered Stephen Wechsler had survived the worst of the early postwar years. Life in Bautzen, the repository for defectors, was still Spartan, but there was no hunger. The painful reconstruction of an advanced industrial society was under way. But the demand for increased production with accelerated work norms persisted and would lead in June 1953 to a labor uprising. That event tried the ideological commitment of staunch socialists, who had to work hard to find solidarity with a socialist dream in the face of a workers' revolt. Wechsler's faith in socialism was not shaken, but he faced in those early days a realization that as a young Jewish New Yorker he had cast himself into a vastly different universe — with little chance of ever reversing course. His new life, however, provided a rare window to peer into a fascinating, complex, and contradictory socialist experiment. Wechsler, now metamorphosed into Victor Grossman, would always be an "auslander," never, of course, to experience the GDR from inside the skin of a native East German, and unlike his neighbors, more than willing to abjure travel to the West. But he arrived there not as a celebrated immigrant, but as an uninvited guest with no perks or privileges, save the "jester's license" afforded a foreigner to offer mildly critical observations. Except for occasional work in film or in celebrity translation, his was a relatively normal life that apparently never drew special attention from official circles or the general public. Wechsler had to struggle with both degrading and uplifting relations with fellow exiles, recycle his schooling and grapple with dogmatic professors, find work, wrestle with outmoded plumbing and heating, build a social life, get married, raise a family, struggle with daily irritations and obstacles from scarce telephones to household chores to workplace conflicts — and suffer rebuff or disinterest when he sought to contribute to the polity. He was no doubt the only one on this earth who could offer comparisons between a worker's lot in the GDR and in Buffalo's industrial plants. He saw the country at ground level, and his experience commands our attention.

The former West Germans have labored assiduously to erase all symbols of the GDR's political and spiritual life and banish from memory the GDR's social experiments which might be of use in dealing with nagging problems in the West like women's equality and family protection. After re-unification, a relentless tattoo of the misdeeds of the Stasi, the state security apparatus, was beaten to drown out ideas that anything of value existed in the GDR worth preserving. But the country's essence was far more than a visitor's troubled image of the often pugnacious and paranoid behavior of the guards at its sensitive borders. In historic perspective, the Germans in the East were called upon to accede to the formation of the GDR under Soviet orchestration and with a landscape made barren by war and forced restitution. Although their revolution was set in motion from without, most of the people were willingly engaged in building a socialist system that spawned the tenth largest industrial economy in the world, at one point encompassing 4,000 publicly owned industrial enterprises, 600 construction firms, 5,000 agricultural cooperatives and state farms, and 86,000 trade enterprises with 30,000 private tradesmen among them.

A vision of a socialist polity was in the marrow of the reds who returned from exile to create "real existing socialism" under Soviet tutelage. From an ideological standpoint, the social net was not just the welfare state div-idend of a centrally planned, state-owned economy; it was the embodi-ment of an unbreakable "unity of social and economic policy." Along with antifascism the social net provided identity and meaning to a state sliced off from its actual historic roots. The social policy provided comprehensive personal and social security—universal health care, extensive childcare, guaranteed pensions, subsidized prices, rentals, and vacations, free occu-pational training and higher education, and inexpensive access to culture and sports. Medical and dental services were rendered without reams of documents and without even a nod to the cash nexus. Women perhaps were the greatest beneficiaries of the social net, with access to abortion (af-ter 1972) and generous paid maternity leave. Each additional birth brought leave time and continuing job protection regardless of the length of ab-sence. Single women with babies were helped by friends, neighbors, and workmates. Little wonder that Wechsler found in the GDR both symbolism and substance to fire his leftist imagination and give him enough comfort and pride in calling that little country his home.

The GDR's greatest attainment in the social sphere was the forging of a largely egalitarian culture where, except for some Party higher-ups, star athletes, and top-rank artists, people lived, interacted, and accumulated at similar levels. The French agriculturist and Pennsylvania colonizer St. John Crèvecoeur, in a paean to New World equality, found that there "the ploughman and the professor received the same questions." At East Berlin's Humboldt University, where I taught history in 1988, I was reminded of Crèvecoeur's observation when repeatedly seeing the open and mutually consultative relationships between department heads and secretaries, senior professors and workers. Marzahn, the sprawling concrete jungle of high-rise buildings (part of Honecker's grand plan to build 950,000 housing units — a plan which contributed to the GDR's near bankruptcy) housed factory workers, tradesmen, cops, apparatchiks, academics, cultural workers, scientists, students, and foreign guests in similar circumstances. As in other neighborhoods of smaller scale, the local pub, supermarket, "Zentrum" department store, and school served the entire community, which pursued its material needs without the pressures of commercialism. A desire for up-to-date consumer goods existed and would grow to become a critical political problem. But day-to-day, there was little time for fetishistic preoccupation with Western commodities. The waiting list for a Trabant auto seemed a lifetime (although there were ways for resourceful people to reduce the waiting period), but the two-stroke little car fulfilled the acquisitive dreams of many East Germans. Not until the GDR disappeared did the commercialization of individual desires, driven by advertising, burst forth and the rush ensue for repainted lemons from the West.

Performance standards were not necessarily the first priority in the GDR workplace. Productivity often gave way to the coffee klatsch, where the sinews of solidarity and mutual support were quietly formed — often in collectives that experienced decades of continuous existence. More overtly political notions of solidarity were encouraged through the state's ideological machinery. Fund raising for liberation movements (Bruce Springsteen's epic 1988 performance in East Berlin under the sponsorship of the Free German Youth was in its conception a "Konzert für Nikaragua") and officially sanctioned peace campaigns won considerable support based on the persuasiveness of those causes. There was a core of loyalty and participation in a society that could often convince a sizable public to engage in projects generated by the state machinery. At the same time, that culture of solidarity filtered down to the apolitical mass in subtle and often incalculable ways. Many GDR citizens who felt the heavy weight of an overbearing and restrictive polity reconfigured the culture of solidarity into an ethos of communal kindnesses, which they proudly contrasted with West Germany's individualistic and competitive "elbows society." In Wechsler's loose estimate 10–15 percent of the public passionately embraced the system and a similar number was strongly opposed, with the remaining 70–80 percent shaping their attitudes based upon shifting personal circumstances. While such numbers hardly constitute a case for a legitimate government, neither are they egregiously at odds with conditions for stability. Many other states survive with less of a modicum of acquiescence. Why then did the GDR disintegrate so rapidly in 1989—leaving Stephen Wechsler feeling that he was "the last of the Mohicans"?

————————

Wechsler's story reveals the gradual accumulation of combustible materials in ordinary life that exploded in 1989, ultimately overwhelming the socialist dream, which was not enough to sustain the desires of an increasingly restive and unhappy majority. While the collapse of the GDR is inseparably linked to the fate of the socialist bloc and to the globalization of capital, the flaws and contradictions of internal political life were also cogs in the wheels that ground to dissolution. Wechsler offers a poignant example of the chill which stifled thought and expression so essential to societal development. The presence of a secretary scribbling notes at a student seminar in 1956 was enough to distract and intimidate him from forcefully voicing his doubts and worries in the tense period following the events in Hungary. That the note-taking had no sinister intent underscores the perceptual insidiousness of an environment where even a false impression of intimidation can coax an individual into silence. For the average East German with no thought of leaving the country, that environment had a more direct impact on his or her behavior than the occasional horrific bloodletting at the Wall.

The roots of such conditions can be traced to the origins of the GDR. From 1945 through early 1947, not many nationalizations were carried out in the Soviet zone, with the exception of Junker land holdings. While there was zealous de-Nazification and ruthless extraction of reparations, the foundation for a separate socialist society had not been fully laid. But each eruption of conflict hardened positions on both sides. The rush to found the Federal Republic of Germany, the incorporation of ex-Nazis into the FRG government, the writing of a constitution which claimed the eastern zone, the formation of NATO, rapid economic development of the FRG, a western currency reform which threatened to drain the east of liquidity as a prelude to financial breakdown — all spurred the rapid development of an East German socialist state on weak economic and political foundations. The Communists and Social Democrats were merged into a single organization, the Socialist Unity Party, with hopes of building broad support among a shattered, demoralized population. Four other parties (Democratic Farmers, Christian Democratic Union, Liberal Democrats, and National Democrats) were harnessed into a National Front. That emerging political apparatus was mobilized to support the creation of a socialist state without ideological choice at the polls. Wechsler's mordant description of a pencil-less polling booth that few used for fear of casting a secret ballot exemplified politics stripped of meaning and vitality. With weak soil for creating a viable socialist society and Western pressures increasing, the emerging East German leadership absorbed the political culture of the postwar USSR — a siege mentality based on real and perceived threats. The separation of powers was rejected, state security proliferated, the judicial system was placed under tutelage, the media were state-controlled, the freedom of science and culture was infringed upon. At least until 1953, distrust and suspicion were becoming institutionalized, even extending to fervent antifascists and Communists who had emigrated to the West rather than to the USSR in the prewar years.

In the period after Wechsler arrived in Bautzen, Marxist cultural life in Berlin was becoming partly unhinged by accusations and small purges. Walter Janka, a pugnacious editor and veteran of the Spanish Civil War, was already in trouble for his grumbling about sclerotic leaders. When Wechsler heard worried leftist foreign migrants to the GDR in 1957 mention Janka's troubles, it all seemed vague and distant. But in cultural circles, the retreat of critical intellectuals into exile and the trials of Janka and others in Hungary's wake cast a pall over the sometimes rich and experimental intellectual life of the GDR. The conflict between self-expression and the state's constraints did produce creative tension which often led, as Wechsler points out, to interesting and valuable work. But an intellectual climate unencumbered by a police mentality was needed to liberate intellectual life to rise to challenges which could assist in cultivating a more probing, self-confident, and committed public. Without that freedom, poets, writers, and musicians who might not have turned against the GDR became estranged from the system and either went into an artistic underground, into exile, or dropped out.

The Stasi has become a universal target of opprobrium. It could be ruthless, as Wechsler noted. But overt threat and terror were not its game. Stasi omnipresence in every nook and cranny of GDR society was aimed at effecting its version of correct socialist behavior. As Charles S. Maier observed, Stasi agents saw themselves as social workers of a sort, assisting in negotiating between the state and the populace to assure the latter's "constructive" role in public life. Citizens were transformed into clients of the state, their well-being determined by their accommodations to the norms articulated by state security. Many Stasi operatives prided themselves on their sophistication and their ability to distinguish rebellious styles like long hair from subversive acts. That posture was more representative of the apparatus than the actions of its demented head, Erich Mielke, with his "smell samples" from the clothing of suspected subversives and his collection of raw files, which to scale, rivaled J. Edgar Hoover's. With tens of thousands of full-time agents and over one million informants, the Stasi's greatest damage was to the very sense of communal trust upon which egalitarian principles relied. However benign the Stasi's style, its ceaseless accumulation of informants, its role in doling out perks such as travel, publication, and promotion in exchange for approved behavior, its rewards for snooping, and its relentless questions about the political reliability of workers, students, and intellectuals fanned discomfort, unhappiness, suspicion, and fear which strained and corrupted interpersonal relations, undermined egalitarianism, gradually enervated public discourse, and pulled more and more citizens into an insulated private sphere.

In the eighties, with escalating economic and political difficulties in the socialist bloc, with globalization more and more piercing the inner defenses of the GDR with commodified culture, with Western TV bombarding the senses with baubles and with images of energetic participants in an increasingly interconnected world, with growing opportunities to travel wrested from the system — awareness of a stagnant, "abnormal" society deepened, especially among young people. The authorities found it harder to extract loyalty based on the old cold war slogans of anti-imperialist resistance and defense of socialism. As in much of the capitalist world, increasing social complexities were reflected in issues of gender, social mobility, self-identity, and personal fulfillment which could not be subsumed under the old orthodoxies. Growing sectors of society were succumbing to ideological exhaustion while many perceived in the proclamations of the old leaders a widening gap between rhetoric and reality. News of joblessness, militarism, racism, and collapsing human services in the West were often met with disbelief or indifference while sunny reports on GDR TV of new hatcheries in Thuringia or new housing in Brandenburg suffered a similar fate.

These developments led to some painful ironies. The GDR's leaders' refusal to trust their own people to help build a participatory civil society spurred a "counter civil society" of semi-underground dissidence. That current emerged in part from the cumulative impact of limiting and controlling self-generated involvement in the polity. The quasi-official Peace Council worked cautiously through other sanctioned groups to produce controlled peace actions, never daring to encourage grassroots antiwar initiatives, much less any questioning of official foreign policy. Similarly, politically freighted activities from environmental protection to trade unionism were held within tight bounds while largely apolitical endeavors from folk music to the study of Native American lore to nature worship normally passed muster. But in the last years of the twentieth century, it became nearly impossible to seal the GDR from both stylistic and substantive aspects of dissidence. Before the dam burst in 1989, the Stasi's fabric of control began to fray as unsanctioned religious, pacifist, and environmental groups gained strength and influence. A semi-underground counter politics and culture, as Wechsler observed, emerged with a creativity, vitality, and attractiveness for which the moribund ways of the establishment were no match. It would be naive to assume that such a dissident "civil society" was not influenced and aided by Western intelligence. But, whatever the degree of outside influence, the GDR's vast security apparatus was ultimately helpless against a widening stream of dissatisfaction and protest. In fact, the Stasi's pervasiveness in a small country contributed to the instability and unrest that it sought to prevent.

Throughout the process of dissolution, the old guard increasingly lost touch with the public and with changing circumstances. That was not without tragic aspects. Much of the ruling party and government leadership had long and heroic records of antifascist struggle and sacrifice. But that painful history probably influenced pinched, undemocratic rule. By their lights, only they could be trusted to guard working-class hegemony and the socialist ideal; having suffered at the hand of fascism, only they understood the costs of vacillation and retreat; only they could be counted on to defend against bourgeois contamination. With such self-righteous and unchecked authority, corruption, petty and large-scale, seeped into official circles. Without a democratic culture, the GDR's relatively high standard of living within the East Bloc and its significant achievement in social policy were increasingly offered by the party and state old guard as patriarchal largesse to the masses. Intentional or not, social benefits served to buy off potential criticism and unrest. The social net certainly had public approval and a degree of democratic and participatory content, but that could not outweigh widespread feelings of being stifled and limited by a rigid and repressive rule.

After the Wall came down, disclosure of the party leadership's fancy hunting lodges and supposedly lush dachas brought forth intense vitriol which accelerated the collapse of the old guard. Those fancy retreats were not very luxurious by Western standards. Wandlitz, the Politburo's country playground, was little more than an upscale Holiday Inn. It's hard to believe that nicely manicured but relatively modest facilities could be the cause of such widespread disgust. Rather, the anger came from a strong feeling of betrayal of the egalitarian ideal and revulsion at perceived hypocrisy in their leaders' claims of moral superiority over the West.

As the GDR disintegrated, a fundamental issue emerged with inescapable clarity: the need for a democratic essence at the core of socialism. Capitalism, to this point, has been able to sustain itself even when democracy weakens. The performance principle, driven by fear of job loss, and productive growth, driven by the system's need for profit maximization, allow capitalism to cohere and achieve degrees of stability. Socialism is theoretically committed to full employment and ending the profit motive — banishing the workers' fear of job loss and the bosses' need for wealth. Without the twin engines of workers' fear and the employers' drive for maximum profits, a socialist system must develop with the support of an overwhelming majority of diverse social forces, or sooner or later it fails.

That failure to achieve democratic participation was especially damaging in the basic area of economic policy, where dialogue, experimentation, and the attainment of mutual trust between citizens and state were required for survival and progress. The trajectory of the GDR's economic development — and ultimate downfall — underscores that essential need.

Forced to give up more than 20 percent of its capital equipment in reparations by 1950, the GDR nevertheless embarked on building an advanced socialist system — and achieving impressive successes. While West Germany was being infused with billions of Marshall Plan dollars, the GDR, with nationalized means of production and an economic plan, boosted industrial production between 1950 and 1974 sevenfold. In 1969 that state with only seventeen million inhabitants produced more industrial goods than Germany with sixty million people had produced in 1936. Such progress suggests that nationalized ownership and central planning could be powerfully effective in capital formation and mobilization of resources to spur revival and growth. But progress came at the price of relatively severe work norms, strict political control, and the required primacy of industrial production over consumer goods due to vast wartime destruction of industrial facilities. After the outbreak of June 1953, there was an easing of demands on labor, expansion of consumer goods and services, and continuing productive growth. Yet, the West German behemoth hovered over the GDR; attractive jobs generated by its "economic miracle" drew East German labor in large numbers. By 1960 alone, over two hundred thousand of the GDR's most productive workers departed while inflated East-marks flowed westward through porous borders. The Wall that went up in 1961, while a public relations disaster, stanched the flow of labor and currency, stabilizing the GDR's system and fostering continued productive growth and advances in social services.

Labor productivity, however, lagged behind the West. Socialism's successes in building the industrial foundations for modern economies was difficult to replicate in the next stage of soft goods manufacturing, where the need for innovation, efficiency, and receptivity to the market superseded the mobilization of large clusters of labor and capital. A nagging contradiction between socialism's tendency toward low consumer goods productivity and the requirement for higher output was extremely hard to re-solve. While the GDR's per capita productivity was the highest in the East Bloc, its limited access to the West's advanced technology further hindered its ability to approach Western standards. Yet, with a respite provided by the Wall and with movement toward limited economic reform in the USSR, a vigorous, self-critical debate broke out in the GDR's leading cir-cles over the substance and direction of its economic policies. That resulted in some reforms: decentralization of decision-making in selected areas, limited use of market mechanisms to determine societal preferences, mate-rial incentives, calculation of profit as a measure of performance, setting prices based on real input costs, and expansion of privately owned handi-crafts and services. Those reforms were reasonably successful despite bot-tlenecks and shortages resulting from inherent problems in coordinating exchanges between enterprises under the central plan and those respond-ing to the market. That golden age of sorts demonstrated that private own-ership was not necessary to build a growing and stable socialist economy.

In 1968 the GDR's leadership saw in the Prague Spring in Czechoslova-kia a specter of pluralism, capitalist restoration, and the disintegration of the socialist bloc. The GDR was the most zealous proponent of the War-saw Pact's removal of Alexander Dubcek's reform government, a position that disquieted a large segment of East German opinion. That crisis in-creased debate in East Germany's upper echelons between proponents of market mechanisms and those of state planning. Meanwhile, the economy continued to make respectable gains. Between 1968 and 1971 there was a spurt in growth (nearly 6 percent annually), with investment in new tech-nologies for metallurgy, petroleum products, and data processing achiev-ing good results.

In 1970, Poland was shaken by a wave of strikes culminating in the use of force to end unrest at the Gdansk shipyard. For the GDR, economic and political questions had become increasingly intertwined and inseparable. In 1971, Erich Honecker replaced Walter Ulbricht as leader of the ruling SED. The ascendance of the veteran of ten years in a Nazi prison was seen as a step forward for reform based on greater orientation toward consumer goods and improvement of living standards. That priority was confirmed at the SED 8th Party Congress that year. But the most likely means of fi-nancing a generous and extensive social policy would be exposure to the world market, including large infusions of borrowed capital. At the same time, pressures were building to pull back from the sixties' economic reforms. Concern over signs of instability in the socialist bloc and frustration over failure to find a smooth relationship between central planning and market mechanisms led to cutting back on decentralized decision-making and constricting small crafts and services. Later those decisions would have serious consequences for the survival of the GDR.

In 1969, Willy Brandt formed the first postwar Social Democratic West German government. He then initiated his "Ostpolitik" to widen economic and political ties with the East, especially the GDR, as a means of opening new areas for investment and to nudge the socialist states to liberalize their economic policies (and ultimately gravitate to capitalism). The FRG recognized the GDR (but its constitutional claim to all of Germany remained); both states entered the UN; trade between the two Germanys grew exponentially with the GDR granted technical assistance and huge loans. Under those circumstances, East German living standards continued to rise in the seventies. Incomes increased by one-third, savings doubled, retail trade rose by 56 percent, 40 percent of all households had a car, and 88 percent had television.

But beneath the surface, profound changes were taking place that would bring upheaval over the next quarter-century. The epoch of the 3rd Internationale which spanned much of the twentieth century was coming to an end. While the GDR was enjoying stability and international acceptance, the costs of the social net were increasingly financed by funds freed up by foreign loans for other purposes, especially from the West German government. In 1973 the head of the State Planning Commission, Gerhard Schürer, warned Honecker that the GDR's debt was escalating and that by 1980 it could rise to more than 20 billion deutsche marks. Honecker ordered the suppression of his report. At a critical moment, the GDR leadership chose to silence debate and hide disturbing facts from the public.

Schürer had a proposal which might have broken the spiraling debt. Among the states of the Council for Mutual Economic Assistance (CMEA), the East European trade body, the GDR had made the greatest strides in microchip technology. It could shift priorities to invest heavily in developing that technology to modernize the socialist bloc's rusting industrial plant. In return, it could collect "valuta" or convertible currency to pay down its debts to West Germany and import high-quality technology and consumer goods from the West. However, there was one important qualification: massive subsidies for the social net would have to be shifted to costly microchip development. Such a decision would have had serious political consequences. Rather than foster a public debate on such a hard choice, Honecker kept the issue from his own Politburo, not just from the people of the GDR. A small circle of advisers was paralyzed by the problem; it could not find the will or the words to openly explain the country's growing difficulties and to explore with the public possible cutbacks in the social net to achieve long-term gain. Nothing was resolved; the reforms of the sixties were fading from memory as centralization tightened — and the GDR sank deeper into debt.

During the seventies the West experienced severe crisis. For the United States, Vietnam brought tragic loss in blood and treasure; Watergate had shaken faith in a democratic polity; labor militancy was rising; revolutions struck from Ethiopia to Angola to Central America. In the economic sphere, the vast postwar industrial structure in the United States and other advanced states had become enervated rust belts; "Fordist" mass production had driven up inventories; the carefully constructed postwar global monetary system had been torpedoed by Richard Nixon, who allowed the dollar to float on international markets; the Organization of Petroleum Exporting Countries (OPEC) had achieved cohesion that allowed it to constrict the production of oil and threaten the viability of industrial states.

Faced with a compelling need to restructure the capitalist system, the Western states, especially the United States, launched a major overhaul of their productive apparatus — willing to act with a ruthlessness that was antithetical to socialist ideology and thus could not be matched by socialist states. Downsizing, mergers, and buyouts of industries, forced unemployment, intensified efforts to curb unions, and utilization of new technologies from robotics to fiber optics characterized the restructuring of world capitalism. As the West entered a new period dominated by computers and high-speed transmission of information, the division of labor and production shifted from largely national entities to a global platform. Capital broke free from national boundaries to effect an unimpeded flow across national borders, nesting in areas that permitted profit maximization and then often moving on.

For the socialist countries, globalization was devastating. Saddled with resistant bureaucracies and unable to bear the political costs of restructuring, lacking capital to transform hulking industries into svelte high tech enterprises, unable to compete in a global marketplace with goods that were utilitarian at best, the socialist states became caught in a painful contradiction. They needed access to global capital and markets, but also needed to insulate themselves from growing dependence on those very same forces in order to prevent bankruptcy and collapse. The CMEA as a whole began to reel from globalization. The cooperative organization had been formed originally to facilitate a rational division of production and exchange within the socialist bloc. Each state was to emphasize production of its most valued products for exchange within the community. Theoretically, the entire socialist system would benefit from exchanging each country's best products, thus improving living standards, eliminating redundancies, and effecting significant savings. But globalization and the growing gap in scientific and technological development between east and west virtually destroyed intrabloc cooperation. Pressed for hard currency to purchase Western technology and goods, each state began selling its most valued commodities to the West. This situation ruptured internal bloc cohesion, resulting in an overall lowering of industrial performance and living standards. The socialist bloc's share of world trade diminished sharply as it could not compete in world markets with its often unglamorous goods, especially against the inexpensive products of the Asian tiger economies that combined high tech with cheap labor. The ominous situation was worsened by changes in the raw materials needs of advanced countries moving to new technologies. Both Third World and relatively underdeveloped socialist states faced shrinking markets for their raw materials, which were less and less compatible with the West's changing requirements.

Throughout the eighties, the GDR fell farther behind in global competition. Unable to keep pace with the growth of labor productivity in the West due to introduction of computer technology, the GDR saw its market share of engineering exports fall from 3.9 percent in 1973 to 0.9 percent in 1986. Hopes for servicing debts and importing goods through robust exports were fading rapidly.

With few natural resources, the GDR had depended upon Soviet oil and gas at subsidized prices. In 1987, however, the USSR, now shifting its sale of oil and gas to the West at world market prices, informed GDR officials that it would no longer subsidize the price of energy sources shipped to East Germany. The GDR would either have to forgo energy purchases from the USSR or be forced to sell to the Soviets whatever was valuable enough to sell on the world market to buy advanced technologies. The Hobson's choice was between selling to the West for technology or selling to the Soviets for energy. Either way, the consequences were bleak. By 1990, the fading Soviet regime was accepting only hard currency for its oil and gas. By that time, the GDR had already suffered through heavily reduced energy purchases from the USSR and was forced to rely heavily on pollutant lignite. By 1988, GDR health officials were hospitalizing children stricken with respiratory ailments for weeks on end. That was the only alternative to spending billions in hard currency, which it did not possess, to clean up the environment.

With all that, the GDR celebrated the 750th anniversary of Berlin in 1987 with appropriate pomp, but as Wechsler points out, with a spirit both ironic and joyful. The small country still ranked among the top industrial powers in the world, but its economy was increasingly dependent upon the strangling accumulated debt to the FRG and other Western creditors. Its interest on the debt alone was now one and one-half times greater than its receipts from sales to the West. Under such circumstances, the social net began to fray. Medical services, once the jewel in the GDR's social crown, now suffered defection of doctors, aging equipment, and declining care. At Humboldt University an old hand-cranked adding machine was not a museum piece but essential equipment in the comptroller's office. Despite massive investment in new housing, housing stock in most cities suffered dangerous neglect. This was especially true of cities like Leipzig, which did not benefit from the sort of favors bestowed upon Berlin. Leipzig later experienced the most strident protests against the government. Dissatisfaction among a widening public over growing shortages — unthinkable in the previous decade — was spreading to all sectors of society. Despite the gradual increase in the number of East Germans allowed to visit the West, the Berlin Wall (as well as the tightly patrolled border with West Germany), always an irritant to most in the GDR, became increasingly suffocating and intolerable — especially in light of Honecker's occasional declarations that the Wall would continue to stand for at least another one hundred years if conditions did not change.

The rapid disintegration of the GDR, it turns out, was foretold in the unraveling of the socialist bloc, in the devastating effect of globalization, and in exhaustion from relentless Western pressure. When Hungary, the most eager of CMEA members to move to a capitalist-oriented market, opened its border with Austria, tens of thousands of vacationing East Germans made their way to the West. Soon thereafter, Mikhail Gorbachev came to Berlin to celebrate the GDR's fortieth anniversary, warning that those who did not change with changing history would be doomed to fall behind. That statement probably signaled that the Soviets in promoting a "common European home" were seeking to end the division of Europe and open a qualitatively new political and economic relationship with the West, especially the FRG. That surely did not bode well for the Soviet commitment to the survival of the GDR and deepened growing fear and suspicion about Soviet intentions among the GDR's old guard.

Wechsler tells the story of dissolution from his exceptional vantage point. He was in Leipzig when the now famous Monday night demonstration turned from "we are the people" to "we are ONE people" and a palpable odor of neo-Nazism was in the air. He saw how the opening of the Wall brought a qualitative change in mass consciousness; it was now possible to step into hitherto forbidden zones confident that huge crowds would mitigate danger. Once on the other side of the Wall, throngs of Ossies were exposed to the Kurfürstendamm's opulence. Traffic also flowed in the opposite direction. Helmut Kohl's CDU and the SPD rolled eastward with computers, faxes, copy machines, and deutsche marks. The SED, responding to necessity and to the full-throated pleas of its own rank-and-file, sought ways to preserve a socialist structure by purging the old guard and instituting a democratic polity led by the respected Dresden leader Hans Modrow. Carl Bernstein, reporting from East Berlin in January 1990, found in young and old alike "an abiding love of East Germany" and a fervent desire to preserve socialism and its version of a beloved community. But it was too late. The surge of feeling for "the socialism that we were taught, not the socialism we got" could not withstand the march to reunification built on a dream of getting a piece of West Germany's perceived abundance. A broadly based "Round Table" sought to formulate a new, democratic constitution, but the dissident members seemed determined to pursue merger. Modrow understood that reunification was inescapable and sought ways to establish unity on the basis of two sovereign states with equal rights. Gorbachev believed that he had an agreement with FRG Chancellor Kohl that a period of gradual reunification would commence with the withdrawal of Soviet troops from East Germany. But an election in March 1990 gave 17 percent of the vote to the remnants of the old SED (now the Party of Democratic Socialism) and installed a government which essentially took its orders from the FRG and sped the rapid accession the GDR to the Federal Republic.

Wechsler provides a vivid picture of the methodical steps taken by the victorious Kohl government to wipe out the economic, social, and cultural structures of the GDR after the political defeat of the ruling SED. Such a thorough erasure did not have to happen. The GDR's property was public in character and was formally detached from the party leadership. Theoretically, it could have remained public at least for a time (even if subsidized by the FRG)—providing jobs and income to a deeply wounded people. That is not what happened. While there were huge financial transfers from west to east, the GDR's property and assets were sent to the west and into private hands on an unprecedented scale. In 2000, unemployment in the west was 8.2 percent while eastern joblessness was officially listed at 17.8 percent. Industries that had a sliver of potential competitiveness with West German firms were systematically dismantled. Surveys by west German researchers in 2000 showed that 53 percent of east Germans between the ages of eighteen and fifty-nine had been unemployed one or more times by 1998. Wide-scale demolition of the east's major industries has transformed the former GDR from an industrial region into a vessel of service industries. But small businesses (snack stands, used car lots, video stores) that sprang up during the *Wende* are falling by the wayside. Poverty levels in the east have increased more than threefold from 1990 to 1999 (determined to be 50 percent of the average income in the east). Every tenth person in eastern Germany is living in poverty. Social decline is measured in decreasing birth rates (in 1994 births were at 50 percent of 1989 levels) and lower life expectancy. Reunification has actually accelerated the gap between rich and poor. Eastern Germany now counts 260 people earning more than a million deutsche marks annually—a thin layer compared to 25,000 millionaires in the west, where the impact of globalization and the drain from high taxes and job competition stemming from reunification has also opened a wide disparity between rich and poor.

One of the most troubling and contentious issues in the wake of the GDR's collapse is the rise of skinhead and neo-Nazi groups in the east.

Some in the FRG have pointed to the GDR's insular society with its patriotic rhetoric as spawning the ugly ultranationalism that underpins much of neo-Nazism. But there is a fundamental flaw in that ideologically freighted claim. The most prominent age group (young men in their teens and early twenties) among the neo-Nazis today were children when the GDR dissolved. The postwar neo-Nazi surge moreover is an all-German phenomenon with roots in the west. The long trail of harboring and utilizing ex-Nazis extended deeply into the FRG, as Wechsler's *Democratic German Report* revealed. While West German educators exposed their youth to the Holocaust and the horrors of Nazism, sometimes semi-apologetically, they rarely explored the economic and social roots of fascism and the measurable self-interest of working-class and middle-class young people in fighting that scourge. Moral appeals to guilt have often left West German youth feeling assailed and resentful while changes in all-German and world society continue to breed skinheads and neo-Nazis at the extremes. The GDR did cleanse its society of Nazis; it did engage its youth in symbolic dedication to oppose Nazism. It had earned the right to call itself the "antifascist state." But at times it stretched its legitimate claims beyond credible bounds, as when it denied that a Nazi mentality could be born and nurtured in the soil inherited from Hitler's Germany. The result, as Wechsler noted, was gradually weakened and ineffective anti-Nazi education, abetted by a generational change in the teaching force.

In today's Germany, there are widespread feelings of loss and purposelessness in a society that has plunged into globalization at the cost of high levels of joblessness and loss of identity. The pursuit of an integrated Europe has also nurtured new waves of right-wing nationalism and often murderous antiforeign racism. Politicians now openly question the soiling of German homogeneity by Third World immigrants while some intellectuals now grouse about what they view as incessant demands for atonement for Nazism. Wechsler claims that the neo-Nazi incubus was imported to the east after the Wall came down. There is evidence to support that. But the rapid and fairly widespread embrace of neo-Nazism in the east also reflected the rapid deterioration of social life there and the staggering dead end in employment and educational opportunities since reunification. For some of the young in particular, the lack of jobs and hope has become the goad to capitulate to neo-Nazism with its scapegoating and sick illusions. That plus the GDR's weaknesses in anti-Nazi education add up to a volatile and dangerous mix. A united Germany would do well to end finger-pointing and devise a united strategy to end an ugly all-German phenomenon.

For eastern Germans, reunification has unquestionably brought more formal democracy and greater obeisance to individual dignity. The supply of goods and services has increased on a scale unthinkable before 1989. Giant strides have been taken in infrastructure improvement—especially in communications and transport. Recently, real wages and pensions have begun to rise, though they are still far below western levels. On the other side of the balance sheet are the loss of social rights, joblessness, less social security, and rising rents and prices. On a psychological level, eastern Germans complain of the coldness of unified German society, the lack of community, the widespread arrogance, profiteering, social division, and red tape that Wechsler describes. Surveys by western German agencies have shown that eastern Germans give the GDR higher grades in social security, protection against crime, equal opportunity for women, education, health, and housing.

Yet, there is little or no thought of returning to authoritarian and hierarchal structures of the GDR. The eastern Germans will never go back, but neither will they settle indefinitely for second-class status in a united country. History certainly has not come to an end, and the search for a more just, humane Germany goes on. In that search, the GDR experience cannot be erased and will continue to be a vital reference point.

Stephen Wechsler remains an unbowed leftist who admits that it is difficult to disentangle internal failures from external attack in assessing the causes for the GDR's dissolution. But on balance, he believes that the country's collapse was caused by relentless Western pressure on economic, military, cultural, and psychological fronts to dismantle socialism and restore capitalism. There is no doubt that the economic and military strength of the FRG and NATO, along with their extensive propaganda machinery, contributed to bleeding the GDR of many of its most productive citizens. West Germany's ambition to swallow the GDR was undisguised. The power and reach of the FRG and globalized capital drew East Germany and the entire socialist bloc irresistibly into the global system on fatally disadvantaged terms. With all that in mind, Wechsler's arguments are force-

ful. At the same time, the internal political culture which ultimately alienated and deflated a majority, among them many who wished to participate
in building democratic socialism but were never invited, remains entan-
gled with and inseparable from the external pressures. Perhaps it is impossible to determine the reasons for the dissolution of the GDR (and the entire socialist bloc) without grappling with parallel and intersecting internal
and external factors. Nor is it productive to assess the GDR (and the entire
experience of twentieth-century socialism) in terms of balancing the good
and the bad. In the end, that little country's substantial social achievements
were not enough to prevent its dissolution. In coming to grips with that,
one perhaps needs to go beyond the positive and negative to locate the crucial dynamics which drove the GDR to collapse. The interplay of social
forces with institutional structures — economic circumstances shaped by
history, the status of citizen consent, the weight of cold war competition,
the impact of globalization — must all be considered.

Was the GDR fated to collapse? Wechsler notes that it pulled itself out
of the ashes of World War II to build a powerful industrial state. Had its
leadership persisted in fashioning creative and effective adjustments and
reforms in the face of changing circumstances, had it recognized the insep-
arability of a democracy and socialism, had it invited its citizens to share in
grappling with its problems, had it sought to at least consider ways to apply glasnost and perestroika to its own society after telling its citizens for
years that the Soviet Union was the pure embodiment of socialism — perhaps it might have had the strength and support to survive for a time. Yet
we still are unable to reliably assess the freedom of socialist states to chart
new paths in a world dominated by powers eager to contain and eliminate
systems of public ownership. Wechsler pleads for the moral superiority of
a society where sufficiency and an unhurried, humane workplace are valued
above the frenzy of high productivity. Yet, for the socialist project to advance, it will have to find a way to combine unpressured, humane labor relations with the ability to attain levels of productivity that satisfy both the
material and spiritual needs of the people. The GDR's experience underscores the fact that the socialist project has barely scratched the surface in
seeking to realize its material aspirations and spiritual values.

Wechsler's ideas and experiences raise important questions. Whatever
the pain felt from the abuses of the GDR and other socialist states, he could
draw sustenance from the fact that at the end they were committed to

building a just society. He could also balance the transgressions and out-right crimes of socialist states against brutal antidemocratic actions, bor-dering on the criminal, of the advanced northern countries. Those are compelling arguments; but ultimately for socialism to win support, it would have to cleanse its own house of pain and injustice without reference to the crimes of the West. He struggles with the need to think for himself, but also feels the need to accede to collective decision-making in order to avoid paralysis. The experience of the GDR suggests that the mere exis-tence of collective leadership does not automatically assure just rule. Such bodies can become insular, self-serving, and corrupt. Movements for trans-forming change, in digesting the experience of the first wave of socialism in the twentieth century, will probably have to ascribe greater sovereignty to individual conscience and thought within their ranks. Wechsler's plea for leaders who can listen and be responsive should be taken a step further. A regenerated socialist project would most likely have to insist on mecha-nisms and norms to remove from power ineffective, unresponsive, or cor-rupt leaders and leading bodies.

Stephen Wechsler reminds us that the relative democracy of most north-ern countries rests on the prosperity derived from the impoverishment of the southern hemisphere. In today's globalized economy, that condition is omnipresent. Capital's race to the bottom — to find the lowest wages, lax-est environmental rules, and most accommodating regimes — has brought back long-forgotten diseases like sleeping sickness, has rekindled child la-bor on a massive scale, has placed greed above dissemination of cheap drugs to combat the AIDS pandemic, has prostrated countries without raw materials for new technologies, has spread hunger and social disloca-tion, and has brought about unprecedented gaps between rich and poor — all of which create the swamp that breeds terrorism. The northern coun-tries have by no means escaped that dislocation. Some Berlin streets are now dotted with young women from Romania, Moldova, or the Ukraine who have been uprooted by economic catastrophe and now sell their bod-ies to survive. Thus, Wechsler pleads for the reconstruction of the world's economic and cultural foundations to create a more equitable distribution of wealth and to establish principles that place human survival and progress far ahead of private gain. Agree with him or not on the GDR, his plea for the human race to finally construct the human epoch compels us to con-sider the ways and means to get there. There is no greater task.

SELECTED BIBLIOGRAPHY
(Including Notes on Sources)

While general histories of the forces that frame Stephen Wechsler's life — the American left, the cold war, and the rise and fall of the German Democratic Republic — are abundant, there is no comprehensive narrative of the left and Communist youth movements in the forties and fifties. Robert Cohen, *When the Old Left Was Young: Student Radicals and America's First Mass Student Movement* (New York, 1993), tells the story of Wechsler's thirties' antecedents. Kim Chernin's *In My Mother's House* (New Haven, Conn., 1983) and Carl Bernstein's *Loyalties: A Son's Memoirs* (New York, 1989) touch upon the complexities of parent-child relationships in Communist families during the McCarthy years. David Horowitz's *Radical Son: A Generational Odyssey* (New York, 1997) and Ronald Radosh's *Commies: A Journey through the Old Left, the New Left, and the Leftover Left* (San Francisco, 2001), written by converts from the left to the far right who talk about their upbringing in Communist and left environments through the prism of their latter-day ultraconservatism. Peter N. Carroll, *The Odyssey of the Abraham Lincoln Brigade: Americans in the Spanish Civil War* (Stanford, Calif., 1994), captures the passion of Americans who volunteered to fight Franco and the emotions of those who supported them. There is no published history of the Labor Youth League. The quote from Leon Wofsy, national chair of the LYL, is from his pamphlet *For a New Youth Organization Dedicated to Education in the Spirit of Socialism* (New York, 1949), p. 3.

Harvey Klehr and John Earl Haynes, *The American Communist Movement: Storming Heaven Itself* (New York, 1992), is a relatively recent survey of the Communist Party and other left organizations from an anticommunist perspective. William Z. Foster, *History of the Communist Party of the United States* (New York, 1952), is a partisan party history by one of its most prominent long-time leaders. Michael Brown, Randy Martin, Frank Rosengarten, and George Snedeker, eds., *New Studies in the Politics and Culture of American Communism* (New York, 1993), is a series of essays that achieve a considerable degree of balance. Two works covering the Communist-led left during the forties and fifties — partly critical, partly sympathetic — are Maurice Isserman's *Which Side Were You On? The American Communist Party during the Second World War* (Middletown, Conn., 1982) and *If I Had a Hammer: The Death of the Old Left and the Birth of the New Left* (Urbana, Ill., 1987). Julia Dietrich, *The Old Left in History and Literature* (New York, 1996), contains a chapter that tidily sketches the cultural milieu of the postwar left. Among many memoirs of Communists who were active in the forties and fifties, Al Richmond's *A Long View from the Left: Memoirs of an American Revolutionary* (Boston, 1973) stands out as particularly well written and perceptive.

Among the most comprehensive studies of the anticommunist hysteria in the late forties and fifties is David Caute, *The Great Fear: The Anti-Communist Purge under Truman and Eisenhower* (New York, 1978). Albert Fried, ed., *McCarthyism: The Great American Red Scare, A Documentary History* (New York, 1996), contains much valuable material on the repressive climate of the forties and fifties. Studies on the impact of McCarthyism on U.S. social and cultural life include: Griffin Fariello, *Red Scare: Memories of the American Inquisition* (New York, 1995); Stephen J. Whitfield, *The Culture of the Cold War (The American Moment)* (Baltimore, 1996); Jim Tuck, *McCarthyism and New York's Hearst Press* (Lanham, Md., 1995); Aaron L. Friedberg, *In the Shadow of the Garrison State* (Princeton, 2000); Paul S. Boyer, *By Bomb's Early Light: American Thought and Culture at the Dawn of the Atomic Age* (Chapel Hill, 1994); and Richard M. Fried, *Nightmare in Red: The McCarthy Era in Perspective* (New York, 1991). Victor Navasky, *Naming Names* (New York, 1980), remains a definitive text on the content and reach of congressional assaults on free speech. Frances Stoner Saunders, *The Cultural Cold War: The CIA and the World of Arts and Letters* (New York, 2000), is a path-breaking study of the CIA's ideological subversion of culture in Europe and the United States. Ellen Schrecker, *No Ivory Tower: McCarthyism and the Universities* (New York, 1986), chronicles capitulations to McCarthyism at Harvard and other schools. Schrecker's *Many Are the Crimes: McCarthyism in America* (Boston, 1998) explores the impact of McCarthyism on the labor movement, Hollywood, politics, and other aspects of the nation's life. There is presently no study of the military's treatment of leftist GIs during the Korean War. Information on the Supreme Court's ruling overturning undesirable discharges on political grounds can be found on the Internet at http://www.fedworld.gov. The Court ruling of March 1958 for the plaintiffs was in two consolidated cases brought by veterans who had received undesirable discharges. The cases were *Harmon v. Brucker* and *Abramowitz v. Brucker* (both 355 U.S. 57). Howard Abramowitz, a former Labor Youth League member, had received a medal for valor in Korea and had later been given an undesirable discharge.

In 1961, D. F. Fleming published his two-volume work, *The Cold War and Its Origins* (London and New York, 1961). Without extensive access to archival materials and working mainly from secondary sources, Fleming nevertheless produced a sweeping, judicious study whose analyses and conclusions have largely withstood the test of time. Additional studies that were consulted are: Walter LaFeber, *America, Russia, and the Cold War: 1945–1952* (7th edition, New York, 1993); Ronald E. Powaski, *The Cold War: The United States and the Soviet Union, 1917–1991* (New York, 1998); Lloyd C. Gardner, Walter LaFeber, and Thomas J. McCormick, *Creation of the American Empire* (New York, 1973); and Jules Davids, *America and the World of Our Time* (3d edition, New York, 1970). One of the best general surveys of the origins of the cold war is Thomas G. Paterson, *On Every Front: The Making of the Cold War* (New York, 1979). Other studies which focus on the antecedents of the cold war are John Lewis Gaddis, *The United States and the Origins of the Cold War* (Rev. ed., New York, 2000), and Randall Woods and Howard Jones, *Dawning of the Cold*

War: The United States' Quest for Order (Athens, Ga., 1991). Daniel Yergin, *Shattered Peace: The Origins of the Cold War and the National Security State* (Boston, 1978), is an absorbing study of the formation of a cold war ideology. Other studies of the shaping of the cold war are Richard J. Barnet, *The Roots of War: The Men and Institutions behind U.S. Foreign Policy* (New York, 1973); and Lloyd C. Gardner, *Architects of Illusion: Men and Ideas in American Foreign Policy* (Chicago, 1970). A left perspective on the origins of the cold war is Joyce Kolko and Gabriel Kolko, *The Limits of Power: The World and United States Foreign Policy* (New York, 1972). Nikolai V. Sivachev and Nikolai N. Yakovlev, *Russia and the United States: U.S.-Soviet Relations from the Soviet Point of View* (Chicago, 1979), presents a Soviet perspective on the cold war. An exhaustive academic study of the Soviet role is William Taubman, *Stalin's American Policy: From Entente to Détente to Cold War* (New York, 1982). Mikhail Gorbachev's *Memoir* (New York, 1996), a generally neglected but hugely useful memoir, discloses Gorbachev's understanding of the terms of Soviet disengagement from the GDR. Gar Alperovitz, *The Decision to Use the Atomic Bomb and the Architecture of an American Myth* (New York, 1995), provides exhaustive background for the fears that many on the left felt after Hiroshima.

Two very different books constitute essential reading on the rise and fall of the German Democratic Republic. Charles S. Maier's *Dissolution: The Crisis of Communism and the End of East Germany* (Princeton, 1997) is a vital study which draws heavily upon recently opened GDR archives. While Maier undervalues the positive aspects of the GDR, he does note repeatedly that both the east and west blocs faced daunting problems in the last decades of the twentieth century. His archival research uncovered hitherto undisclosed economic data which clarify the nature of the GDR's economic implosion. Peter Marcuse's *Missing Marx: A Personal and Political Journal of a Year in East Germany, 1989–1990* (New York, 1991) is a diary of his sojourn in the GDR at the time of its collapse. Written in the rush of events, it lacks scholarly paraphernalia, but contains many shrewd and penetrating insights into GDR life which at times escaped Maier.

A recent study which utilizes newly available archival materials is Mike Dennis, *The Rise and Fall of the German Democratic Republic* (New York, 2000). Martin McCauley, *The German Democratic Republic since 1945* (New York, 1983), is a general history written nearly a decade before unification. A standard compendium of statistics is Countries of the World Information Series, *Information GDR: The Comprehensive and Authoritative Reference Source of the German Democratic Republic* (New York, 1990). Works on the East German economy include the official GDR *Statistical Pocket Book of the German Democratic Republic* (Berlin, 1982); Raymond Bentley, *Technological Change in the German Democratic Republic* (Boulder, Colo., 1984); Irwin W. Collier, *Connections, Effective Purchasing Power, and the Real Product in the German Democratic Republic* (Berlin, 1985) and *The Estimation of Gross Domestic Product and Its Growth in the GDR* (Washington, D.C., 1985); and Reinhard Pohl, *Handbook of the Economy of the German Democratic Republic* (Farnborough, U.K., 1979).

Among the works in English on East German social, educational, legal, and cultural life are: Lorna Martens, *The Promised Land? Feminist Writing in the German Democratic Republic* (New York, 2001); Nancy Lukens and Dorothy Rosenberg, eds., *Daughters of Eve: Women's Writing from the German Democratic Republic* (Lincoln, Nebr., 1993); H. G. Huettich, *Theater in the Planned Society: Contemporary Drama in the German Democratic Republic* (Chapel Hill, 1978); David Rock, *Voices in Times of Change: The Role of Writers, Opposition Movements and the Churches in the Transformation of East Germany* (New York, 2000); Helmuth Stoecker, *Socialism with Deficits: An Academic Life in the German Democratic Republic* (Münster, 2000); Daniel John Meador, *Impressions of Laws in East Germany: Legal Education and Legal Systems in the German Democratic Republic* (Charlottesville, Va., 1986); Karen Hammerlund Lukas, *The Educational System of the Former German Democratic Republic: A Special Report, 1991* (Washington, D.C., 1991); Timothy R. Vogt, *Denazification in Soviet Occupied Germany: Brandenberg, 1945–48* (Cambridge, Mass., 2000); and Marilyn Rueschemeyer, *The Quality of Life in the German Democratic Republic: Changes and Developments in State Socialist Society* (Armonk, N.Y., 1989). Two useful studies from UNESCO are K. Korn et al., *Education, Employment and Development in the GDR* (Paris, 1984), and Hans Koch, *Cultural Policy in the GDR* (Paris, 1975). Henry Krisch, *The German Democratic Republic: The Search for Identity* (Boulder, Colo., 1995), explores the psychological dimension of East German nationality. Studies of GDR politics before and/or after the *Wende* include: David Childs, *The Fall of the German Democratic Republic: Germany's Road to Unity* (New York, 2001); Jorg Swoboda, *The Revolution of Candles: Christians in the Revolution of the German Democratic Republic* (Macon, Ga., 1996); J. K. A. Thomaneck and James Mellis, eds., *Politics, Society, and Government in the German Democratic Republic* (New York, 1989); and John R. P. McKenzie and Derek Lewis, *The New Germany: Social and Political Challenges of Unification* (Exeter, U.K., 1995). M. E. Sarotte, *Dealing with the Devil: East Germany, Detente, and Ostpolitik, 1969–1973* (Chapel Hill, 2001), is a very recent study of FRG-GDR relations in the critical late sixties and early seventies; Philip Zelikow and Condoleezza Rice, *Germany Unified and Europe Transformed: A Study in Statecraft* (Cambridge, Mass., 1995), is a triumphalist study of the strategies of Helmut Kohl and the Federal Republic to effect unification. Critical and self-critical analyses by the Party of Democratic Socialism, successor to the ruling East German Socialist Unity Party, are in PDS National Executive, *Five Years of German Unification* (Berlin, 1995), and in the bimonthly *PDS Newsletter,* published in English. A comprehensive examination of postunification social problems is contained in the Society for the Protection of Civil Rights and Human Dignity, *Human Rights in East Germany* (Berlin, 1994). While stridently tendentious and hostile to the GDR, two articles on the World Socialist Web Site (<wsws.org>) contain useful data: Peter Schwarz, "Stalinism in Eastern Europe: The Rise and Fall of the GDR," and Verena Nees, "Ten Years after German Reunification: A Balance Sheet." Audrey Choi, "The Democratization of East Germany: A Dream of Waking Reason," *Radcliffe Quarterly* (March 1990), is a perceptive view of East German ambivalence on the eve of unification. Carl Bernstein's observations on the East German mood during the *Wende* is in "Voices of East Berlin," *Time,* January 22, 1990.